The Collected Essays of Harvey Leibenstein

Volume 1
Population, Development and Welfare

Edited by

Kenneth Button
Department of Economics
Loughborough University

EDWARD ELGAR

Published by
Edward Elgar Publishing Limited
Gower House
Croft Road
Aldershot
Hants GU11 3HR
England

British Library Cataloguing in Publication Data
Leibenstein, Harvey *1922--*
  The collected essays of Harvey Leibenstein.
  1. Economics
  I. Title   II. Button, Kenneth
  330

  ISBN 1-85278-151-3 *v.1*
  ISBN 1-85278-163-7 *v.2*

Printed and bound in Great Britain at
The Camelot Press Ltd, Southampton .

Contents

Editorial Preface

Selecting the forty-four papers contained in these two volumes has been no easy task. Harvey Leibenstein has been a prolific writer since his first article appeared nearly forty years ago and the contents of these *Collected Essays* affords the opportunity to reproduce only part of this substantive output. Hopefully, however, they provide ready access to those seminal pieces which are now so readily cited in debates on fertility or industrial efficiency but more than that, they are intended to reflect the breadth of the work of Professor Leibenstein and the importance of the questions that his varied work raises.

Putting together a collection of this kind is a team effort and this is particularly true given the geographical distances involved between Cambridge, Massachusetts and Loughborough, Leicestershire. It was made doubly difficult by Harvey Leibenstein being seriously injured in a major car accident in 1987 and from which he is still recovering. The completion of these two volumes would, therefore, never have been possible without the considerable help and encouragement of Margaret Leibenstein. Equally, Louise Frederickson has not only been a vital point of contact at Harvard but has also provided invaluable help in the gathering of material and information. Again without her assistance the whole venture would soon have floundered. On the European side of the Atlantic, a large number of people have, in different ways, helped in ensuring the successful completion of these volumes and my thanks are extended to all of them. In particular, Keith Blois at Templeton College, Oxford University devoted considerable time to checking and commenting on material and I am especially grateful for this.

Kenneth Button
February 1989

Harvey Leibenstein: A Brief Biographical Sketch

Economists are often viewed as rather narrow individuals concerned with technical issues which apparently have little relevance for everyday life. Harvey Leibenstein, while an economist by training and instinct, is something of an exception. He has certainly contributed, as most eminent economists have, to advances in several key areas of economics, most notably demographic economics and industrial organization, but beyond this, his research has actively led to increased integration of approaches and theories from outside of the discipline into mainstream economic thinking.

He was born in Russian in 1922 but his parents moved to Canada when he was three years old. His initial training in economics was at Northwestern University, Evanston where he obtained his Bachelor and Master's degrees in 1945 and 1946 respectively. It was at Princeton University, however, that he began his academic work in earnest under the watchful eyes of Jacob Viner, Frederich Lutz, Oscar Morgenstern, Ansley Cole and Frank Notestein, all of whom, with the exception of Viner, served on his Ph.D. committee. His research was to focus on demographic economics. In 1949, while pursuing his doctoral studies at Princeton, his interest in development problems, and with population questions in particular, had been stimulated by a period spent as Social Affairs Officer in the Population Division of the United Nations. His responsibilities there involved spending much of his time assisting Alva Myrdal with her work - work which clearly had a bearing on his own, later studies.

His Ph.D. dissertation, which was completed by 1951, looked at *Selected Aspects of the Theory of Demographic - Economic Change* and formed the basis of his first book, *A Theory of Economic - Demographic Development*, which was published by Princeton University Press in 1954. Interestingly enough, his doctorate came after the publication of his first major article in the *Quarterly Journal of Economics* (in 1950). This piece, dealing with bandwagon, snob and Veblen effects, subsequently assumed the status of a classic in the field of consumer theory and still remains compulsory reading for many university microeconomics theory courses.

In 1951, Harvey Leibenstein moved west to become Assistant Professor in the Economics Department at the University of California at Berkeley. At about the same time be became involved in consultancy work for the Rand Corporation, and, in particular, studied matters relating to Soviet-style economic systems. From this stemmed two further, albeit rather specialized, books both published in 1954; *Proposal for the Development of a Theory of Economic Growth for a Soviet-Type Economy*, and *Economic Development and the Rate of Interest under Dictatorial Conditions*.

As time progressed he took up the position of Social Science Research Council Faculty Research Fellow at Berkeley, a post he held from 1956 to 1959. This position afforded more time to pursue his own specific research interests and resulted in the production of a series of major articles (see Volume 1 of the *Collected Essays*) focusing particularly on questions of unemployment, investment and economic development. The ideas he generated at this time certainly did not go unnoticed as correspondence from several key black African leaders (including Hastings Banda who was being held in Gwelo Prison in what was then the Federation of Rhodesia and Nyasaland) testifies.

He also began his wide range of travels whilst based in the Bay Area. Unlike some academics who research and teach on questions relating to the problems of economic underdevelopment, Harvey Leibenstein has always been a ready traveller, usually preferring extended stays in a country to a brief and fleeting visit. In 1957, for example, he spent time in Mexico and worked on the material for what subsequently became *Economic Backwardness and Economic Growth: Studies in the Theory of Economic Development*.

Parallel to his growing involvement in the economic development debates which were attacting considerable attention in the late 1950s and 1960s, Leibenstein also interested himself in industrial organization. Much of his early work, although carefully presented and adding incrementally to conventional economic analysis, showed little of the major insights which were to characterize his later writing. His *Economic Theory and Organizational Analysis*, which appeared in 1960, certainly reflects his growing interest in the way organizations operate and decisions are reached but its focus is on the interface between classical microeconomic theory and organization theory rather than a direct questioning of the cost minimization postulate which was to come later. Interestingly, however, the study does critically discuss the conventional idea of profit maximization objectives. This concern with the reality of the maximization postulate reflects the importance of Leibenstein's earlier contact with Herbert Simon and Anatol Rapoport whilst an instructor at Illinois Institute of Technology in the late 1940s. Later, however, as discussed in the Introduction to Volume 2 of the *Collected Essays*, he clearly distinguishes his approach from that of the mainstream Behavioural School although he is in general sympathy with its ideas. His work has been primarily, although not exclusively, concerned with questions of efficiency rather than with the objectives and goals of management.

Perhaps the concept Harvey Leibenstein is most widely associated with is 'X-efficiency' - that difficult to quantify deviation from cost-minimization which, in particular, characterizes non-competitive markets. The story of how the concept was first conceived in the mid 1960s and subsequently acquired its remarkably apt name is set out in Volume 2 of the *Collected Essays*. In itself this story is amusing and interesting but perhaps of greater importance is the degree to which it reflects on the approach to academic analysis which typifies Leibenstein's work. His interests are wide and range from particle physics, to the history of philosophy and mathematics. This tends to lead him to look for patterns of behaviour and to examine events and data rather than just rely, as many theoretical economists do, on pure deductive logic. His work reflects at least as great an interest in the underlying postulates as in the logic of an argument although the latter is always followed through meticulously. Leibenstein's subsequent refinement of X-efficiency theory, and its incorporation into the broader notion of 'micro-micro theory', is particularly illustrative of this thoroughness.

At about the time his seminal paper on X-efficiency appeared in the *American Economic Review*, an important change was to occur in Leibenstein's life. Berkeley in the late 1960s was an exciting place if one was a young activist interested in trying to immediately right the perceived injustices of the World. This, however, had its costs on the academic community. Student unrest was widespread and academic work disrupted. Those concerned with deeper issues and, in particular, conducting the scientific work necessary to bring about a longer term understanding of how society functions found it an unsettling place to work. Leibenstein, who had been made a full professor at Berkeley in 1960, and had been honoured as a Guggenheim Foundation Fellow in 1963, was invited to Harvard University as a visiting professor in 1966-67 and accepted. In the following year he was offered the Andelot Professorship of Economics and Population at Harvard. In a sense, this was an 'offer he could not refuse'. Besides the obvious aptness of the position for someone with his interests, the move to Cambridge promised to enable him to conduct his research and to carry on, uninterrupted, with his teaching. He accepted the post and has held this position at Harvard ever since.

It has been at Harvard that he has both refined his earlier theories and substantially added to them. Interestingly, while many economists with the numeracy of Harvey Leibenstein may have chosen to gain greater acceptance of their ideas among their peer group by recourse to increased sophistication in the mathematic formulation of their theories, Leibenstein has not followed this route. Certainly, there is a simple mathematical appendix on X-efficiency in *Beyond Economic Man* (written jointly with Peter Kalman), but this is not really representative of the more recent work he has done.

Rather, Leibenstein has pursued a less technical approach in trying to understand better how decisions are reached and has brought to bear on his work concepts drawn from management science, game theory, philosophy and psychology. Insights are gained not by the application of ever more abstruse and complex mathematics but rather by the synthesis of theories and ideas from a range of disciplines. The result has been a succession of papers and books over the past twenty years which have considerably enhanced our understanding of industrial organization in the latter part of the twentieth century.

Research output, and paper counts in particular, are now fashionable criteria for judging the worth of an academic. There is a tendency, in this world of 'brownie points', to forget that university professors also have wider responsibilities and not the least of these is to their students. Harvey Leibenstein has always been an enthusiastic teacher, and unlike many academics has enjoyed this aspect of his work. He has put at least as much intellectual energy into course development as he has into his research and academic writing. Courses on both economic development and population topics have been given regularly to Harvard students, and one on microeconomic theory has been refined over the years. A generation of students have been confronted by Professor Liebenstein's 'Socratic' approach to teaching and have enjoyed and benefited from the stimulation of thought which active participation in debate engenders.

At a somewhat more elevated level, many eminent academic economists have benefited from being his doctoral students and included among these are Robert Cassen (Director of Queen Elizabeth House, Oxford University) and Nachum Gross (Professor of Economics at the Hebrew University). Other doctoral students have moved outside of the academic world including; Ali Wardhana (former finance minister for Indonesia), Widjojo Nitisastro (adviser to the Indonesian government) and Timothy King (Head of the Population and Human Resources Division at the World Bank).

Although, while there is an almost universal tendency these days to place weight on published output, Harvey Leibenstein's pronounced influence on development matters has been as much through the way he has encouraged and helped his students as by his voluminous and important contributions to the academic literature - which total some nine books listed below' and over seventy major papers to date.

While relatively stable in terms of career moves for a leading American academic (although some might argue that there are few other places to go if you have been at Berkeley and Harvard!), Harvey Leibenstein could never be described as a stay at home. He always enthusiastically made full use of vacations, sabbaticals and study leaves. Some have been spent at other US institutions and, indeed, in 1978-79 he spent the year as a member of the Institute for Advanced Study at Princeton University working on the application of the theory of games to co-ordination problems. This period saw the development of a germ of an idea which was to re-emerge more fully grown in Harvey Leibenstein's most recent book, *Inside the Firm: the Inefficiencies of Hierarchy*.

Professor Leibenstein has also always been an inveterate international traveller. His main academic positions have provided the bases from which to travel and develop his ideas abroad. (These periods away have also provided the opportunity to gain inspiration and material for his oil painting and sketching - a not inconsequential consideration.) Mention has already been made of his stay in Mexico but this is merely the tip of an iceberg. He has spent considerable amounts of time in England - in London and at Oxford and Cambridge Universities - as well as in Rome, and in Haifa and Jerusalem. Athens was his base whilst completing some of his work on returns to scale in education and on development issues. In Turkey he examined questions of population. At Kyoto University in Japan, where he was the Distinguished Visiting Professor of Economics, he worked on X-efficiency and questions pertaining to inefficiencies of hierarchy. Issues of development and population claimed his attention in New Delhi (where he also ran a seminar for Indian Fulbright recipients). In Beijing, China he lectured to academics and civil servants on population theory, and yearly visits to Klosters, Switzerland allowed him the luxury of uninterrupted time to write while still being able to indulge in his two favourite physical activities, tennis and skiing. In addition he has visited Peru, Ecuador, Brazil, Belgium, Yugoslavia, Taiwan and Thailand. Such travel has generated a storehouse of examples and illustrations upon which he can draw to substantiate an argument as well as providing conducive places to work and meet with fellow researchers.

List of Books Published

A Theory of Economic - Demographic Development, Princeton University Press, Princeton, 1954.

Proposal for the Development of a Theory of Economic Growth for a Soviet-Type Economy, RAND Corporation, Santa Monica, 1954.

Economic Development and the Rate of Interest under Dictatorial Conditions, RAND Corporation, Santa Monica, 1954.

Economic Backwardness and Economic Growth: Studies in the Theory of Economic Development, John Wiley, New York, 1957.

Economic Theory and Organizational Analysis, Harper & Row, New York, 1960.

Beyond Economic Man: A New Foundation for Microeconomics, Harvard University Press, Cambridge, 1976.

General X-Efficiency Theory and Economic Development, Oxford University Press, New York, 1978.

Inflation, Income Distribution and X-Efficiency Theory, Croom Helm, London, 1980.

Inside the Firm: the Inefficiencies of Hierarchy, Harvard University Press, Cambridge, 1987.

Introduction and Acknowledgements

1 Introduction

Dividing the academic work of Harvey Leibenstein into neat boxes is no easy matter. He has written on a wide range of subjects over nearly forty years and has never confined himself to the traditionally narrow boundaries of economics. In particular he has concerned himself very much with issues of economic development and population, indeed he very aptly holds the Andelot Professorship of Economics and Population at Harvard University. Further, Leibenstein's seminal work developing the theory of X-efficiency and, more recently, applying the Prisoner's Dilemma paradigm to economic behaviour is both extensive and is itself very wide-ranging.

Pragmatism, however, means that some form of division is necessary if the importance of his contributions to economics are to be fully appreciated. Equally, given the large output Leibenstein has generated since his first article appeared in the *Quarterly Journal of Economics*[1] in 1950, a degree of selectivity is inevitably necessary.

In this volume of the *Collected Essays* the emphasis is very much on issues of population, and in particular the micro-economics of fertility, and the links between population and economic development. This is supplemented by a number of key papers which extend the discussion of economic growth and development to embrace issues of enterpreneurship and technical progress.

The companion volume to this (*X-Efficiency and Micro-Micro Theory*) contains Harvey Leibenstein's main theoretical contributions to the debate on non-allocative efficiency and a selection of articles applying his idea of X-efficiency to a variety of micro and macro economic issues. Some papers could comfortably fit in either volume. Professor Leibenstein's extensive work on economic development has, for example, clearly made him aware of the proclivity of developing economies to suffer from X-inefficiency[2]. The allocation of material between volumes is, therefore, somewhat subjective (as indeed is the selection of papers itself) although it is hoped that a sensible framework emerges.

Given these facts, some comments on the selection and the rationale for the division of material adopted seems in place. These brief comments are in no way meant to offer a series of short abstracts of the papers selected, although in some cases a brief précis is given, but rather to provide a contextual background to the various articles and papers. They also give some, albeit very incomplete, guidance to the numerous other articles by Harvey Leibenstein for which there is insufficient space in this volume.

2 The Selection of Papers

This volume contains some nineteen published and one unpublished papers which span the years from 1955[3]. The umbrella title, *Population, Development and Welfare*, may be somewhat misleading in that it could be taken to imply a set of disparate and disconnected papers. Certainly the subject matter is, in a sense, diverse. Further, Professor Leibenstein's views have evolved over time in the light of new evidence and as his theories have been refined.

There are, however, important common threads which run through the essays contained in this collection. Perhaps the most important of these is the characteristic Leibenstein approach of trying to advance economic understanding by moving away from some of the traditional assumptions of micro-economics. The framework adopted is based, instead, on a careful assessment of how the world behaves and frequently relies upon the penetrating use of salient facts and data to substantiate an argument. The papers also share a common theme in their persistent concern with human welfare - the theoretical developments relate to establishing a basis for a clearer understanding of human behaviour and not just to the creation of new techniques of analysis.

The material selected is intended to offer a blend of Harvey Leibenstein's theoretical and applied work. In several instances, empirical or advocative papers have been selected in preference to others on a similar theme but of a more technical orientation. The less overtly theoretical pieces being given precedence in such cases because they offer insights into Leibenstein's wider interests in policy formulation and economic welfare.

Questions centred around the economic theory of human fertility, especially in relation to the Third World, have taken up a considerable amount of Harvey Leibenstein's time over the years. His thesis in the mid-1950s[4] (which is set out as a more complete theory in his 1975 *Quarterly Journal of Economics* paper contained in Part I of this collection) went against much of the conventional wisdom of the day in arguing that sustained fertility decline was, in general, quite likely to occur as incomes rose. His approach, which only claims to be an explanatory vehicle and not a *strictly predictive one, is to move away from trying to explain family size per se* to consider the question of why a typical family may decide to limit itself to say three children rather than four. The model avoids many of the restrictive assumptions of the Hicksian microeconomic world of Chicago and Columbia and does not rely upon rational calculations for every aspect of reproductive activity. Instead, the roles of culture, status and group influence are perceived to be of central importance. Essentially, such factors play an important part in a sort of cost-benefit analysis of the value of an additional child.

The framework of analysis developed in 1957 is set in the wider context of fertility theory in his *Journal of Economic Literature* paper of 1974[5].

The paper offers a critical assessment of his own work to that time as well as critiques of other schools of thought. In the sense that the paper is essentially a critical survey, it does not offer a completely new theory but it does provide a rather rare attempt to bring together a set of diverse theories and also goes on to show how Professor Leibenstein perceives his own ideas as developments from them. This approach is further extended in the final paper in Part I of the collection (the 1981 article from the *Population and Development Review*). Here we see a rather fuller integration of Leibenstein's views on population and his theory of inert areas[6]. It also offers some insights into how work from other disciplines could be more completely integrated with economics to produce a more satisfactory theory of fertility.

The papers in Part II of the collection are concerned with the interaction of population growth and economic development[7]. A central element in the arguments presented is that it is not the rate of population growth *per se* which is important in influencing economic growth but rather the nature of that growth. While rapid population growth is seen as detrimental to economic development it is not an insurmountable obstacle. Labour skills, training and education[8] are treated as key components of the production function while such elements are often ignored or glossed over in simpler models which usually treat labour inputs as homogeneous[9]. There are also, extending the theme of papers in Part I of the collection, counter-pressures on population growth as economic growth takes place.

This theme is extended beyond developing countries to consider the links between population growth and the expansion of the U.S. economy (in the 1972 paper reproduced from the *Report of the Commission on Population Growth and the American Future*). The negative impact of a rapidly expanding population is countered by the flexibility and energy which accompanied its youthfulness and by growth in other factors of production.

Part III of the collection gathers together some of Harvey Leibenstein's work on economic development. The question of population growth is raised again in several of these papers but the contributions are distinguished from those in the previous section because their approach is more general. Population growth, in these cases, is set in a wider context and is only one element in the development process.

The 1966 paper reproduced from *Kyklos*, provides a good guide to Leibenstein's pragmatic approach to economic development issues. It considers the 'Friedman Test'[10] of economic theories too limited a guide to the usefulness of theories of economic development. It is difficult, for example, to specify all key relationships in an exact quantitative fashion and, further, there may be no universal theory of development which applies to all conditions or a general theory which is applicable at all stages of development even within one country. Leibenstein, therefore, comes down in favour of viewing theories of development as what are termed *sample* relationships relevant to a particular situation or time. Such relationships should be credible. The usefulness of theories derived in this way is that they can help diagnose existing problems and indicate the types of remedial policy which, although not universally applicable, may be of relevance.

The majority of the remaining papers in Part III concentrate on specific problems in stimulating economic development. Looking at issues of investment policy, underemployment, development planning etc. the papers are far from uncontroversial and indeed, since they are in the main seeking to raise questions concerning conventional thinking about the appropriateness of traditional neo-classical approaches to development, this is hardly surprising[11]. In particular the idea developed in several of these papers[12] is that in a poor country with abundant labour it may not be desirable to maximize the labour/investment ratio if long term per capita living standards are to rise over time. Alternative strategies may bring forth higher levels of reinvestment and urbanization (with accompanying falls in the birth rate).

The final paper (which has not been published elsewhere) in this Part of the *Collection* looks at the economics of the kibbutz. It examines the success of a rather different approach to economic development and considers why over a relatively long period the kibbutz has outperformed the rest of the Israeli economy. The role of certain forms of non-pecuniary rewards in stimulating economic growth is a central theme of the paper and provides Leibenstein with further ammunition for questioning some of the underlying assumptions of traditional development theory.

The two papers in Part IV focus on the role of entrepreneurship in a developing economy. The basic arguments are set out in the *American Economic Review* paper of 1968. Production functions and markets for factors of production are particularly incomplete in less developed economies[13]. Thus, the theory of competition with automatic market clearance is a poor description of reality. Instead the entrepreneur fulfils an important role as an 'intermarket operator'. The paper advocates that development economists consider the responsiveness and motivations of the particular countries they are concerned with. The more recent paper written jointly with Patrick Kaufmann ties in with this theme by examining the potential of business format franchising as a means of motivating local entrepreneurship in developing countries. The conclusions are not altogether optimistic in terms of possible distributional and cultural impacts.

The concluding two parts of the book contain somewhat older material relating, in turn, to Harvey Leibenstein's work on Production Theory and on Economic Welfare. These are, in the main, technical papers concerned with clarifying certain aspects of economic theory although Leibenstein's concern is rather more with the relevance of this theory in practice.

The *Review of Economics and Statistics* paper of 1966, for example, focuses on the usefulness of the incremental capital-output ratio in enhancing our understanding of economic growth. The conclusions suggest that the early Keynesian growth model was deficient in that the real link was from growth to the incremental capital-output ratio rather than the reverse as it explicitly assumes. In typically pragmatic fashion Professor Leibenstein, therefore, questions the usefulness of the incremental ratio as a planning instrument. We also find in the paper on long term welfare criteria a concern with 'questions which are of an empirical and researchable nature' rather than with the technical aspects of deducing conclusions from established criteria.

3 Acknowledgements

The following kindly gave permission for the reproduction of material in this collection:- American Economics Association; Banca Nazionale del Lavoro; Basil Blackwell Ltd; Indian Economic Journal; John Hopkins University Press; John Wiley and Sons Inc; Journal of Development Planning; Macmillan Press; Prentice Hall; Resources for the Future; Review of Economics and Statistics; St Martins Press; The Population Council; and the University of Chicago Press.

Notes

1 This is reproduced in the companion volume.
2 Indeed, much of the recent empirical work by others attempting to evaluate the quantitative importance of X-efficiency has been conducted in relation to developing economies. Non-monetary rewards play a larger part in the economic activities of such countries and institutional structures, coupled with high transaction costs, tend to create an environment in which a high degree of shelter grows up to cushion producers from the need to seek maximum efficiency.
3 It does not, however, contain material taken directly from the several major books Professor Leibenstein has contributed on the subject. In particular these are, in chronological order:- *A Theory of Economic-Demographic Development* (Princeton University Press, Princeton) 1954; *Economic Backwardness and Economic Growth: Studies in the Theory of Economic Development* (John Wiley, New York) 1957; and *General X-Efficiency Theory and Economic Development* (Oxford University Press, New York) 1978. Some of the ideas originating in essays contained in this volume are developed further in these books.
4 See *Economic Backwardness and Economic Growth: Studies in the Theory of Economic Development, op. cit.*
5 This paper was not without critics, see for example, M.C. Keeley, 'A Comment on "An Interpretation of the Economic Theory of Fertility"', *Journal of Economic Literature*, Vol.13, 1975, pp.461-8, and for Harvey Leibenstein's response see, 'On the Economic Theory of Fertility: A Reply to Keeley', *Journal of Economic Literature*, Vol.13, 1975, pp.469-72.
6 It also ties in closely with his work on the Prisoners' Dilemma (see papers in Part III of the companion volume covering, *X-Efficiency and Micro-Micro Theory*).
7 This has been a long term interest of Harvey Leibenstein. For a report on some of his early work relating population growth and economic development couched in terms of a Malthusian equilibirium framework, see the summary of his paper to a conference of the Econometric Society held in Eugene, Oregon in 1952 (*Econometrica*, Vol.21, 1953).

8   He calls this the 'quality replacement effect' since the entrants to the labour force are more skilful than those already in it or leaving. The arguments are spelt out in more detail in, H. Leibenstein, 'The Demographic Impact of Nurture and Education on Development', in *International Population Conference, 1969*, (International Union for the Scientific Study of Population, Leige), 1971, pp.1937-55.

9   Inadequate appreciation of this fact is one reason Leibenstein is sceptical of results generated by some economic studies of the merits of birth control, e.g. H. Leibenstein, 'Pitfalls in Benefit-Cost Analysis of Birth Prevention', *Population Studies*, Vol.23, 1969, pp.161-70.

10 Milton Friedman holds that the predictive ability of an economic theory should be the main guide to its validity, see M. Friedman, 'The Methodology of Positive Economics', in *Essays in Positive Economics*, (Chicago University Press, Chicago), 1953, pp.3-43.

11 Critical comments have been provided by H. Neisser, 'Investment Criteria, Productivity, and Economic Development: Comment', *Quarterly Journal of Economics*, Vol.70, 1956, pp.644-7; J.E. Moes, 'Investment Criteria, Productivity, and Economic Development: Comment', *Quarterly Journal of Economics*, Vol.71, 1957, pp.161-4; H.H. Villard, 'Investment Criteria, Productivity, and Economic Development: Comment', *Quarterly Journal of Economics*, Vol.71, 1957, pp.470-71; and G. Ranis, 'Investment Criteria, Productivity, and Economic Development: An Empirical Comment', *Quarterly Journal of Economics*, Vol.77, 1963, pp.175-9.

12 See also the following not included in this volume; W. Galenson and H. Leibenstein, 'Reply to Mr Moes and Mr Villard', *Quarterly Journal of Economics*, Vol.71, 1957, pp.471-5 and H. Leibenstein, 'Investment Criteria and Empirical Evidence - A Reply to Mr Ranis', *Quarterly Journal of Economics*, Vol.77, 1963, pp.175-9.

13 This ties in closely with the underlying explanation for X-efficiency discussed in contributions contained in the companion volume.

Part I
Fertility

[1]

THE ECONOMIC THEORY OF FERTILITY DECLINE

Harvey Leibenstein

Are children inferior goods? One would think so if (1) one thought of children as durable goods, and (2) one noted (a) that higher income groups "buy" fewer children than lower income groups and (b) that in the course of economic development (per capita income growth) family size declines. Since income differentials between different groups in developing countries are sometimes twentyfold or more and since per capita income grows by the same magnitude during economic development, this would imply, at first blush, that children are indeed extremely inferior goods.

The analogy of children as durable goods strains reality. Nevertheless, in the last decade a group of economists (Becker, Mincer, Willis etc.[1]) have used this analogy, but have correctly shied away from the idea of children as inferior goods. Hence, they have had to argue that family size should normally rise with income except for a countervailing quality or price (of the mother's time) effect. The main point of this paper is to present an alternative economic theory of family size determination that does not employ or lean heavily on either of these hypotheses.

The theory to be expounded is primarily designed to explain the decline in fertility that accompanies sustained economic development. In addition to (1), a general reconsideration of the author's

1. See No. 2, Part II, *Journal of Political Economy*, LXXXI (March/April, 1973).

previous theory of fertility (published in 1957),[2] this paper (2) attempts to handle explicitly a criticism [3] on the quality of children, and (3) introduces a sketch of a new theory of consumption based on social status considerations that are critical to the explanation of the utility cost of children. In our theory, differential knowledge of contraception is not involved in the explanation of differential fertility.

The theory to be presented is *not* to be considered as a "total" explanation of fertility. We do not know what part of fertility change can be accounted for by largely noneconomic factors, nor do we know whether the relationship of noneconomic to economic factors is additive or of a more complex nature. What we shall try to convey is that economic development implies and is accompanied by conditions that induce fertility decline to a sufficient degree so that enough fertility change is explained for the theory to be meaningful and of interest to an understanding of the process of development.

I. Typical Behavior Versus Critical Marginal Behavior

Two types of arguments are frequently presented against an economic theory of fertility. (1) People in underdeveloped countries do not use modern contraceptive means and hence do not limit their family size. (2) Fertility behavior is culturally determined and, to some degree, random or spontaneous and hence is not amenable to economic calculation.

We dwell only briefly on the first point. The high fertility rates in underdeveloped countries are considerably below their biological maximum — probably 40–60 percent below the Hutterite level.[4] Therefore, even in instances where fertility is traditionally high, there is a considerable degree of control. Furthermore, there exists a wide variety of traditional child spacing and family size controls — deferred marriage, abortions, taboos on sexual intercourse, long periods of lactation, coitus interruptus etc. One need not specify all possible means. Innumerable means have been known in the past. Furthermore, all means are substitutes to some degree

2. Harvey Leibenstein, *Economic Backwardness and Economic Growth* (New York: John Wiley and Sons, Inc., 1957), Ch. 10.
.3. Gary S. Becker, "An Economic Analysis of Fertility," in *Demographic and Economic Change in Developed Countries* (Princeton: NBER, Princeton University Press, 1960).
4. United Nations, Department of Economic and Social Affairs, *Demographic Yearbook, 1969* (New York, 1970), pp. 222–34. See also T. J. Eaton and A. J. Mayer, "The Social Biology of Very High Fertility Among the Hutterites," *Human Biology*, XXV (Sept. 1953), 206–64.

THE ECONOMIC THEORY OF FERTILITY DECLINE   3

for all other means. Finally, we can point to the fact that many of the countries that achieved their fertility decline earlier did so prior to the widespread distribution of modern contraceptive practices.[5]

For an economic theory to be valid, one need not assume that *typical* behavior is "rational." It is sufficient that behavior at critical junctures be of a "rational" type. Assume that the age of marriage and the birth of the final child depend on calculated considerations, although all intervening fertility behavior is "spontaneous." Note that under these conditions *average* typical behavior appears to be nonrational, but marginal behavior is rational. If the start-stop points are determined by calculation, then clearly fertility is determined, despite the fact that spacing will have a random component. In addition, it is not required that all households behave this way. If a reasonable proportion do, then an economic theory that depends on rationality is significant.

This paper is motivated in part by the belief that if a population has homogenous tastes (i.e., not dependent on status or "life style"), it is implausible for the cost of children, especially those attributed to "quality" or mother's time, to account for the inverse relation between family size and income level, given the large income differentials that exist and the income growth that occurs in developing countries.

The alternative that suggests itself, and the one that we shall employ, is that populations are divided into social status groups that have different tastes, who may to some degree have different desires for children (but not simply because of an income difference), and who especially see the whole cost structure of their expenditures, including expenditures for children, from the viewpoint of vastly different preference structures.[6]

---

5. T. Paul Schultz, "An Economic Model of Family Planning and Fertility," *Journal of Political Economy*, LXXVII, No. 2 (March/April 1969), 163–180. Schultz refers to a paper by Alvin J. Harman, which "finds no evidence in the Philippines that reported knowledge or use of contraceptive methods is associated with lower fertility after controlling for various socioeconomic determinants of desired fertility and stratifying by age. This study is based on individual family records for some 7,000 Philippine households in 1968" (p. 27).

6. Two of my students, Lee Edlefsen and Samuel S. Lieberman, carried out an econometric study based on data from Iran, which substantially supports the view taken here. As far as I can judge, from a general viewpoint, this is also the view taken by Richard Easterlin in a recent article. See (1) Lee Edlefsen and Samuel S. Lieberman, "An Econometric Model of Differential Fertility in Iran," Research Paper Number 2, March 1974, Center for Population Studies, Harvard University, Cambridge, Massachusetts; and (2) R. Easterlin, "Toward a Socioeconomic Theory of Fertility," in S. J. Behrman, *et al.*, eds., *Fertility and Family Planning: A World View* (Ann Arbor, Michigan: University of Michigan Press, 1969), pp. 127–157.

4   *QUARTERLY JOURNAL OF ECONOMICS*

The above remarks should not be taken to imply that the direct and indirect costs of children are not important, or that they are not likely to be higher in higher income groups than in lower ones, but simply that they are not sufficient to carry the weight of the entire decision process to determine the observed inverse relation. What will be attempted is to present an analysis that allows for an expanding number of variables within a relatively simple framework in order to capture the complexities of the situation under various circumstances.

II. Development, Occupational Shifts, and Status Shifts

Fertility is significantly influenced by events that accompany economic development. We present a brief stylized view of the development process and consider its impact. Basic to the development process is a persistent shift of labor (and households) out of agriculture into urban pursuits so that the ratio in agriculture changes from over 80 percent of the population to less than 20 percent. In general, the labor force shifts into manufacturing up to a maximum of 35 percent, while the rest moves into nonrural tertiary pursuits that include a vast variety of services such as trade, banking, and transportation.[7] These labor force shifts are associated with increases in education per worker, on-the-job training, and with a considerable increase in the amount of human capital per worker and per household member. Also, the work force becomes more highly differentiated in terms of (1) occupation, (2) skill content or education, and (3) assets per household — all of which are likely to be indexes of status.

We shall emphasize two aspects of the process of urbanization and occupational shift: (1) the shift of greater proportions of the population into higher socioeconomic statuses than would have been the case had the country remained at its lower income level; and (2) the simultaneous growth of per capita income. We shall argue that while *both* of these factors influence (a) the *utility* attached to children and (b) the *utility* of the typical expenditure patterns of households, which in turn determines the *utility costs* associated with children, the status-shift effects and income effects play very different roles and may even affect fertility in opposite ways.

7. See P. Bairoch and J. M. Limbor, "Changes in the Industrial Distribution of the World Labour Force, by Region, 1880–1960," *Essays on Employment*, Walter Galenson, ed. (Geneva: International Labour Office, 1971), especially pp. 34–40, for a summary of the relevant data.

THE ECONOMIC THEORY OF FERTILITY DECLINE 5

III. THE INTERSTATUS-INCOME RATIO COMPRESSION EFFECT

The elements that normally enter into socioeconomic status include signs of wealth, occupation, housing, education, residential location, political or military power, and hierarchical and other titles. Some elements are given at birth, while others are achieved. Many external manifestations of status have to be maintained through expenditures — i.e., the maintenance of a unique "life style," to use a modern term. In our analysis we distinguish ordinary consumption expenditures from *status* (or life style) goods and expenditures. The household's view of status depends on a reference group of "important others" who influence the consumption decisions of the household. The utility of such expenditures are in part a reflection of expectations of explicit or implicit approval or disapproval of the important others. We live in social groups. Beyond basic sustenance, consumption has a broad social status (life style) basis.

For present purposes status depends on (1) occupation, (2) education, and (3) consumer durable assets. We assume a status hierarchy. A household in a higher status is not always associated with a higher income, although the mean income for a higher status group is usually higher than that of a lower one. For ease of exposition consider a three-status–two-period model as illustrated in Table I. The two periods may be viewed as approximately fifteen years

TABLE I

Status		Period 1			Period 2		
		Income (1)	Status expenditures (2)	Nonstatus expenditures (3)	Income (4)	Status expenditures (5)	Nonstatus expenditures (6)
(Lowest)	1	100	40	60	200	100	100
	2	200	100	100	300	210	90
	3	300	150	150	350	300	50

apart. The numbers in column (4) compared to those in column (1) illustrate the interstatus-income ratio compression effect.[8] This is a well-documented, almost universal phenomenon that has been studied extensively by labor economists. For example, in a developing country an engineer might earn twenty times the income of an agricultural laborer, while in a high-income country the ratio might be reduced to three.

8. See Harold Lydall, *The Structure of Earnings* (London: Oxford University Press, 1968), pp. 163–99.

Now we assume that the income distribution remains more or less constant in the long run. Thus, if households move disproportionately to higher statuses between the two periods, and simultaneously interstatus-income ratios fall, then it is possible to retain approximately the same income distribution. The relative income compression effect will be compressed all the more if the income distribution becomes more equal as development occurs.[9]

Consider some of the possible consequences of relative income compression on consumption patterns on the basis of the following (reasonable) hypotheses: (1) Families have a strong desire to avoid a fall in status. (2) Some families will want to emulate those in higher statuses for themselves or for their children. (3) Services are disproportionately involved in "status goods." That is, the higher the status, the greater the expenditure on status goods that involve services. Since the general wage rises, we expect services to be more expensive in period 2 than in period 1. For example, educational costs would probably rise between the two periods. (4) Families try to maintain a strong status differential through their expenditure patterns. To start, assume that households attempt to keep the relative expenditures on status goods in the same proportion.

The four hypotheses lead to the conclusion that if status goods are a significant portion of income, then a considerable squeeze on the proportion of the budget spent on ordinary goods takes place. If those in status 1 consume the same amount of status goods in the second period as was consumed by status-2 families in the first period and if the differential is maintained, then status-2 families have to double their expenditures on status goods. If previously they spent 50 percent of their income ($100) on status goods, they will now have to spend twice as much. If, in addition, the price of status goods rises because services cost more, then an even higher proportion has to be spent on status goods. A lower proportion is thus available for nonstatus expenditures. We shall argue that to the extent there is a utility cost of children [10] that is distinct for each status, the utility foregone for an nth-order child could be higher in a higher status than in a lower one.

A more general way of viewing the matter would be in terms

9. See Simon Kuznets, "Economic Growth and Income Inequality," *American Economic Review*, XLV (March 1955), 1–28. Kuznets indicates that income distribution is likely to become more unequal in the earlier stages of development as the high-productivity industrial sector expands relative to the low-productivity agricultural sector, but that in the later stages of development income becomes more equally distributed.

10. In terms of the utility of the consumption foregone.

of income elasticities of demand. We distinguish between the *intra-status structure* elasticity for status goods and the *interstatus* elasticity. By the interstatus elasticity we have in mind the change in the demand for status goods for a given change in income as we move from one status to another. In general, it seems reasonable to assume (1) that the interstatus elasticity is greater than the intrastatus elasticity, and (2) that at some point the interstatus elasticity may become greater than one. Thus, a movement from one status to another involves an increase in the proportion spent on status goods. Is the interstatus elasticity affected by the extent of the income differential compression? It would seem reasonable to believe that the greater the compression, the easier it is for lower statuses to emulate higher ones, and the more sharply the desire of households in higher statuses to differentiate themselves from lower ones by increasing status expenditures. Thus, as compression increases, the greater will be the interstatus elasticity of demand. Hence, the greater the compression effect, the smaller will the proportion be of the budget available for nonstatus goods. If children are primarily a substitute for nonstatus goods (i.e., the fewer the children, the more the nonstatus goods that are enjoyed), then we can readily see that the utility cost of an nth-order child can become high as the compression effect proceeds if we make suitable (and to my mind reasonable) assumptions about the relative utility of income in different statuses.

IV. STATUS AND OTHER *IMU* GOODS

A critical part of our analysis is based on a simple and unique theory of consumer behavior that differs from conventional theory in that not all goods are subject to diminishing marginal utility from the first unit. In the theory to be sketched [11] we posit the existence of goods that are subject to *increasing* marginal utility up to some level and to normal diminishing marginal utility beyond that level. As a shorthand we shall refer to these as *IMU* goods. We distinguish four types of such goods (in terms of certain basic characteristics): (1) consumer durables subject to physical indivisibili-

11. The theory of consumption sketched here will be elaborated in detail in a forthcoming paper. James Duesenberry, in his *Income, Saving, and the Theory of Consumer Behavior* (Cambridge: Harvard University Press, 1949), denies the validity of the usual theory based on independent preferences and discusses the relation between consumption and social status (see pp. 28–32). He argues, as I do, that status expenditures are higher for higher income groups (p. 113). However, he does not develop a theory of the *increasing* marginal utility for some status goods.

ties or significant economies of scale for some reason; (2) what we shall call "commitment" goods; (3) status or "life style" goods; and (4) "target goods" in the sense that there is some target quantity or expenditure that is especially significant for some reason and anything less than the target amount is of little utility. These categories and the characteristics they emphasize are not distinct. Some expenditures may fall into all four categories to some degree. Some consumer durables that are indivisible in some sense may be ordinary goods. However, an expenditure on such an indivisible commodity (e.g., an automobile) is subject to a significant discontinuity. Spending $100 on automobiles yields zero utility if the minimum unit cost is $1,000. Furthermore, if there are economies of scale, then one may obtain increasing marginal utility per dollar spent up to some point.

Consider the following example. Suppose that someone takes a foreign language course given in monthly units. After six months he can receive certification indicating a certain level of proficiency useful for normal conversation. The person may feel that any number of lessons are useful but that hitting the minimal conversational proficiency level is especially important. For such a person the marginal utility of each lesson increases until the critical proficiency level (his target) is reached. Beyond that point diminishing marginal utility sets in. The person is *"committed"* to a certain minimum expenditure. We shall argue that by and large status maintenance expenditures are commitment goods in the sense indicated, although some may not be of this type. Needless to say, it is not the physical nature of the goods that makes them commitment goods, but rather the way people feel about them and about status.

Suppose that housing is a status good and that some people feel that "appropriate" housing determines their status and that they will be judged by others accordingly. Hence, at less than a certain minimal expenditure on housing, they feel that status is not maintained or that it is seriously jeopardized. In that case there is likely to be increasing marginal utility to housing expenditures at least up to the status maintenance level. Of course, housing provides utility as shelter, but it also provides *additional* utility as a status good. Since many types of goods serve as status indicators, to maintain status these goods have to be purchased to some degree. Also, some expenditures *on* children (e.g., clothing, schooling, health care, toys etc.) operate as status goods.

An important analytical possibility is that the utility for some set of goods depends on the deviation from some set of accepted

THE ECONOMIC THEORY OF FERTILITY DECLINE   9

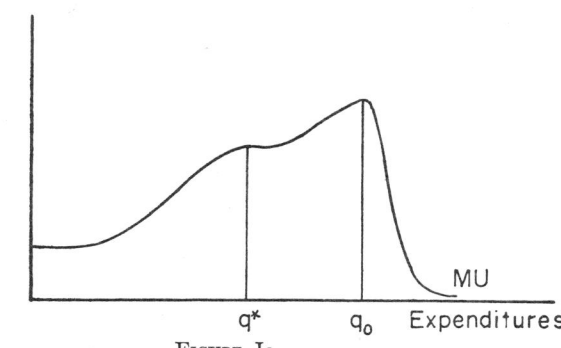

FIGURE Ia

consumption "norms." In other words, what matters, at least in part, is the relative consumption level rather than the absolute level. Certain classes of consumption may be related to such psychological magnitudes as the sense of self-esteem or significance, or of attainment etc., so that comparison with others is the critical criterion that scores. The basic idea is illustrated in Figure Ia. We show marginal utility per dollar spent (price is given) on the ordinate and expenditures on the abscissa. (This is indicated by MU in Figure Ia.) q^* is the class norm. We can readily imagine that there may be consumption or expenditures for which people feel that they would like to reach or exceed the class norms. Utility rises rapidly until the point at which the class norm is reached, although the maximal marginal utility may be at a point greater than the class norm, say at q_0. In other words, the optimal quantity from a comparative viewpoint is larger than the class norm by a given degree. This will vary by households. Essentially, the relation of utility to class norms adds nothing new analytically to our analysis. It is simply another illustration as to why some commodities for some households might be IMU goods.

An important type of *commitment*, which occurs especially in higher statuses and increases with status, is the provision for old-age security. This is frequently looked upon as one of the utilities for children, but for higher income groups it could be viewed as a significant expense. Clearly, the amount of provision for old-age security depends on the life style one is used to and hence also the life style one wishes to live in during old age. Thus, this commitment component operates in the same way as the status or IMU goods would operate.[12]

12. Ronald Freedman points out the degree to which old-age security may have influenced the falling Japanese birth rate. He writes:

10   *QUARTERLY JOURNAL OF ECONOMICS*

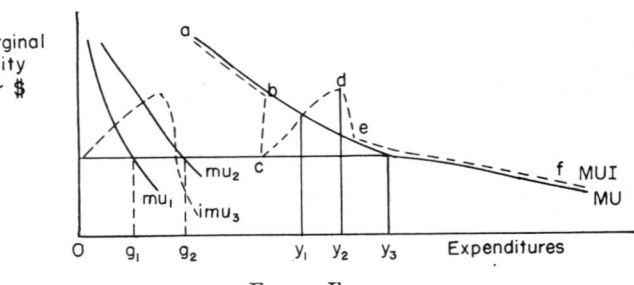

FIGURE Ib

Expenditures on commitment goods are different from ordinary expenditures in the same sense that long-run costs differ from short-run costs. Once the commitment is made, it continues for some period of time even if "tastes" change. Thus, a man may buy insurance for his wife when he loves her and retain the insurance when he ceases to do so — although if he had it to do over again, he would not make the commitment. Similarly, expenditures on children involve *minimal* commitments that do *not* reflect tastes in the sense of temporary feelings towards the child, but reflect simply the *fact* of the responsibility involved in the child-parent relation, and the life style that determines the degree of the appropriate minimal (and optimal) expenditure *commitments* for different types of status goods.

We now turn to show the significance of *IMU* goods on the marginal utility of income (for savings is viewed as a type of expenditure). In Figure Ib, mu_1 and mu_2 are the marginal utility curves for ordinary goods 1, 2 etc. (prices are given). Suppose that only ordinary goods existed. Then *MU*, the lateral summation of the curves mu_i, for all i, is the marginal utility of income curve. (Of course, these curves are for *only* one set of prices. The curves have to be redrawn for each price change.) If income is y_3, then utility

---

Recent Japanese data provide a striking illustration of the close relation between norms about dependence on adult children and the course of fertility. Between 1950 and 1961 the Japanese birth rate fell spectacularly from 28 to 17 per 1000. In the same period the biennial sample surveys by the Mainichi press posed to a representative cross-section of the population the question: "Do you expect to depend on your children in your old age?" In 1950 a majority, more than 55 percent, answered "definitely yes." The proportion giving this answer declined steadily in five succeeding surveys, reaching 27 percent by 1961. It is rare that public opinion on a matter this vital changes so steadily and rapidly and just as rare that we have statistical data with which to document the trend.

See Ronald Freedman, "Norms for Family Size in Underdeveloped Areas," *Population and Society*, Charles B. Nam, ed. (Boston: Houghton Mifflin Company, 1968), p. 222.

maximization requires that the utility for the marginal dollar spent on every commodity be equal. Hence the expenditures on commodities 1 and 2 are shown by og_1 and og_2. The

$$\sum_{i=1}^{i=n} og_i = y_3.$$

Now consider what happens when we introduce an *IMU* good shown by the broken line imu_3. As we proceed down our marginal expenditure function, we can no longer proceed by *marginal* dollars spent. At each point what we must ask is whether there is an expenditure of some size whose marginal utility is low but whose total utility is larger than would be obtained by continuing expenditures on diminishing marginal utility goods. In Figure Ib this occurs at the point b. The new curve is *MUI* (i.e., marginal utility of expenditures inclusive of *IMU* goods). We note a curious result here in that it is possible for the marginal utility of a higher income y_2 to be higher than that of a lower income y_1. We shall also see that the hump in the curve cde will have an important bearing in determining family size.

V. Intrahousehold Distributions and Commitment Claim Drift

In previous sections we treated the household as a unit. However, in order to see how pressures accumulate to maintain (or pursue) status through the purchase of status goods it is useful to examine the processes of *intra*household claims, whether implicit, subdued, or explicit, and to consider the interactions of *intra*household claim compromises among family members and *inter*household emulation through demographically similar individuals. We shall see that the process to be described is likely to lead to proportionately greater pressure toward the purchase of status goods as we proceed up the income-status scale — with the exception of the very top status levels. The analysis to be presented complements the discussion in Section IV.

What happens to claims on family income by family members as household income increases? Three elements that are likely to play a role are (1) the nature of the resolution of conflicting claims prior to the income increase; (2) the degree to which the other households in the same "social influence group" (SIG) have also had income growth; and (3) competitive appeals for fairness. We shall consider claim pressures from the viewpoint of the net contributor (parent) and refer to others in the household as claimants. Also, suppose that under normal circumstances, each member, above some minimum age, wants as much as possible of the *increase* in household income (i.e., apart from empathy for the abnormal circumstances of some particular family member).

Family members are likely to have certain preferences about the *form* in which the share of family income comes. Thus, a net receiver would normally prefer (1) money grants over goods in kind (of equal value) if transaction costs are trivial, and (2) long-term money commitments over short-term money grants. At the very least, a person can buy the family-chosen commodity bundle, or he could purchase one that he prefers. We may think of a short-term money grant to a family member as an allowance, and a commitment as a money grant that is repeated periodically without negotiation. Ideally, one would prefer the option to renegotiate the commitment upwards but not downwards. On the other hand, the net contributor (or both parents), will frequently want some control over at least part of the income share allocated to a family member. Hence a compromise usually has to be worked out on the "form" of the family income share that goes to a specific member.

A family member's utility depends on (1) the amount "spent" on him or her, (2) the "form" of the expenditure, and (3) the nature of the negotiations and subsequent relations that result in the expenditure. In Figure II, the curve marked P_1 indicates the parent's willingness to trade some degree of control over the expenditure of the claimant for a greater amount of the expenditure. The curve

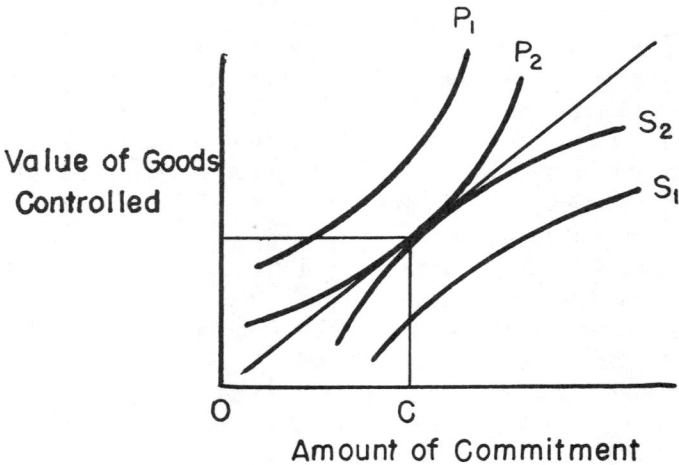

FIGURE II
OC = "Controlled-Commitment" Agreement

THE ECONOMIC THEORY OF FERTILITY DECLINE   13

P_1 approaches an asymtote, since there is a maximum amount the parent is willing to spend. The claimant's (say, a son's) indifference curve S_1 is shaped in the opposite way reflecting the son's (claimant's) desire to give up some of the expenditure if less parental control is exercised. Curves P_1 and S_1 represent loci of "control-commitment" mixes where no unpleasantness is felt by P or S. The parent who is in ultimate control of the purse strings, can always "impose" a solution by his willingness to undergo a given degree of unpleasantness. Thus, if the curves P_1, S_1 do not have any contact points, then there are other curves that may be viewed as moving towards each other, but at the same time curves closer to each other involve degrees of dissatisfaction on both sides. P_2 and S_2 have a tangency point, which reflects a cooperative solution. Both P_2 and S_2 are functions of current family income. If income was higher, the son would expect more and be more dissatisfied with the existing solution, and the parent would probably be willing to yield more (i.e., the P_1 curve would move to the right).

Unwelcome compromises may have been imposed on at least some family members, since all must ultimately yield to the income constraint. It is as though the net contributor has built a dike to dam the wave of claims. But the dike overflows once the potential claimants perceive an increase in income. Claimants rush to renegotiate. The net contributor may find it hard to struggle against the onslaught, especially since in some cases some family members may aspire to a higher social status in making their claims.[13] We must keep in mind the asymmetry that exists in this connection — many aspire upwards but few aspire to a fall in status.

If we define total claim elasticity as the ratio of the increase in all claims to the increase in income, then claim elasticity in the previous case is most likely greater than unity. Consider especially the case in which all households in a given social influence group (SIG) [14] receive an increase in income. Once the family agrees to live in a style somewhat similar to those who are in its SIG, many areas of discretion are narrowed. Family members with similar demographic characteristics (age, sex, etc.) will to some extent have to be equipped with similar material goods. The very meaning of

13. This may occur because as the process of economic development proceeds social status jumping gradually becomes a more readily visible phenomenon.

14. The term SIG and social status group will be used interchangeably. The appropriate social influence groups may differ considerably in different cultures. Hence, in doing empirical work in order to test this theory identifying the appropriate social influence groups, or optimal proxies for such groups, may be a very important and distinct aspect of the empirical problem.

belonging (and especially *demonstrating* belonging) to a given SIG implies some similarity in the type of expenditure patterns.

If there should be disagreements between net receivers and net contributors about the allocation of family income, the standards set by the group — or examples of specific members of the group but outside the family — will frequently be invoked as reference points and arguments in appeals for "fair shares." Suppose that for family members in a SIG there is (1) a modal allowance and (2) a modal expenditure. For a specific household each family member argues for at least the *perceived* modal allowance and expenditure. Not receiving the allowance may be viewed as questioning whether the parents in control are living up to the image of the particular SIG to which they directly or indirectly claim to belong. The process of competition between households and between demographically similar household members puts pressures on those who control household income to treat their own members no worse than they are treated in other approximately similarly placed households.

It should also be noted that outsiders to the household will seek and acquire commitments from family members. Leases, mortgages, school fee arrangements, credit payments, club memberships, and so on frequently take the form of intermediate length commitments entered into by household members with outsiders. In general, we should expect that the proportion of household income that goes to all commitments rises with increases in socioeconomic status. The reason for this is that to a considerable degree one needs either to be a commitment recipient or to have a fairly high income before one can safely and easily become a commitment payer. There is a necessary relationship between the steadiness of income receipts (or the level of permanent income) to the household and its ability to supply commitments. In the world of the day laborer receiving an irregular wage, there are likely to be many fewer commitments to household members (or outsiders) than in the world of the professional receiving an annual salary. In brief, a relatively stable income stream to the household permits the household to undertake stable commitments to both household members and outsiders, and this capacity increases as we go up the socioeconomic scale. In the course of economic development job formalization and professionalization increases, which in turn increases the ability of all groups to grant commitments.

Can interdependent and interacting claim structures be explosive? Suppose that all members sequentially raise their claims by some relatively small amount. If the average size allowance is used

THE ECONOMIC THEORY OF FERTILITY DECLINE   15

as an argument and if some claims are met, then the average allowance will gradually rise, which in turn becomes an excuse for higher claims to be met so that we have, on the whole, a general upward claims drift. However, there are strict upper limits to such drifts. If many household members make such claims, then fairly soon the competing claims exhaust family income, and not all claims can be met. At this point some claims are not met, and when enough of such claims cease to be met, then it becomes clear that other claims are relatively excessive and the comparative "fairness" appeal no longer works. Thus, the point at which the upward claim drift equilibrium settles can frequently lead to a level of expenditures for the average SIG family that will be on the verge of exhausting the income increase. Households whose incomes (after the increases) are less than the representative household's income will face more pressure from claimants than in the case for households with more than the representative amount.

Suppose for a moment that the marginal income elasticities of claims and commitments for a group of households are greater than unity. The lower the household income within a socioeconomic status group, and the lower the *increase* in income, the greater the marginal elasticities. One can see that in this case the absolute amount left to net contributors (one or both parents) may be no greater than before the income increases. To the extent that this type of intrahousehold pressure builds up, one can readily see that an increase in household income (when other incomes rise simultaneously) will not yield much of a decrease in pressure, and will for many households produce an increase in pressure to grant commitments to family members to maintain or pursue status, and to enter into commitments with outsiders, so that on balance, the portion of the anticipated income stream left for family size expansion may be proportionately or absolutely less than before.

VI. On the Price Inelasticity of Status Goods

In discussing status (and other *IMU*) goods in different statuses, we argued that the possible larger service component in the consumption patterns in higher statuses meant that the price of status goods might rise as the interstatus relative income compression proceeds. We now want to suggest that the characterization of status goods given in Figure Ia and in the preceding discussion implies that such goods are likely to be highly inelastic with respect to price.

16   *QUARTERLY JOURNAL OF ECONOMICS*

Diagrammatically, the relation between ordinary and status goods may be represented by the following strange-looking "kinky" indifference curve in Figure IIIa. The two goods are g, the ordinary

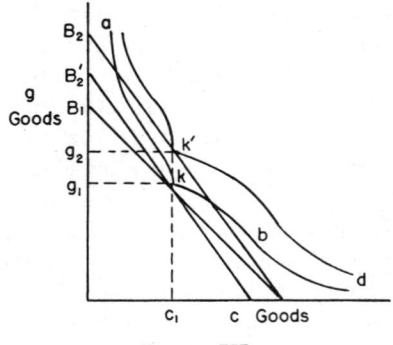

FIGURE IIIa

good (representing all ordinary goods) and c, the status or commitment good. The portion of the indifference curve ak represents the counterpart of increasing marginal utility of c goods, namely, the increasing marginal rate of substitution of c goods for g goods. As we move along kbd, some degree of diminishing utility of c goods sets in. On segment bd, the indifference curve resumes its normal concave shape and reflects the *diminishing* rate of substitution of c goods for g goods.

B_1 and B_2 in Figure IIIa are alternate budget lines. Because of the kink at point k, we note that for some price changes the commodity bundle desired c_1g_1 remains the same if we exclude the income effect kk'. B'_2 represents the budget line that compensates for the income change inherent in the price changes. As drawn, Figure IIIa illustrates the important *possibility* of a complete lack of a substitution effect, although c goods are relatively more expensive. Other possibilities along the same lines are shown in Figures IIIb and IIIc.

In Figure IIIb the same idea is reflected as in Figure IIIa except that only one portion of the indifference curve reflects an increasing marginal rate of substitution. This reflects a single target value rather than a double target value, such as a minimal one and an optimal one, for status goods of the type illustrated in Figure Ia. Figure IIIc suggests that without a kinky indifference curve but with increasing marginal rates of substitution we may still have very low price elasticities of demand. In figure IIId we illustrate

THE ECONOMIC THEORY OF FERTILITY DECLINE   17

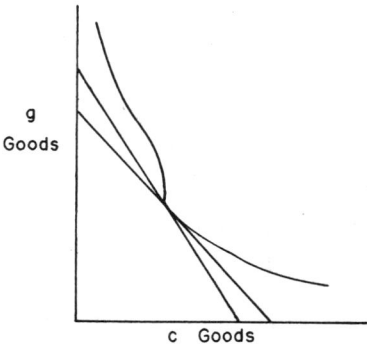

FIGURE IIIb

FIGURE IIIc

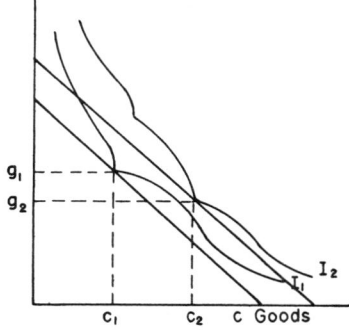

FIGURE IIId

an indifference map in which an increase in income results in a disproportionate increase in the demand for status goods in accordance with the arguments in Section III.

VII. Interstatus Total Utility Differentials and the Utility Cost of Children

One of the difficulties in comparing the costs of children for different households under different circumstances is in determining what we should reasonably assume about the relative utility of income. Three possibilities come to mind: (1) Equal total utility for the rich and the poor and proportional dollars spent imply the same marginal utility. (2) The utility *per dollar* is the same for the rich and the poor, and diminishing marginal utility with respect to dollars at the same rate, so that the marginal utility of a dollar is necessarily lower for the richer individual. (3) A greater total utility for the rich (and higher status households) and proportional declines in marginal utility. A priori and intuitive knowledge, as well as a great deal of survey data marshalled by Easterlin, suggests that on the average higher income groups are somewhat happier than lower income groups.[15] As a consequence, it seems inappropriate to make the equal total utility assumption. We are thus left with a second or third alternative. It seems intuitively plausible, but impossible to prove, that if a higher status person had the same income as a lower status one (not necessarily the same assets), a marginal dollar to a higher status person would have less utility than to a lower one if all goods were ordinary (not *IMU* goods.) In what follows, this will be the assumption we shall use. However, it can easily be shown that the results could be qualitatively similar on the basis of the second assumption.

We now introduce the concept of *average equal utility expenditure units* (to be referred to as *AEU* units). Suppose that the total utility of the higher status person is one and one half times that of the lower status person. We then compute what would be the equiv-

15. Richard A. Easterlin, "Does Economic Growth Improve the Human Lot?: Some Empirical Evidence," in Paul A. David and Melvin W. Reder, eds., *Nations and Households in Economic Growth: Essays in Honor of Moses Abramovitz* (Palo Alto, California: Stanford University Press, 1974). Easterlin finds that higher income groups are by various survey measures happier than lower income groups, but that this does *not* change over time as per capita income increases. The data are consistent with the argument presented above that, as income increases and the relative income compression occurs, the "need" for status goods increases disproportionately, and more "needed" status goods do not contribute more happiness, so that total utility within a status does not change markedly.

THE ECONOMIC THEORY OF FERTILITY DECLINE 19

alent number of dollars for a higher status person that would yield the same utility as one dollar for a lower status one. This enables us to use average equal utility expenditure units to compare the decisions of higher status and lower status households. Let y_1 and y_2 be the incomes for the two households, and TU_1 and TU_2 their total utilities. Then an *AEU* unit is defined as $\dfrac{Y_2}{TU_2} \Big/ \dfrac{Y_1}{TU_1}$ . . . .

For instance, if incomes are \$300 in the higher status household and \$100 in the lower one and total utilities for the higher income are 200 and 100 for the lower one, then an *AEU* unit will represent \$1.50 for the higher income and \$1 for the lower income.

In Figure IV the abscissa indicates the equivalent utility ex-

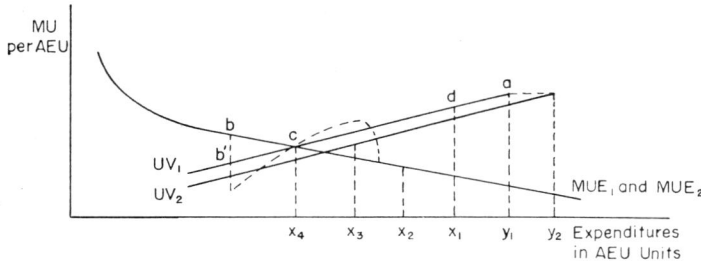

FIGURE IV

AEU = average equi-utility units
MUE = marginal utility of expenditure curve for both individuals
y_1 = income for status 1
y_2 = income for status 2
UV_1 = marginal utility for children in *AEU* units for status 1
UV_2 = marginal utility for children in *AEU* units for status 2.

penditures units. The ordinate represents marginal utility. We assume that for *AEU* units, marginal utility falls just as rapidly for higher and lower status individuals. We can easily relax this assumption to obtain similar results, but that would only complicate the exposition unnecessarily.

The curve *MUE* is the marginal utility of expenditures (in *AEU* units) for the two households. The curves marked UV_1 and UV_2 are the utility values of children for the lower and higher status, respectively. We read the utility value of marginal children from right to left as indicated by the arrow. The area adx_1y_1 represents the utility value of a first child in the household in status 1. We assume that in terms of *AEU* units the utility value of an nth-order child is the same. The arbitrarily assumed equal distances,[16] $y_2 y_1$, $y_1 x_1$, $x_1 x_2$ etc., are the average utility costs of children in terms of equi-utility expenditure units. As a first step we assume that the cost of child rearing is the same for the two groups in terms of AEU units. Of course, this means that in dollars it is higher for the higher status.

We can now read off the results in Figure IV. The first point to observe is that if all goods were ordinary goods, then the family size for the higher status household would be larger than for the lower status household. This can be seen by comparing the equilibrium points at which the relevant MUE and UV curves intersect. As drawn, the higher status household would have 4.5 children, and the lower status one only 4 children. It is noteworthy, once we introduce status goods (i.e., IMU goods), that the situation reverses itself. We see that the lower status household chooses four children, while the higher one would choose three children. The higher status MUE curve has the "status-goods-IMU hump," which raises the marginal utility cost of children for higher status households. In other words, a fourth child will mean sacrificing the high-status-goods utility. Thus, in the case illustrated, a larger family could threaten the status position of the higher status household.[17]

In interpreting Figure IV we should keep in mind that the cost of children for lower status groups during the period in which the economy is less developed has as an offset the earnings of children. It makes more sense to look upon it this way rather than to look upon these earnings as part of the value we attribute to children. This offset is likely to be lower as we go up the status scale and as education increases. For very high statuses it dwindles to zero.

Now let us relax for a moment the assumption that children in each status cost the same in terms of equi-utility expenditure units. Suppose they cost more in the AEU units for the higher status. Clearly, in this case the qualitative result is similar. The higher status would have even fewer children than otherwise. The situation is more complex if for the higher status there is a lower average

16. Equality of distances is assumed for ease in exposition only. A more realistic figure would show the cost of the first child about twice the size of the second, but subsequent distances could be approximately equal or declining somewhat. See Thomas J. Espenshade, "Estimating the Cost of Children and Some Results from Urban United States," Preliminary Paper No. 4, February 1973, International Population and Urban Research, University of California, Berkeley, pp. 15 ff.

17. We can introduce a small-status-good hump on the MUE, curve, say, between the points b' and c without changing our conclusions. The main point is that the higher status will spend a higher proportion on status-IMU goods.

THE ECONOMIC THEORY OF FERTILITY DECLINE 21

expenditure cost in *AEU* units per child. In that case whether or not the situation reverses itself (compared to the no-status-goods assumption) depends on the degree of the lower cost for the higher status. It is clear that, while we cannot prove necessarily that higher status (and higher income) households will have fewer children, we show the possibility and argue the probability that this will be the case. Further, we indicate the way the relationship between utility costs and status-goods expenditures leads to such conclusions. Given the arguments presented in connection with the phenomenon of the relative status income compression, it would appear likely that, even if at the outset of development higher status family size was the same as lower status size, the relative income compression and its impact on status-*IMU* expenditures would eventually lead to a fall in family size for the higher status household.[18]

VIII. On the Utility of Children

It will facilitate discussion if we divide the desire for children into three categories — low-, medium-, and high-parity children. By low parity we have in mind zero–three children, medium parity represents four–six children, and high parity will represent seven or more children. We have argued in the previous section almost entirely on the basis of utility cost considerations. A question that arises is whether the significant variable is not the utility *value*, so that the entire explanation could be based on a decline of the utility value (benefits) of children (a) as we move from lower to higher statuses and (b) as per capita income increases.

Now the hypothesis we will argue is that, while the utility and desire for high-parity children unquestionably declines in the course of development, the utility and desire for medium-parity children is probably *not* very much lower, and as a consequence what has to be explained is how economic costs induce a reduction in actual

18. The relatively rich within a status will have approximately the same utilities and utility costs as the average household in the status, but a lesser budget constraint, and hence will be able to afford and desire more children than the representative household. Hence, birth rates are positively associated with income *within* a status, but not *between* statuses. This is consistent with Deborah Freedman's findings for the United States. See Deborah Freedman, "The Relation of Economic Status to Fertility," *American Economic Review*, LIII (June 1963), 414–26. See also Eva M. Bernhardt, "Fertility and Economic Status — Some Recent Findings on Differentials in Sweden," *Population Studies*, XXVI (July 1972), 175–84. For some occupations very low-income groups in the occupation have relatively higher fertility rates. This may be because (a) occupation by itself is a poor proxy for status and (b) income (or characteristics that vary with income) is also part of the defining characteristic of status.

family size from the medium parity that would be desired to the low parities that actually occur. Some empirical evidence buttressed by theoretical considerations suggests that a plausible argument could be made that the desire for children would not have declined beyond the high middle parities, say 4.5 to 5 children, were it not for the utility costs. Thus, we shall want to show that, while there is reason to believe that the value of high-parity children has declined, there is very little reason to assume this for low- and middle-parity children.

In an interesting experiment reported on by Namboodiri,[19] it was found that people with relatively low family size, when asked their ideal family size if they had all the income necessary to support any number of children, desired somewhere between 4 and 5 children. One could even argue that such an experiment involves a bias on the low side. To a considerable degree people take their cues about the correct number of children from others in the same social status. Something like a "band-wagon effect" occurs. Thus, if most households are having between two and three children, that fact influences the desired number. The influence would be very different if most households had, say, between five and six children. Thus, if everybody in a given social status had all the income necessary to support their ideal family size, then overall family size would be higher, and the cues that influence them with respect to the "proper" number of children would also be higher.

We now consider some of the specifics involved in the utility value of children. Consumption utility reflects the extent to which parents want children as sources of personal satisfaction. How this utility varies with status increase or income growth is difficult to say. We are concerned only with the utility of a third or higher parity child. As income increases, there are increasingly available alternative sources of satisfaction that are potential substitutes for the consumption utility of high-parity children. However, not to bias the theory unduly, we shall assume that consumption utility

19. See N. Krishnan Namboodiri, "Some observations on the Economic Framework for Fertility Analysis," *Population Studies*, XXVI (July 1972), 185 ff. This is based on a pilot study in North Carolina where the income range of the two middle categories was between $7,000 and $13,000 per year. Other studies show similar results. See the review of some of these data in Easterlin, *op. cit.*, pp. 140–44. See also Judith Blake, "Family Size in the 1960's — A Baffling Fad," *Eugenics Quarterly*, XIV (March 1967), 60ff. It is likely that the no-income-constraint-family-size preferences for countries whose per capita incomes are less than, say, $1,000 would frequently be considerably higher.

is constant or does not fall significantly with respect to status increases or income increases.[20]

A significant sociological concomitant of development is the attenuation and eventual disappearance of the extended family system, in the sense of a kinship system in which there are exceedingly strong bonds of mutual obligation and support. Sociologists have emphasized the extended family as a significant instrument in establishing and maintaining large family norms. The following quotations summarize the essence of the argument.

> In most pre-industrial societies a wide range of activities involve interdependence with kinsmen. . . . These include production, consumption, leisure activity, assistance in illness and old age and many other activities covered by non-familial institutions in modern societies. To simplify greatly: large numbers of children are desired if the values considered worthwhile are obtained through familial ties rather than through other social institutions. . . . This, in turn, depends on the division of labour between the family and other social institutions and on how much the performance of important functions by the family depends on the number of children produced in it.[21]

> Islam partakes of the pro-natalist social forces that exist generally in peasant and pastoral societies. . . . Sons are valued for many purposes: for continuity of family line and land-ownership; for contribution to agricultural labor; to strengthen family numbers in village rivalry and strife; for support in old age; for religious intervention at and after death. As in other developing societies . . . , the joint family system in Islam buffers the direct burdens of childbearing on the parents.[22]

It seems natural to give these notions an economic interpretation. The extended family system is an arrangement whereby the kinship group provides an informal trading system of desired *services* for its members through a system of mutual obligation. Among these services are insurance against economic disaster, insurance against the consequences of some children not working out well, old-age security, and insurance against the economic disabilities of failing health. It also provides inexpensive baby-tending services, a locus of leisure time activities, health-tending services, as well as a pool of labor skills that may be traded informally in emergencies and part of whose value lies in the existence of a *variety* of skills.

The persistent migration to urban areas that accompanies de-

20. Namboodiri's data do show a 20 percent difference approximately between high and low education (4.1 versus 4.8 children) and a similar difference with respect to income. However, these differences would be less if there was no differential "band-wagon" effect.

21. Ronald Freedman, "Norms for Family Size in Underdeveloped Areas," *Population and Society*, Charles B. Nam, ed. (Boston: Houghton Mifflin Company, 1968), pp. 220–21.

22. Dudley Kirk, Factors Affecting Moslem Natality," Nam, *op. cit.*, p. 235.

velopment leads to the dispersal of nuclear families so that the extended family is attenuated and eventually disappears as members of the group find it impossible to maintain their obligations to trade informally nonmarketed services. Hence, such services have to be provided either by the market or within the *nuclear* family. To the extent that some can only be provided more cheaply within the nuclear family, this will *increase* the demand for children rather than the other way around. Not only is there an insurance motivation to maintain reasonably high parities for nuclear families, especially with respect to the provision of old-age security, but also internal baby-tending services and bases for leisure activities and affective relationships that previously were provided (cheaply) for the most part within the extended family. To some degree, higher status groups can rely more on the market, especially for servants, for such services. The point to be stressed is that even as the extended family becomes attenuated, counteracting forces come into play that prop up the desire for fairly large (medium- to high-parity) nuclear families in the absence of economic constraints.

It would take too much space to work through all of the influences and assess what we know about these factors. Some of the major *probable* relations are suggested and summarized in Table II, which indicates the importance of six significant factors on the desire for medium- and high-parity children as status and per capita income increases. The table allows us to separate quickly the status-rise effects from the income-growth effects. In general, almost all of the variables work in the direction of reducing the utility of high-parity children. However, this is not the case for medium-parity children.

Both for status increases and for increases in income, there are factors that work in opposite directions in terms of their impact on the desire for medium-parity children. Especially noteworthy is what is likely to happen as per capita income increases. At least three factors are likely to stimulate an increase in the desire for children, especially as the extended family attenuates. These are (1) the value of children as a source of old-age security, (2) as a vehicle that maintains and provides nuclear family status, and (3) as a means of providing *insurance* with respect to the previously mentioned variables. On the other hand, the utility of children falls as an input that meets extended family obligations and as a contributor to family earnings. It is difficult to assess how it all nets out. It seems probable that even if on balance the desire for children does decline to some degree, the decline is not great enough to explain

TABLE II

Factor	Impact of factor on desire for children as status increases		Impact of factor on desire for children as per capita income increases	
Children as a source of:	Medium-parity children	High-parity children	Medium-parity children	High-parity children
1. Family labor or family income	declines with status: cost offset to cost of child rearing	declines with status: cost offset to child-rearing costs	declines with income: cost offset	declines with income: cost offset
2. Old-age security	constant or increases with status	constant with status	increases as extended family declines if inadequate family provision by government	decreases markedly as non-family security systems come into play
3. Extended family obligations	constant or rises with status, higher statuses frequently have greater awareness of extended family obligations	probably unimportant at high status	declines with income as extended family declines with income	of no importance as income rises
4. Insurance (against some children not capable (e.g., unemployed) or willing to contribute adequately items 1, 2, 3, or 5)	probably constant with status	probably unimportant with status	constant with income, may decline with very high increases	becomes trivial with high incomes
5. Contributions to nuclear family status maintenance and welfare	probably constant with status	probably unimportant as status rises	increases with income as extended family declines	probably unimportant
6. Impact of mortality decline effect	declines unimportant with status, son preference theory questionable	declines considerably with status	decreases as income increases	unimportant or trivial except for very rapid declines from previously very high rates

sufficiently the shift from a demand for almost high-parity children to low-parity children.

A theory that has to be disposed of is the idea that son preference plus declining mortality rates can explain fertility decline. The essence of the argument is that households want a target number of *surviving* sons (say, two). Because of the high mortality risk they need a higher number of male births (say, three) for two to survive, and given the sex mix that nature offers, a large family size occurs. As mortality rates decline, the risk aspect changes, and fewer male births are required. This should lead to the finding that households that have males born early (e.g., three boys out of the first three births) should have a smaller family size. Repetto [23] has marshalled as much data as he could find on the subject. He found that the expected relation held. For instance, families whose first three births were all males had higher fertility rates than those who had only girls. Clearly, the theory is wrong. My hypothesis is that households behave like gamblers with loaded dice. Where son preference is high, a household that finds that nature has awarded it with a string of, say, its first three, conceptions that are all males, feels that nature has loaded the dice in its favor, and it keeps on playing to cash in on the winning streak.

IX. COMBINING UTILITY AND UTILITY COST RELATIONS

On the basis of ordinary utility analysis, it follows that the utility of a marginal child, for a *given income* and *status*, falls with respect to increases in the number of children. Other things equal, utility costs are likely to rise (for given money expenditures) as we shift to higher order births. If expenditures on a fourth and fifth child are the same, then the utility cost for a fifth child will be higher than a fourth. The indirect marginal opportunity cost (say, to the mother in terms of *partial* income foregone) is likely to be approximately the same unless spacing is compressed when there are more rather than fewer births. This last is a possibility in some cases. Also, higher income foregone at slightly older ages is an additional complication. These possibilities are probably more than adequately accounted for if we assume at first that the utility costs of *higher* order births are at least the same as birth-order increases.

We can aggregate for every household the individual utility and utility cost relations. Given the jth's household income y_j, status

23. Robert Repetto, "Son Preference and Fertility Behavior in Developing Countries," *Studies in Family Planning*, IV, No. 3, (April 1972), 70–76.

THE ECONOMIC THEORY OF FERTILITY DECLINE   27

level s_j, and the per capita income of the economy y^* to indicate the economic environment in which the household finds itself, we can determine the fertility behavior of the household.[24] The five basic functions are

(1) $U_{ij} = f_{ij}(y_j, s_j, y^*)$,

(2) $U^c_{ij} = F_{ij}(y_j, s_j, y^*)$,

(3) $y_j = fy(y^*)$,

(4) $s_j = f_s(y^*)$,

(5) $y^* =$ given exogenously,

where U_{ij} is the utility of the ith child for the jth household and U^c_{ij} is the utility cost. Since some households move from one status to another as per capita income changes, we assume that at each level of per capita income y^* determines the status of household j. That is, y^* is a proxy for the factors that determine the distribution of occupation in the economy, and the educational requirements to which the supply of labor responds.[25] With y^* given, and hence status determined, equations (1) and (2) determine the fertility behavior of the household.

As long as $U_{ij} > U_{ij}^c$, the household will have an incentive to have an ith child. If U_j is a monotonic-decreasing function with respect to the number of children, and U_j^c is a monotonic-increasing function with respect to the number of children, y^* and s_j given,

---

24. In contrast to Becker, the "quality" of children is handled indirectly in this model. My theory is in the spirit of Duesenberry's quip that "Economics is all about how people make choices. Sociology is all about why they don't have any choices to make." Quality is determined indirectly as a consequence of the household's reaction to its status. This seems to me to reflect more accurately what occurs in reality. I doubt whether any significant proportion of, say, middle class households consider that they have a valid option to choose between fewer children educated at their status level, and *more* children nurtured and educated at a lower level.

Ultimately, this question can only be answered by empirical research. In part, it is also a scientific tactical problem that involves the determination of the optimum set of assumptions. If the quality variation *within* recognized groups is found to be exceedingly small, then it might be convenient to develop the theory without the quality variable as part of the household decision-making mechanism. Also, following the principle of Occam's razor, if the theory does quite well without a quality variable, it may be best to leave it out. There may be problems for which it may be useful to have quality as a household decision-making variable. However, with respect to the problem at hand, my tentative approach is to have quality in terms of education, job training, and nurture enter by the back door.

25. We could develop a more realistic looking model in which the occupation of household j depends on some previous year's per capita income, and similarly education could be a lagged function of income in the past and so on. While such a model would appear to be more realistic, it would probably add little to the essential points we are trying to make.

then the number of births for the household is determined at the point where $U_j - U_j^c$ is a minimum.

We shall refer to the intersection of curves U_{ij} and U^c_{ij}, with respect to the variations in status or y^* or both, as the birth-order switch point. Up to the per capita income level (or whatever the independent variable is) of the intersection, the household is in favor of the ith birth, and beyond the switch point it is against it, or vice versa. That is, for other configurations of the two curves, the household may switch from being against the ith birth to being in favor of it. More than one switch point may exist.

For each status we visualize a representative household whose relations (1) and (2) are the averages of all households j. We introduce the concept of a representative household decision-making unit to simplify the exposition of the theory. Such a household would desire the average number of children of all households in the status. For the representative household j, its level of $U_{ij} = f_{ij}(y^*_k)$ is the average of the utility levels for the ith child of all households in status k, where y^*_k is the per capita income for all households in the status. We assume that y^*_k increases as y^* increases.

Consider what the utility and utility cost functions look like for the representative household in a nonextreme status.[26] We have argued that if consumption utility is constant with respect to increases in income (as per capita income increases) and the nonconsumption utilities decline slightly as income increases, then the utility function will look like the one marked u_6 in Figure V.

We shall begin our analysis as if there are no status-*IMU* goods in the utility cost functions. In that case we have argued that

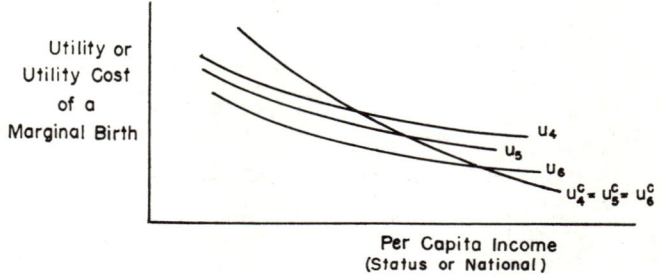

FIGURE V

26. Extreme statuses sometimes do not follow the generalizations for nonextreme statuses. However, they are frequently unimportant numerically. For references see the citations in Freedman, *op. cit.*

THE ECONOMIC THEORY OF FERTILITY DECLINE   29

the actual cost is likely to be a decreasing proportion of income. Furthermore, the utility cost is likely to decline. The probable diagram for this case is illustrated in Figure V. Even though the utility function for children declines somewhat, it seems likely that the utility cost functions will decline more rapidly as per capita income increases. The result is increasing fertility with increases in per capita income.

The alternate situations in which the utility cost functions include status-*IMU* goods are illustrated in Figures VI and VII.

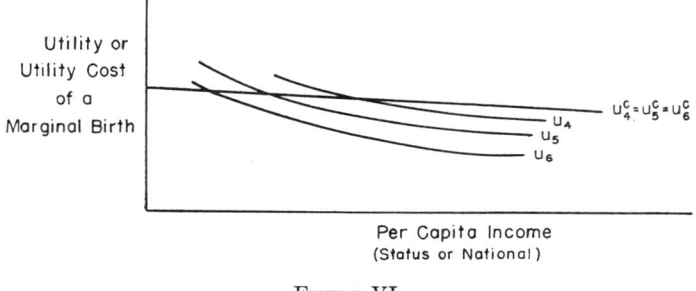

FIGURE VI

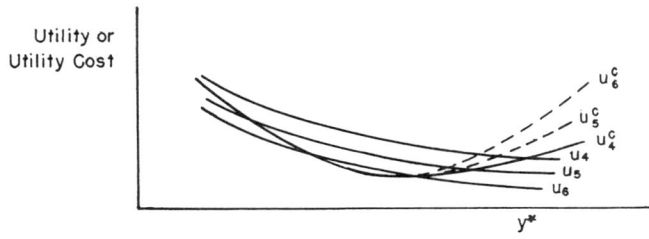

FIGURE VII

The utility cost function presents difficulties. Status expenditures rise as income increases. However, the status expenditures may not rise sufficiently compared to the income increase to imply an increase in utility cost at the higher income. We assume in Figure VI that the utility costs are also negatively inclined, but that they do not drop as rapidly as the utility functions. Now for each set of U_i and U_i^c (in each status) there is a "switch point" income level, up to which the household favors an ith child $(U_i > U_i^c)$ and beyond which $(U_i^c > U_i)$ the household is against an ith child.

The utility curves for higher parity children are drawn below each other in Figure VI in accordance with the arguments previously advanced. The utility cost curves probably should be drawn above each other, but the extreme case, in which the utility costs for a third, a fourth, and a fifth child are the same, simplifies the graphical analysis. If the utility cost curves cut the utility curves from below, then it is clear that the relation of the switch points to income will be such that family size falls as income increases.

We now leave the situation of a single status and consider the economy as a whole. Once again we use the concept of the representative household, this time for the entire economy. But we keep in mind that the representative household now changes status as per capita income rises. In general, we expect that the distribution of households shifts, on the average, so that smaller proportions remain in lower statuses associated with higher fertility rates, and higher proportions are in higher statuses associated with lower fertility rates. Figure V and VI can be reinterpreted as representing the typical household of the economy as a whole, but we now have an additional reason for expecting to have the utility function negatively inclined. Also, the *status-shift* effect should result in the utility cost function to be positively inclined or less negatively inclined.

A final possibility worth considering is the one in which the utility cost function first declines and then rises with increases in per capita income. In the illustration in Figure VII the U-shaped utility cost curve at first cuts the utility curves from above. If we examine the birth-order switch points, we see that this involves a situation in which the initial consequence of development (per capita income increase) is an increase in fertility, but this trend eventually reverses itself and shifts to a sustained decline in fertility.

The possibility shown in Figure VII is that the status-*IMU*-goods hump, so to speak, becomes relatively more important as we move towards higher parity children. In other words, higher parity children require that the household give up some of its status goods, and furthermore, in accordance with our previous analysis, this possibility may increase with income. This is illustrated in Figure VII by the broken lines that reflect higher parity utility costs. It is possible that considerations of this kind may have led to the very rapid drop in fertility in a country such as Japan during the postwar period.

We have shown that the use of utility cost curves that are functions of status and income will, in general (but not invariably), lead to patterns of immediate or eventual sustained fertility decline as a consequence of development. It is to be noted that the assump-

THE ECONOMIC THEORY OF FERTILITY DECLINE   31

tions behind the theory do not have built into them sufficient and necessary conditions for fertility decline. But the arguments presented suggest that the parameters of the functions, taking status-IMU goods into account, are probably such as to be consistent with fertility decline in the course of economic development. Nevertheless, the theory allows "reversals" in the fertility trend to set in if status goods become relatively cheap or relative income compression ceases as per capita income rises. This is consistent with the sort of turning points in the fertility trend that have been observed in the developed countries since World War II.

HARVARD UNIVERSITY

[2]

An Interpretation of
The Economic Theory of Fertility:
Promising Path or Blind Alley?

by HARVEY LEIBENSTEIN
Harvard University

MOST economists are, or until recently have been, blissfully unaware that some of their colleagues have been spending a good deal of time and scarce research funds in applying Hicksian micro-theory to explain *their* (mankind's) intimate behavior. These neo-classical theories of human fertility are in sharp contrast to the Malthusian viewpoint. Malthus's view was a quasi-biological one which set great store on the "passion between the sexes" and similar urges. Some modern theorists *seem to* put equal store in cool rational, carefully calculated decision making in this aspect of human behavior. A number of attempts have been made to "test" empirically the capacity of the theory to explain fertility differentials. At this point, the reader from another branch of our discipline might like to know how the theory has fared. Have the confrontations with empirical evidence turned out to be in conformity with the theory or not, and if not, has the theory been discarded into the dustbin of interesting, promising, but unfortunately invalid ideas?

The reader will have to be patient. There are a number of theories that fit into this general class (broadly defined). Not all have met attempts at verification. For the bulk of theories brewed from the Hicksian model of the household and molded at Columbia or Chicago to fit the family size choice decision, the basic answer that emerges is that for the most part the facts do not appear to be in conformity with theory. However, the theorists show no signs of discarding the theories. Watchers of theory-fact confrontations in other branches of economics will not be surprised at this outcome.[1] Nevertheless, an analysis and brief survey of this field is of interest. Is it a promising new branch of economics or a blind alley?

I. Introduction

Before going into analytical detail, a bit of potted history to orient the non-specialist reader might be helpful. (The reader should note that I am probably not a dispassionate observer in this arena. As an early contributor I watched with some interest how various theories fared, but until recently, a decade and a half after the event, I have not been seriously tempted to come to the defense of my initial effort.) However, this is not a detailed review and analysis of the attempts to develop an "economic" theory of human fertility. There is only space enough to consider some important highlights of the problem, but hopefully it can serve as a useful introduction for further reading.[2]

---

[1] S. J. Latsis [37, 1972], basing his work on I. Lakatos [36, 1970], argues that economic theories are composed of a hard core and a protective belt. What look like data-theory confrontations are rarely critical since the "protective belt" allows for reinterpretations of the theory or the facts or both so that the "hard core" is rarely seriously threatened.

[2] For excellent summaries of the literature see G. Hawthorn [29, 1970], R. A. Easterlin [17, 1969], and W. C. Robinson and D. Horlacher [56, 1971]. See also the reading list in the *Journal of Political Economy: Supplement*, March/April 1973. (This brief romp through the more readily observable peaks of theory and evaluation is not a substitute for the carefully mapped surveys mentioned.)

457

II. *Some Potted History of Recent Eco-Soc Pop Theories*

For ease in exposition, some shorthand terminological devices are necessary. I will refer to all who work or have worked on human population problems as *demographers,* irrespective of their background or training, and to those whose work draws significantly on, or is molded in accordance with, micro- or macroeconomics as economists. In addition, I will refer to those whose work appears to be inspired by, or draws on, Gary Becker's two famous articles as the Chicago School of Theorists whether or not they had anything to do with the University of Chicago. These are convenient and probably easily understood shorthand devices in the field.

To some of those who had been laboring in the vineyards of demography for decades, the efforts of economists in the sixties and seventies to develop a theory of fertility must have appeared like the invasion of a horde of primitives on a technologically advanced community proclaiming loudly their intent to reinvent the wheel. In fact, the demography profession was not devoid of theory or theorists. Indeed, there was a profusion of theories, as well as a vast amount of empirical information about the determinants of fertility prior to the descent of economists into this particular arena. One can understand the disdain of some demographers for these efforts,[3] some of which suggested that the economist in question had not bothered to assimilate very much of the earlier findings. A great deal

of information was known about the causes of differential fertility and changes in fertility over time prior to the 1960's. As social scientists go, the demographers had a pretty good record. They had their period of fairly successful predictions as well as their deserved comeuppance when the reversal of the fertility trend after World War II proved their predictions of impending negative population growth in the U.S. and Western Europe premature. Like many social scientists before them they were able to ride a trend with ease and delight but came-a-cropper at a turning point. The soul searching that followed was chastening and scientifically stimulating and useful.

The difficulty with the profusion of theories that existed was that they were neither systematic, coherent, nor general [U.N., 60, 1953]. There were a great many bits and pieces of useful knowledge (as well as misleading correlations) that the practitioner had to sort out by himself. Everytime one thought one had hold of a good generalization, an inconvenient study would show up that appeared like a counter example. Probably the counter examples were taken too seriously by the sociologists and statisticians who made up the bulk of the practitioners.

Sociologist-demographers took the bits and pieces of knowledge in their stride, but economists would have found these bits and pieces aesthetically unfulfilling.[4]

A. *The Theory of the Demographic Transition*

A major exception to the bits and pieces was what became known as the Theory of Demographic Transition. It had a grand sweep, made interesting predictions, had a considerable empirical basis, and some logical appeal. Certainly it could serve as an organizing schema for further study. Its

---

[3] A personal observation may not be out of place here. Demographers and population economists appear to be a touchy and sensitive group. By and large they like their own theories, stances, policies, or viewpoints, and are readily resistant to alternatives. This stems, in part, from the fact that people interested in the so-called population problem have frequently gotten into the related disciplines involved out of a strong emotional commitment. Thus, competing viewpoints do not always obtain the fairest of hearings. Although I believe this is not too far off the mark, some of the major contributors are exceptions to this characterization.

[4] For example, Kingsley Davis' book on India and the Royal Commission Report in 1949 showed quite a profound knowledge of the determinants of differential fertility [11, 1951].

elements are simple and we could do worse than start with a compressed summary of its essentials.[5]

As a theory of social evolution, the Transition Theory carries on the tradition of biological determinism from the school of Social Darwinism. The relevant aspects of the Theory fall into three stages. Stage I starts with the assumption that prior to modernization life was brutish, means were scarce, and longevity was short. Hence, death rates were high. This is critical. As a consequence, only those societies that developed mores and institutions consistent with at least equally high birth rates survived. Their institutions and mores had a high degree of stability to sustain high birth rates and were resistant to change.

Stage II declares that modernization, associated public health methods, improved diet, etc. lead to the gradual reduction of mortality. No one resists good health and increased longevity. Hence, mortality fell, but fertility was resistant to the early blandishments of modernization. Ergo, mortality fell, fertility remained constant and population growth rates increased and reached unusually high levels compared to the average of past centuries.

In Stage (Act) III, fertility finally succumbs to the allurements that accompany modernization. These are many and varied and will be discussed later. The final outcome is the gradual descent of fertility rates towards falling and low mortality rates.

The critical part for our purposes is Stage III. It could have many variants. Most important, it is a skeleton that allows for considerable filling out. Many reasons associated with modernization can be put forth to account for fertility decline during this stage. Indeed many were put forth and some of the reasons looked good. (On the whole demographers turned out to be a very critical group and scutinized most of the

reasons put forth carefully and mercilessly.) Here are some of the better looking reasons. The fall in fertility is a consequence of modernization, which is associated in particular with the following influences on fertility: 1) the rise in education of women and the consequent change in their role and values; 2) the increase of female participation in the non-agricultural labor force and the consequent reduction of the importance of the child rearing role; 3) sustained reduction in infant mortality; 4) a decline in traditional religious beliefs which supported high fertility norms; 5) urbanization with its secularizing influences and alternatives to traditional behavior patterns; 6) the increase in compulsory education and the decrease in the use and value of child labor; 7) increases in the rights of women and changes in their roles outside the home; 8) attenuation of the extended family system; 9) introduction of superior chemical and mechanical contraceptives; 10) the development of old age and other security systems outside the extended family; and 11) increases in socioeconomic mobility, etc. This is a very partial list, but with respect to any of these factors a *plausible* argument can be developed about how these elements contributed towards reducing desired *and/or* actual fertility.

The theory depends heavily on the reduction of *desired* fertility. It suggests that a reduction in desired fertility will, through some *means,* be translated to a *considerable* extent in a fall in actual fertility. It is of special interest to note that by and large the argument does not depend on the introduction of contraceptive technology. Some of the significant fertility reductions in Western Europe were achieved prior to, and without the aid of, large scale dissemination of chemical or mechanical contraceptive means. Furthermore, population control existed in some sense prior to the Demographic Transition, since European fertility rates prior to industrialization were less than 60 percent of biologically

---

[5] See A. J. Coale [10, 1973] for the most recent restatement of the theory.

maximum rates, or of the high fertility rates achieved by the Hutterites.[6]

While the theory of the Demographic Transition is of importance to demographers (including those trained as economists), it is not the sort of theory that fits the mind-set of the theoretically trained economists. It was, and is, in a very different intellectual mold than microeconomic theory. For the most part it seems like a grand historical generalization buttressed by a variety of *ad hoc* causal assertions.

B. *Leibenstein Theory 1957*

My own work was influenced by the feeling of an important lack of even a semi-formal explanatory structure of Stage III in the demographic transition theory. My 1957 theory of fertility (developed in the early fifties and published as part of a book on economic development[7]) addressed itself primarily to the possible explanation of fertility decline in the course of sustained per capita income growth [40, 1957]. The essence of the model is the presumption that families would balance utilities against disutilities ascribed to an nth child in order to determine whether a family wanted an nth child. The emphasis is on the higher birth orders. I am not interested in explaining why a family might want the first two children. It is enough to try to explain why a representative family might want to shift from a five to a four child completed family if its income (and that of the economy) is higher rather than lower. Thus, for the most part, rational decisions need be assumed only for marginal children, as it were. The

theory does not lean on rational calculation for every aspect of reproductive activity.

To be brief, the theory assumes that an nth child is wanted for three types of utility: 1) consumption utility, 2) work or income utility, and 3) security utility, each type of utility to be very broadly interpreted. "Consumption utility" means the child is wanted for itself rather than for the services, goods, or income it can provide for the household. Two types of disutility of an nth child were envisaged: 1) the disutility arising out of the direct cost involved in feeding, housing, clothing, and schooling a child, and 2) the disutility arising out of the indirect costs which involve income earning (and other) opportunities foregone by the parents in raising an nth child. It is assumed that the utility of an nth child is less than that of an $n-1$ child. Consumption utility is assumed constant with respect to income, while work and old age security utility declines with income. Thus, the sum of the utilities of an nth child, as illustrated in Figure 1, where n is fairly high, is presumed to decline as income increases.

It is somewhat more difficult to say anything clear-cut about the disutilities. While direct costs rise with income, the disutility of bearing these costs in terms of the utility of goods given up to bear these costs (out of a higher income) need not rise. The indirect costs could be very important given the extent to which an nth child interferes with parents' income earning capacities or the utilities associated with other activities given up as a consequence of having an nth child. In general, it is assumed that in utility terms these costs probably do not decline as income rises. It is impossible to deduce that children should *necessarily* be fewer as income grows. However, it is possible to use this framework in order to draw the relationships in such a way that, in general, the outcome is such that as per capita income grows the number of high parity children for the representative family falls. The diagram below indicates the type of

---

[6] The Hutterites are a small fundamentalist religious group who on the average have more than 10 children per family. See J. W. Eaton and A. J. Mayer [19, 1953], Coale [10, 1973], Hawthorn [29, 1970], and others.

[7] In my model I also considered what I referred to as the "infant mortality hump." That is, the *initial* transitional effect of falling infant mortality rates as income per capita rises is to increase the expected "child utility years" per birth. But, I argued, eventually it becomes clear to parents that the utility costs of caring for this extra load outweigh the benefits.

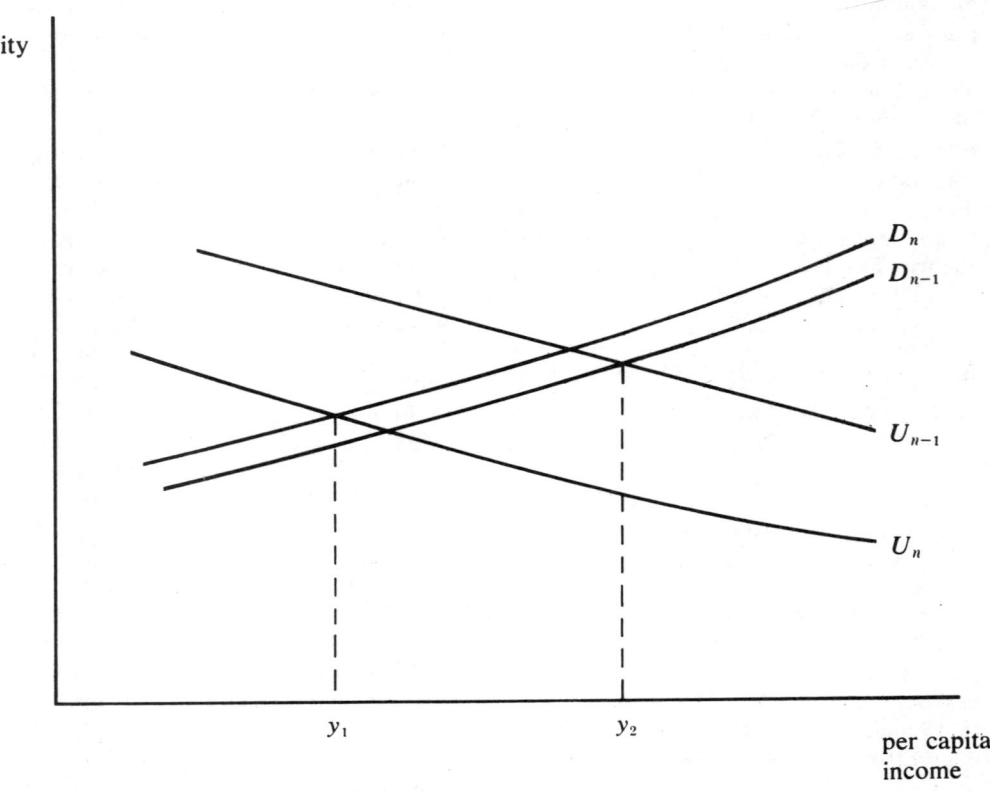

Figure 1.

U_n = Utility associated with nth child.

D_n = Disutility (utility cost) associated with n child.

y_1 = Income beyond which representative household would decide *not* to have an n child.

y_2 = Income beyond which representative household would decide *not* to have an $n-1$ child.

explanation attempted. As developed, the theory was seen as an explanatory vehicle rather than as a predictive device, and one that could readily be expanded or compressed by adding (especially the utility of the perceived benefits of children) or reducing the number of variables that entered as arguments in the utility or disutility functions. (See [Leibenstein, 41, 1973] for an example of an expanded version of the earlier theory.)

C. *The Chicago School Theories*

Gary Becker's paper published in 1960 had some similarities with mine and some conspicuous differences [4, 1960]. It became fairly controversial (at least to economists and demographers outside of Chicago and Columbia), but it also inspired a great deal of useful work in the area. Becker applied the Hicksian version of micro consumption theory to family fertility behavior and came up with some exceedingly interesting interpretations. Microeconomic theory tells us nothing about how people feel about the utility of children. In fact, the theory does not even tell us that it is legitimate to apply it to entities which are not bought and sold. Becker argued that we should view children the same way that the household views the purchase of a durable good, and that it makes its decision "as if" it made calculations for a commodity whose end result was a stream of utilities over time and a stream of costs, given income and price. Becker applied the theory to the differential fertility of different income groups in American society. Why do richer families have fewer children than those with lower incomes? Becker argued that children were not inferior goods and hence as income rose people would, in fact, want more children. Much of the evidence on differential fertility showed that the opposite was the case. The reason according to members of this school, is that the "price" of children is not a constant, and the price effect is more important than the income effect. According to Becker the reason the price effect was more important was because higher income families wanted "higher quality" children. Other members of this school looked for and found different price effects they considered more significant.

We will consider later whether or not these arguments are plausible. For the present it is important to note an intriguing aspect of the structure of the theory. It presented (and still presents) economists with a puzzle, which in turn stimulated a good deal of research, and hopefully some enlightenment. If what was needed was a significant price effect to counter the positive income effect of the demand for children, then it is possible to either accept the quality argument, think of other positive price effects, or augment it by a number of "price" effects. Thus, an intellectual climate was created in which a good deal of theoretical and empirical research could be done within a given framework.

Let us dwell on the basic "puzzle." Assume that the representative family in each income group has the same tastes as in any other income group. Of course, a higher income group will purchase a different bundle of goods than a lower one, but this could be explained by the higher income and not by preference map (*e.g.,* taste) differences. If any commodity is not an inferior good, then with more income the household should purchase more of it. Presumably there is no reason to believe that children are inferior goods, hence if the price is constant then higher income groups can afford more children and should want more children. (Empirical evidence suggests that among very low income groups budget constraints are indeed operative.) For some western countries the lowest income occupations frequently show lower average family size than some of the higher income occupations. But as income rises it becomes difficult to visualize that there are other commodities which yield satisfactions similar to those obtained from children and are superior substitutes to children. But in fact higher income groups do generally have fewer children. Hence the puzzle.

Is the puzzle quantitative or qualitative? The mere fact that children may cost more for those with higher incomes is not a sufficient explanation. The price effect has to be significant enough to counteract the income effect. Thus, if we limit ourselves to economic solutions to our puzzle we must try to find empirically significant price effects. But non-economic or socioeconomic solutions are also possible.[8]

Let us look at some of the other "price effect" arguments. If higher income groups want children of higher quality and higher quality bears a cost, then this *may* be a solution. Other "solutions" have to do with the cost of time.[9] The argument here is that time is equivalent to money, and higher income groups have a higher time cost in child rearing than lower income groups and that this has "price effect" consequences. Some contributors (*e.g.*, J. Mincer [47, 1963]) emphasize that higher income groups have more education than lower income groups and therefore the opportunity cost to the mother, since childrearing may prevent her from working, would be greater for higher income groups. There are three aspects to the previous argument: 1) children limit the labor force participation of the mother; 2) the desire for labor force participation should be higher where the income potential of the wife is higher; and 3) the higher wage involves a greater opportunity cost foregone if education and wages are higher. In other words, for higher income groups a higher proportion of wives would wish to participate in the labor force and they would "lose" more by doing so.

The quality and opportunity cost price effects need not be substitutes, they may be additive.[10]

A possible argument that does not seem to have been explored extensively is the relative time costs of *commodity consumption* compared to "child services" consumption. As we move up the income scale goods take more time to consume which competes with baby tending time. There is little empirical investigation to suggest whether this hypothesis is either significant or valid.

The essence of the situation can be seen on the basis of elementary indifference curve diagrams. In Figure 2 the lines b_0, b_1 represent the budget lines between material goods and children for associated incomes y_0, y_1. The curves w_0, w_1 are welfare indifference curves whose slope at

---

[8] A non-economic argument that Becker suggested is that lower income groups have less knowledge of contraception and hence despite the fact that they want fewer children they do not know the means. In general, the survey data collected by sociologists does not support this view. This data suggests that higher income groups very frequently want fewer *desired* children. A more sophisticated version of this argument is that more convenient means of contraception are costlier. To some degree both of these arguments may be true but it seems unlikely that their effect is significant as a general explanation since beyond some point the cost of contraceptive means turns out to be a very small part of family budgets compared to lifetime childrearing costs.

[9] In this area Chicago School contributors also indicate their intellectual debt to Becker's 1965 article on the cost of time. Others have used time cost arguments prior to 1965. My 1957 model also employed the opportunity cost of parental time as part of the indirect costs of children [39, 1957].

[10] Recent contributions of the Chicago School are assembled in a Supplement to the *Journal of Political Economy* March/April, 1973, entitled "New Economic Approaches to Fertility." On the whole, the volume made up of papers from contributors invited to an *NBER* conference has a very "clubby" feel about it. For the most part only those within the inspirational framework of the school appeared to have been invited. The work would have gained in catholicity and the juxtaposition of competing scientific frameworks and ideas if scholars like R. A. Easterlin, A. J. Coale, Deborah Freedman, and others had been included. It is also of interest that in the overall survey by T. W. Schultz, the results of the confrontation between theory and empirical evidence is not emphasized. Rather, claims made about the promise of the theoretical contribution are stressed. Also, in the agenda for further work the socioeconomic aspects, namely those associated with the influence of group membership and the possibility of variable taste patterns, are not mentioned. Finally, it should be mentioned lest the wrong impression be given, that not all of the authors agree with each other, and some of the work is at a remove from the central formulations of what we have referred to as the Chicago School. This seems to be true of the papers by T. Paul Schultz, Rueben Gronau, and to some degree the exceptionally interesting paper by Y. Ben-Porath. Ben-Porath takes a methodologically different stance than say, B. Gardner, or D. N. DeTray. The latter use the theory to make predictions, and check how well their econometric exercises fit, while Ben-Porath appears to use the theory as an analytical framework in order to examine and discuss his empirical work.

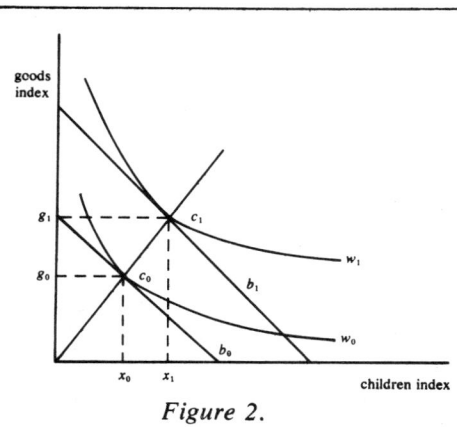

Figure 2.

each point represents the psychic trade-offs between goods and children. The convex (from the origin) shape of the welfare curves suggests diminishing *marginal* satisfaction for additional children, and a diminishing rate of substitution of children for goods as we move along the X axis. It seems clear that if the relative prices of children and goods are constant and the welfare curves have similar shapes, *i.e.,* the slope tangent to any two successive curves does not change very markedly as we move along any ray from the origin, that more children would be desired with

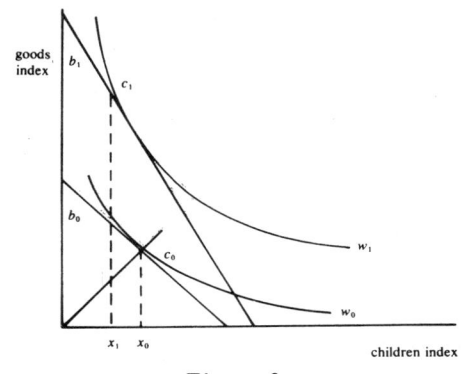

Figure 3.

more income. Comparing tangency points c_2 and c_1 in Figure 2 we see that under y_1 more children and more material goods can be enjoyed than under y_0.

To get other results requires, as illustrated in Figure 3, that the cost of children rise very steeply *vis à vis* goods, as income rises. Hence, the steep slope of the budget line b_1 compared to b_0. The alternative possibility of unusual changes in the shapes of the successive indifference curves will be examined later.

D. *Other Theories and Contributions*

Although space limitations prevent comprehensive and detailed consideration of other theories, theorists, and contributions, some indication must be given of the directions of work that seem noteworthy to the present writer—even if a short list must be selective and arbitrary. Promising and interesting contributions have emphasized the following:[11]

(1) *Infant mortality effects:* These may be viewed as independent theories or, as in T. Paul Schultz's work, as part of a larger model. In its simplest version, households desire a *target* number of surviving children. Increased income decreases mortality and increases the chance of survival. As a result fewer births are desired to achieve the same number of surviving children. This argument can be strengthened by thinking in terms of a target number of sons. With increases in the probability of survival, considerably fewer births are wanted in order to have, let us say, two surviving sons. See D. M. Heer and D. A. May [30, 1968], and R. Repetto [55, 1972].

(2) *Socioeconomic status:* A number of theorists, both sociologists and econo-

[11] Some contributions are of interest not because they emphasize a particular direction of research but because they attempt a high degree of comprehensiveness of variables within a fairly complex model. Robert J. Willis' contribution in the *Journal of Political Economy: Supplement* March/April 1973, deserves special attention from this viewpoint.

mists, have emphasized the effect of socio-economic status or social class on the taste for children or the preferences for material goods or on the relation between the two. See J. A. Banks [3, 1954], R. A. Easterlin [17, 1969], and D. S. Freedman [21, 1963].

(3) *Threshold values in income and/or education:* A few investigators have stressed the hypothesis that there is a threshold value in income and/or education before the frequently observed inverse relations between fertility, and income, or education take effect. Some have argued that prior to the threshold value there is a positive relation between income and the other two variables. See P. B. Gupta and C. R. Malaker [27, 1963], Easterlin [18, 1972], and J. Encarnacion [20, 1973].

(4) *Changes in norms and institutions:* This has involved mostly the work of demographers who have stressed the importance of the extended family system, caste, religious sanctions, cultural factors, and other institutions and their relations to norms which in turn determine family size ideals, and which to some degree are altered by the process of modernization [22, Freedman, 1964].[12] The influence of various types of group membership frequently turns out to be important in such analyses but changes in the proportion of group membership as well as their nature alter aggregate fertility behavior.[13] Easterlin (1969) has argued that what sociologist-demographers call norms is equivalent to what economists look upon as preference maps. However, it remains to be demon-strated whether one to one correspondences could be worked out between these sets of notions in the senses in which they are used in different disciplines.[14]

The arguments put forth by Banks, J. S. Duesenberry, and Easterlin (and Leibenstein [41, 1973]) deserve special mention since each in its way touches on a social influence group aspect of the problem. Banks argued that the English middle classes in the 1870's cut back their fertility in order to maintain their standard of living [3, 1954]. In other words, he saw the effort to maintain what could be viewed as a "target standard of living" being threatened or complicated by an excessive number of children. Duesenberry and B. Okun, in their brief comments on Becker, contested the idea that parents are free to choose how much they spend on children, and argued that socioeconomic groups establish social conventions that circumscribe to a very high degree the extent to which expenditures on children can be varied [15, 1960]. Easterlin adopted Duesenberry's ideas and argued that the effect of income also affects tastes, preferences, and norms for the disposal of income. Based partly on earlier findings, Easterlin argued that on the one hand increased income may enable the family to support more children, but on the other hand it will tend to lower fertility because the status effect of increased income raises the relative desire for material goods [21, Freedman, 1963 and 23, Freedman and Coombs, 1966]. It is of interest that this class of considerations is ignored, for the most part, by the Chicago School.

It seems to me reasonable to assume that people in different socioeconomic statuses or other types of social groupings possess different tastes, and that these tastes are such that they shift towards a higher prefer-

[12] Such factors are emphasized by the Princeton Studies on the demographic transition in Europe, in terms of provinces as units (rather than countries). The result is to qualify the concept of the demographic transition and to weaken the idea of a strictly economic interpretation. See Coale [10, 1973, pp. 62, 63].

[13] Ben-Porath's work separates groups by the broad geographic background of their origins which reflects the notion that group membership in some sense is significant.

[14] Adelman and Morris demonstrated through the use of factor analytic techniques that indices representing social and political structures of fifty-five developing countries accounted for 57 percent of interstate fertility differences [1, 1966].

ence for goods as against children, as we go up hierarchically recognized social groupings.

The reason for such shifts in tastes is not clear, but to some extent they are likely to be associated with education, cultural trends, and the type of socio-cultural influences found in occupational grouping. Economists may, as a first step, want to accept such shifts in tastes as given without determining the reason. A more complete analysis would require that we try to understand the factors behind such taste changes. On the other hand, it has been argued that from an econometric viewpoint, it is easier to carry out empirical analyses if we do not assume different tastes for different groups. But it is difficult to see why we should allow econometric convenience to dictate the nature of our theories.[15]

The recent work of Easterlin is especially noteworthy [18, 1972]. In it he separates the demand and supply elements (in utility terms) for children from the demand and supply element for the regulation of family size. Thus, the end result depends on two classes of forces, those that determine the difference between what would be the "naturally" conceived and desired number of children, and those that determine the degree of regulation of fertility that will be "purchased" in order to determine *actual* family size. Easterlin's work is especially noted for its catholicity of approach, and for a high degree of success in assimilating a wide variety of empirical and theoretical contributions, both economic and sociological, into a manageable and systematic amalgam.

Other work of promise involves questionnaire studies and related inquiries which attempt to determine directly the degree of *felt,* and/or *appreciated* economic benefits of children, and the *felt* burdens of children

to households in developing countries. See Eva Mueller [48, 1972], J. Fawcett [20a, 1972], and T. and S. Poffenberger [53a, 1969]. These works are of interest since they confirm that at least in the cases of the few studies involved, households do seem to be aware of the utilities of children in a reasonably well articulated sense, and furthermore, they are connected with family size differentials.[16]

III. *Some Evaluative Comments*

How should we evaluate the results? Whose results? Let us look at the Chicago School. There is a certain coherence in their work. They follow the same body of inspirational doctrine and have certainly made a significant impact on the work of American economists in the population field.

The reaction one has to the Chicago School depends in part on the stance we believe they take. Consider three possible stances: 1) playing intellectual games; 2) developing scientific theories whose destiny depends on confrontations with the empirical world—a hard-nosed stance in this area would say that if the facts falsify the theory, the theory should be discarded; and 3) modes of analysis, under this approach the theory is not put "on the line" as it were, but it is viewed as a convenient framework (or "straightjacket" by some lights) for analyzing empirical data.

In terms of "playing games," the Chicago School theory does not score badly. They have developed an interesting intellectual game. Anyone may enter, although not everyone can count on getting his results published. The game has a significant educational function. It does introduce economists to some aspects of "the population problem." But even as a population studies game it should not be taken too

[15] See the comments by Robert E. Hall, and by Margaret G. Reid in the *Journal of Political Economy: Supplement,* March/April 1973.

[16] Richard Anker's doctoral dissertation is especially interesting in this connection [2, 1973, cf. pp. 155 and 228].

seriously. There are other interesting intellectual games that should be played in this area. Some of them are well advanced. There are forecasting games, age-structure consequences games, games that stress sociological variables, or historical variables, and so on. Clearly, there is something to be said for the broad gauged intellectual athlete. A strong case could be made for the need for decathelon types rather than sprinters.

If I view the Chicago School theory as a potentially falsifiable scientific contribution then I have to express a mixture of scepticism and gratitude. First, the sceptical remarks. My feelings about the shortcomings of the approach are based on gross empirical and methodological grounds. The broad facts available suggest that the price effect is very unlikely to be significant enough to explain the negative relation between significantly divergent income groups and fertility.[17] Consider, for simplicity, a relatively high versus a relatively low income group in the same economy (say, in which the representative household's high income is four fold that of the lower one) or a four fold change in income over time. We take two critical basic explanatory variables in turn.

1) *Quality of children:* The basic quality that will determine the earning capacity and other non-hereditary traits of children is likely to be education. Most educational costs are provided by the state and hence free to the household in many countries. Therefore, this cost is unlikely to be a significant deterrant. The indirect costs, such as income opportunities foregone by the children being schooled, are likely to be

insignificant if the law requires a high level of compulsory education, and if parents can only sequester for themselves a small proportion of such earnings. These opportunity costs are likely to be much more important to low income households. Hence, on this ground one could not imagine the quality aspect being the critical influence that induces the much higher income group to have fewer children. The cost of a few more years of education per child whose direct costs are paid for largely by the state seems unlikely not to be covered by the large income differential initially assumed.

2) *The price of time:* The variants of the theory where the price effect depends on the value of the mother's time is highly culture bound. In some cultures, most women in medium and higher income groups in urban areas do not work. If they do not work for cultural reasons then mother's time cannot be a significant factor. In any event, we have to separate the fertility experience for non-working mothers as against working mothers. If we take only non-working mothers' groups then it is quite likely that the inverse relationship still holds.

Most important, the net opportunity cost of a mother's time is not what she would have earned had she been able to work, but the substitute babytending costs of servants, grandparents, or other substitutes for the mother's childrearing activities during her absence. These data are available. The "babysitting" costs are approximately the same for an nth child, whether the family is relatively rich or poor. Clearly, the high income family is more readily able to afford the babysitting costs than the low income one.[18]

---

[17] Budget studies for England, 1940, suggest that actual expenditures on education increase by exceedingly small amounts as income varies from £250 to over £800 per annum, *e.g.*, it increases from £6 out of £350 to £21 out of £650. The cost variation as the number of children increases appears to be quite trivial at all the income levels considered. See A. Henderson [31, 1949].

[18] A study in Syracuse, New York, on the use of time shows an exceptionally small variation in all household work when one changes from two child families to four-six child families. For example, 8.4 hours are used in two child families and 8.7 hours in four-six child families. See Kathryn Walker and Margaret Woods [63, 1972].

If we use education to explain the value of mother's time (apart from the babysitting cost argument) then education by itself is likely to be the significant explanatory variable (rather than its presumed indirect effect on the value of mother's time). In other words, education has a significant impact on tastes rather than on the value of time. In cultures where servants are readily available, the marginal cost of babysitting may be almost zero. Finally, consider the fact that infant mortality rates are lower for higher income groups, hence the costs of "producing" a surviving child are lower for such groups and therefore we should expect the higher income group to have more surviving children rather than less. Even if the costs of a marginal child are somewhat higher for higher income groups, they do not seem to be very much higher so as to make a significant impact on the income differential between the higher and lower income groups.

As a convenient mode of analysis, the Chicago School theories are useful but limited in their range. I would opt for theories that stressed the influence of different social groups, their taste differences, whether these groups are open or closed to new entrants, and on the relationship between economic events and the movement between social influence groups.

The theories we have just criticized from an immanent viewpoint (*i.e.*, within the theories' frameworks) have made a contribution to population studies. They have enabled scholars to focus on an important and tantalizing aspect of the problem in a systematic and orderly way. No doubt, these theories have stimulated a great deal of research, some of which will turn out to be useful. For those who are not fond of these theories they have provided provocative ideas to react against. Perhaps of greater importance, the Chicago School theories have provided a coherent research frontier at which economists can readily enter. As an aside, it has provided

employment for econometricians and computers.

From my personal viewpoint, it has pointed up an underdeveloped aspect of my 1957 theory of fertility. While I like to believe that my theory was sufficiently general so as to avoid some of the pitfalls of overly specific assertions, nevertheless it did not grapple sufficiently with the problem of why the disutility of the cost of children should be sufficiently high so as to lead a) higher income groups to have fewer children, and b) the population as a whole to have fewer children as incomes rise in the course of economic development [40, Leibenstein, 1957].

The other theories discussed in highly compressed form are too varied to assess in detail. At this stage of our knowledge theories should put primary emphasis on their ability to explain fertility phenomena rather than on predictive power. At the same time we cannot focus on everything that comes to mind that may possibly influence fertility. Hence, it seems to me, we should focus on 1) trying to explain relatively large fertility differences, and 2) turning points rather than trends.[19] Therefore, the work on attempting to determine "threshold values" of independent variables seems to me to be important and promising. In addition the relation between social influence groups and tastes are so critical, and come out so clearly as being important in a number of investigations, that theories which include social group influences, directly or by implication, are likely to be more

---

[19] In a recent paper Göran Ohlin makes the point (in discussing the consequences of infant fertility decline) that "this is one reason to suspect that a fertility decline is latent even where birth rates have not yet begun to fall." See G. Ohlin [53, 1973]. This is an important insight into one of the frequently ignored functions of theory—to show what is latent in a set of circumstances although the facts appear to show otherwise. The latent elements may or may not manifest themselves depending on the intervening events. Thus, latency and predictions are not the same thing.

Leibenstein: An Interpretation of the Economic Theory of Fertility   469

promising than those which exclude them. Also, one has to separate discretionary choice points from largely nondiscretionary behavior. Easterlin's recent work seems to be of considerable interest in this connection. Finally, I would emphasize a point made by Norman Ryder in his evaluation of Willis, to the effect that "the economic theory of fertility is too important to rely on secondhand data, devised for other purposes."[20] From this viewpoint, the attempts being made to measure directly, through survey techniques, how people view the benefits and burdens of children and their relation to fertility behavior seems interesting, promising, and worth encouraging.

IV. *Methodological Analysis*

The Chicago School theories, as well as some other models, can be faulted to some degree on methodological grounds. Whether or not these observations appeal to the reader may depend on his or her methodological tastes. As formulated, many of the models are in the tradition of "as if" theorizing. That is, the nature of assumptions are not taken seriously, and the theory presumes that people behave as if they are *buying* consumer durables in a well organized market and in a calculating manner at every step of the way. As Easterlin has pointed out, the existing theory is an unbelievably sexless subject,[21] considering the detailed nature of the "production function." The simplicity requirements of theory construction may necessitate a model of "as if" theorizing which appears unreal, but this does not mean that we should employ "as if" theorizing as a license with which we are

[20] *Journal of Political Economy: Supplement,* March/April 1973, p. 69.
[21] Cf. Easterlin [18, 1972, p. 3]. A colleague who follows this type of theorizing has conjured up the image of every couple having a miniature Wang calculator under their bed on which they work out the balance of the streams of expected benefits and costs, etc., prior to a decision.

allowed to choose our assumptions at will irrespective of whether or not they go counter to observed experience, or whether or not the "as ifs" are really required by the necessity of maintaining some degree of simplicity.

The essence of the "as if" theorizing in this class of models is to rely on presumed *implicit* trade. This is very different from the usual objectives of micro theory which is to explain *explicit* trade. The contrast between implicit and explicit trade is very important for our purposes. Explicit trade involves a number of important observables. If someone trades yams for bananas (or for gold) the following aspects are usually likely to be seen, heard, and sometimes even smelled: 1) the objects traded, 2) the bargaining procedure used, 3) the actual exchange that takes place, 4) the price involved, 5) the comparison between this price and other prices in similar trades, 6) the relation between qualities of commodities and their prices, and 7) the detailed nature and organization of the market. In addition, people can usually discuss in a meaningful and easy way, and in economic terms, why they did not purchase more or less of the given goods involved under specific conditions. All of this is in sharp contrast to the presumed "market" for children. People do not "buy" children. It is not at all clear what the objects traded are. This difficulty arises not only because of the impossibility of assessing the quality characteristics of children, but most important, one cannot see what is given up in order to obtain a child. Neither the bargaining procedure nor the actual exchange is observable. No one knows what the price involved really is. We cannot compare it with other prices. Furthermore, we cannot say anything about the detailed nature and organization of the market. Are we to presume that the market is competitive without any important externalities or collusive arrangements, etc.? It not only strains the imagination to argue that people behave "as if" they are buying consumer durables, but the very nature of the market is vastly different. Even using such words as "market" is questionable in this context. Hence, it is dangerous to presume that the mode of decision-making is similar and that we simply have to transfer the well developed microeconomic mold and its presumed thought processes from one area to another.

The assumption of implicit trade allows us to say almost anything we please about how decisions are made without being able to check against observables. Consider an example from another field. Suppose I do not show up for work one day and my wage is deducted accordingly. An implicit trade theorizer may argue that a normal exchange relationship took place, that I have a preference for leisure over work, and that the value of this leisure was greater than the pay for a day's work. This sounds very plausible. No observable trade is involved. The exchange was imputed. In fact, it may turn out to be false. On emerging to go to work I may have slipped on an icy driveway, twisted an ankle, and spent the day in bed. In other words, there is obviously a qualitative difference between theories based on implicit trades compared to explicit trades, *or other explicit* observable events. Where implicit trades are involved, we are making many more assumptions about the nature of reality and we have to be much more careful that there is some concordance between behavior assumptions and observed behavior.

To return for a moment to my theory, I think I am saying something different than the Chicago School theorists if I argue that some people take into account the utilities and disutilities that they associate with a *marginal* child (but not necessarily with intramarginal children), as against the assertion that people, in making decisions determining their family size, behave in the same way as they behave in the market for consumer durables. I would assert that

my statement is a much weaker statement that fits the results of survey research. The way we state our theories is not just semantic quibbling. Rather, it involves necessary precautions against bringing over wholesale the decision-making thought processes from one area where they may be applicable to another where they are not. Precautions are especially necessary in this field because the market is fictional. The elements entering into the "decision-making process" are more subtle and at a greater remove from sense data than in normal trade. Hence, our simplified behavioral pictures have to be elucidated in such a way as to suggest, to as great a degree as possible, the means and areas where we can check behavior assumptions against sense data. Naturally, we have to compromise between the simplicity required for manageable theories and the complexity of observed reality. But we should not use the need to theorize as a license to presume anything we please.

V. *Towards a More Adequate Theory*

In my view, a narrowly construed strictly economic approach is unlikely to be successful. Income differentials, as we go up the socioeconomic status scale, are much more significant than the increase in the costs of children. In the course of development, incomes increase over twenty-fold, and the costs of child rearing need not increase proportionately. *As usually viewed,* the cost of children do not appear to be the basis for a sufficient explanation. Kuznets has concluded that:

> it still remains true that the timing of the broad association between modern patterns of mortality and fertility and modern economic growth, is *not* close. The economic growth processes undoubtedly provided opportunities for reducing mortality and *raised the inducements and requirements for lower fertility* [35, Kuznets, 1973]. (My italics.)

Where do these inducements come from? Do such changes involve altered views of the significance of the costs of children so as to really form sufficient inducements for fertility decline in order to explain the rough association, with variable lags, between fertility decline and sustained development? While the normal interpretation of such costs does not appear sufficient, a social standard influence group theory of cost *pressures* enables us to work out an explanation that appears to be broadly consistent with the facts to the extent that we know them.

The determinants of fertility are manyfold. Some causes of fertility changes are historically unique, others depend on socioeconomic and cultural variables. No single aspect offers a complete explanation. Nevertheless, it seems reasonable to seek a partial explanation in the economic changes, and their *social* concomitants, involved in the process of modernization. Part of the phenomenon of fertility change can be accounted for by the direct choices of the population in the process of determining the number of children they desire. These in turn depend on an assessment of the benefits (in terms of utility and/or satisfaction, broadly defined) and costs (also in terms of utility and/or satisfaction) that are attributed to children during significant *marginal* controllable situations.

A sensible theory must take into account competition between the budgetary demands for expenditures on children versus pressures for other expenditures as the *social* and *economic* circumstances change in the course of economic development.[22] Where do these pressures for *other* expenditures come from? *Social* and *economic* influences must not be considered in isolation. The basic notion is that economic changes influence the social status of families. As a consequence of the changed social status situation, tastes change not only for children, but simultaneously for a) goods that compete with children, and b) the goods and services involved in the nurture of children. To see how this works out, we have to reconsider the conventional theory of consumption. The "textbook" theory of consumer behavior essentially assumes that the household operates as if it were an individual. Intra-household conflicts play no role. Either concensus or dictatorship reigns. Within the limited space available, I want to sketch a very different picture of household behavior.

Conventional micro theory is dominated by the notion that diminishing marginal utility holds as more of a good is consumed. If tastes and prices remain constant it follows that diminishing marginal utility holds as expenditures increase. The notion to be stressed here is that increasing marginal utility (IMU) exists, for *some quantity segments,* with respect to both goods and expenditures.[23] The basic arguments follow:

---

[22] Much of this section contains in extremely abbreviated form some of the ideas of the author's current theory of fertility [41, Leibenstein, 1973]. A technical and detailed version of this theory will be published in the *Quarterly Journal of Economics*, Fall, 1974. Also contained in this section, in highly compressed form, are some basic ideas of a different theory of consumption which are spelled out in detail in a forthcoming paper. (See footnote 23).

[23] The normal assumption of diminishing marginal utility as we consume more is true only if targets are not involved. Where targets are involved, part of the marginal utility curve can rise. For example, Tenzing and Hillary obtained much more satisfaction from the last hundred feet in their climb to the summit of Everest than from any previous hundred feet. Consider an antibiotic for which a certain minimum amount, say 20 grams, is certain to stop infection but less will not. Surely the twentieth gram will be associated with a higher utility than the 19th or 18th. There is no reason why socially determined consumption targets should not operate in a similar fashion. Unfortunately, conventional theory does not take phenomena of this type into account. It is of interest that in a well known article by Friedman and Savage, a segment of their *total* utility-income function implies increasing marginal utility of expenditures. However, they seem to invent their function out of the blue and do not relate it to individual goods or to expenditure components. Their concern was to explain insurance purchases and gambling simultaneously [25, 1948].

1) Human beings create standards for themselves and others. We are a specific goal aspiring species. To meet a consumption standard implies reaching a target or goal, and goals of this type are important to many individuals.

2) The population is divided among socio-cultural groups to which households belong, and which influence the *target* living standards and family size preferences. For simplicity, we assume that each household is a member of only one such social influence group (to be referred to as SIG). These are not the same as SES groups (socioeconomic status groups), because cultural and historical elements influence SIG membership, but they are frequently (but not invariably) highly correlated. For brevity in exposition we assume a perfect correlation.

3) SIG's help create achievable *common* standards for members. To some extent such groups are hierarchical. Households in lower groups find it difficult to achieve standards set by higher groups. Intra-group standards make certain commodities "target goods." The behavioral characteristic stressed is that for some household members achieving the target consumption level is very important. The existence of a target creates the possibility of increasing marginal utility up to the target level, or up to what may be deemed as an optimal consumption level. Common targets may involve expenditures on health, insurance, education, housing, and means of transport.

4) Standards and targets are frequently associated with commitments that household members make a) to themselves, b) to others, or to both. Commitments usually involve a sense of obligation towards achieving a target expenditure to (or for) household members or outsiders. The obverse of commitments are claims that family members make on family income earners, as well as claims by outsiders (charitable institutions, the state,

etc.). The consequence of all such commitments is that a portion of the household's budget, involving the sum of target commitments, is associated with a feeling of pressure to meet the commitments. Increasing marginal utility is likely to be operative at least up to the point where some minimum level of obligations is keenly felt. In general, many such commitments will have critical minimum values.

5) Individuals and households express their sense of status through observable expenditures. Not all family members need have such interests. It is sufficient for some to have them in order to influence the family as a whole to express their status via some portion of their expenditures.

6) Each SIG has a different representative household income, and each social influence group determines a *target* standard of consumption for some important class of goods. As we move towards higher income SIG's, the target consumption level of representative households is likely to get more important. At least two reasons come to mind why higher status households may find that a higher proportion of their income goes into targeted commitments than lower status ones. In the higher status household it may become necessary a) to spend more on target commitments to be *sure* to express status membership, and b) higher status family members demand more in terms of commitments from the household budget both to express status and for other purposes.[24] This results, in part, from the

[24] Lydall, among others, has shown that the relative incomes of hierarchically recognized occupational groups become compressed in the process of development. For our purposes this would imply that if a higher status household (assuming it is related to a higher occupational grouping) tries to maintain its *relative* life style and economic status it must more than proportionately increase its expenditures on "status goods." Thus each new generation as it enters the status group of its parents (for the large proportion

Leibenstein: An Interpretation of the Economic Theory of Fertility   473

taste differences of people in different classes, who in turn are influenced by the occupation and education of group members. As we go up the income scale it is possible for household members to make proportionately higher claims since the bare necessities of life can now be achieved by increasingly lower proportions of income. However, it is not argued that the proportion spent on commitment goods is *necessarily* higher in status α than in β (where the average income in α is higher than in β) but that empirically it frequently turns out this way for most nonextreme statuses.

7) The process of *inter*-household competition and emulation within a SIG, and frequently between demographically similar household members, puts pressure on those who control household finance to treat similarly placed household members no worse than they appear to be treated in competing households. Such a process creates an upward drift in commitments to family members as household incomes rise (when most household incomes within a SIG rise simultaneously). This can result in claimants making demands for greater commitments to them from the household resources until the sum of the increases in all commitments exhausts the increase in income. Thus the ratio of non-commitment income may actually fall as income within the group rises.

The possibility that households in a higher income group would have *fewer* children than those in a lower income group once an increasing marginal utility of expenditures bulge (IMUE) is introduced, *but not otherwise,* is illustrated in Figure 4. The abcissa indicates expenditure units in terms of the average expenditure

per child between the representative household in the two groups. If the expenditure per child in α is twice that in β, then each unit on the abcissa would indicate twice as many dollars for the higher group as for the lower one. The curve marked UC stands for the utility of expenditures on children. This curve is drawn from the budget constraint line B to the left in order to reflect that the marginal utility of children substitutes for the utility of expenditures on other goods. MUE_α and MUE_β are the marginal utility of expenditure curves for the representative households in status α and β respectively. One can readily see that the number of children will be determined at the point of intersection of the expenditure curve and the cost of children curve.

The broken lines on MUE_α and MUE_β indicate the increasing marginal utility "humps" in the two cases. Without the humps household α has more children than β shown by $a'B > bB$. However, once the increasing MUE humps are introduced, a reversal sets in, and with the humps household α has fewer children than β, *i.e.*, $ab < bB$.[25]

These ideas are also illustrated in Figure 5 below, in which the axes are similar to those in Figures 2 and 3. Three budget lines are shown. The lowest one represents a low income SIG while the two higher ones, B_2 and B_3, represent the budget lines for higher income households in the *same* higher income SIG. The household represented by B_2 should be viewed as the representative household in that SIG, while household B_3 belongs to the same SIG but has a larger family income. As the budget lines and the indifference curves

---

[25] In Figure 4 it is assumed that the utility of children function UC is the same for both households. For the purpose of showing the difference that the increasing MUE "hump" can make, this seems adequate. The same thing could be shown if the utility of children was assumed to be somewhat higher for household β than α. But there is no point in cluttering up the Figure with additional curves.

---

that do) may find it more difficult to maintain the sense of relative status on which they were nurtured [44, 1968].

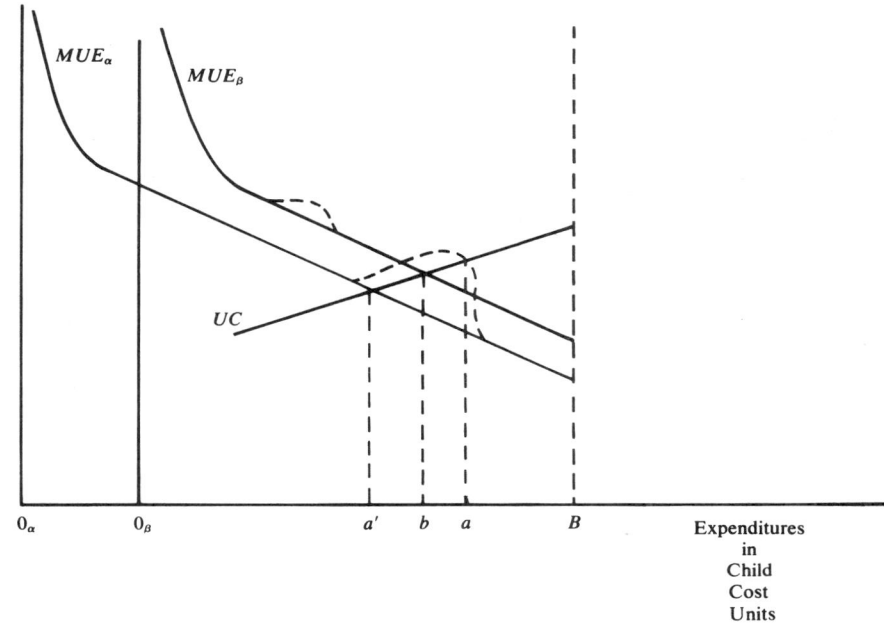

Figure 4.

$0_\alpha B$ = Budget constraint for α representative household.

$0_\beta B$ = Budget constraint for β representative household.

are drawn we observe that: a) taste patterns are different for the low income SIG
as against the high income one; b) the
target consumption level is higher in
proportion to the income level for the
higher SIG rather than the lower one; and
c) the point at which there is the transition
from the increasing to decreasing rate of
substitution (included to reflect the IMU
segment for goods) is an important element in determining the neighborhood of
the tangency position between the budget
line and the indifference curve, and hence
in determining desired family size. As
illustrated, the results are consistent with
the idea that the representative household
of the higher income group will have fewer
children than that of the lower income
group. However, within SIG's, households

that have an income level above that of the
representative household will want more
children than the representative household. In general, if we choose socioeconomic groups, such as occupational groupings, as proxies for social influence groups
we find that the empirical evidence supports the generalization that the higher the
income level of the group (except for
extreme income groups) the fewer the
average number of children per family,
but *within* such groups the reverse holds
[29, Hawthorn, 1970, pp. 84–6].

Also it seems likely that as income constraints impose burdens on maintaining
consumption standards so that fewer children are actually born, *actual* fertility
performance will set a new reference
standard for appropriate family size which

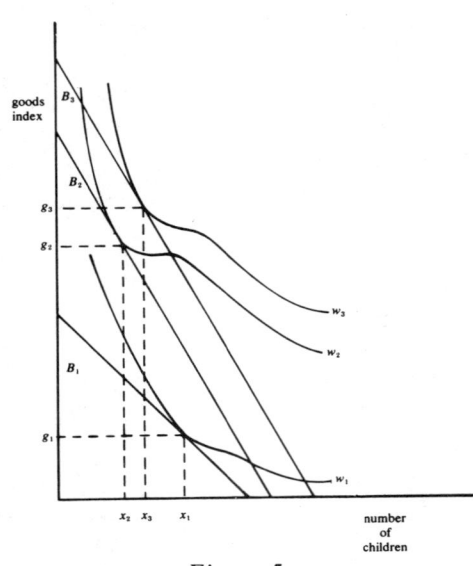

Figure 5.

will determine what people *feel* are the appropriate (or ideal) number of children apart from income considerations. In other words, the income constraints effect not only the actual number of children households will have for a given preference map, but in the disequilibrium state, if SIG members find that, on the average, member households are having less children than anticipated, this fact will in turn influence preference maps in the next period, and so on until a new equilibrium is reached.[26]

For the economy as a whole, the course of fertility will depend in part on a) the degree to which SIG's are open or closed,[27]

and b) the movement of households between SIG's. Among the persistent consequences of economic development are increases in the educational level, net migration to urban areas, and structural changes in the demand for labor which results in a systematic reapportionment of the labor force so that a higher proportion enters higher status groups.[28] Thus households are reapportioned towards statuses whose fertility is lower.

It is to be noted that the theory we have just sketched does not presume rational and calculating behavior with respect to every birth. It assumes that there is a higher degree of substitution between the extent to which people indulge themselves in "causual" decision-making and the point at which economic constraints force, or create strong pressures for, calculated decision-making. Households may be relatively irrational in determining the spacing of most of their children but a calculated decision may be forced upon them in deciding their ultimate family size (*e.g.,* at some point a housewife may decide on an abortion for the nth pregnancy where the $n - 1$ births were unplanned.) Only critical marginal decisions need be calculated, not all decisions or even seemingly representative ones need be.

REFERENCES

1. ADELMAN, I. AND MORRIS, C. T. "A Quantitative Study of Social and Political Determinants of Fertility," *Economic Development and Cultural Change,* Jan. 1966, *4*(2), pp. 129–57.
2. ANKER, R. B. "Socio-Economic Determinants of Reproductive Behavior

[26] See the author's paper, "Bandwagon, Snob, and Veblen Effect in the Theory of Consumers' Demand," for the analysis of approximately parallel phenomena with respect to the interdependence demand for goods [39, Leibenstein, 1950].

[27] The importance of open versus closed SIG's has been stressed by sociologists. See E. D. Driver [14, 1973]. See also R. E. Kennedy [34, 1973], for an application of such ideas (open versus closed groups) to the explanation of fertility differences between Northern and Southern Ireland.

[28] Of course the functional economic benefits of children as a source of labor power, income, old age security, and so on also decline as a consequence of the legal and socioeconomic changes that accompany development.

in Households of Rural Gojarat, India." Doctoral Dissertation, Ann Arbor, University of Michigan, 1973.

3. BANKS, J. A. *Prosperity and parenthood*. London: Routledge and Kegan Paul, 1954.

4. BECKER, G. "An Economic Analysis of Fertility." In National Bureau of Economic Research, *Demographic and economic changes in developed countries*. Princeton, N.J.: Princeton University Press, 1960, pp. 209–40.

5. ——, "A Theory of the Allocation of Time," *Econ. J.*, Sept. 1965, *75*(299), pp. 493–517.

6. BEHRMAN, S. J.; CORSA, L. JR. AND FREEDMAN, R., eds. *Fertility and family planning: A world view*. Ann Arbor: University of Michigan Press, 1969.

7. BLAKE, J. "Are Babies Consumer Durables? Critique of the Economic Theory of Reproductive Motivation," *Population Studies*, 1968, *22*, pp. 5–25.

8. BOURGEOIS-PICHAT, J. "Les Facteurs de la Fécondité non Dirigeé," *Population*, May–June 1965, *20*(3), pp. 383–424.

9. CARLSSON, G. "The Decline of Fertility: Innovation or Adjustment Process," *Population Studies*, March 1966, *20*(2), pp. 149–74.

10. COALE, A. J. "The Demographic Transition Reconsidered," *International population conference*. IUSSP. Liège, 1973 Vol. 1, pp. 53 ff.

11. DAVIS, K. *Population of India and Pakistan*. Princeton: Princeton University Press, 1951.

12. ——, "The Theory of Change and Response in Modern Demographic History," *Population Index*, Oct. 1963, *29*(4), pp. 345–66.

13. DEMENY, P. (1968). "Early Fertility Decline in Austria–Hungary: A Lesson in Demographic Transition," *Proceedings of the American Acad-*

emy *of Arts and Sciences*, 1968, *97*(2), pp. 502–22.

14. DRIVER, E. D. "A Population Policy Model: Structure and Some Empirical Verifications," *O.E.C.D.* Paris, Sept. 1973.

15. DUESENBERRY, J. S. AND OKUN, B. "Comment," in Universities-National Bureau Committee for Economic Research: *Demographic and economic change in developed countries*. Special Conference Series. Princeton: Princeton University Press, 1960, pp. 231–4.

16. EASTERLIN, R. A. *The American baby boom in historical perspective*. New York: National Bureau of Economic Research, Occasional Paper no. 79, 1962.

17. ——, "Towards a Socioeconomic Theory of Fertility: A Survey of Recent Research on Economic Factors in American Fertility." In BEHRMAN, S. J.; CORSA, L. AND FREEDMAN, R., eds. [6, 1969].

18. ——, "The Economics and Sociology of Fertility: A Synthesis." Paper prepared for *Seminar in early industrialization*, Princeton, 1972.

19. EATON, J. W. AND MAYER, A. J. (1953). "The Social Biology of Very High Fertility amongst the Hutterites: The Demography of a Unique Population," *Human Biology*, 1953, *25–6*, pp. 206–64.

20. ENCARNACIÓN, J. "Family Income, Education Level, Labor Force Participation, and Fertility." Unpublished paper, 1973.

20a. FAWCETT, J., ed. "The Satisfaction and Costs of Children: Theories, Concepts, Methods." *Report of Workshop, East–West Center*, Honolulu, April 27–29, 1972.

21. FREEDMAN, D. S. "The Relation of Economic Status to Fertility," *Amer. Econ. Rev.*, June 1963, *53*, pp. 414–26.

22. FREEDMAN, R. "Norms for Family Size in Underdeveloped Areas," *Proceedings of the Royal Society of London,* 1964, B 159, Part 974, pp. 220–45.

23. ——— AND COOMBS, L. "Economic Considerations in Family Growth Decisions," *Population Studies,* Nov. 1966, *20*(2), pp. 197–222.

24. FRIEDLANDER, D. "Demographic Responses and Population Change," *Demography,* Nov. 1969, *6*(4), pp. 359–81.

25. FRIEDMAN, M. AND SAVAGE, L. J. "The Utility Analysis of Choices involving Risk," *J. Polit. Econ.,* August 1948, *56*(4), pp. 279–304.

26. GOLDSTEIN, S. AND MAYER, K. "Residence and Status Differences in Fertility," *Milbank Memorial Fund Quarterly,* July 1965, *43*(3), pp. 291–310.

27. GUPTA, P. B. AND MALAKER, C. R. "Fertility Differentials with Level of Living and Adjustment of Fertility, Birth and Death Rates," *Sankhyā* (Calcutta), Nov. 1963, B*25*(1–2), pp. 23–48.

28. HAJNAL, J. "European Marriage Patterns in Perspective," in GLASS, D. V. AND EVERSLEY, D. E. C., *Population in history.* Chicago: Aldine, 1965, pp. 101–43.

29. HAWTHORN, G., *The sociology of fertility.* London: Collier-Macmillan Ltd., 1970.

30. HEER, D. M. AND MAY, D. A. "Son Survivorship Motivation and Family Size in India: A Computer Simulation," *Population Studies* 1968, *22*, pp. 199–210.

31. HENDERSON, A. "The Cost of Children," *Population Studies,* Sept. 1949, *3*(2), pp. 130–50.

32. JAMES, W. H. "Estimates of Fecundability," *Population Studies,* July 1963, *17*(1), pp. 57–65.

33. ———, "Fecundability Estimates: Some Comments on M. Henry's Paper," *Population Studies,* Nov. 1964, *18*(2), pp. 181–86.

34. KENNEDY, R. E., JR. "Minority Group Status and Fertility: The Irish," *American Sociological Review, 38*(1), pp. 85–96.

35. KUZNETS, S. "Population Trends and Modern Economic Growth—Notes Towards a Historical Perspective." Paper prepared for the United Nations Symposium on Population and Development, 1973.

36. LAKATOS, I. "Falsification and Methodology of Scientific Research Programs." In LAKATOS AND MUSGRAVE, A. E. eds. *Criticism and the growth of knowledge.* Cambridge: Cambridge University Press, 1970.

37. LATSIS, S. J. "Situational Determinism in Economics," *British Journal of Philosophy of Science,* 1972, *23,* pp. 207–45.

38. LEASURE, J. W. "Factors Involved in the Decline of Fertility in Spain, 1900–1950," *Population Studies,* March 1973, *16*(3), pp. 271–285.

39. LEIBENSTEIN, H. "Bandwagon, Snob, and Veblen Effects in the Theory of Consumers' Demand," *Quart. J. Econ.,* May 1950, *64,* pp. 183–207.

40. ———, *Economic backwardness and economic growth.* New York: Wiley; London: Chapman and Hall, 1957.

41. ———, "The Economic Theory of Fertility Decline." Research Papers Series: Harvard Center for Population Studies. Harvard University, 1973.

42. LEWIS-FANNING, E. *Report on an enquiry into family limitation and its influence on human fertility during the past fifty years.* Papers of the Royal Commission on Population I, London: H.M.S.O.

43. LORIMER, F. "The Economics of Family Formation under Different Conditions." In UNITED NATIONS DEPARTMENT OF ECONOMIC AND SOCIAL AFFAIRS, *World population conference*

478   *Journal of Economic Literature*

1965, II, Fertility Family Planning.
New York: author, 1967, pp. 92–95.

44. LYDALL, H. *The structure of earnings.*
Oxford: Clarendon Press, 1968, pp.
163–99.

45. MASON, K. O.; DAVID, A. S.; GERSTIL,
E. K.; LINDSEY, Q. W. AND RELES-
CEN, M. *Social and economic corre-
lates of family fertility: A survey of the
evidences.* Research Triangle Park,
N.C.: Research Triangle Institute,
1971.

46. MAULDIN, W. P. "Fertility Studies:
Knowledge, Attitude, and Practice,"
Studies in Family Planning. Population Council, New York, June 1965, 7,
pp. 1–10.

47. MINCER, J. "Market Prices, Opportunity Costs and Income Effects." In
CHRIST, C. F., ed. *Measurement in
economics: Studies in mathematical
economics and econometrics in mem-
ory of Yehuda Grunfeld.* Stanford:
Stanford University Press, 1963, 67–
82.

48. MUELLER, E. "Economic Motives for
Family Limitations: A Study Con-
ducted in Taiwan," *Population Studies,*
Nov. 1972, *26*(3), pp. 383–403.

49. MUSALLAM, B. *Sex and Society in Is-
lam, The Sanction and Medieval Techniques of Birth Control.* Dissertation,
History Department, Harvard, 1973.

50. NAG, M. *Factors affecting human fertility in non-industrial societies: A
cross-cultural study.* Yale University
Publications in Anthropology, 66. New
Haven: Yale University, 1972.

51. NAMBOODIRI, N. K. "Some Observations on the Economic Framework for
Fertility Analysis," *Population Studies,* July 1972, *26*(2), pp. 185–206.

52. OHLIN, G. "Mortality, Marriage, and
Growth in Pre-Industrial Populations,"
Population Studies, March 1961, *14*(3),
pp. 190–97.

53. ———, "Economic Theory Confronts
Population Growth." Paper presented

at the International Economic Association Conference on the Economic Aspects of Population Growth, Valescure,
France, September 1973.

53a. POFFENBERGER, T. AND POFFENBER-
GER, S. *Husband—wife communica-
tion and motivational aspects of pop-
ulation control in an Indian village.*
C.F.P.I. Monograph series no. 10.
New Delhi, India: Central Family
Planning Institute, 1969.

54. RELE, J. R. "Fertility Differentials in
India: Evidence from a Rural Background," *Milbank Memorial Fund
Quarterly,* April 1963, *41*(2), pp. 183–
99.

55. REPETTO, R. "Son Preference and Fertility Behavior in Developing Countries." In *Studies in Family Planning,*
April 1972, *3*(4), pp. 70–76.

56. ROBINSON, W. C. AND HORLACHER, D.
"Population Growth and Economic
Welfare." Reports on population/fam-
ily planning no. 6. New York: Population Council, February, 1971.

57. SCHULTZ, T. P. "An Economic Model
of Family Planning and Fertility," *J.
Polit. Econ.,* March/April 1969, *77*(2),
pp. 153–80.

58. SPENGLER, J. J. "Values and Fertility
Analysis," *Demography 3*(1), pp. 109–
30.

59. SZABADY, E. *World views of population problems,* Budapest: Akademiai
Kiado, 1968.

60. United Nations Department of Economic and Social Affairs, *The determinants and consequences of population
trends.* New York: author, 1953.
ST/SOA/ Series A/17; 53. XIII.3.

61. ———, "Conditions and Trends of
Fertility in the World," *Population
Bulletin of the United Nations,* no. 7,
1963, New York: author, 1965. ST/
SOA/Series N/7; 64. XIII. 2.

62. VIELROSE, E. "Family Budgets and
Birth Rates." In SZABADY, E. ed.
World views of population problems.

Budapest: Akademiai Kiado, 1968, pp. 359–63.

63. WALKER, K. AND WOODS, M. "Time Use for Care of Family Members." Working Paper No. 1, Cornell University, Ithaca, New York, September 21, 1972.

64. WRONG, D. H. "Trends in Class Fertility in Western Nations," *Can. J. Econ. Polit. Sci.,* May 1958, *24*(2), pp. 216–29.

65. ZAREMBKA, P. *Toward a theory of economic development.* San Francisco: Holden-Day, 1972.

[3]

Economic Decision Theory and Human Fertility Behavior: A Speculative Essay

Harvey Leibenstein

Either explicitly or implicitly, almost all explanations of human fertility have some decision-making ideas at their heart. At the very least, decision-making plays a partial role. This is almost of necessity the case if (1) choice is in some way involved in fertility determination, and (2) we view "non-decisions" as decisions, that is, as a type of "passive" choice making. (More on this point later.) All of this is especially clear in economic theories of human fertility—maximization is the explicit decision-making criterion and forms the central element of such theories.[1] Of course, the maximization postulate is taken from standard microeconomic theory and carried over to the theory of fertility. Whether or not it is applicable to fertility theory does not depend on the appropriateness of the maximization postulate in standard micro theory. However, in my view there is room for a weakening of the postulate in both areas.

Equally important, most population policies also implicitly have decision-making, or some specific view of how decisions are made, as their basis. Unless planners and policymakers want to make decisions blindly, or purely on the basis of political expediency, then some vision involving decision-making as part of human fertility is required. It is difficult to see how this could be avoided. Hence, work involving a somewhat different approach as to how decisions are made can be of central importance to the rational determination of population policies and population plans. This is not to suggest that in fact actual population planning is carried out on the basis of a theory of human fertility. Most plans are probably very much of an ad hoc nature.[2]

What follows is a speculative essay concerned with some implications of maximization as a decision rule and with the possibility and possible fruitfulness of introducing alternative decision schemes. In the alternative, maximization is not denied; however, it is also not assumed to be universal. Outlines of a different decision theory are set forth. The general approach we will take is a *process* view of decision-making. Different processes of decision-making may or may not be consistent with maximization. We will see that this approach can yield very different views of the fertility decision process and that it allows us to ask different questions about decision-making as such. We also hope to connect this approach to ways of developing specific research programs to help us deepen our understanding of this basic element of fertility research.

Decision-making processes
and fertility

It is useful to recall the distinction made by Herbert Simon[3] between substantive rationality and process rationality and, by implication, between substantive and process decision theories, whether rational or not. Substantive rationality can be equated with "after-the-fact" rationality. It is as if any decision procedure used will always result in an optimum solution. Process rationality, by contrast, would indicate the procedures that would lead to optimum decisions.

Economic theory assumes rationality but fails to spell out the way decisions are made. While there are a large number of economic theories of fertility, they all have a certain common basis. They are all substantively rationalistic. The theories differ on the variables that are considered, but they are similar in their *implicit* view of how decisions are made. Substantive rationality allows for a wide variety of possible interpretations. It even allows for various interpretations of the possibility of different interpretations.

Consider the postulate of maximization. Is this a complete assertion or an incomplete one? In other words, is maximization meaningful without stating what it is that is to be maximized? Clearly there are two possibilities here. We can argue that people make decisions so that the result is the best possible outcome; that is, we assume that they know how to obtain their momentary objectives, whatever they may be. Or, it is possible to argue that the only meaningful scientific assertion involving maximization is an assertion that specifies what it is that is to be maximized, such as profits, or utility, or value of assets. Both of these assertions are in some sense defensible. With regard to the first, we can argue that it is not possible to specify *what* is to be maximized because different people have different objectives, and furthermore the same individual will have different objectives at different points in time. On the other hand, we may argue that if, indeed, this is the case (i.e., the objectives are always in flux), it implies that no generalization can be made about the objectives of individuals and that saying that individuals maximize does not really help. Even if it is argued that maximization is meaningful as a behavioral statement, it becomes completely untestable. Unless we know *what* it is that is being maximized, we cannot—even in principle—determine whether maximization is taking place. Thus, if we want testable assertions, then at the very least we have to assert that individuals are maximizing something specific, although what is being maximized need not be the values of a single variable, but may be a fairly complex function.[4] As used, maximization is frequently an incompletely stated postulate.

Consider the case of the maximization of utility. Here it would appear that we are specifying what it is that is being maximized. Once again we can face similar problems to those discussed under the case where we do not specify what it is that is being maximized. It all depends on how utility is interpreted. If nothing is said about the nature of utility or about the components of utility, then we really cannot have a testable statement about what it is that is being maximized. Any outcome can be interpreted as the consequence of maximizing utility. Clearly this is no more helpful than simply asserting that the person is maximizing. What is necessary is to give some content to the idea of utility so that we have an idea whether the outcome fits the content or not.

But what content and how much content about utility is required? While this question cannot be answered in detail, we can say something about the criterion that should be met if the content is to be deemed adequate. At the very least the content should be sufficient so that we can visualize types of behavior that would falsify the assertion that a person maximized utility which had the specified content. The content can be of three types: it can indicate something about the structure of utility, such as, that it follows a law of diminishing marginal utility; or something about the structure of preferences, such as that it follows a transitivity rule; or something about the components that determine increases or decreases in utility.[5] Of course, not all assertions about utility will be adequate to permit testability even in principle, let alone in practice.

The next question that arises is what leads to maximization. At this point it becomes useful to consider how many procedures are involved in trying to carry out a maximizing decision. Here is a list, but it is probably a partial list for a great many problems: (1) Obtain all the correct information up to the point where the additional cost of information is greater than the additional gain; (2) Analyze the distinctiveness of the particular choice situation; (3) Determine, on the basis of external information, the options available; (4) Determine (dredge up), on the basis of "internal information," all of the additional options; (5) Work out a preference ordering for all relevant options, or work out the utilities associated with different options; (6) Make assessments on the basis of correct logical or mathematical principles; (7) Do not avoid details, but do not get unduly caught up in worrying only about details; (8) Avoid irrelevant emotions associated with options or with other elements of the choice process; (9) Avoid irrelevant considerations, facts, and so on; (10) Do not follow others in making choices—consider the uniqueness of your own situation; (11) Do not rationalize any particular choice after the fact; (12) Delegate tasks to others where delegates can do an acceptable job at equal or lower cost; (13) Have an optimum periodic reassessment plan especially for decisions involving different periods of time. Although this is not necessarily a complete, detailed set of procedures, nevertheless one can see that a procedural view of any specific decision suggests that maximizing behavior is far from simple.

Once we consider the fact that actual decisions involve procedures, then we have to examine how we can combine this idea with maximization. What is the status of nonoptimal procedures when maximization is assumed? Do they represent impossible procedures, or procedures that simply do not take place; do they involve trivial deviations from the optimum, or are they to be viewed as mistakes? If we accept the tautological interpretation of maximization, then nonoptimal procedures are not used, or they are mistakes, or what may appear as nonoptimal really is optimal if we take objectives and costs into account.

For purposes of this discussion, we can ignore the question of mistakes.[6] Presumably mistakes can happen for both optimal and nonoptimal decision-making. But let us suppose that someone uses a procedure that is nonoptimal from an outsider's viewpoint. According to the tautological interpretation, this procedure could be shown to be optimal if we understand the real objective involved rather than the presumed objective. Or it would be argued that the nonoptimal procedure is really optimal since what would be viewed as the optimal one involves special, unobserved costs in these particular circumstances. Clearly any tautological interpretation is not useful because it eliminates testability of the propositions. It would appear to be simpler to avoid a tautological interpretation and to consider a wider decision process that permits nonoptimal procedures.

Attempts to improve our understanding of fertility have led different authors to consider different variables, but not different decision processes. The approach developed by Becker and Willis emphasizes income, price, and child-quality changes as explanatory factors in fertility, on the assumption that tastes are given, once and for all.[7] Price changes include changes in the costs of children and the opportunity costs of the mother's time. A number of other writers—Freedman and Leibenstein—have emphasized social status as a variable that may imply different categories of consumption expenditures.[8] Other writers have put emphasis on endogenous taste changes,[9] or on some type of knowledge, or have put stress on human capital and wealth as factors. Still others have emphasized the labor productivity of children, or remittances, or children as a source of old age security, or children as a means of avoiding or reducing risk.[10] Thus we obtain different theories by positing different variables and different behavioral relations, but the decision process remains implicit.

Why should decision procedures be left implicit? If the implicit procedure theory could do everything an explicit one could do, then there would appear to be no point in loading additional intellectual baggage on to our theories without purpose. But it is precisely because we feel that the existing theory explains only a very small amount of the variance in fertility, and because it leads to some results that do not accord with observation, that we are interested in widening the approach to include procedural elements.

A word about the nature of tests in this area may be helpful. Maximization theories are usually of a micro nature; however, the tests, for the most part, involve "macro results." That is, the theory concerns how a specific family would behave under specific circumstances. The test involves looking at statistics about how a population behaves on the average, apart from the behavior of specific families that determine the average. Suppose that the theory suggests that the cost of children is higher for wives with more education, since they sacrifice more by rearing children rather than working. We then look at whether, in a population, families with more highly educated wives, on average, have fewer children, other things equal. We usually do not look at whether there are instances for which the reverse is the case. Suppose that in 40 percent of the households, women with higher education have more children, other things approximately equal. This would appear to go against the theory if it were viewed as theories are usually viewed in the natural sciences. However, it does not show up if we use only macro tests for micro theories. In addition, the macro results, while consistent with the maximization hypothesis, are also consistent with nonmaximization. The mere fact that women take into account the opportunity costs of bearing and raising children does not imply that they take these costs into account to the degree they would if maximization were practiced.

We have seen from the above arguments that the macro result cannot test maximization.[11] The question to keep in mind is whether we get any further by using a decision procedure involving a nonmaximization or occasional nonmaximization approach.

On the consequences of decision processes in fertility theories

The essentials of any social science theory are the variables and relations that specify behavior. If we add decision processes, then we have a more complex theoretical structure. Thinking of decision processes as separate entities, it is evident that theories may differ because their variables and relationships are different but the decision processes are the same; or they may differ because the variables and relationships are the same but the decision processes are different. Or, all elements may differ. Looking at the fertility determination problem from this enlarged view, we can see that the lack of agreement between theory and observation may depend on more than the variables usually considered. It may depend on the decision processes involved.

Simply as an exploratory procedure the introduction of decision processes would seem to be an approach worth considering; at the very least, it may have heuristic value. It is easy to conceive of fertility as a function of such variables as the age of the population, the average income level, the education level, the occupational distribution, the locational distribution, and some aspects of its past history. If we change the variables, we expect to get different results. But we must keep in mind that in general we include variables either on the basis of experience or because general knowledge of human behavior indicates they are likely to have an influence. For instance, it is certainly not difficult to give reasons why age, income, or education should influence the number of children a family would want. However, by the same token it is reasonable to argue that we would want to include decision procedures. It clearly makes a difference whether the couple feel free to make a decision on the basis of careful calculation of their own interest, or whether they do so simply by emulating the behavior of others who are, in some sense, in their reference group. Readers can readily find plausible reasons for either of these decision procedures, as well as for others that might come to mind.

One of the most important areas that the decision process approach could help to illuminate is the treatment of information. Clearly, in some sense or other, information processing is essential in making a decision. This is true even if the processing involves no more than deciding to ignore new types of information. Thus, even if the inputs are the same, different decision processes can obviously lead to different results. Of considerable importance is how the decision process operates as a sieve for various types of information that become available. Within a single context, different procedures may select different types of information. In addition the procedures will determine the extent to which there is a search for new information. Insofar as information determines whether an optimum or nonoptimum solution results, different procedures will lead to different deviations from optimality.

We have already suggested earlier that decision-making, whether of the maximizing or nonmaximizing kind, may involve a great many procedural steps. The number of procedures would depend on the specific content of the decision problem. Thus we cannot simply shift from a substantive theory to a detailed procedural theory. Such a theory would be too concrete. Furthermore, it would probably be too complex. What we can do, however, is attempt to develop a theory based on a few procedural classes. Each class would be abstract: it would not indicate the detailed procedures used but would suggest various ways in which decisions are actually made.

Passive (or inertial) versus active decision-making

What follows is a brief statement of a theory of the decision process. To start with we distinguish between *active* and *passive* (or inertial) decision-making.[12] We assume that active decision-making is infrequent. Day-to-day behavior is on a routinized basis. Passive decisions usually involve routine behavior. It may be viewed as behavior "within a holding pattern." However, events occur, and if the event is strong enough and has a significant impact on the assessment of the decision-maker about the outcomes of behavior, then the impact of the event forces itself on the attention of the decision-making entity. In this way the event may activate the idea that a new, *active* decision may have to be made. Of course, the retention of existing routines is one of the options in the new decision. But there is a distinction to be made between retaining an existing routine *after* considering switching to alternatives, and proceeding with existing routines *without* considering other possibilities. The main point of all this is that we need a theory about how procedures for considering nonroutine behavioral options are activated.

One way of looking at passive decision-making is from the viewpoint of the inert area concept. We assume that within certain bounds of certain variables the routines in behavior that occurred in the past simply continue. Only if the changing data (i.e., the circumstances that surround one's life) go beyond the lower or upper bounds of the inert area does a stimulus arise for active decision-making. If we visualize that for the most part most changes in data are limited in their variance so that most of the time the inert area bounds are not pierced, then we would expect that most periods are passive decision periods. In other words, active decisions are considerably less frequent than they could be were it not for the force of inertia.[13]

A question that arises concerns the relationship between optimality and passive decision-making. Even if one were a maximizer, it would be silly to try to respond to every change in data no matter how small. Clearly in many instances the cost of active decision-making would be greater than the advantage to be gained by trying to respond to very small changes in data. Should one change one's diet every time a single item changes its price by a penny? Obviously not. Thus many instances of passive decision-making may in fact represent maximizing behavior. In a similar vein, an argument could be made that one should not attempt to monitor all changes in data. The cost of very frequent monitoring may be greater than the value of the additional information. However, there are limits to such arguments. One has to have some monitoring and hence a monitoring plan. In fact, what is required is that a maximizer should attempt to work out an optimal monitoring plan. Since most people do not have such plans, it is reasonable to presume that most people do not attempt to maximize in this sense.

In any event it seems reasonable to want to investigate the extent to which people behave in terms of routine—that is, within inert areas—because they take into account the variety of costs involved in active decision processes. Among these are (1) the cost of collecting new data, (2) the cost of assessing data, (3) the "stress" costs of decision-making,[14] and (4) the set-up costs of initiating new activities, and other (unclassified) costs of decision-making. To start with we will assume that most passive decision-making is not of the maximizing type. To many people, simply listing the procedures needed for them to determine their optimum passive decision period would suggest to them that many of their own personal passive decision phases are nonoptimal.[15]

Thus we will revert to our general hypothesis that it takes relatively striking changes to activate or stimulate active decision procedures. The stimulus required depends in part on the personal characteristics of the decision-maker. There are a great many reasons for nonoptimal passivity.[16] We consider only a few in order to suggest more fully than otherwise the sort of things we have in mind. Different degrees of laziness and lethargy may be appropriately descriptive for some personality types. Other descriptive phrases, such as torpor or contentment, may come to the minds of some readers. But this general class of reasons is not the only one.

There may also be rational reasons for deferring decisions. Some of the obvious ones that come to mind are: (1) with more time more information may become available; (2) more time would enable an individual to search for more alternative options; (3) if it is not clear that there is any advantage to making a decision now versus deferring it to a later date, then it makes sense to defer it. However, an important distinction must be made between simply letting a decision opportunity slide by, so to speak, and *actively* deciding against making certain decisions now. In other words, there is such a thing as an *active*, rational decision to defer. We want to separate this last from the general notion of inertial (passive) decision-making.

An active avoidance of the consequences of decision-making may also play a role of maintaining the passive state. The fear of external or internal conflicts is frequently important. An attempt to make a decision may lead to conflict between husband and wife. Since such conflict is frequently unpleasant, one avoids it through passive decision-making. The type of external conflict just mentioned will strike many as obvious (once mentioned), but internal conflict may work in a similar manner. The classic case of Buridan's ass comes to mind. For humans, one would expect a decision to be made when hunger became sufficiently severe. The more familiar cases are those where the prospect of a certain type of decision brings up alternatives that are unpleasant to consider or assess. Somebody in love with two potential mates is more likely to remain unmarried than someone in love with one potential mate.

On the advantages of models that contain routine decision-making

Our general hypothesis is that a high proportion of the fertility rate is determined by "non-decision decisions," that is, passive or inertial decision-making. One of the important empirical research needs, at present, is to determine whether this is so, and to determine in which contexts passive decision-making is more important than in others. Research of this type would probably involve two elements: (1) determining the routine behaviors associated with passive decision-making, and (2) assessing the extent to which such behaviors contribute to fertility. For example, in some contexts age of marriage and length of the lactation period may be determined primarily on the basis of well-established conventions to which most of the population adheres. In such a case, we would have the raw materials with which to estimate the degree to which the passive decisions involving these two elements contribute to fertility.

At this point, if not before, the reader may well ask what a theory of fertility that stresses passive decision-making can add to our knowledge. Here I would like to express a dogma—the passive decision dogma. For most groups routine behavior, which is the expected type of behavior under passive decision-making, predominates. Of course, enunciating the dogma does not make it so. But suppose it is true, what follows? The implication is that to explain most behavior we have to understand routines and why routines are established. Our theory attempts to provide a framework for doing just that. Also it may help to explain why existing empirical studies based on nonroutine behavior result in such low R^2s. In other words, even when the empirical studies appear to give the appropriate directional results, they seem to explain a very small proportion of the variance. This also means that when behavior is studied for which maximization is assumed, the actual result is a correlation of a very mixed type of behavior that involves passive behavior as well as changes in behavior. This result cannot help but distort the changes in behavior that take place.

We would also expect that where most behavior is highly routinized it should be easier to make predictions. This is not to say that we expect the future to be exactly like the past. The results we may look at may involve routine procedures whose outcomes differ over time because of changes in some variable that is well understood. For instance, consider a population with a disequilibrium nonstationary age structure. Suppose that age-specific fertility is determined by routines that follow fairly rigid norms. These norms may determine the age of marriage, average frequency of intercourse, average periods of lactation, and so on. Thus, as the age structure changes, the overall fertility rate will change even if the age-specific rates remain the same. Similarly other compositional variables (e.g., the proportion of the population in rural versus urban areas) may change in a systematic way that may determine the routine types of behavior followed. If we take these considerations seriously it can readily be seen that introducing a large measure of routine-like behavior is likely to facilitate the analysis of events and attempts to make predictions.

Once we consider nonroutine options, the next question arises: How do we choose among the old routine pattern and new, nonroutine options? But this hides some important steps: the search for alternative options, and the evaluation of new options. To what extent do we carry out such search procedures? Finally, there is the choice mechanism itself. Let us assume that this can be represented by a lexicographic ordering and decision procedure. By this we have in mind that we place options within a hierarchy. Lower steps in the hierarchy are tried out earlier. But each step will have a cost (or disutility) associated with it. If the cost is too high, then we proceed to switch to a higher step. An example would be the following four-step hierarchy: (1) Choice on the basis of some ethic. (2) Choice on the basis of some type of conventional behavior. (3) Choice on the basis of partial calculation. (4) Choice on the basis of full calculation. Within each step there is a preference ordering of the options. Also, each step is considered sequentially. If the cost for that step is below a certain threshold value, nothing more happens. The choice is made from the options within that step. Otherwise there is a movement to the next step.

It is of interest to view this approach in terms of the well-established psychological law known as the Yerkes-Dodson Law.[17] Under this law, effectiveness increases with stress up to a point, and beyond that point effectiveness decreases as stress continues to increase. In a similar sense, we may visualize decision-making as a form of behavior under which effectiveness (closeness to optimality) of the decision increases in some sense with the pressure determined by the environment.

It is easier to indicate what we have in mind if we limit ourselves to environmental pressure. For low environmental pressure, individuals may follow habitual or conventional behavior of some sort. As pressure increases, there is a consideration that perhaps behavior should be changed. Beyond some point, say when the pressure gets beyond the inert area bounds, active decision-making is triggered. At this point the individual may first search for a new convention by a variety of means. Some that come to mind are to observe how others behave in similar circumstances, or to inquire about such behavior, or to seek some sort of authoritative advice. Thus a new convention may be chosen. In the next stage, activated by still greater pressure, there is a set of partial calculations, some of which are more extensive than others. For instance, in a partial calculation the direct costs of children may be taken into account but not the indirect costs. Finally, calculation may be fairly complete and the result approximates maximization. There is psychological experimental evidence that as motivation increases decision performance comes closer to maximization.[18] This seems to be closely related to the notion that pressure, from whatever source, will result in a movement toward procedures closer to maximization.

Of course, beyond some point pressure may be too great for objective sensible behavior. The emotions related to very high degrees of stress influence the result so that effectiveness declines.[19]

The situation can be somewhat more complex than just indicated. In addition to switch costs, there may be trade-offs between elements on different steps. Thus, Step 2 may contain ethical components from Step 1. Similarly, Step 3 may contain both ethical and conventional elements from Steps 1 and 2. In other words, a shift to a lower level in the hierarchy does not necessarily imply the complete abandonment of elements at higher levels. A partial non-maximization theory of decision-making of this type can have interesting implications for the understanding of fertility. As a first step, emphasis should be on routines, and especially on conventions. Unlike habits, which are of a personal nature, conventions are useful because they involve widely shared routines within the community.

In the usual approach to analysis of fertility behavior, the investigator considers certain data he or she assumes to be important and implicitly assumes that the data are equally important to the decision-making entity. But this may not be the case. Consider a situation in which four variables—parental income, parental education, labor earnings of children, and nurture costs of children—are assumed to determine family size. Now, let us suppose that only education and income are taken into account by the actual decision-makers. In other words, changes in the earnings opportunity for children and cost of nurture do not result in any changes in fertility decisions. It is not important for our purposes to consider whether we have selected the best variables in order to suggest the nature of the case. What is important is that *not all* the variables that the investigators consider important may be taken into account by the actual decision-makers. Hence, one reason that we want a decision theory is to determine whether variables viewed as likely decision variables from the outside are in fact decision variables from the viewpoint of the decision-maker.

More difficult to handle are those situations for which the same variables are considered by the investigators and the decision-maker, but in which they are assigned different levels of importance. Some variables may be discounted by the decision-maker and hence play a small role in actual decisions, whereas other variables may be amplified by the decision-maker compared with the importance attributed to them by the investigator. These problems are in part avoided by our approach, which uses conventions as decision procedures. To the extent that such conventions are employed, they are likely to be shared and to be similarly perceived by both investigator and decision-maker.

We can also imagine situations in which decision-makers act in a routinized manner (i.e., passive decision-making), while the investigator would expect an altered decision in view of a change in some data. We can apply the theory of inert areas[20] to this type of behavior. In this instance the theory would suggest that, within certain bounds, changes in data do not result in changes in behavioral decisions. The bounds may be different for different variables. As a result, many events of the outside world would have no influence on fertility decisions when they influenced the economic circumstances of the household under consideration.

In essence, inert area behavior is behavior that is insulated from outside events. Of course, there are limits to the nature of the events from which it is insulated. Two aspects of such behavior need to be studied: (1) the extent to which intermediate fertility variables in some sense can be interpreted as routinized behavior; and (2) where the former is the case, the extent to which outside events have a tendency to break up such routine. Of special interest in this connection are the group of four variables determined by John Bongaarts to explain most fertility variation: age of marriage, lactation, use of contraception, and use of abortion.[21] If conventional behavior is sufficiently widespread then it may be of interest to experiment with attempts to combine estimates of the proportions of the population whose behavior is controlled by conventions that determine the Bongaarts variables—that is, age of marriage, length of lactation period, noncontraception, and nonabortion. On this basis simple models can be constructed to estimate convention-determined fertility. It would be of interest to see how much of actual fertility could be explained by employing such methods.

A problem we have not considered is intrafamily conflict and conflict resolution. The view taken here is that, where intrafamily decisions are concerned, some sort of traditional principal agent assignment has taken place, in the sense that certain members have the conventional role of making decisions for other members of the family. This ignores the possibility of conflict in decision-making and the related use of power of some sort as a means of conflict resolution. This is unquestionably a significant problem and deserves a great deal more research than has already been done.[22] However, it seems to me that priority should be given at this stage to the problem of individual decision-making, and only after that is resolved to some degree, should we be concerned with conflict and conflict resolution.

Coordination, Prisoner's Dilemma, and routine behavior

A theory of choice based in large part on routines or, more specifically, on choice according to habits and conventions, may appear to some to be overly simple. The decision-maker has to recognize a context and, once such recognition is made, to apply the habit or convention involved. It is as if the context operates as a stimulus for the routine. While such an approach may appear naive, it appears less so if we attempt to understand the types of problems that habits and conventions essentially solve. While the behavior patterns are indeed simple, the problems to which they provide solutions are in fact fairly complex. This argument will be elaborated in this section.

There are two basic problems that routine behavior, especially conventions, solve: (a) multi-equilibrium coordination problems, and (b) Prisoner's Dilemma problems. We turn first to the multi-equilibrium aspects. A great many problems require coordination between individuals. Some coordination problems imply unique solutions, while others may have a multiplicity of possible solutions. If A and B have to meet and A arrives at the airport at a specified time, and that is the only time that A's plans allow him to meet with B, then the only possible solution may be for B to meet A at the time of arrival and carry out their business at that time and location. There is a sense in which such a problem is fairly easy to solve. Communication may be necessary so that B knows where A will be, but if B is available at that time then the coordination problem is solved. Furthermore, no other time will work. Obviously, if A and B have a variety of times available, say, during that same day, then clearly they have to solve a slightly more complicated coordination problem. They have to choose a mutually convenient time, although there may be a multiplicity of such times. This is a one-time-only problem with a one-time-only solution. The more interesting cases are those types of situations that repeat themselves periodically, where some signal is possible for repetition, and where there are a multiplicity of possible solutions. In those cases, we will argue, conventions are necessary.

The most clear-cut case of the need for conventions where there are a multiplicity of solutions, and where the need for solutions is recurrent, is language. The capacity for speech requires that individuals make sounds so that they are understood by a variety of other people. It is clear that more than one sound can be given certain meaning. Hence agreement of sound–meaning connections is important. The possible connections are not unique. It is these agreements that we refer to as conventions.[23] Furthermore, the family of agreements among a group of individuals using the same set of agreements forms a language. Thus a language may be seen as a complex set of conventions.

Many other examples come to mind. We will consider a few of them. Mealtimes are frequently highly conventional within a culture. Here, too, there are different possibilities. Different cultures and different countries may have different mealtimes, but it is frequently necessary for certain groups within cultures to have similar mealtimes. Since mealtimes are associated with ends and beginnings of other types of activities, such as the division between sleeping and work, or work and leisure, it is necessary to have agreed-upon times for meals since that also implies agreed-upon times for other activities. While biological and other influences may also play a role in determining the mealtime conventions, it is nevertheless true that somehow conventions arise and solve the coordination problems necessary in determining mealtimes. Here, too, it is important to observe that what may appear as an effective solution at one time in history may turn out to be a costly one in some other time, although it may persist into a period when it ceases to be economic or rational. For example, the meal siesta custom in Mediterranean countries made sense in rural or small-town environments, but it no longer makes sense in the urban environment of capital cities, where long periods of transportation are necessary to carry out the midday meal siesta activities. Closely related to mealtimes are the conventions for work hours, or conventions for keeping shops open, and times for carrying on other business activities. Clearly here some variety is possible but coordination is required.

Once a convention that solves a coordination problem exists, the problem is no longer seen as such. The problem is a forgotten and *hidden* problem. No one views it any more as a problem. Instead individuals simply become aware of the convention and behave according to it. The individual learns the convention, finds that behavior in accordance with it seems to "work," and hence continues to behave in accordance with the convention. In other words, this is a choice procedure that has a positive utility payoff, and normal experience reinforces this perception. Nevertheless, it is important to keep in mind that the particular convention is not necessarily optimal. It may very well be suboptimal, but it would be too costly for any individual to attempt to introduce a superior convention.

In the Prisoner's Dilemma type of problem, the situation is somewhat more complex.[24] Let us review briefly the three characteristics of these problems. First, no individual controls all the variables. Second, the outcome depends on the joint choice of a number of individuals. Third, when each one attempts to do as well as he possibly can, the outcome is the worst outcome possible rather than the best. From this point of view, the "rational solution" to a Prisoner's Dilemma problem is the opposite of the invisible hand theory, under which individual maximizing behavior maximizes social welfare.

We now turn to an example of a Prisoner's Dilemma problem that is relevant to problems of fertility. Consider an ethnic group in which each household (i.e., family) is eager for the group or people to survive indefinitely. If we start with the assumption of fairly high mortality rates, then the group requires fairly high fertility rates to survive. However, each individual household may feel that a high fertility rate for them requires a per family member level of living lower than they would desire. As a result each household in fact desires low fertility rates for themselves, but each would like to see that all other households carry out practices that result in high fertility rates. Thus there is the usual conflict between group objectives and individual family objectives. This is illustrated in the payoff table below.

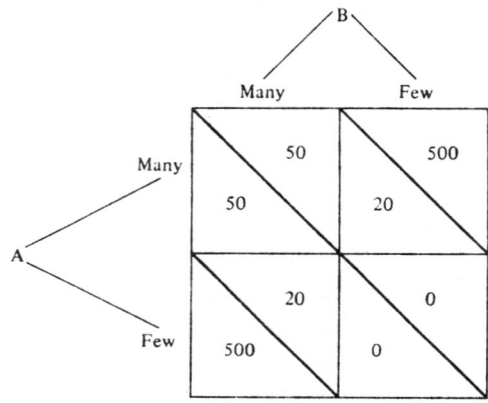

A represents the household we are concerned with and B represents the typical household of all *others*. The two choices available involve many children and few children. If A chooses to have many children and B chooses to have many children, this will guarantee group survival. On the other hand, if A prefers to have few children while everybody else has many, this puts A in a better position since for A this implies both group survival and a high standard of living per family member for A. The reverse is of course true for B. If each behaves so that both have few children, then of course the group does not survive and the worst situation occurs. In the payoff table above, the numbers in the various cells indicate the utilities attributed to the two choices. The exact utilities are of no importance. What really matters is the ordering and general magnitude. As the payoff table is arranged, it is clear that if each family chooses what is best for their household, then survival does not take place and, as a result, the worst situation occurs. We next consider how conventions of various types may solve this problem.

Even if households wish to have relatively few children, they may still be bound by convention in their behavior. In other words, within limits, conventional behavior may dominate or override behavior desired on the basis of private preferences. In most cases, the force of convention is so strong that private preferences do not really enter as a serious option on a conscious level.

In other cases, what would be the private preferences if the conventions did not exist are rationalized into other preferences that are consistent with conventional behavior. Hence, appropriate conventions can eliminate the Prisoner's Dilemma (worst) outcome. Strong conventions that determine or influence the age of marriage, the channeling of sexual activity within marriage, and the length of the period of lactation may determine a fertility outcome that would be entirely different from the outcome in the absence of such conventions.

Surviving civilizations are likely to have developed high-fertility conventions. Civilizations that have not survived may not have developed them. Clearly it is useful to know the nature of these conventions, even if one does not know the exact Prisoner's Dilemma problem that they may temporarily have "solved." Of course, it is not surprising that such conventions continue to hold sway after mortality rates decline and the need for such conventions no longer exists. Thus the very high rates of population growth that have been observed during the middle half of the twentieth century are probably the consequence of lagging conventions that effectively solved problems in the past.[25] Once the convention is in place, the problem becomes hidden. The existence of a previous Prisoner's Dilemma problem is completely forgotten when fertility rates decline; that is, it is the problem and not the previous solution that is no longer apparent.

It may appear to some readers that the ideas just developed go counter to the belief that high fertility rates are to be explained by the discounted benefits of children being greater than the discounted costs. This is a difficult issue to address. In my view, it is hard to know in particular situations when in fact net benefits exceed costs. However, even where this is so, conventions remain significant. Consider the case where children are viewed as a source of labor earnings. Even if one could show that there is a net gain to the household from the labor of the *nth* child, the outcome still depends on the convention (custom) that determines the extent to which a child's earnings can be appropriated by the parents. Also, even if it is true that there is a net benefit *on the average* when we consider children as a source of labor, it is not necessarily true for the marginal family. It may be true for a portion of the work force but not for the entire work force. Strong conventions, however, operate for both the average household and the marginal household.

We should not view conventions as overriding all pressures based on calculation. In other words, convention will not necessarily persist in the face of very long-run advantages to ignoring the convention. But conventions are likely to persist to some degree, and for some period of time, during which they are no longer rationally supportable. This helps to explain the persistence of relatively high fertility rates in the presence of conditions that, in the absence of marriage, lactation, and related conventions, would be conducive to relatively low-level fertility.

It is of more than passing interest that the seeming transitions from one population epoch to another appear like a succession of Prisoner's Dilemmas, in which the "solution" of one dilemma becomes the basic element that sets up the next one. Thus, the high-fertility conventions that solve the survival dilemma in the high-mortality phase become the basis of the adverse result in the low-mortality phase. Finally, the calculated low-fertility solution of that phase leads to apprehensions of nonsurvival in the modern developed country phase. Examples of this last are West Germany, France, and some Eastern European countries, where the net reproduction rate is considerably below unity.[26] However, it would take us too far afield to consider these matters in any detail.

Comment on psychological and related literatures

It seems clear to the writer that on many of the issues raised in this paper the psychological literature should be of great interest. However, forays into that literature proved to be rather disappointing.[27] A good deal of the literature on decision-making appears to be essentially of a normative nature; it usually attempts to indicate a wide variety of steps that have to be taken in order to make various types of *complex* decisions. Frequently, these steps are compared with behavior in various types of experiments. However, the experiments usually do not permit individuals to make decisions in any way they please. Rather the experiments suggest in one way or another some of the ways in which these decisions *ought* to be made, or they constrain some of the elements in the decision-making process. On the whole, the experiments involve decisions that are relatively unique, and that are frequently concerned with complex aspects of the decision process. Indeed, one of the major works on decision-making (Janis and Mann)[28] indicates specifically that they are only interested in complex decisions.

There are scholars who seem to love complexity. They equate complexity with methodological sophistication. Also, they appear to view simplicity with suspicion and equate it with naivete. Such scholars, were they physicists in the eighteenth and nineteenth centuries, would have viewed Newtonian mechanics as absurd, given its basic simplicity. Such views are not limited to individuals. Yet, from my viewpoint, this general attitude is basically wrong. Simplicity should be welcomed when and if it is found. Complexity should be of scientific interest primarily if it can be viewed as being made up of a combination of essentially simple underpinnings.

Pure demography (of the type developed by Lotka) is essentially based on an extremely simple and admittedly naive behavioral relation, namely, that mortality and fertility are functions of age. A great many of the measurements used in demography are of a similar nature. While they are frequently viewed as purely statistical measures, in fact they are based on extremely simple behavioral relations. As long as we are aware that the real world does not follow completely the behavioral relations, no great harm is done in using such measurements to advantage.

The approach developed in this paper, which places great stress on repetitious behavior, may appear to some readers as essentially naive. Yet it seems to me that it is basically this type of behavior that may account for most of the fertility behavior that takes place. Furthermore, it would seem desirable to understand simple types of behavior before we move on to more complex variants. Of course, one could go too far in the direction of simplicity. Nevertheless, the mere fact of emphasizing behavior that may be viewed as simple is not by itself in any way damaging to the essential nature of the theory involved. Quite the reverse would appear to be the case.

Intensive village studies

Decision processes could be studied in a variety of contexts. For our purposes, it would seem desirable to start such studies as part of intensive village studies. Several reasons come to mind: (1) Those living in a village in a developing country are likely to exhibit a considerable amount of routine behavior, and hence this would appear to be a desirable context within which to study passive decision-making. In other words, the general hypothesis is that so-called traditional behavior is likely to involve a great many passive decisions. (2) In general, in the initial stages of such research, it would seem desirable to choose contexts that avoid the variety of behavior and complexities found in urban life. (3) Perhaps the most important reason for doing village studies is that most of the population of low-income developing countries lives in rural villages.

The basic advantage to a single village study is the possibility of intensity. There is a trade-off between intensity and representativeness. If fewer than several hundred people are interviewed or studied, then the statistics that result cannot be representative of a more general fertility picture. Can we get something in return for the lack of representativeness? One way of viewing the matter is to consider the situation as a trial run for larger studies that will be representative. Another way of looking at it is to see whether we can learn something simply as a consequence of putting more resources into each person interviewed or observed.

The essence of the approach that we are developing is that it is more important to find out what will *not* change with respect to relatively small changes in the economy, than what will change. In doing village studies there may be direct, as against indirect, approaches involving the examination of these questions. An example of the direct approach is simply to ask a selected group of individuals a set of questions and to make judgments on the basis of the responses. The indirect approach would be, in part, simply to observe events as they take place, or to make judgments about other information available concerning the culture and the society. We would then use such information to develop hypotheses and check inferences. On an a priori level, very little can be said about which approach one should employ. It would seem reasonable to assume that both would have their uses. However, the direct approach is much easier to illustrate by a variety of examples, and hence we examine this approach in greater detail below.

Clearly the age of marriage and the proportions married are significant determinants of fertility. In some societies, especially in the early stages of development, the age of marriage may be determined by social convention. We can readily imagine a set of questions that would attempt to elicit information of this type. They are presented only for purposes of illustration. Here are some of the questions that might be asked of women in a village study. (1) At what age did you marry? (2) Is there an expected or traditional age of marriage in your group? (3) Do parents normally expect their daughters to marry at some particular age? If so, at approximately what age? (4) Would you have married when you did if the family from which you came was (a) 10 percent poorer, (b) 10 percent richer, (c) 20 percent poorer, or (d) 20 percent richer? (5) Do you have relatives (brothers, sisters, cousins) who failed to get married at the expected age, or expected time, because of adverse economic conditions? (6) Can you recall any such conditions, or any economic reversals that took place? Of course all such questions would have to be carefully worded so that they were clearly meaningful to individuals within the particular culture. Such phrases as "economic conditions" would probably have to be given very specific content. For instance, for those engaged in farming, the content might be in terms of good versus poor harvests, share-cropping rents, prices of crops, and so on.

In this set of questions, the clearly implicit attempt is to relate age of marriage to possible changes in level of income. However, other variables can also be examined from the same viewpoint. For example, changes in level of education may also be studied in connection with the same intermediate variable.

The critical element in any such project must be an attempt to discover the decision processes that are used by the household members. One could develop a variety of decision-making theories even using only the relatively few components we have considered. Two types of components are involved: different circumstances may activate the sense that a decision has to be made; and the steps in the hierarchy of the lexicographic ordering may be different for different individuals. If decision processes differ for different individuals, then the research effort would require that we attempt to relate different processes used by different individuals to such possible elements as age, education, economic status, and so on.

An additional step in the research procedure is to examine the extent to which the variables usually considered in fertility theories play a role in the actual decision processes used. As a result, data on such variables as benefits and costs of children, the time allocations of household members, household wealth, options open to the parents, and so on, would have to be collected and analyzed at the same time that we study decision processes. However, the data collected would now be analyzed in terms of how and to what extent they enter decision processes. Of course, once the usual data were collected they could also be analyzed along more conventional lines. In fact, it would be of considerable interest to compare the results of the conventional analysis with the results obtained by including decision processes, and especially passive decision-making. While we cannot tell until we try, it seems likely that studies of this kind could lead to the development of fertility theories (including nonmaximizing, maximizing, passive, and active decision processes) that would have greater explanatory and predictive power than the current models.

Notes

1 See the review in Theodore W. Schultz (ed.), "New economic approaches to fertility," *Journal of Political Economy* 81, no. 2, part II (March/April 1973). See also G. Becker, "An economic analysis of fertility," in *Demographic and Economic Changes in Developed Countries,* National Bureau of Economic Research (Princeton: Princeton University Press, 1960), pp. 209–240.

2 In fact, it probably is avoided much more frequently than not. See S. C. Jain, F. Joubert, and J. K. Satia, "Management of national population programs," in *World Population and Development*, ed. Philip M. Hauser (Syracuse: Syracuse University Press, 1979) for a recognition that fertility theories involve decision elements (p. 586); however, their list of 15 major managerial perceptions and concerns (p. 599) does not mention such elements.

3 Herbert A. Simon, "Rationality as process and as product of thought," *American Economic Review* 68, no. 2 (May 1978): 1–16.

4 See Milton Friedman, "The methodology of positive economics," in *Essays in Positive Economics* (Chicago: University of Chicago Press, 1953), pp. 3–43. For an alternative view more consistent with that of the present writer, see Herbert A. Simon, "Problems of methodology—Discussion," *American Economic Review* (May 1963). See also S. J. Latsis, "Situational determinism in economics," *British Journal of Philosophy of Science* 23 (1972): 207–245.

5 D. M. Grether and C. R. Plott, "Economic theory of choice and the preference reversal phenomenon," *American Economic Review* 69, no. 4 (September 1979): 623–638.

6 See George J. Stigler, "The Xistence of X-efficiency," *American Economic Review* 66, no. 1 (March 1976): 213–216 on mistakes, and on the tautological interpretation of maximization.

7 See Robert J. Willis, "A new approach to the economic theory of fertility behavior," *Journal of Political Economy* 81, no. 2, part II (March/April 1973): S14–64.

8 Deborah Freedman, "The relation of economic status to fertility," *American Economic Review* 53 (June 1963): 414–426; Harvey Leibenstein, "The economic theory of fertility decline," *Quarterly Journal of Economics* 89, no. 1 (February 1975): 1–31.

9 Richard A. Easterlin, "Fertility and development," *Population Bulletin of ECWA* 18 (June 1980): 5–40.

10 Mead Cain, "Risk and insurance: Perspectives on fertility and inequality in rural India and Bangladesh," Center for Policy Studies Working Paper no. 67 (New York: The Population Council, April 1981).

11 Some micro theories have been tested against micro data. To the extent that this has been done, some of the strictures above do not hold.

12 "Passive" and "active" may not be the best terms. They are used here differently than in some of the psychological and sociological literature on decision-making. In that literature "passive" and "active" are related to the extent to which an individual participates in family decision-making. See Paula E. Hollerbach, "Power in families, communication and fertility decision-making," Center for Policy Studies Working Paper no. 53 (New York: The Population Council, January 1980).

13 For a somewhat expanded treatment of the inert area idea and its relation to population, see Harvey Leibenstein, "Beyond economic man: Economics, politics, and the population problem," *Population and Development Review* 3, no. 3 (September 1977): 190–191, 195–197.

14 D. E. Broadbent, *Decision and Stress* (London: Academic Press, 1971), especially pp. 109–112.

15 Of special interest on various aspects of decision deferral is R. M. Corbin, "Decisions that might not get made," chapter 3 in *Cognitive Process in Choice and Decision Behavior*, ed. T. Wallsten (Hillsdale, N.J.: Lawrence Erlbaum Associates, 1980).

16 A paper by Geoffrey McNicoll contains ideas that somewhat overlap with those developed here. However, in my view, bounded rationality and routine behavior are not quite the same. However, there may be instances in which they turn out to be very similar. See Geoffrey McNicoll, "Institutional determinants of fertility change," *Population and Development Review* 6, no. 3 (September 1980): 441–462.

17 The Yerkes-Dodson Law seems to be so well established among psychologists that the citations to the original experiments (1908) are rarely made. See Broadbent, cited in note 14, p. 454. For a more general treatment see John W. Atkinson and David Birch, *Introduction to Motivation* (New York: Van Nostrand, 1978).

18 W. Edwards, "Reward probability, amount and information as determinants of sequential two-alternative decisions," *Journal of Experimental Psychology* 52 (1956): 177–188; S. Siegal and D. A. Goldstein, "Decision-making behavior in a two-choice uncertain outcome situation," *Journal of Experimental Psychology* 55 (1959): 150–155.

19 Broadbent, cited in note 14, pp. 453–456.

20 See Leibenstein, cited in note 13, pp. 183–199.

21 John Bongaarts, "A framework for analyzing the proximate determinants of fertility," *Population and Development Review* 4, no. 1 (March 1978): 105–132.

22 See Hollerbach, cited in note 12.

23 David Lewis, *Conventions* (Cambridge: Harvard University Press, 1969).

24 There is now a large and rich literature on the Prisoner's Dilemma problem. The basic analysis can be found in R. D. Luce and H. Raiffa, *Games and Decisions* (New York: Wiley, 1957). See also A. Chammah and A. Rapoport, *Prisoner's Dilemma* (Ann Arbor: University of Michigan Press, 1965). Sometimes n-person Prisoner's Dilemmas are referred to as "social dilemmas." For an excellent treatment see Robyn M. Dawes, "Social dilemmas," *Annual Review of Psychology* (1980): 169–190.

25 In this connection the paper by Moni Nag, "How modernization can also increase fertility," *Current Anthropology* (October 1980): 571–587, is of considerable interest.

26 Philippe Ariès, "Two successive motivations for the declining birth rate in the West," *Population and Development Review* 6, no. 4 (December 1980): 645–650.

27 For a review of this literature see Paul Slovic, Baruch Fischoff, and Sarah Lichtenstein, "Behavioral decision theory," *Annual Review of Psychology* (1977): 1–39.

28 I. L. Janis and L. Mann, *Decision Making* (New York: Free Press, 1977).

Part II
Population Growth

IV

The Impact of
Population Growth on Economic
Welfare–Nontraditional Elements

Harvey Leibenstein

In an age when there is unusual concern about the population explosion one
would think that the concern arises as a result of a solid understanding of the
consequences of population growth on the economy. However, much of what
is normally understood about the consequences of population growth depends upon the classical approach to the problem. The primary mode of
analysis involves inferences about output based on the impact of population
growth on the ratios of the traditional inputs of land, labor, and capital. Only
in recent years have we had hints that we may be on the wrong track. The
viewpoint taken in this paper is that a more useful approach is to consider the
problem in terms of a number of nontraditional elements that are likely to be
important in determining the rate of economic growth. To be specific, our
analysis will emphasize the impact of population growth on those acquired
qualities of the population that are important to output and its growth.

The Classical Mold of the Population-Resources
Problem

The essence of the classical mode of thinking is to emphasize physical
resources in relation to population; therefore, land and capital are the basic
resources considered. Behind this mode of thinking is the notion of a unique
production function. That is to say, there is a one-to-one relation between the
inputs for land, labor, and capital and the output that results—for every set of
inputs there is a unique and determinate output. Since it is usually argued
that land and other natural resources are fixed, then at some point the rela-

*Harvey Leibenstein is Member of the Center for Population Studies and
Andelot Professor of Economics and Population, Department of Economics,
Harvard University.*

79

tion between a growing population and fixed natural resources must lead to diminishing returns per person, other things being equal. Even if we allow for the fact that capital is, in some sense and to some degree, a substitute for natural resources—given the belief that capital becomes a successively less adequate substitute as more capital is substituted for resources—diminishing returns to population growth appear to be valid and reasonable. In principle, output per worker must *eventually* decline as the population grows. The one ameliorating influence is the application of new inventions to the production process.

At first blush, this view seems so reasonable that it is difficult to believe that it could be faulted. Probably most reasoned arguments about the hazards of population growth to economic welfare depend in one way or another on arguments of this type. Such arguments appear to have special relevance for developing countries where the bulk of the output takes place in the agricultural sector and where it often appears that the genuine limiting factor must be cultivable land. In what follows it will *not* be argued that these traditional considerations are of no importance. Far from it. Rather, the thrust of the argument is that such considerations are less important than one would have believed 2 decades ago and that in most instances they are not the factors of prime importance.

The endless stream of arguments about the applicability of neo-Malthusian models rests on two major elements:

1. The consequences of technical change resulting from an endless flow of inventions enable us to avoid indefinitely an approximation to the state of Malthusian equilibrium.

2. The fertility assumptions employed in the neo-Malthusian models no longer hold in view of contemporary contraceptive technology.

Although the second objection is probably a weak one,* the first one seemed to be strong and to have considerable basis in fact. As a consequence, the neo-Malthusian debate frequently turned on whether one happened to be an invention-innovation optimist or an invention-innovation pessimist; i.e., whether one believed that the current rate of material inventions would continue or one believed that this, too, was subject to considerable diminishing returns. The experience of the last half century or so supports the technological optimists. Extrapolating from countries and periods within the last 50 years, during which fairly rapid growth has taken place, it would appear that at least *potential* economic growth is greater than the rate of population growth. The argument of the technological pessimists depends on theory rather than experience, i.e., on the belief that some resources such as land are in fact fixed and that, in fact, the substitutes for such resources are likely to be considerably inferior to the fixed resources so that diminishing returns are likely to result.

*Contraceptive technology has no bearing if families *want* to have many children, say between four and six.

The "Residual" and the Acquired Quality of Labor

Research carried out by economists in the last 15 years suggests that, for the most part, growth cannot be explained by increases in the traditional inputs of capital, land, and labor. Although most of this research has been carried out in developed countries, studies by Kuznets refer to periods when the developed countries were relatively underdeveloped.

What has been called the "residual"—that part of economic growth that *cannot* be explained by increases in traditional inputs—comprehends most of the economic growth that takes place. This finding is of great importance. This paper will argue that it is a critical element in any reinterpretation of the neo-Malthusian viewpoint, or of any set of relations between population and resources, or on the impact of population growth on economic development. (Although there has been considerable speculation about the nature of what we may call the "residual" inputs and although we know with some degree of definiteness what some of them must be, we cannot say what all of them happen to be.)

According to Kuznets (1), no more than 10 percent of the growth rate (in a number of European countries, Australia, and Japan) can be accounted for by the traditional inputs.* Kuznets concludes

> ... that the direct contribution of man-hours and capital accumulation would hardly account for more than a tenth of the rate of growth in per capita product—and probably less. The large remainder must be assigned to an increase in efficiency in the productive resources—a rise in output per unit of input, due either to the improved quality of the resources, or to the effects of changing arrangements, or to the impact of technological change, or to all three.

There are a number of studies of the residual. For the most part they concern advanced countries, and the results are frequently less extreme than those found by Kuznets. Nevertheless, it is rare that less than 50 percent is explained by the residual. Traditional inputs explain less than one half, and frequently considerably less than one half, of the growth. †

In addition, some recent studies suggest from a different angle that capital accumulation is relatively unimportant as a contribution to growth. (We

---

*Although the countries used by Kuznets are today developed, the starting period of the analysis (e.g., Norway 1865-74) frequently goes back to a time when they were relatively underdeveloped.

†A number of these studies are summarized in the O.E.C.D. Journal, *Productivity Measurement Review.* See especially (2, 3).

A recent fascinating paper by Krueger (4) shows "that three variables normally associated with the concept of human capital can explain more than half the difference in income levels between the United States and a group of less developed countries for which data are available."

should keep in mind that usually population growth is less than one third of the rate of capital growth.) In a study by the author (5) it has been shown that the incremental capital output ratio varies, in almost all cases, inversely with the growth rate. Patel (6) shows this to be the case for developing countries. A reasonable inference from these studies is that in most cases neither capital nor labor of the existing quality is the major force in growth. Hence, we stress those qualities of the population that result in the improvement of the quality of labor through education and other means of skill acquisition, and those elements that lead to the introduction of innovations and technical change.*

Incentives and Effort Responses

Among the qualities of a population that are likely to be of importance in affecting productivity per worker is the responsiveness of the population to incentives. We may think of it in terms of the degree and directions of effort that the population is willing to put forth in response to the incentives that exist and those that it creates. The rate of population growth is in some sense related to these elements, at least in terms of the impact of differences in family size on nurture and education.

The basic idea to be developed is that human inputs, essentially varieties of labor including management and entrepreneurship, can put forth different degrees of effort in response to different incentives both within firms and in the economy at large. Effort should *not* be interpreted here in a narrow physical sense, although physical effort is one dimension.

Some of many possible dimensions of effort are listed below:
1. various physical activities, each activity being a different dimension;
2. the act of choosing between different activities;
3. the degree of care in carrying out such activities;
4. scanning the "information field" inside and outside the firm;
5. various "search activities," i.e., looking for a new means of performance in terms of techniques of production or characteristics of the product;
6. the degree of perseverance in carrying out activities;
7. the degree of cooperation with co-workers.

Whereas all types of effort are important in production, it is probably true that the forces employed to introduce innovations are the ones that are most significant in promoting economic growth. Such efforts are likely to involve the search for and development of information on new techniques of production and the marshaling of the other inputs required to introduce innovations. This last point is far from trivial. Knowledge of a potential innovation might not be sufficient to induce the entrepreneurial efforts to marshal all of the inputs necessary to put the innovation into effect. Whether the innovation

*A good deal of the evidence is summarized in a paper by Morgan(7).

takes place is likely to depend on three elements of the quality of labor: the actual skills of the labor force which depend upon on-the-job training and formal education; the incentives that exist in the economy; and the degree to which individuals respond to such incentives. Needless to say, incentives also enter the picture in determining the accumulation of physical capital as well as the accumulation of human capital (i.e., education and skills). The point is that part of the acquired qualities of the population that determine development depend upon motivational elements.

If the rate, structure, and pattern of population growth, and its consequences, are in any way related to psychological attitudes concerned with incentives and responsiveness to incentives, then we may obtain a connection between population growth and some of the determinants of economic growth. This relationship may be important despite the fact that there may be aspects of the problem that are exceedingly difficult to measure. We must also include the "negative efforts" to production—the efforts put forth by various people to resist change, to resist the adoption of innovations, whether through legislation, the support of constraints, featherbedding practices, and so on. There is almost no direct evidence on how incentives and degrees of responsiveness to incentives are related to different rates of population growth. As we proceed we shall see that some tenuous clues exist on this matter in the literature on semistarvation, and on the relations between family achievement and family size. There are suggestions that psychological variables, such as apathy in the case of hunger and verbal skill formation in the case of "overcrowded" families, may be of importance. There is also in the literature some exceedingly tenuous evidence on the consequences of maternal deprivation. On this, however, it is exceedingly difficult to know whether it is of any importance from a macro (overall) viewpoint in *any* economy, or whether the incidence is always so small as to be irrelevant for our purposes.

The important aspect of all this is not that the facts themselves—or their possibilities—are especially new. What is of interest in recent research is that it has been shown that the incentive-responsiveness elements are likely to be of great importance (8) in understanding increases in production, although, unfortunately, the relations of these elements to population growth are, at present, not known.

Micro-Demographic Effects*

Associated with the economic state of the system at any time there are a set of demographic characteristics which affect various aspects of the nurture

*A brief version of this section was presented at the General Conference, London, September 1969, of the International Union for the Scientific Study of Population.

process and schooling. (See Figure 1.) The nurture and schooling processes have economic consequences which in their turn alter the economic state of the system and may alter some of the demographic causative variables. The system can be viewed, *in part*, as an internally self-generating system. That is, it is a system in which individuals at any time not only transmit their genetic fertility and mortality potentialities in a systematic way to subsequent generations but also transmit certain social, cultural, and physical characteristics. However, it is not a completely self-contained system since part of the economic changes—probably the greater part—are determined outside the demographic system and are, from the point of view of the demographic system, an autonomous set of influences.

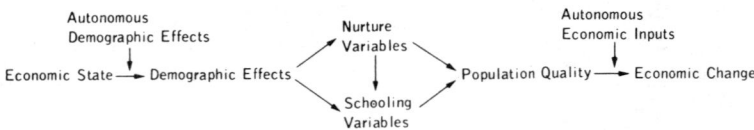

Figure 1. The impact of demographic variables on the economic state of the system.

Now, we delineate what may be viewed as a set of demographic causative effects:

1. *the age-structure-dependency effect*; this effect has been analyzed in detail by Coale and Hoover (9);
2. *the sib-number effect* which considers the consequences of the number of children per family;
3. *the sib-spacing effect*;
4. *the parental-mortality effect* which considers the effects of the possibility of one or both parents being absent during the nurture or schooling period;
5. *the replacement effect.* *

All but one of these listed effects of a greater rather than a lesser rate of population growth are detrimental to the acquired economic quality of the labor force. The main idea is that the quality of the labor force depends (in part) on the growth rate of labor, which in turn depends on the growth rate of the population. The relation between the quality of an input and its

---

*A fairly complete list of demographic effects would also include:
6. *the population-resource ratio effect*
7. *the congestion effect*
Both are likely consequences of population growth. However, these matters will not be treated in this paper.

growth rate is a rather unusual one.* We do not know enough about the facts to examine this element in more than a suggestive way. The discussion that follows suggests that the sib-number effect, the sib-spacing effect, and the parental-mortality effect are all detrimental to the quality of the work force, but we do not know to what degree. The replacement effect, considered at the end of the paper, may operate in the opposite direction from the other effects considered, in some cases.

THE NURTURE-NATURE BORDERLINE: INTELLIGENCE AND FAMILY SIZE

An interesting qualitative aspect of the problem involves the imprecise borderline between nurture and genetic inheritance. A large (although controversial) literature has accumulated which suggests that, on the average, children that come from families with relatively few siblings or with no siblings do disproportionately better at intellectual and related pursuits than those with many siblings (10). Also birth order is in some degree connected with intellectual achievement—on the average the higher the birth order the greater the achievement. It has not been determined whether any of this contains a genetic component.

At present we know little about the relation between population quality, entrepreneurial capacities, innovating capacities, and contact with siblings. There are some data that suggest that an unusual proportion of those who have considerable intellectual achievements to their credit were either only children or from families in which there was a relatively large age gap between siblings (11). It seems plausible that the ability to think abstractly would be developed earlier or would on the whole be greater if children learned the concomitant verbal skills either from adults or from siblings considerably older than themselves (12). Although it is difficult in fact to separate the level of intelligence from acquired skills, there is evidence to suggest that a child's intelligence level can actually be raised by a culturally nurturant upbringing or by training (13), or by the kinds of environmental stimuli available in an urban setting (14, 15); and that there is a connection between family size and intellectual capacity. Intellectual capacity with the attendant ability to manipulate abstractions that typifies educated intelligence is unquestionably important to economic development. It is evident in the contribution of professionalized skills to the economy; i.e., in the work of engineers, lawyers, doctors, architects, and teachers at various levels. It seems likely that acquired intellectual capacities are also related to managerial skills. It would appear then that the smaller the rate of population growth and the smaller the family size, the greater the extent to which these skills could be developed.

*To some degree this idea is found in the concept of "embodied technical change."

SIB-NUMBER AND OTHER FAMILY-SIZE EFFECTS*

The number of siblings in a family is likely to be important with respect to at least two elements of nurture: nutrition (16, 17) and preschool training. It may also be important in terms of the existence, or absence, of maternal deprivation, but this is not at all clear. With respect to all three of these effects there is some impressive case study evidence although we do not know how widespread these cases are from a statistical viewpoint. Other things being equal, we would normally expect that the number of siblings will determine the nutrition of children and hence the greater the sibling number, the greater the likelihood of malnutrition in low income families (16, pp. 142-143).

For example, J. A. Scott (18) studied a cross-section of children attending ordinary day schools in London. He collected data in 1959 on height and weight of pupils and then linked the results of their "eleven-plus" examinations (verbal reasoning test) with the data. Table 1 shows that as the number of children in the family increases, mean height, weight, and intelligence scores tend to decrease. (Two exceptions—intelligence of a two-child family in 1 G and + height + weight of a four-child family in 1 B.) Conversely—". . . children who belong to small families tend to do better in intelligence tests than children from larger families, and that children from large families are not so tall (or so heavy) at any given age as those from small families."

In Table 2 Scott shows that as average intelligence increases so does the average height. Table 1 shows that intelligence is related to family size and that height is also related to family size. The question is raised as to which of these two variables (height or family size) has the greater influence on intelligence. Table 3 shows that intelligence increases with height and decreases with family size.

Scott therefore says the data suggest that the most intelligent child will be found in the small family.

Similarly, it has been shown that the greater the sibling number the less the effectiveness of informal preschool training on linguistic skills or I.Q. (17, p. 130).†

---

*See also J. D. Wray, "Population Pressure on Families: Family Size and Child Spacing," in this volume, especially the tables.

†There is a large literature on these matters which shows an inverse relationship between intelligence and aspects of family size such as sib number, etc. See (10, 11). Results are questioned by Blackburn (18). See the symposium edited by Scrimshaw and Gordon (19), with report of experiment by Harold Skeels, pp. 353-354. See also Patton and Gardner (20), with report by Thomas, Springfield, Illinois, 1963, in which six cases are cited in which extreme maternal deprivation has been associated with retardation of physical growth and delayed skeletal maturation. However, this last may be the consequence of the accompanying malnutrition rather than maternal deprivation as such.

TABLE 1

Mean Height, Weight, and Standardized Score, by Sex, Year of Examination, and Family Size

Group[a]	Family Size (Number of Children in Family)	Number of Children in Class	Age at Measurement (Years)	Mean Height (cm.)	Mean Weight (kg.)	Mean Standardized Score
Boys 1 B	1	336	11.25	144.2 ± .37	37.01 ± .36	99.9 ± .83
	2	399	11.26	143.4 ± .34	35.23 ± .33	99.1 ± .76
	3	202	11.25	142.4 ± .46	34.13 ± .45	97.5 ± 1.02
	4	79	11.24	142.8 ± .76	34.63 ± .74	96.5 ± 1.71
	5 or more	72	11.27	140.2 ± .78	32.47 ± .78	93.1 ± 1.79
	All	1,088	11.25	143.2 ± .20	35.35 ± .20	98.5 ± .46
Girls 1 G	1	307	11.26	145.3 ± .43	38.67 ± .45	101.8 ± .82
	2	412	11.23	144.8 ± .37	37.08 ± .39	102.4 ± .71
	3	196	11.24	143.9 ± .54	36.15 ± .56	99.5 ± 1.03
	4	106	11.25	142.7 ± .74	34.62 ± .77	97.8 ± 1.40
	5 or more	60	11.23	140.4 ± .98	32.76 ± 1.02	93.9 ± 1.86
	All	1,081	11.24	144.3 ± .23	36.88 ± .24	100.8 ± .44

Junior Leaving (11+) Examination in 1959

[a]Children were divided into four main groups:
  1 B   Boys born between September 1947 and August 31, 1948;
  1 G   Girls born between September 1947 and August 31, 1948;
 11 B   Boys born between September 1948 and August 31, 1949;
 11 G   Girls born between September 1948 and August 31, 1949.

Source: Scott (18).

TABLE 2

Mean Heights[a] of Children from One-Child and Two-Child Families, by Intelligence Score

Verbal Reasoning Standardized Score	Group I				Group II			
	Boys (B)		Girls (G)		Boys (B)		Girls (G)	
	Number of Children	Mean Height	Number of Children	Mean Height	Number of Children	Mean Height	Number of Children	Mean Height
70-86	151	141.8 ± .56	97	142.7 ± .75	92	137.5 ± .68	59	134.6 ± .84
87-95	147	143.1 ± .56	142	144.1 ± .62	126	138.4 ± .58	101	136.7 ± .64
96-104	169	143.9 ± .53	162	145.3 ± .58	157	138.5 ± .52	153	138.1 ± .52
105-113	142	144.7 ± .57	179	145.7 ± .55	135	139.5 ± .56	137	138.7 ± .55
114-140	126	146.0 ± .61	139	147.1 ± .63	158	139.8 ± .52	190	139.3 ± .47
All	735	143.0 ± .25	719	145.2 ± .28	668	138.8 ± .25	640	138.0 ± .25

[a]Standardized for age by simple linear interpolation—Group IB and G 11-25 years and Group II B and G 10-25 years.

Source: Scott (18).

TABLE 3

Average Verbal Reasoning Standardized Scores by Height
and Family Size—Data of Group II G

| Height (cm.) | Number of Children in Family | | | |
| | 1 | 2 | 3 | 4 or More |
	Average Verbal Reasoning Score[a]			
Less than 130.0	96.2 (19)	101.2 (35)	97.5 (16)	94.5 (33)
30.0- 134.9	102.1 (58)	100.4 (88)	101.4 (52)	94.1 (55)
135.0- 139.9	108.4 (70)	107.0 (119)	102.4 (80)	100.7 (44)
140.0- 144.9	108.5 (54)	106.0 (104)	105.9 (37)	99.9 (44)
145 and over	108.5 (43)	107.5 (50)	106.5 (28)	102.8 (16)

[a]Figures in parentheses are numbers of children in each class.

Source: Scott (18).

Maternal Deprivation

Whereas the degree of maternal deprivation may depend to some extent on sib number, it is more likely to depend on sibling spacing and on the maternal morbidity and mortality rates. The effects of extreme maternal deprivation are drastic and impressive in the sense that they affect linguistic skills, I.Q. scores, and success in later life (19-21); the existence or absence of apathy; such physical aspects as height and weight (16, pp. 136-137); as well as the normal immunity from various diseases which is believed to be derived from breast feeding in the early nurture period (19, p. 23).

In 1943 and in subsequent years, Goldfarb (cited in 22) had an opportunity to study communities of children in institutions. Of thirty children aged 34 to 35 months, fifteen who had been brought up in institutions had I.Q.'s lower by 28 points than those of the remaining fifteen who had been in foster homes from the age of 4 months.

Spitz (22) gives the name "anaclitic depression" to the state of dazed stupor found in children deprived of maternal care. The child is apathetic, silent, and sad; he makes no attempt at contact; in many cases he suffers from insomnia; he loses weight and becomes prone to recurrent infections; there is a rapid drop in the developmental quotient. Of the ninety-five children studied by Spitz, this type of depression was observed in almost 50 percent.

Follow-up studies are of particular interest. One of the most important was carried out by Goldfarb who chose two groups of children of similar heredity. Those in the first group had been brought up in institutions until the age of 3 and then placed in the care of foster parents, whereas those in the second group had been handed over to foster parents from the outset. In all cases separation had taken place within the first 9 months of life. The lack of intellectual ability, and particularly the ability to conceptualize, were particularly marked in the group sent to an institution at an early age (22).

On the effects of the length of the intersib interval Anastasi (11) reports on a French study in which

> . . . there were 1,244 two-sibling families . . . both siblings had been tested. These were separated into "long interval" and "short interval" sibships, the latter being defined as those falling at or below the median interval. On the intelligence test, the children with long intersib intervals obtained significantly higher means, these differences persisting within each of the five occupational categories into which the sample was subdivided. With long intersib intervals the scores approximated those of only children —with short intersib intervals, they approximated the scores obtained by 3-child sibships.

Nutrition

It should be stressed that the economic consequences of different levels of nutrition, especially with respect to calories, is probably on a sounder basis than many of the other aspects we have considered. There has been a considerable amount of work on the relationship between the calorie intake and work capacity, and to some degree on the relation between calories and actual output. Unfortunately, the studies involved have not been carried out in less developed countries; therefore, some transference of results is necessary from wartime conditions in advanced countries to the less developed countries. The validity of the transference is to some degree an open question. A good deal of the work is summarized by Keller and Kraut of the Max Planck Institute of Physiology (23). It is of some interest, perhaps, that the relation between calorie change and output change per worker in Germany differed, as we might expect, for different types of work, but the degree of the change for relatively heavy work is quite striking. For example, in a group of coalminers an increase in calories by 33 percent appeared to be associated with a 40 percent increase in output. For steelworkers a 33 percent reduction in calories from an 1,800-calorie level was associated with a slightly larger percentage reduction in output. Although such numbers are at best only suggestive, they nevertheless indicate that at the lower calorie levels, say beginning with 1,800 calories per day and moving downwards, calorie reduction and output reduction may be proportional to each other. One must add, however, that even if it were known that this relationship is true for agriculture in cases where considerable disguised unemployment, or observed unemployment, exists, the reduction in physical capacity per man need not result in an actual reduction in total output. It may simply mean that more of the unemployed become absorbed in the work involved.

Economic Consequences

The economic consequences of all these effects are not entirely clear. Both the sib-number and sib-spacing effects seem to diminish physical size, linguistic skills, relative immunity from disease, and I.Q. (17, p. 130). It should be emphasized that these elements are not entirely separate from one another. Nurture effects will also affect the consequences of formal schooling in the sense that the capacity to absorb formal schooling will depend to a great degree on the nurture aspects.* Thus what appears as part of the economic returns to formal schooling is in fact a return to nurture, since it is the nurture elements that determine the capacity to take advantage of formal schooling. The main element to be noted is that a greater rate of population growth will set in motion demographic causative effects all of which have an adverse impact on economic growth.

The argument presented is that higher rates of population growth (compared to lower rates) are associated with (a) a younger population and hence a higher dependency ratio, (b) usually a higher average sib number, (c) usually closer sib spacing, and *probably* (d) a greater number of pregnancies per woman and *perhaps* higher maternal mortality and morbidity. (This last depends upon the degree to which the higher rate of population growth is a result of lower mortality rather than higher fertility.) The impacts of these four demographic effects on dependency, malnutrition, degree of maternal deprivation, speech and personality formation, I.Q., and on success indicators are all adverse to economic growth and the average *acquired* economic quality of the labor force.

For the most part the data are only suggestive, providing clues to the importance of the elements considered. Unfortunately, there is a lack of statistical information as to how important these elements are from a macroeconomic viewpoint. We do not know what rates of population growth at what level of per capita income will lead to what degree of malnutrition or

*Tanner (16, p. 211) states that Douglas in 1960 reported from a sample of children in Great Britain that "early maturers had gained significantly more successes than late maturers in the examination for entry to secondary schools at age 11. Not only were their test papers better; the reports of the teachers upon their behavior in class also favored them." However, the later maturers catch up when they reach their physical growth spurt.

other detrimental nurture effects or how widespread these effects are on the population.* It may very well be that, despite the dramatic nature of some of the clinical cases, the percent of the population affected in this way may be small. In what follows it will be assumed that the three effects already considered have, in fact, a small impact; for the most part the implications of the replacement effect will be traced.

THE REPLACEMENT EFFECT

The rate at which a population transmits acquired characteristics to subsequent generations will depend in part on the growth rate of the population and its age structure. This is readily seen if we assume that all quality improvements take place among the lower age groups and not the higher ones. For example, nurture and schooling improvements are, for the most part, likely to enter the system during early ages. To the extent that entrants into the work force are of higher quality (i.e., higher education and acquired skills, etc.) than those that leave through retirement or death, the average quality of the labor force improves more rapidly if the rate of population growth is higher (other things equal) rather than lower.

*There is some evidence on the effects of starvation that can lead to interesting calculations. For example, Keys (24) determines experimentally the reduction in physical capacities as a consequence of "semistarvation," e.g., a shift from 3,000-plus calories to about 1,600 calories leads in 12 weeks to a decrease in strenuous physical work capacity to 52 percent of the nonstarved group, and, at the end of 24 weeks, to a decrease equal to only 28 percent of the nonstarved group. Of course the initial level based on the diet of well-off American students is unusually high. Perhaps the work capacity is not much lower for a standard below the U.N. Food and Agriculture Organization (FAO) norm but above Colin Clark's (25) calculated norm for west Asia. If so, then we might readily visualize an agricultural family producing grain that would yield 9,600 calories per family per day. Calculating children as two thirds of adults, this would lead a three-child family to have approximately 2,400 calories per adult-equivalent whereas something close to a six-child family would reduce the intake to the semistarvation level of about 1,600 calories. At this level we might apply Keys' results with qualifications. In the Carnegie experiment mentioned by Keys, men's physical capacities were reduced trivially when on a 2,000 calorie low-weight-maintenance diet. See Brown (26) for actual nutritional reference diets, pp. 36, 142-143. See also Clark (25, pp. 123-129). If we raise Clark's figures by some 25 percent for the greater weight and height of Americans to tally with Keys' data, we obtain a norm of about 2,300 calories.

It seems probable that the greatest effects of "semistarvation" are the psychological ones. In Keys' experiments, *apathy* was a major consequence of semistarvation. It was highly correlated with such psychological elements as lack of ambition, decrease in self-discipline, decrease in mental alertness, and a decrease in concentration. On a self-rating scale the increase in apathy and the related psychological characteristics was roughly calibrated at about 1.75 on a range between no apathy (0) and extremely more apathy (5). This was approximately half of the amount of the sense of tiredness reported. Of course, it is very difficult to determine the economic significance of these results, but they are suggestive of the possible relationship between poor diet and the type of resultant characteristics that inhibit economic change.

Among the important factors affecting economic growth are, first, the work skills of the population and, second, the attitudes of the population. The attitudes of the work force are shaped by religious, social, cultural, and political traditions which for the most part are transmitted by the process of nurture, informal education as well as formal training. Among the basic attitudes that affect growth are those that determine degree of adherence to traditional occupations and procedures (9, pp. 108-109). Such attitudinal changes will usually influence the degree of labor mobility, the extent of participation by women in the work force (27), and the age at which people normally enter the work force. In addition, they will affect the willingness of people within a given occupation to accept new techniques, equipment, or new organizational forms. In view of these considerations we visualize an economic quality replacement effect in the sense that those who enter the economically active population have a higher productive capacity than those who leave, and hence they increase the average quality of the labor force.

The extent of quality improvement depends, in part, on the rate of population growth. To see the nature of the possibilities involved, consider some examples based on the following assumptions:

1. Education of a formal or informal nature takes place prior to entry into the labor force.

2. Education expenditures are assumed to be consumption expenditures by the parents of those being educated.

3. There are constant economic returns to education with respect to numbers of people educated.

4. The years of education per person are an independent variable.

5. The mean annual income of those with more education is greater on the average than those with less.*

Figure 2 illustrates what can happen to income per worker under sets of alternative assumptions that emphasize the differences between stationary versus growing populations. In cases I and II we have stationary populations in which 2 percent enter the work force each year and 2 percent leave. Those who enter are assumed to have twice as many years of education and three times the associated income levels as those who leave. In the third case 2 percent exit the work force every year and 5 percent enter every year. Note, for example, that at the end of 25 years the per worker income of the stationary population is $150 (assuming an initial income in year zero of $100) compared to $176 for the case in which the population increases 3

---

*See Appendix Table A for some sample ratios for a number of developing countries. The assumptions are admittedly extreme since they assume that the entire income differential is a consequence of education. However, the nature of the assumption does not invalidate the main point which is to examine the consequences of the entrants to the work force having different productive capacities than those who leave.

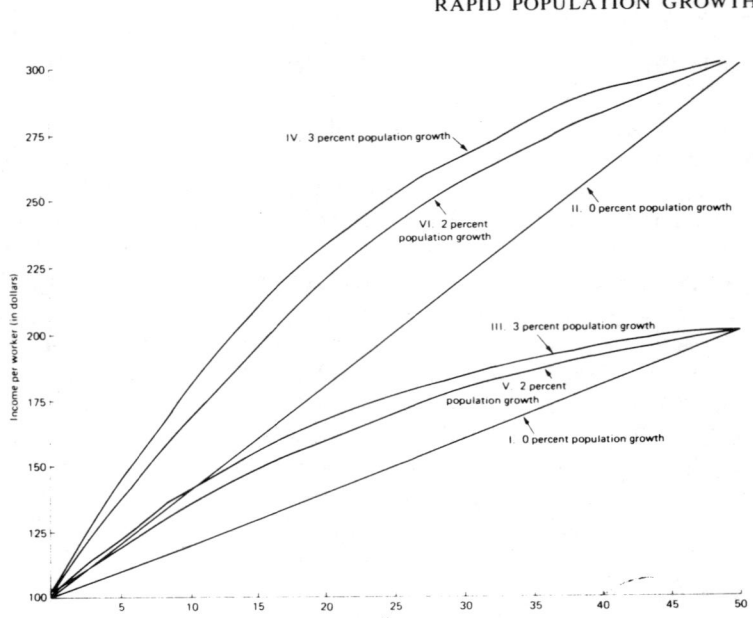

Figure 2. Income per worker at 0, 2, and 3 percent population growth over 50 years.

percent per year. The income per worker is approximately 16 percent higher for the rapidly growing population at the end of 25 years. If we assume a three to one ratio in income of those entering as against those leaving (case IV), the per worker income is 25 percent higher at the end of 25 years. However, at the end of 50 years, when full replacement takes place under all assumptions, the per capita income is the same for all rates of population growth. This, however, omits the likelihood that during this 50-year period further increases take place in the education of those who enter compared to earlier entrants and hence the replacement effect continues to operate until the point is reached where the productivity of those who enter ceases to be higher than the productivity of those who leave.* Also, the illustration omits the effects of higher savings and investment out of the higher income per worker on income growth.

Of course the results depend on the assumption. But we can weaken some of our assumptions without altering the general point made. For example, assume that beyond some point there are diminishing returns to education at

*A model in which there was a gradual shift from 10 percent of the entrants receiving 6 years of education to 100 percent over a period of 10 years gave approximately similar results for the twentieth year. In other words, the 3 percent growth population earned more than 25 percent more income per worker than the stationary population in year 20.

a given level. In that case the replacement effect is somewhat less efficient, but up to a point it still operates in the same direction. The general case is illustrated in Figure 3 in which the X axis represents "general-capital," i.e., physical capital plus human capital. We assume that human capital is the more important component and the major productive element in general-capital. The rays from the origin represent constant ratios of labor and general-capital and they result in a constant income level per worker. If L_0 is the

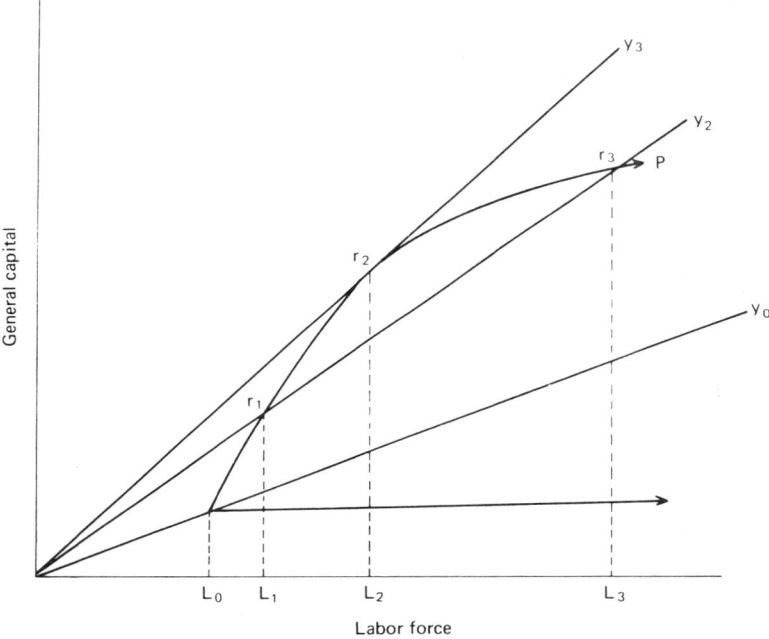

Figure 3. Growth of labor force and general capital.

initial amount of labor and Y_0 is the initial income per worker, then the horizontal arrow shows the consequences of labor force growth under the classical assumptions and constant returns to scale. If education *per person* is an independent variable and a greater number of people implies a higher level of education per worker on the average, then the path of labor force growth is shown by the curved line marked *P*. The tangent of this path with one of the income rays yields the optimum growth of the labor force for the period. It can readily be seen that if actual labor force growth falls short of the optimum labor growth, then the analysis implies the desirability of an increase in the rate of population growth. The figure illustrates the possibility that the lower rate of population growth of r_1 leads to a lower income per worker than the greater rate of population growth r_2.

Expenditures on education in most cases will probably not increase in direct proportion to the number of young people in the population.* Taxing capacity will depend somewhat on real income per person. There are many alternative claims on public revenues. These conflicting claims will vary with the rate and pattern of population growth. In a largely agricultural population, the greater the rate of population growth, the less land per man; the greater the degree of fragmentation of holdings, and usually the smaller the output per man. Also, high growth rates will normally increase the burden of dependency (9, pp. 332-333) and decrease *potential* taxable revenues. Population growth may raise population replacements to a higher production capacity per person, other things equal, *but* it may simultaneously make it more difficult to provide a given amount of education for the same proportion of children entering the population (9, pp. 247-249).

Intuitively we should expect that as population grows, *beyond some rate*, that education per person declines. Under this assumption we have two opposing forces at work. On the one hand, a greater rate of population growth yields a greater replacement effect, but on the other hand, a greater rate of population growth reduces education per person. In principle, the balance of forces can still be in favor of the replacement effect. Thus in Figure 3 the intermediate rate of population growth r_2 yields the highest income per worker.[†]

Educational Inputs

Educational inputs are unlike traditional inputs. Although we know in a general way that education pays off from a productivity viewpoint, we do not know much about the marginal productivity of education. Calculations of the returns to education have been of the *average* returns to marginal years of education. What we do not know very much about are the *marginal* returns to marginal years of education. The author's view is that it is not at all impossible that the marginal returns for some marginal years of education may be zero when a given type of education expands very rapidly.[‡] Education is also complicated by the fact that its inputs are diverse, its quality is rarely constant, and many of its influences on productivity are indirect. This may be one of the reasons why very general types of education, which frequently

---

*See (28) and Gavin Jones, "Effect of Population Change on the Attainment of Educational Goals in the Developing Countries," in this volume.

[†]r_1, r_2, and r_3 are rates of population growth associated with the alternate amounts of labor force increase L_0L_1, or L_0L_2, or L_0L_3.

[‡]An unpublished study by the author on returns to education in Greece leads him to believe that this may have occurred with respect to secondary education for the period 1960-64.

appear to be unrelated to given vocations, seem frequently to yield relatively high rates of return. We cannot readi'y assume that we can inject educational inputs and harvest productivity outputs at the other end of the pipeline.*

Similar to education and information, but much more elusive, are the inputs responsible for technological change—especially entrepreneurial capacities. The innovation rate will depend on the perception and the ability to take advantage of economic opportunities, and hence on entrepreneurial capacities. Returning to some assumptions discussed earlier, we might recall that not all inputs necessary for production are marketed and that some are not available to all individuals. Hence, only some people are entrepreneurs. They are likely to be the ones who are able to fill the gaps in necessary inputs or capable of creating substitutes for unavailable inputs, and, in general, are able to perform as "input completers."[†] Once again entrepreneurship is an elusive input and not easily augmented in the sense in which traditional inputs are augmentable.

The main point of the previous remarks is that, although with the traditional inputs we were able to rely on a production function which is a one-to-one correspondence, in the sense that if we add something tangible to our stock of inputs, we can visualize obtaining at the other end a tangible output. Once we deal with the nontraditional inputs, we can no longer have confidence in such simple input-output relationships.

CONJECTURES AND CONCLUSIONS

In a broad sense human investment—the activities that create the essential changes in the acquired economically valuable qualities of the work force—must be the critical element which determines whether or not population growth in any particular case has adverse economic consequences. Even the process of capital accumulation is not a mechanical one. Obviously entrepreneurial qualities (which are for the most part acquired qualities) are essential elements in the process. Economic growth requires more than the accumulation of capital goods of the type already in use. New types of productive instruments have to be created; new occupations learned, induced, generated, and filled in new contexts and locations; new types of risks have to be assumed; and, to some degree, new social and economic relationships have to be forged. Hence, the characteristics of the population that are transmitted from generation to generation through nurture and education become the vital factors that determine the rate of growth. But the transmission of such characteristics does not result in a replica of the previous generation's occupational skills, and attitudinal characteristics. The transmission process creates the potential for change.

*For a summary of existing knowledge in this area see Bowles (29).

[†] For a fuller treatment of these matters see the author's (30).

In most instances, economies do not operate at their productive and technical upper bound. Developing countries do not have to invent new techniques. They can borrow techniques and types of capital that already exist. (Of course, in detail, some research and experimentation is frequently necessary to adapt broadly known techniques to specific local conditions.) In view of these considerations, the finding that traditional inputs account for only a small proportion of the growth that takes place is hardly surprising. The old Malthusian argument that additions to the population come into the world with additional hands but without the additional capital or land necessary to produce at the same level as their forebears is not entirely true. The nurture and educational system can create to some degree the additional capital necessary. Whether this "human capital" is adequate or not depends upon the rate of transmission of known and new skills, and the simultaneous introduction of other types of capital into the population. (The word *skill* is used in its broadest possible sense in this context.) The rate of growth of physical capital may be to some extent a function of the growth rate of human capital. The basic argument is neither pro- nor anti-Malthusian. Rather it suggests that the traditional approach misses to a considerable degree the fundamental processes which determine whether or not given rates of population growth are adverse to economic growth.

The point emphasized in this paper is that the research of the last 15 years shows that whereas the output that results from traditional inputs may not be entirely trivial, it is nevertheless not nearly as important as the contribution to output that results from nontraditional inputs. Many of the nontraditional inputs have an elusive quality about them. They cannot be handled from an analytical viewpoint as easily as the traditional ones. The basic conjecture of this paper is that the assumption of a one-to-one correspondence between inputs and outputs is no longer tenable once one gives primary importance to nontraditional inputs. What is new is the rather persuasive evidence that the nontraditional inputs are usually more significant than the traditional ones, and hence the relations between population growth and nontraditional inputs should in most cases become central to the analysis of the "population-resources" problem.

For the most part, this paper is only suggestive. The overall results are inconclusive since we really do not know very much about the economic magnitudes of the demographic factors that are detrimental to economic growth, as against those that are helpful. This lack is especially true of the effects other than the replacement effect. The replacement-effect type of argument is of interest since it suggests that even in developing countries, there may be situations and periods for which relatively high rates of population growth *may* involve some demographic effects that are helpful to economic growth. Whether the beneficial effects are ever the predominant ones is hard to say, but it is a possibility that cannot be entirely ignored. In examining the replacement effect, we do not imply that a 0 percent population growth should attempt to increase its rate of growth to reach the 3 percent level.* Our conclusion is that, other things equal, a population growing at 3 percent will have a temporary advantage over a population growing at 0 percent, in terms of a positive replacement effect, but this advantage cannot be achieved by a gradual increase in the rate of growth of a slower or non-growing population. It simply implies that the more rapidly growing population has a positive aspect which counteracts the negative aspects of rapid growth, and that this aspect is less significant in the slow-growing population.

Whether or not the replacement effect is of interest depends on the acceptability of the assumptions, especially with respect to the assumptions: (a) that the costs of education are consumption costs rather than investment costs, and (b) that the level of education per person provided for later entrants (rather than earlier entrants) is unaffected (or less than proportionately reduced) by positive rates of population growth. We do not have the space here to consider all the possibilities.

Two important qualifications must be made in considering the replacement effect. First, the replacement effect may be negative as well as positive. In other words, if the demographic effects considered in the previous sections are in some sense transmitted from one generation to the next, then a more rapid rate of replacement may lower the acquired economic qualities of such a population. Second, it must, of course, be remembered that even the positive replacement effect must be considered as only one element among many others—most of which probably inhibit economic growth. The positive replacement effect is delineated primarily in the interest of achieving a balanced approach to the question of assessing the consequences of population growth.

*Jones and Gingrich have developed a model in which practically no advantage is gained on the basis of the replacement effect by a population increasing its rate of growth gradually. See (31).

APPENDIX

TABLE A

Schooling and Earnings

Country	Age	Years of Education		Ratio Col. (4)/ Col. (3)	Years of Education 11	Ratio Col. (6)/ Col. (4)
		0-1	5-6			
(1)	(2)	(3)	(4)	(5)	(6)	(7)
Mexico	32	$560	$1154	2.06	$2080	1.45
Colombia	32	$397	$1430	3.60	$2601	1.81
Chile	n.a.	n.a.	$101.4	n.a.	$194.0	1.81
India	32	850 Rupees	1500 Rupees (7 years)	1.76	2565 Rupees	1.71
Venezuela	23-65	3750 Bolivars	7500 Bolivars	2.00	18,000	2.4

n.a. = not available

Sources: Mexico and Colombia (32), Chile and India (33), and Venezuela (34).

REFERENCES

1. Kuznets, Simon, *Modern Economic Growth.* New Haven: Yale Univ. Press, 1966. pp. 80-81.
2. Aukrust, O., "Investment and Economic Growth," *Productivity Measurement Rev*, February 1959. pp. 35-53.
3. Niitamo, O., "Development of Producitivity in Finnish Industry, 1925-1952," *Productivity Measurement Rev*, November 1958. pp. 30-41.
4. Krueger, Anne O., "Factor Endowments and *Per Capita* Income Differences among Countries," *Econ J*, September 1968. pp. 641-659.
5. Leibenstein, Harvey, "Incremental Capital Output Ratios in the Short Run,"*Rev Econ Stat*, February 1966. pp. 20-27.
6. Patel, S. J., "A Note on the Incremental Capital-Output Ratio and Rates of Economic Growth in the Developing Countries," *Kyklos*, 1968, Fasc. I. pp. 147-150.
7. Morgan, Theodore, "Investment Versus Economic Growth," *Econ Devel & Cult Change*, April 1969. pp. 392-414.
8. Leibenstein, Harvey, "Allocative Efficiency vs. X-Efficiency," *Amer Econ Rev*, June 1966. pp. 392-415.
9. Coale, Ansley, and E. M. Hoover, *Population Growth and Economic Development in Low Income Countries, a Case Study of India's Prospects.* Princeton: Princeton Univ. Press, 1958.

10. Altus, William D., "Birth Order and Its Sequelae," *Science*, January 7, 1966. pp. 44-49.

11. Anastasi, Anne, "Intelligence and Family Size," *Psychol Bul*, May 1956. pp. 187-209.

12. McCarthy, Dorothea A., "Language Development in Children," *Manual of Child Psychology*, L. Carmichael, ed. New York: John Wiley & Sons, 1946. pp. 558-559.

13. Haggard, E. A., "Social Status and Intelligence," *Genetic Psychol Monographs*, Vol. 49, 1954. pp. 141-186.

14. Jones, H., "The Environment and Mental Development," *Manual of Child Psychology*. L. Carmichael, ed. New York: John Wiley & Sons, 1946. p. 655.

15. Smith, S., "Language and Non-Verbal Test Performance of Racial Groups in Honolulu before and after a Fourteen-Year Interval," *J Genetic Psychol*, Vol. 26. pp. 51-93.

16. Tanner, J. M., *Growth at Adolescence*. Oxford: Blackwell's 2nd ed., 1962.

17. Tanner, J. M., "Galtonian Eugenics and the Study of Growth," *Eugen Rev*, September 1966. pp. 127-128.

18. Scott, J. A., "Intelligence, Physique, and Family Size." *Brit J Prev Soc Med*, October 1962. pp. 165-173.

19. Blackburn, Julian, "Family Size, Intelligence Score, and Social Class," *Population Studies*, June 1947. pp. 165-176.

20. Scrimshaw, Nevin S., and John E. Gordon, eds., *Malnutrition, Learning and Behavior*. Cambridge: M.I.T. Press, 1968. pp. 353-354.

21. Patton, Robert Gray, and Lytt I. Gardner, *Growth Failure in Maternal Deprivation*. St. Louis: C. C. Thomas, 1963.

22. Lebovici, S., "The Concept of Maternal Deprivation: a Review of Research," *Deprivation of Maternal Care; a Reassessment of Its Effects*. World Health Organization Public Health Papers, Vol. 14. Geneva, 1962. pp. 75-95.

23. Keller, W. B., and H. A. Kraut, "Work and Nutrition," *World Review of Nutrition and Dietetics*, G. H. Bourne, ed. New York: Hafner Pub. Co., 1962. Vol. III.

24. Keys, Ancel, *Biology of Human Starvation*. Minneapolis: Univ. Minnesota Press, 1950.

25. Clark, Colin, *Population Growth and Land Use*. London: Macmillan, 1967. pp. 123-129.

26. Brown, Lester R., *Man, Land and Food*. Washington, D.C.: U.S. Dept. of Agriculture, Economic Research Service, Regional Analysis Division, 1963. pp. 36, 142-143.

27. International Labor Organization, "The World's Working Population, Some Demographic Aspects," p. 173.

28. Harbison, Frederick H., and Charles A. Myers, *Education, Manpower, and Economic Growth, Strategies of Human Resource-Development*. New York: McGraw-Hill, 1964. p. 19.

29. Bowles, Samuel, *Planning Educational Systems for Economic Growth.* Cambridge, Mass.: Harvard Univ. Press, 1969. Chs. 1-3.

30. Leibenstein, Harvey, "Entrepreneurship and Development," *Amer Econ Rev*, May 1968. pp. 72-83.

31. Jones, Gavin, and Paul Gingrich, "The Effects of Differing Trends in Fertility and of Educational Advance on the Growth, Quality and Turnover of the Labor Force," *Demography*, Vol. 5, 1968. pp. 226-248.

32. Carnoy, Martin, "Aspects of Labor Force Mobility in Latin America," *J Human Res*, Fall 1967. pp. 528-9.

33. Selowsky, Marcelo, "Education and Economic Growth: Some International Comparisons," *Economic Development Report No. 83.* CIA, Cambridge, Mass.: Harvard Univ. p. 49, Table 14, p. 60, Table 19.

34. Shoup, Carl S., *A Report. Fiscal System of Venezuela.* Baltimore: Johns Hopkins Press, 1959. p. 407.

[5]

Chapter 10

POPULATION GROWTH AND THE TAKE-OFF HYPOTHESIS

BY

HARVEY LEIBENSTEIN
University of California

I. INTRODUCTION

LIKE Pirandello's 'Six Characters in Search of an Author' Professor Rostow has given us an interesting historical hypothesis in search of a theory.[1] While this quip exaggerates the case, since the *Economic Journal* (1956) articles do have many statements about economic behaviour, nevertheless, I believe it is correct if we interpret 'theory' in a narrow sense. The central hypothesis, and this is all that I shall be concerned with in this paper, is that at some point in a country's development events may occur that will considerably speed up its rate of growth, and that when this persists for two or three decades[2] the country then enters a stage of self-sustained growth. This hypothesis is worth considering on many grounds, not the least of which is that Rostow has succeeded in clothing it in a language that gives his hypothesis great suggestive and evocative power.

Some writers have been tempted to use the analogy of an aeroplane for the take-off. If I were the inhabitant of an island whose last contacts with civilization were as it was a century ago, and if a ship-wrecked sailor suddenly appeared and told me about heavier-than-air machines that flew, and if he explained that for flight to take place the flying entity had to have wings of a certain shape (the pre-conditions), and that it had to be travelling at a certain speed before it left the ground, then I would indeed find this an

---

[1] By a theory I have in mind a clearly stated set of equations, or their verbal counterpart, *including behaviour relations*, that would lead to a definite set of conclusions consistent with at least some observations.

[2] All of my references to the Take-off Hypothesis are based on the March 1956 article in the *Economic Journal*. Whether or not the 'two or three decades' part of the hypothesis is correct is a matter for historians to debate. I take it that this part of the hypothesis was meant to be interpreted elastically. I shall so interpret it here.

170

Leibenstein — *Population Growth and the Take-off Hypothesis*

interesting relationship, one which would lead me to think about aeroplanes and how they function. Nevertheless, it would not be a 'theory' of aerodynamics. In short, it would be an hypothesis based on observation that would inspire me to look for the theory, but it would not of itself suggest the theory. I go out of my way to develop this point because I am sympathetic with Rostow's central hypothesis.[1] But, if the hypothesis is true there is still a great deal to be done; namely to develop the theory with which this inductive hypothesis is in conformity. In other words, one of the deductions from such a theory should be the historical hypothesis that Rostow has given us.

My job in this paper is to consider the population element in connexion with economic development in general and the 'take-off' hypothesis in particular. In the absence of a theory it is difficult to analyse whether what we know about the population element fits the hypothesis. I could probably invent models in which it would fit the hypothesis and others in which it would not. Yet, on the whole, I think that the population element is really important for a theory of development consistent with a take-off type hypothesis, and I trust that the following remarks will suggest that this is the case.

The discussion that follows will be suggestive rather than rigorous, since in the space allotted it is clearly impossible to consider in detail a large number of alternative theories and to examine the population element in each of them. Since the population variable is only one of many in any theory of development we shall have to allude from time to time to some of the other variables in the system, but this will be done rather sketchily for the reason just given.

Many authors on development seem to treat population growth as an exogenous and autonomously determined variable that represents a hurdle to *per capita* income growth. In the discussion that follows I will argue that viewing population growth entirely as an autonomous variable is not a view that is likely to be consistent with the take-off hypothesis. On the other hand, population is not an entirely endogenously induced phenomenon. I shall argue that both elements (autonomous and endogenously induced population growth) are involved simultaneously, that they are to a great extent inversely related to each other, and that this view of the matter is most likely to be consistent with a take-off type hypothesis.

---

[1] I am, in a sense, committed to being sympathetic since the type of theories that I have attempted to develop in the past have been in conformity with what I interpret to be Rostow's central *non-gradualist* position. Cf. my *Economic Backwardness and Economic Growth*, John Wiley and Sons, New York, 1957.

The Economics of Take-off into Sustained Growth

II. THE TAKE-OFF HYPOTHESIS IN A CONSTANT POPULATION ECONOMY

Would the take-off hypothesis hold in an economy in which the size of the population remained constant irrespective of other social and economic changes that took place? This is, of course, an artificial situation since the same forces that promote economic growth are also likely to induce demographic changes. Nevertheless, it is desirable to consider this question as a first step in determining the rôle that population plays in a process of economic growth for which the central hypothesis is true. The hypothesis is presumably a denial of gradualism — a denial of the possibility that an economy can grow in a sustained fashion without several decades of accelerated growth. Is this likely in the absence of population growth?

The empirical evidence seems to suggest that almost all countries, including the most backward, do have a positive rate of net investment, at least on the average over periods such as decades.[1] Those who are prone to make inductive generalizations on this score suggest that on the average this might be at least 5 per cent. This implies that with a capital-output ratio of 3 or 4 to 1 such economies could grow at rates in excess of 1 per cent. Superficial deductions from this suggest that in the absence of population growth, all backward economies would have positive rates of *per capita* income growth. Indeed, one might argue that these rates would be higher than we have just stated because in the absence of population growth the burden of dependency would probably be lower. The level of consumption might therefore be less, and as a consequence, the rate of investment would be higher.

On the other hand, we must consider the possibility that the causal nexus could work the other way round. It may be that it is the fact of population growth that induces the rate of investment necessary to maintain that level of population growth and not vice versa. That is, in the absence of population growth a positive rate of net investment would not show up. One could invent arguments that would suggest that this might be the case. For example: Entrepreneurs invest in anticipation of demand. Population growth signifies an expansion of demand. The ones who invest and save are, in a backward economy, likely to be the same people. The reason they save is because they invest simultaneously, and if that investment did not take place the difference would

[1] Cf. the evidence summarized in Simon Kuznets' *Economic Growth*.

Leibenstein — Population Growth and the Take-off Hypothesis

simply be spent on consumer goods. The vast majority in a backward economy does not save anything at all, and investment is carried on by entrepreneurs who are forced to save as a consequence of their desire to invest. Thus, the argument might run, an economy that behaves in this fashion would not grow in the absence of population growth.

While it is possible to develop a model in which the economy would not grow with zero population growth, it seems hardly likely to me that this would be a realistically plausible model. In other words, it is hard to believe that *gradual* development would not take place in an economy with a constant population. To begin with, population growth is not the only factor that stimulates investment, and as a consequence, the absence of population growth would still leave other forces that could act as stimulants. From time to time one would expect that cost-reducing innovations would stimulate investment. In addition, with an unequal distribution in income there would surely be some people whose incomes were sufficiently large, and their sacrifice in current consumption sufficiently small, that they would have an inducement to invest. Of course, others would disinvest simultaneously, but this influence is likely to be less without population growth than with it. At the same time, other possessors of capital would want to maintain their existing standard of living and output and hence would replace their capital when it wore out. Gradual improvements in organization and discoveries of various sorts that are the outcome of experience would also add to the productive capacity of the population. In addition, occasional windfall gains, such as an especially good harvest, might leave people with a temporary surplus for still further investment. All in all, I suspect that the *likelihood*[1] is that in the absence of population growth, economies would experience gradually rising *per capita* incomes, and in several centuries such gradually rising *per capita* incomes would lead to reasonably high levels of *per capita* income.

In fact, this last has not generally occurred in the backward economies of the world. What has happened often seems to have been expansion of the economy without growth in *per capita* income. We might deduce from the previous discussion that this expansion was not stimulated entirely (if at all) by population growth. On the contrary, the historical evidence would seem to suggest the exact opposite type of economic causation. In other words, it was the rate of population growth, whether or not induced by economic

[1] There is no necessity about this argument. It is based on what appears to me as reasonable likelihood.

The Economics of Take-off into Sustained Growth

expansion, that ate up the fruits of expansion and resulted in expansion in the aggregate sense without much improvement per head.

If this last argument is correct, then a take-off type theory would not hold for a constant population economy. In other words, it seems likely that in such an economy there would be innumerable patterns of growth, some more gradual than others, that are both conceivable and likely. There would seem to be no special reason on these grounds to have a rapid period of *per capita* income growth before an economy could take off into self-sustained growth.

It is of interest that the previous discussion was mostly about the investment function and not the population growth function. This is the area in which one of the main difficulties of discussing the take-off really lies. Since the take-off hypothesis does not specify an investment function it is very difficult to argue whether or not population growth is crucial to the theory. For it is mostly in relation to an investment function that the importance of population growth to economic growth can become evident. We have suggested some *ad hoc* reasons why investment might take place at low rates of growth with a constant population. If we look at some of the existing growth models other reasons become evident. For example, a growth model of the Joan Robinson type,[1] in which investments depend on the magnitude of the profits, would yield a similar result. There is nothing about the model that determines a specific division between wages and profits, and for some divisions gradual growth rates would be possible. In other words, there is no reason to believe that a constant population economy implies a stationary state.

Similarly, investment models that depend on the accelerator do not necessarily imply the take-off thesis if the population is stationary. There is no special reason why the accelerator should work if the rate of growth is relatively large and not when it is rather small. Once again, there is nothing about the accelerator theory *per se* that implies the impossibility of very gradual growth.

III. AUTONOMOUS POPULATION GROWTH AND THE TAKE-OFF

A nice feature of population growth for a take-off type hypothesis is that it creates an obvious reason — though not the only reason by any means — why low rates of investment do not work. Low rates of investment imply low rates of aggregate income growth,

---

[1] Joan Robinson, *The Accumulation of Capital*, Macmillan, 1956, Book II.

Leibenstein — Population Growth and the Take-off Hypothesis

and the low rate of aggregate income growth may not be sufficient to overcome the rate of population growth. Hence, the familiar phenomenon of expansion of the economy and expansion of the work force without at the same time any increase in *per capita* income. If, for a moment, we assume a given level of population growth — say 2 per cent — then the rate of investment has to be sufficiently high so that aggregate income expands at more than 2 per cent.[1] It is quite possible that unless an economy gets used to such higher rates of investment for quite a period of time it will not learn to sustain such a high rate and will not permanently be able to exceed this rate. Only if it has a sustained experience of *per capita* income growth will it be able to sustain through its own operations a higher growth rate than the rate of population. Whatever one might think of this view of the matter, it surely must seem clear that with the population element thrown in it would be easier to develop a theory of growth consistent with a Take-off hypothesis than it would be without the population element.

But how should we treat the population element? Consider first the population variable as a completely exogenous element. There is the commonly held view that the rate of population growth is determined by factors that have little if anything to do with changes in economic variables. Mortality rates are presumed to be determined by advances in sanitation, public health, and medicine, and fertility rates are determined by sociological and cultural conditions unconnected with the level of income. This view of the matter must also imply that the rates of population growth that we observe in backward economies have increased over time. On purely statistical grounds this would appear to be the case since the current population of the world would be inconceivably large if it had been growing at $1\frac{1}{2}$ to 2 per cent say, for the last two thousand years.

But suppose for a moment that the autonomous population growth rate is constant, say, at $1\frac{1}{2}$ per cent per year. This would imply that economies must maintain a growth rate in aggregate income of $1\frac{1}{2}$ per cent, or failing to do so, to suffer steadily diminishing levels of *per capita* income. We might expect that some economies with favourable resource endowments should be able to exceed that level of growth. Others would hit this level of growth, while still others would fall behind. The histories of such countries would, therefore, fall into three categories: (1) Some countries would enjoy increasing levels of *per capita* income, some at quite gradual

---

[1] As far as I could tell, Professor Rostow seems to see population as an *autonomous* factor that is an obstacle to *per capita* income growth. (*Economic Journal*, 1956.)

The Economics of Take-off into Sustained Growth

rates, (2) others would just maintain a constant level of *per capita* income, and (3) for still others their *per capita* income level would be getting perpetually worse. But it seems that the third and first groups do not quite fit the facts to the extent that we know them. Relatively few countries have had steadily worsening *per capita* incomes starting at low level, and few countries have experienced *very* gradual growth. In other words, if the rate of population growth is nothing more than an obstacle to *per capita* income growth then it is difficult to understand why there should not have been quite a few countries that have experienced *sustained per capita* income depression. The obstacle theory of population growth is not completely helpful to a take-off hypothesis. If an obstacle exists then it is simply necessary to overcome the obstacle by a little bit and we are over it. It is not necessary for the rates of investment to soar considerably above the obstacle before it can take-off into sustained growth.

Also, and most important, the obstacle theory is not consistent with the common phenomenon experienced in backward economies, that of economic expansion in the aggregate sense without *per capita* income growth. This last statement simplifies the facts somewhat, but it is really not too far from the truth. Of course, even in backward countries *per capita* incomes have fluctuated considerably, and in many cases the secular trend may have been a slowly rising one. But these fluctuations in trend magnitudes are surely exceedingly small compared to the *differences* in *per capita* income that exist between advanced and backward countries and the differences in the rates of growth in *per capita* income that must exist between the advanced and backward countries.

In other words, if a non-gradualist take-off hypothesis is correct, then we might as a first approximation consider the *per capita* incomes of the non-take-off countries to be approximately constant (as a secular trend). But, if this is the case, then it is surprising that so many backward countries should have investment rates that just enable them, in the long run, to maintain their level of *per capita* income. But it is surprising only if we insist on maintaining the hypothesis that population growth is entirely an exogenously determined obstacle to development.

Furthermore, if countries that are still backward are able to sustain a rate of income growth equal to the rate of population growth, then we might expect that in an earlier period they should have been able to sustain a rate of income growth greater than the rate of population growth since the autonomous rate of population growth was lower in earlier periods. But, if that were the case,

Leibenstein — Population Growth and the Take-off Hypothesis

then the history of such countries should have been that of growing *per capita* income up to some point after which the growth should have stopped and a reversal of the trend should have set in. In fact, the evidence does not seem to suggest that this has generally been the case. It is certainly not clear that *per capita* incomes in the low income countries of the world are for the most part lower today than they were in the pre-war period.

The conclusion we come to on the basis of these speculations is that both on theoretical grounds and on historical grounds it would seem difficult to maintain simultaneously the complete exogenous population growth hypothesis and a non-gradualist take-off hypothesis.

IV. INDUCED POPULATION GROWTH

Prior to the post-war advances in public health it seemed clear to demographers that the level of consumption was a significant determinant of the rate of population growth. The argument went roughly as follows: In low income, tradition-bound countries fertility rates were normally very high. The culture of these countries had to be such as to emphasize the virtue of fertility. Great prestige is commonly attached to child bearing. Societies that did not develop such cultural patterns were doomed to disappear in view of the high mortality rates. Hence, societies that did survive must have had built in within them a social and cultural structure that enabled them to sustain very high fertility rates. This implies cultural patterns in which there is no resistance to factors that reduce mortality rates but in which there is considerable resistance towards those elements that reduce fertility rates. As a consequence, the initial impact of rising consumption levels was on the reduction of mortality while the fertility rate within marriage remained roughly constant.

The possible connexion between rising consumption levels and falling mortality rates is easy to see. Rising consumption levels, almost by definition, imply improvements in food consumption, in shelter, in sanitation, in medical care, and so on. Clearly, on this ground we would expect an improvement in mortality rates — especially in those instances where the initial mortality rates were exceedingly high. This, in part, explains the fact that the greatest fall in mortality rates is usually at first in the lowest age group. But not all consumption is private consumption. A considerable amount of sanitation, public health facilities, and medical care facilities are governmental matters. And with rising *per capita* incomes it is

The Economics of Take-off into Sustained Growth

surely easier for governments to provide more of these facilities than when incomes are stationary or falling.

In addition to the mortality effect it is conceivable that to a limited extent increases in *per capita* income in low income countries may induce an increase in the fertility rate. This may happen indirectly by improving the health of mothers and potential mothers so that the number of live births increases for the same number of conceptions. Second, there is probably an indirect effect in that high incomes result in a reduction in the average age of marriage. This, of course, does not exhaust the possibilities. But on the whole it would appear that while rising fertility rates are possible their magnitude and effect on population growth is likely to be smaller than the long run impact of falling mortality rates on population growth.

The impact of population growth on economic variables is at least two-fold. First, there are the classical diminishing returns. Some resources in backward economies are relatively fixed, and — other things being equal — population growth will decrease the amount of income obtainable *per capita* with increases in the labour force. Diminishing returns may also hold even if capital grows at the same rate as population since capital is not a perfect substitute for natural resources.

The second impact on population growth is via the burden of dependency. Since a significant impact of falling mortality rates is on the very low age group the ratio of children to adults is likely to increase (at first) as a result of falling mortality rates.[1] This in turn is likely to increase the amount consumed out of income and to decrease the savings rate accordingly.

Given the foregoing factors that increase population growth, and the effect of population growth on savings and output, we have the elements necessary for a Malthusian type model. The increased rate of population growth induced by a *per capita* income rise leads to increased difficulty in expanding output, and in a reduction in the rate of savings and investment. But, of course, the mere statement of these effects is not enough to establish a Malthusian type model that would lead to a return to a previous level of *per capita* income once there was a deviation from it. It is also necessary that the magnitude of the effects be in the right ranges.

In a simple Malthusian type model an increase in *per capita* income may be deemed to have two effects: On the one hand it induces an increase in the rate of population growth, but on the other hand, out of a higher income may come a higher rate of

[1] We assume here that mortality rates are high to begin with.

Leibenstein — Population Growth and the Take-off Hypothesis

savings and investment. For the Malthusian model to work it is
necessary that at some point, although not necessarily immediately,
the income-reducing effects of population growth be more significant
than the income-raising effects of the induced investment that may
result out of the increased *per capita* income. If, on the other
hand, the income reducing effects of population growth are trivial
and the induced investment is always positive then, of course,
gradualism will always work. Economies could then advance at
various rates and no special take-off to sustained growth would be
necessary. It is thus clear that the mere admission of a relationship
between changes in *per capita* income and the rate of population
growth is not sufficient for a take-off theory. It all depends on the
magnitudes of the parameters.

But let us assume for a minute that the population effect in our
theory is significant. Would this give us a theory of the take-off?
*It would appear that all that it could explain is the persistence of
self-sustained backwardness.* In other words, and this is the important point, what we have here is a vehicle for explaining self-
sustained backwardness, but not one for the explanation of the
transition to self-sustained growth. By the very nature of demographic phenomena there is a limit to the magnitude of induced
population growth. There is a biologically determined upper limit
to the fertility rate and there is, at any time, a lower limit to the
mortality rate. Hence, beyond some point increases in *per capita*
income will lead to no further increases in the rate of population
growth. If somehow the rate of investment could get to be sufficiently high, then it could overcome the growing population hurdle,
and at some point if the high rate of investment could sustain itself,
then self-sustained growth could be assured. The missing link,
however, still appears to be a properly worked out investment
function. The contribution that the population variable makes is
to help explain why low rates of *per capita* income persist. But
since there is an upper limit to population growth, we need better
understanding of the investment phenomena to explain the take-off.

We have left out of consideration the possible neo-Keynesian
effect of population growth. We argued that population growth
will have only a dampening effect on further income growth. However, it has been argued, especially in the 1930's, that population
growth stimulates investment. But this is true only if there is a
clear separation between investment and savings, and if the inducement to invest is not limited by limited savings. Certainly one
gets the impression that in low income economies limited savings
are the consequence of high rates of consumption, and not the

The Economics of Take-off into Sustained Growth

consequence of low rates of investment; by contrast, in the Keynesian analysis of depression in advanced economies saving is low because investment is low and not because real income *per capita* is low. For the most part an increase in demand does not come about simply because there is an anticipation that there will be more mouths to feed. Anticipated increases in demand come about mostly because of the anticipation of more purchasing power which in turn implies more income. Thus, it is anticipated increases in income that we might expect to induce investment. Only to a very limited degree would we expect the fact of population growth to induce greater investment in a backward economy.

We have presented two views of the population factor: Population growth as an autonomous variable, and as an induced variable. In both views positive rates of population growth are a retarding influence on *per capita* income growth. But in the former case population was seen as an exogenously determined *obstacle* that is there to begin with, whereas in the latter view population growth can be viewed as an element that is induced to *race* against capital growth and aggregate income growth. Now it has been argued that in the post-war period, given the advances in public health, etc., the '*exogenous obstacle*' rather than the '*race*' view may be said to predominate. While this is probably true, the important point to consider is that these two aspects of the phenomenon are not independent of each other. To the extent that population growth becomes autonomous, to that extent the 'induced race' aspect becomes less important. But, in general, it seems to me that the induced aspect does not disappear. In sum, we might say that whereas countries that have developed earlier had to overcome a population hurdle which to a great extent *raced* along with their attempts at development, low income countries that develop today find that the population-growth hurdle is already reasonably high in the early stages, and that more than in the past they have to strain to maintain their existing level of *per capita* income.

V. THE QUESTION OF FERTILITY DECLINE

I have refrained from discussing fertility decline because it usually sets in in the later stages of development. It is not likely to occur in the state of sustained backwardness, nor is it likely to be significant in the *early* take-off period. There is, however, one possibility worthy of consideration in connexion with the take-off. Demographers speak of the gap between the onset of sustained mortality

Leibenstein — Population Growth and the Take-off Hypothesis

decline (as a consequence of economic betterment) and the beginning of sustained secular fertility decline.[1] Now, from our viewpoint,
one of the interesting aspects is the belief that the length of the
demographic gap has become shorter and shorter. Thus, while the
length of the gap may have been about seventy years in countries
whose take-off was in the middle of the nineteenth century, it has
been reduced in some cases to no more than two or three decades
in countries whose take-off is in the twentieth century. These
notions are, of course, very rough and approximate because it is
exceedingly difficult to measure the beginning of a trend when it is
surrounded by considerable cyclical fluctuation. Nevertheless, this
view does suggest the possibility that the onset of fertility decline
may occur sometime within the take-off period, if we view the
take-off as Rostow does, as taking approximately three decades.
Furthermore, it is possible that (at least in some cases) fertility
decline gives that extra push to sustained growth necessary for a
successful take-off. It is clearly very difficult to know whether, in
fact, this is so because so much depends on the relative magnitudes
of the various influences determining population growth, the impact
of population growth on income growth and investment and on the
factors that determine the rate of investment. It is worth noting
in this connexion that the study by Coale and Hoover suggests that
fertility decline may have a considerable impact on growth by
making available something like 40 per cent more savings per year
due to the smaller burden of dependency associated with falling
fertility rates. In addition, my own studies have suggested to me
that once fertility decline sets in it could be very rapid, and that
it is likely to change the burden of dependency in a significant
manner.[2]

Quite a few theories have been developed by demographers as
to why fertility decline takes place. This is not the place to go into
a detailed analysis of these sometimes conflicting theories. However, it may be useful if I try at this point to outline briefly a theory
of the connexions between fertility decline and development.

Fertility decline reflects the changing desire of parents with

[1] We employ the concept of sustained secular fertility decline despite the fact
that in the post-war period fertility rates have risen in advanced countries. This
is not the place to try to explain that phenomenon. The general view, however,
is that a period of fertility decline does set in in the course of development, although
beyond some point there may be a reversal in the trend. Since we are not concerned primarily with the demography of highly advanced countries, we shall
continue to use the phrase 'sustained fertility decline'.

[2] See the author's *Economic Backwardness and Economic Growth*, chapter 14.
See especially Ansley J. Coale and Edgar M. Hoover, *Population Growth and
Economic Development in Low-Income Countries*, Princeton University Press, Prince-
ton, New Jersey, 1958.

The Economics of Take-off into Sustained Growth

respect to children, and this changing desire is induced, in part, by changing external circumstances. The economic changes may, therefore, be viewed as contributing factors to such changing circumstances. It seems to me that to some extent fertility decline is probably connected with the changing production functions that are the consequences of economic development. Income growth implies increasing productivity which in turn implies a higher degree of specialization, and hence an increase in the variety of occupations available. The effect of economic development is not only to increase the degree of specialization but also to increase the size of firms, the variety of firms, and the hierarchical structure within firms. At the same time, more types of consumer goods and a larger variety of capital goods are usually introduced into the economy, which results in a large increase in the variety of distinct job opportunities available. As this increase in the variety of job opportunities is likely to be concentrated in the more urban, rather than rural areas, the possibilities and advantages of economic mobility grow with development. This implies that new occupations and career patterns become desirable to various individuals. Furthermore, the occupations and career patterns available to individuals are no longer those traditionally carried on by members of the family. In sum, economic development creates a changing production structure which in turn increases the opportunities for and incentives to geographic, occupational, and social mobility.

Now the consequences of these effects is to create motives that are conducive to fertility decline. For example, geographic mobility weakens and eventually destroys dependence on the extended family system that commonly predominates in the backward economy. The nuclear family which gradually develops in the more urbanized sectors faces long-run security problems for which early marriage is a disadvantage. In the same vein, the new occupational opportunities and career patterns that become discernable create a positive inducement for the sort of mobility that is most easily attained if a person is single or if family size is small. Without extending this argument too much one could readily see that the consequences of development that we have mentioned are likely to instigate the sort of demographic behaviour that reflects a more rational (i.e. non-traditional) outlook towards family planning. Another side of the picture is that economic development is associated usually with increases in educational level, both as a demand and supply phenomenon, which in turn enables members of the population to behave in ways that are more and more responsive to economic conditions.

Leibenstein — Population Growth and the Take-off Hypothesis

In any event, it seems clear that populations in advanced countries become relatively *responsive* to the economic environment in the determination of their family size. It is this element of responsiveness that probably is associated with fertility decline when economic conditions seem to warrant it that explains in part the increases in fertility in periods of prosperity at the more advanced stages in the process of development. If this view of the matter is correct then it may be reasonable to suppose that the take-off period may engender sufficient responsiveness at some juncture, which in turn induces fertility decline and facilitates the take-off further.

VI. CONCLUSIONS

I have tried to suggest where population growth could fit into a theory consistent with a take-off type hypothesis. The main point is that the take-off hypothesis denies gradualism and probably implies a pre-take-off stage of sustained backwardness. The population growth element enters as a factor that helps to explain the relative high degree of stability that we may attach to the state of self-sustained backwardness. Also, I have argued that while population growth is an obstacle to development it is by no means an insurmountable hurdle, and therefore, given a sufficient stimulus, we may visualize rates of investment sufficiently high to overcome this obstacle. But population growth is an obstacle to self-sustained growth that cannot be surmounted by very small stimuli to growth, or by stimuli whose effects are of very short duration, but with a sufficient stimulus it could be surmounted. In addition we considered the possibility that the onset of fertility decline may occur during the crucial two or three take-off decades. From that point of view the early onset of fertility decline may help to sustain or to hasten the transition to self-sustained growth.

We argued further that it was incorrect to consider population growth entirely as an exogenous variable, just as it would be incorrect to look upon it entirely as an endogenous variable. Rather, we argued that autonomous and induced population growth operated simultaneously and that the magnitude of one bore in some respects an inverse relation to the other. The obstacles to growth created by both autonomous and induced population growth are probably greater today than they have been in the past, but their maximum magnitude is still sufficiently small so that it could be overcome by a sufficiently large and sustained inducement to greater investment rates.

The Economics of Take-off into Sustained Growth

Finally, an attempt was made to outline briefly a theory of fertility decline and to suggest the possibility that there may in some cases be a connexion between the onset of fertility decline and the necessary minimal push required to enter a period of self-sustained growth.

[6]

THE IMPACT OF POPULATION GROWTH ON THE AMERICAN ECONOMY

INTRODUCTION

This essay presents a view of how economic theory bears on the problem of assessing the consequences on the American economy of alternative rates of population growth in the next 30 years or so. The paper consists of sub-essays on various aspects of the problem which are connected, though not always tightly, with each other. No general theory of the economic consequences of population growth will be attempted. To some extent, both micro- and macro-economic theory can be applied to some aspects of the problem. However, the consequences of population growth involve special features that, to some degree, prove the conventional tools of economic analysis to be brittle in some areas. In part, we will focus on some of these special features. But something more will also be attempted. In addition to considering some of the main elements that should be taken into account in assessing the impact of population growth, we shall also (almost inadvertently) present an impressionistic view of whether or not a relatively low positive rate rather than a zero rate of population growth should be a serious concern of government at the present time. We will also show that, in order to assess consequences of population growth, we have to introduce ideas taken from welfare economics. In fact, welfare economics considerations are bound to play an essential role in any final assessment of the consequences of population growth.

To limit our considerations, we shall concentrate on the following practical question: Will the economic welfare of the average family be lower to any significant degree at the end of the next 30 years if the annual rate of population growth is one-half to one percent compared to a zero rate of population growth?

We will have to consider (1) some of the difficulties inherent in interpreting the question; (2) what basic factors should be kept in mind; and finally, (3) how much stock should be put in some of the extreme assertions about the consequences of population growth made by noneconomists.

Population growth also affects the distribution of income as well as its size and growth. However, we shall not consider the distributional aspects in this essay.

It is to be emphasized that this essay is primarily theoretical and speculative. However, the speculations and some aspects of the theory cannot help but be based on impressionistic empirical assessments. For example, we assume that the rates of capital growth, formal education growth, diffusion of technology, etc., are all greater than the rate of population growth. The overall empirical assessment of the impact of population growth will depend to some degree on these basic empirical presuppositions in the author's mind.

A general view that will emerge is that population growth has a number of desirable economic effects as well as a number of undesirable ones, and that the net result depends on a balance of effects—and probably no single effect is very large. Furthermore, we shall consider possible types of individual and group behavior which themselves set up forces that counteract the adverse effects of population growth at the same time that individuals or groups act to increase population size. In other words, to some extent there are dynamic sequences which both induce population growth and counteract its potential adverse effects.

Also to be considered is whether the presumed adverse consequences on some variable (such as pollution) are in fact *caused* by population growth. In general, it will be argued that some of the main villains in the ecology drama are not associated with population growth per se. Whether or not the reader accepts the general conclusion that the impact of low rates of population growth is likely to be, at worst, only mildly adverse to economic welfare, given our three decade horizon, it is hoped that this essay will focus on those considerations necessary for the eventual measurement of the parameters and variables that will enable us to assess whether the impression presented is statistically correct or not.

The motivation behind casting the problem in the form stated above is that governments cannot work on the solution to all problems simultaneously. More pressing social and economic issues should have priority over others. If it turns out that the possible adverse impact of population growth in the next three decades is a mild one, then perhaps we should concern ourselves with the solution to other pressing problems if focusing on population problems can be deferred and reassessed at a later date.

The reader should note that, in the following discussions, we limit ourselves to the consequences of that portion of population growth that results from *wanted* children. It seems to me that the welfare economics of handling the problem of unwanted children is fairly straight forward. It makes economic sense to provide information and services of various sorts so that unwanted children are minimized. Societies may wish to subsidize (to some extent) such services to some groups in order to indirectly redistribute income, or to garner for others in the society the external benefits of such services. Our concern, however, is limited to those aspects of population growth which would occur, and which do occur, as a consequence of households choosing a family size greater than replacement size. Thus, in all of our discussions, we must keep in the back of our minds the utility (i.e., satisfaction) to the household of having children.

THE NATURE OF THE IMPACT PROBLEM

Ever since Malthus, some economists have been interested in the economic consequences of population growth. Yet, very little progress has been made in this area. When the focus of economists narrowed in the 1870's to the neoclassical concern of the explanation of market price, the consequences of population growth as a problem dropped by the wayside. Population changes are not significant in determining equilibrium prices in the short run.

During the 1920's, there was a flurry of interest in the question of the optimal population. However, the tools of analysis were so inadequate that nothing much was achieved beyond the assertion that there may be a population that yields a higher income per capita (or per something) than other population sizes. The Keynesian revolution of the 1930's, and the post-war interest in developing countries, supported an interest in population growth as an exogenous variable; but, once again, apart from the work of Coale and Hoover[1] on the age structure consequences of alternative population growth rates in developing countries, little was achieved. The lack of accomplishment was, in part, due to the very small number of economists who took an interest in the problem. However, part of the answer may lie in the essential difficulties of the problem itself.

If asked to estimate the economic consequences of a 50 percent increase in the American population in the next 30 years, my initial response would be, "if you can tell me everything else that would happen in the next 30 years, then I could hope to estimate the consequence of a 50 percent increase in the population."

It is possible to make this point in a more technical manner, but the essence of the argument would be the same. There is a vast array of alternative exogenous changes that one can visualize in a period of 30 years. Let us write C_{it} for the i-th vector of exogenous changes which occur in the economy during year t. In a parallel fashion, C_i is the time path of changes of the i-th vector for the 30-year period. Clearly, a given rate and time pattern of population change P_i could be associated with every C_i. It is quite possible that the given population change P_i in association with C_i would give a very different result than P_j in association with C_i, or P_i with C_j. It may be useful to consider briefly some specific possible components of C_i.

Consider technological change. This is especially difficult since we do not know the types of technologies available in the future. For example, if technologies are discovered which use power sources which turn out to be cheap and clean, then the consequences for pollution which would occur as a result of a 50 percent increase in population would obviously be very different than if we limit our answer to existing technologies.

Or, consider capital accumulation. For every rate of capital accumulation, we would get a different effect on output for a given rate of population growth. Similarly, the *composition* of the addition to the capital stock would also influence the outcome. Some types of capital are superior substitutes to natural resources than others. Once again, we can visualize different streams and types of capital accumulations, each of which, associated with a rate of population growth, would yield a different outcome.

Or consider the simultaneous and related impact of the diffusion of new technologies and capital accumulation on economies of scale. Assume that the rate of the diffusion of technology depends in part on the passage of time and, to a considerable extent, on the rate of capital accumulation. An increase in economies of scale would also increase the optimal size of the population from the viewpoint of output per worker. Two alternative possibilities are illustrated in Figures 1 and 2.

Each curve $T_i K_i$ illustrates the association between population size and output per worker for the combination of technology and capital $T_i K_i$. The curves $T_i K_i$ rise as more advanced capital is diffused in the economy and as more capital per worker is accumulated. The path O_t shows the time pattern of optimal population points as technology and population change. Similarly, the line P_t shows the path of population change. An alternative path of optimal population points is shown by O_t'

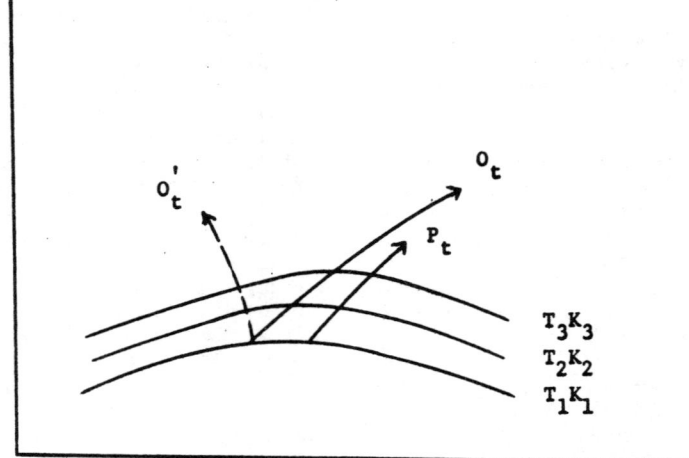

Figure 1

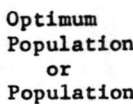

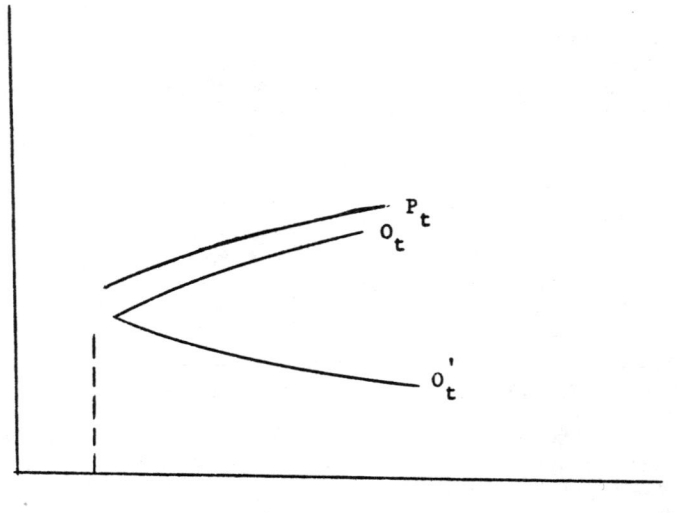

Figure 2

Obviously the impact of population growth is very different if the technology-capital accumulation path follows O'_t rather than O_t. In the first case, there is an increasing deviation between the actual and the optimal population while in the second case these two magnitudes approach each other.

Another difficulty is to determine whether an element is a variable or a parameter. In the discussions above we assumed that capital and technology are determined apart from population growth. But suppose that either capital or the diffusion of technology (or both) varies positively with population growth. Once again, we can visualize outcomes which would be different than in the case in which capital and technological change are exogenous variables.

Changes in tastes may also affect the outcome since tastes affect the values of inputs and outputs. We can define a given set of tastes by assigning to every level of income a predetermined preference structure, and refer to changes in taste when the time stream of preferences, in association with income, changes. Nevertheless, if we find ourselves historically at a given point in the income-taste-time stream, it is hard to determine in advance whether the changes in taste that would occur in the future involve constant tastes in the sense indicated (i.e., a constant evolving set of preference structures) or a change in taste. From the current point in time, every set of evolving tastes for a given increase in the population could lead to a different economic outcome.

It is unnecessary to pursue additional possibilities. The main conclusion that emerges is that, if we are to predict the consequences of population growth, and if we come up with a unique answer, then we simultaneously make a host of other complicated predictions. That is, we are simultaneously predicting, at least implicitly, every change in the parameters over time that influence or could possibly influence the impact of population growth on economic conditions. The longer the time period, the greater the possible variation in the changes in parameters and the greater the possible deviation of any specific prediction about population consequences from what in fact happens. In the light of these conditions, it is easy to understand how the early Malthusian economists came up with the predictions for Europe that turned out to be so very far from the mark.

A QUASI-MALTHUSIAN HYPOTHESIS

We no longer take seriously Malthusian ideas about fertility and mortality in advanced economies. But there is a sense in which the classical notion that, at some point, a very large population presses on the fixed resources to the economic disadvantage of the economy. What follows is an attempt to elaborate the kernel of truth that remains in such Malthusian ideas for an advanced economy.

In Figure 3, we separate the economic gains of population growth from the losses. Both the gains and the losses depend on the size of the population, the

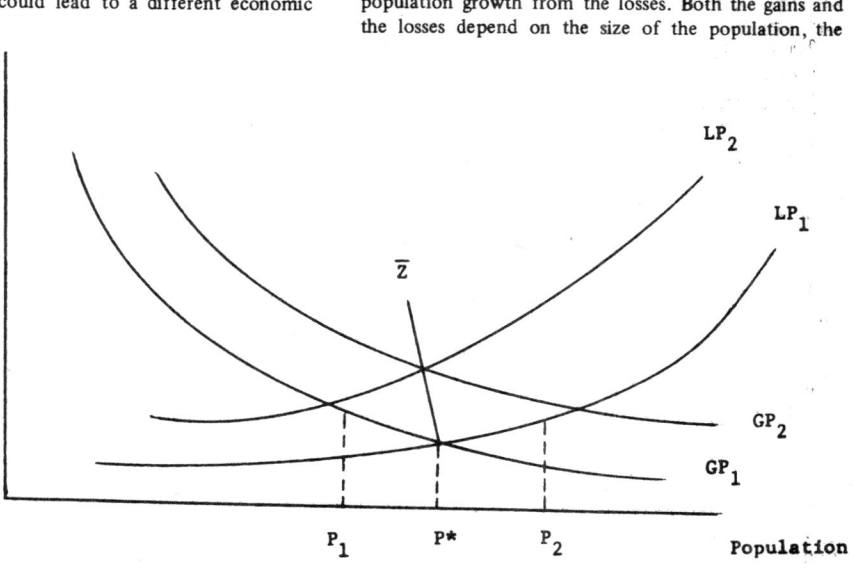

Marginal
Gain or Loss
of Added
Population to
Output per
Worker

Figure 3

population growth rate, and on the rates at which other inputs grow simultaneously. The ordinate represents the marginal gain or loss for a given growth rate of the population (say, one percent per year) to output per worker compared to what that output would have been had other "parametric" inputs grown at the same rate and population been zero. By "parametric" inputs, we have in mind that portion of the inputs whose growth is independent of population size or population growth. This is to be distinguished from functionally related input growth where the inputs increase (or decrease) with population growth.

Alternate population sizes are shown on the x-axis. The hypothesis in its simplest version is illustrated by the two curves GP_1 and LP_1. GP_1 represents the gain from population growth for each level of population size and LP_1 represents the loss, for a one percent rate of population growth. The gains depend on economies of scale and the loss represents the diseconomies involved from crowding on fixed resources and losses from congestion. At the same time, we assume that there is a given rate of capital accumulation, a given "book of technological blueprints," and a given rate of diffusion of new technology. The higher rates at which these three variables (capital, innovation, and diffusion of technology) grow, the less important natural inputs are compared to total inputs and the less the loss to population growth. The higher the growth rate of the three parameters, the higher the GP curves, and the lower the LP curves. Also, beyond some population growth, note that the greater the given population growth rate the lower the GP curve and the higher the LP curve. The point of intersection of the curves GP_i and LP_i marked P* will be further to the right the greater the growth rates of the "external inputs." The essential quasi-Malthusian idea is that the gains from population size are the greater the smaller the population, and the losses are lower the smaller the population size. The transition point P* from net gains to net losses does not imply that output is declining. It simply implies that a point has been reached beyond which output would have been higher had the population size been smaller for a given rate of population increase.

Z is the locus of intersections of the GP_i and LP_i curves for higher rates of population growth. As the curve Z is drawn, it reflects the presumption that the higher the rate of population growth the less the gain from economies of scale, and the greater the loss from the crowding on fixed resources and congestion of various types. It also reflects the idea that it is more difficult to make adjustments at higher rates of population growth than at lower rates. Needless to say, this is

not necessarily true for all situations. We should keep in mind that the gains from population growth include, in addition to scale advantages, the stimulation to the demand of goods and services, and indirectly the decreased cost of maintaining high levels of employment. Thus, it is possible that the curve Z might, to some extent, be positively sloped before it shifts back towards smaller population sizes.

The critical question from our viewpoint is where, on Figure 3, is the United States at the present time. My conjecture is that we are somewhere on the relatively flat area of both curves in a range which surrounds the transition point P*. This is indicated in the graph by the areas between P_1 and P_2. If this is true, then it would imply that, in the near future, neither the marginal gains nor the marginal losses attributable to population growth *as such* are likely to be very large, although at present we cannot tell whether the gains outweigh the losses or vice versa. In my view, a pessimistic assessment of the situation would be to assert that we are somewhere between P* and P_2. However, even in this range, the values of the net losses are probably small compared to other variables that influence output per worker. Subsequent sections will indicate some of the things we have to study to determine whether or not this is true.

Consider briefly some elements on the gain side, GP. It is likely that services which form an increasing proportion of output in the course of economic development are for the most part neutral with respect to economies of scale. Manufacturing as such is probably also neutral. For the most part, manufacturing in the United States has already exhausted whatever gains exist from scale economies. However, services which use a great deal of fixed equipment, or which depend on geography such as communications, advertising, and transport still yield economies of scale vis-a-vis population growth. The same is probably also true of government services which have a fixed cost aspect to them such as national defense, internal security, and so on.

The situation vis-a-vis agriculture is less clear. Here it is possible that the fixed land base might put the consequences of population growth on the loss side. The main instances where losses are involved are the industries that mine natural resources (oil, coal, etc.) and natural recreational facilities.

With respect to fossil fuels, one has to consider the relative rates of discovery of new sources of supply versus the mining of existing sources, and whether or not discoveries, or research and development are to any degree stimulated by demand considerations. Also, international trade of manufactured goods and services, etc., for oil reduces the diseconomies (vis-a-vis population) involved in mining local sources of supply.

In Figure 4, we summarize the information we would have to know if we wish to assess the consequences of different rates of population growth for a given population size. The abscissa represents alternative population sizes while the ordinate represents alternative rates of population growth. The curves Z_i represent "zero *net* population growth consequences" if the index of "external inputs" grow at the rate i. For instance, the point X_1 on Z_4 says that, if the rate of population growth is one percent, then P' is the population size for which there would be a zero net population growth effect if the external inputs grew to four percent. By external inputs, we have in mind the index of input growth for that part of the addition to inputs which are not influenced by population growth. The elements included in our index of input growth are physical capital, human capital, and technological change. We ignore the very difficult problem of suggesting or determining how such an index of input growth would be developed and measured.

The extent of the gains and losses depends on the ability of the economy to adapt to different rates of population growth. For example, it may be easier to maintain full employment with a positive rate of population growth than with a zero rate. There is no way of answering this question at this time, although the general Keynesian view would suggest that an economy is somewhat more robust in terms of maintaining aggregate demand, and maintaining near full employment investment rates, with a growing population rather than a stationary one. It is easier for firms to plan labor demand for an expanding market which includes the effect of population growth than if market expansion depends only on increases in productivity. Thus, for a given population size, the smallest net loss (or largest net gain) may be associated with a positive rate of population growth.

The obverse side of the employment-maintenance argument is the possibility that lower rates of population growth are likely to feed inflationary pressures to a lesser degree than higher rates. This seems like a reasonable proposition simply on the basis that population growth is likely to increase consumer demand, other things equal. However, this notion must be qualified in the sense that it is likely that the factors that determine inflation are only insignificantly influenced by population growth as such. It is certainly true, historically, that inflationary pressures have appeared in countries with very low rates of population growth, as well as those

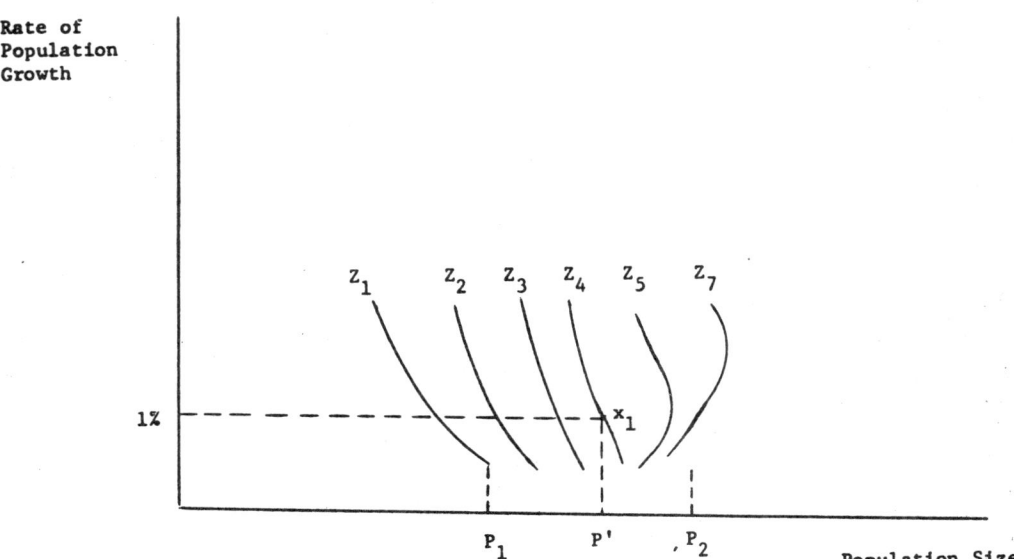

Figure 4

with relatively high rates. It is unknown whether any correlation exists between population growth and inflation, but it is well to keep in mind that most analyses of inflation presume, directly or indirectly, that inflation is primarily connected with the management or determinants of the supply of money rather than with population growth as such:

The utility, or disutility, of congestion per se (apart from the effects of crowding on fixed resources) is difficult to assess. Obviously some people dislike living in densely populated areas. However, it would be rash to assume that this is a representative viewpoint. Successive censuses for the United States reveal that people move out of counties that are losing population and into counties that are more densely populated and that are gaining population. In other words, the observation is in conformity with the hypothesis that, on the average, people prefer to live in a relatively urban environment. As a teacher of mine put the matter, "the country is a nice place to visit, but I would hate to live there."

OBJECTIVES OF ECONOMIC AGENTS, REPLACEMENT EFFECTS, AND THEIR IMPLICATIONS

If other inputs are given, then an increase in the labor force will normally imply a reduction in output per worker since, on the average, workers have less inputs to work with. Even if inputs expand by the same percentage as labor (in terms of initial values), a relative loss might occur because capital and other inputs are imperfect substitutes for a given quantum of natural resources. However, we will argue that the outcome depends on whether inputs are given (or their growth rates are given) apart from population growth, or whether capital growth, etc., depends on population growth. This depends on the objectives of households, firms, and governments, and whether or not we view government as an agent that carries out the objectives of households. Thus, it will be argued that the impact of population growth depends on the objectives of economic agents.

To set the stage for our discussion, consider the following three alternative ways in which we may view the simultaneous increase in population and resources: (1) people come empty into the world, as it were, and the growth in capital and knowledge occur at the same rate independent of the rate of population growth; or (2) each worker who enters the economy is outfitted with as much capital and knowledge as the previous number of workers because an additional worker enters; or (3) each generation that enters the labor force is outfitted with a superior outfit of capital and knowledge

than the previous generation. We shall see that these different assumptions yield different results about the economic consequences of population growth.

To see what is involved, consider education as a human capital input. We shall refer to "general capital" as the sum of human capital (education, etc.) and physical capital. Also, we suppose that output per worker, on the average, depends on the amount of general capital each worker has to work with. Now suppose that each family has the number of children that it wants and that all children are educated to the same level irrespective of family size. This is not an extreme assumption in an advanced economy where the basic consideration is between educating two children at a given level and educating less than three children at the same level. Suppose, for a moment, that education were the only type of capital in existence. Then, every person born is eventually outfitted with the capital to make him as productive as those already in the economy. Since every person brings with him his own capital, as it were, then the fact that we have a positive rather than a zero rate of population growth imposes no loss on anyone else (if there are no external diseconomies of education). It might be argued that, if the additional people were not born, there would be more available to be spent on other members of the family. But whether or not this is a relevant consideration depends on the utility function of the household. If the household maximizes its utility by spending its income in such a way that it raises three children to a given standard of education rather than two, then this is its optimal expenditure pattern and any other expenditure pattern would be inferior.

Of course, education is not the only type of capital. But other types of capital may also depend to some extent on population growth. Suppose that the diffusion of technological information depends on the average level of education, and that this indirectly depends on population growth. This would be so if people are educated only when young so that increases in knowledge depend on the number of young people who are educated. In developing countries where average incomes are very low and population growth very rapid, there is a serious choice to be made between the number of people available and the quality of education. But this is not necessarily a serious consideration in a highly advanced economy where the rates of population growth are relatively low and the actual or potential funds available for education relatively ample. Although families contribute only part of the costs of education, we can view government and its contribution as indirectly carrying out familial objectives and a socially determined redistribution of income.

Physical capital accumulation may also depend indirectly on population growth. Suppose firms invest in order to introduce new or improved techniques, and suppose that the diffusion of technology depends on population growth. In that case, we may view entrants into the labor force as being outfitted, not with average capital, but with the latest type of capital which is superior to the average. If all these suppositions happen to be true—and we do not argue that they are—then population growth would increase output per worker rather than diminish it if input growth is large enough and of the right type. Of course, some of the general capital accumulation is independent of population growth. The point of presenting the string of suppositions above was not to paint a picture that is accurate, but rather one that is partially true so as to argue that the net outcome depends, in part, on how much of the general capital accumulation that takes place is a function of population growth and how much of it is independent of it. It is impossible to guess on *a priori* grounds what the ratio of one to the other is likely to be.

A point not stressed, but one that we may mention in passing, is the hypothesis developed by Kuznets that innovation may in part be a function of population growth. This stems from the notion that the larger the size of the population, the larger the number of geniuses produced. Geniuses of different sorts interacting with each other may contribute innovations disproportionately to their numbers. In other words, the output of geniuses is also subject to positive external benefits that are a function of scale.

Another consideration in this same general area is whether people with larger families work harder, more effectively, more assiduously, etc., than those with smaller families.[2] Obviously, this depends on the objectives of the household. Whether or not such a relation exists cannot be determined on *a priori* grounds. But if it were true to some degree, then this would contribute another counter to the frequently presumed negative effects of a positive rate of population growth. It is not inconceivable that, to some degree, the extent of family obligations in an advanced economy where a large variety of work opportunities exist, should serve as a spur to the application of effort and to the pursuit of superior economic opportunities. Whether there is any substance to this conjecture is not firmly established.[3] Nevertheless, the existence of this possibility undermines the confidence we might have in the notion that relatively low rates of population growth (compared to zero population growth) in an advanced economy are necessarily harmful to economic output. On the other side, it must be recognized that a larger family reduces the number of years the average mother can participate in the labor force.

The final element that fits loosely with the range of considerations covered in this section is what the writer has referred to elsewhere as the "replacement effect." The basic idea has already been alluded to. If education or other forms of human capital are given only to the young prior to entry into the work force, and if its quantity increases over time, then the greater the rate of population growth, other things equal, the greater the rate at which human capital increases. In a stationary and stable population, the entrants to the labor force equal those that retire for various reasons. In the stationary population, the increase in the economic quality of the labor force would depend only on the rate of increase in the human capital given to each successive generation. But in a growing population, the entrants more than replace the retirements and the average economic quality of the population would be higher than in the stationary population.[4] Of course, the significance of this factor would have to be determined empirically, but its existence should be taken into account in any list of counterbalancing effects of a growing population.

ON THE SUBSTITUTABILITY OF CAPITAL FOR NATURAL RESOURCES

Arguments against population growth frequently stress the impact of population growth on the availability and utilization of "natural resources." Some comments are called for in this connection. The most important natural resources are, for the most part, not "natural" (God given) but the consequence of capital accumulation. Cultivated land had to be cleared and altered in many respects before it became a productive asset capable of contributing to relatively high yields per acre. If one were to consider the value of the yield of currently cultivated land, say at the time of Columbus, and its value today, and impute the differential capital values in the two cases, it is likely that over 80 percent or more of agricultural land is the consequence of capital accumulation. To different degrees, similar arguments could be made with respect to other "natural" resources. From this viewpoint, the focus on natural resources exaggerates the negative impact of population growth. For the most part, when productive resources are replaced in the economy, newly created man-made capital is being used to replace old man-made capital.

Even when considering true natural resources, we must keep in mind that there is a very high degree to which capital is a substitute for natural resources. As an economy develops, the technologies available to it increase and, at the same time, the possibilities of substituting man-made capital for other resources increase accordingly. This is not to deny that the process of substitution may involve an increase in the resource cost per unit of output. But this says nothing more than the obvious assertion that population growth will increase the input cost of some commodities. But any single commodity of this type will usually involve only a small proportion of consumer expenditures, and the increase in cost will be a small fraction of total cost. Thus, if 100 percent of consumer spending consists of commodities that fall into this category and the cost increase is one percent, then the total impact is only one-tenth of one percent.

If we consider every type of natural resource, then we should expect, in general, that a fairly high degree of substitutability exists in terms of the utilities created by the commodities produced by these resources. We have already suggested that the greater the technologies available, the greater the degree of substitutability that we should expect of man-made resources for natural resources. If there are many sources of substitutability inclusive of international trade (and this is likely to be the case in a large and complex economy), then we should expect the degree of substitutability to be very high. This is true despite the fact that, if we focus our attention very narrowly on a specific natural resource and a very specific use of that resource, we might find cases in which the degree of substitutability appears to be very low. Nevertheless, the average degree of substitutability for all productive resources may be very high. In addition, we should keep in mind that technological innovations may limit or reduce the value of some types of natural resources. For example, the further development of nuclear power may reduce the value of sources of fossil fuels for power purposes.[5] Even in the case of natural resources used for recreational purposes, a very high degree of substitutability exists if we look at the problem from a sufficiently wide perspective. For instance, swimming pools are substitutes for bathing beaches. The degree of substitutability will depend in part on tastes. For some, the swimming pool with its greater accessability might appear as a superior resource to the more remote beach. Others will prefer the beach. But in addition, one has to consider other forms of recreation as a substitute for either beach or swimming pool activities.

There is the possibility of "bottleneck" resources to be considered. Some resources that have almost no substitutes may be critical for a wide variety of production processes. If such resources exist, then the ratio of such resources per man would have significant consequences for production per man. Prior to the nuclear age, coal and petroleum as the basic source of energy might have been candidates for bottleneck resources. However, at present, there exists the technological possibility of almost unlimited energy. While there are unquestionably serious technological problems involved in substituting nuclear energy for the eventually exhaustible stock of reasonably cheap fossil fuels, there can be little doubt that, in the next three decades, a scarcity of energy as such will not arise as a serious problem.[6]

TECHNOLOGY, URBANIZATION, POLLUTION, AND CONGESTION

This section addresses itself to the common belief that population growth is a major cause of air and water pollution and of urban congestion. There is a sense in which population growth is a contributor, although we may question whether it is a major contributor. Of greater interest is that there is a sense in which population growth has nothing to do with either pollution or many types of urban congestion.

Pollution is the consequence of the techniques (i.e., technology) we use to produce goods and services, and the restrictions or lack of restrictions that society imposes on the use of such techniques. If severe enough restrictions were imposed on the use of techniques of production so that air and water would be pollution free, population growth would not alter the situation. Pollution exists because economic production techniques exist which pollute the environment. For the most part, society makes no attempt to charge the polluters the full cost of the disutilities that they impose on others. It is possible that for most commodities the techniques would still be economic even if full social costs were charged. There is little reason to blame population growth for the fact that governments do not use their powers to regulate the use of technology in order to minimize (or optimize) the pollutants injected into the environment.

For a given degree of control of technology (or lack of control thereof), the degree of pollution may be a monotonic function of the output of the goods or services produced by the pollution technology. Output depends on demand, which in turn is partly a function of income, and for some commodities it is also partly a function of population growth. For example, the demand for automobiles depends largely on income. This explains the fact that there are many more automobiles per 1,000 people in the United States than in other countries. (Indian villages suffer little from the pollution due to automobile exhausts despite their high rate of population growth.) There are commodities, and automobiles may be one of them, whose demand also depends on population size. Nevertheless, it seems to me to be fallacious to focus attention on controlling population growth in order to eliminate or reduce the degree of pollution.

On the surface, the usual pollution argument sounds reasonable. For a given set and sequence of technological choices and a given method of regulation, there is an income effect on pollution and a population effect. It seems reasonable that we should take into account the population effect. Nevertheless, I believe that this is a wrong way of looking at the problem. Consider an example from another area. Suppose that some particular country (say, Great Britain) has rigid exchange rates, an overvalued currency, and an unfavorable balance of trade. It could be argued that such a country should reduce its population size, since this would reduce its imports and improve its balance of trade. But to economists, the obvious and correct remedy is to shift to a flexible exchange rate (or at least devalue) or to something close to an equilibrium exchange rate which would be consistent with an equality between imports and exports. Seeking to solve the problems created by disequilibrium exchange rates by attacking population growth somehow seems the wrong way of tackling this particular problem. Similarly, the economics of pollution is essentially a problem of the cost of goods and services, the allocation of such costs, and the incentives created by charging less than full social costs. Pollution arises, for the most part, as a consequence of the production of goods and services. It seems reasonable that consumers should be required to pay the full cost of these services inclusive of the pollution clean up costs. If the commodity or service involves increasing costs per unit, and demand is in part a function of population growth, then this is simply part of the possible increasing cost aspects which may be a consequence of population growth. These have to be combined with other increasing cost consequences of population growth and weighed against the other decreasing cost elements involved. From this point of view, pollution should not be considered as a unique and separate argument for population control in its own right.

The fact that some particular commodity happens to have a cost structure that involves external diseconomies that are difficult to assess, is not an argument for limiting the number of consumers in general. But that is exactly what we do if we use pollution as an argument in its own right for a reduction in population growth. It is the overall balance of macro considerations that is significant and not the impact of population growth on a single class of commodities.

The appropriate economic approach is to charge the appropriate social costs for commodities. In the case of commodities whose manufacture or use creates pollution, the price should include the cost of modifying technology so that it is nonpolluting, or optimally polluting.[7] It would take us too far afield to work out exact techniques for imposing such costs on those who may prefer more, rather than fewer, children. People should pay for the full costs of the goods they consume out of their income and not through the imposition of artificial restrictions. Regulating family size rather than techniques of production will not eliminate pollution.

Urban congestion is in many respects similar to the technology-pollution problem. Congestion is a consequence of urbanization and poor city planning. Cities in sparsely populated countries such as Australia, Canada, Norway, and so on, frequently suffer from urban traffic congestion as well as other forms of congestion. It is true that for a given degree of urbanization and for a given type of (poor) city planning, population growth will contribute to congestion. But, parallel to the pollution problem, population size is not the basic cause nor is limiting population growth the basic avenue through which congestion can be cured.

Urbanization is the consequence of the technologies employed at high per capita income levels which make possible the production of agricultural commodities with only a very small proportion of the population on the land—frequently less than five percent. There are considerable economic advantages to life arranged in relatively densely populated communities. In part, this is also a reflection of taste. Urban areas and the activities involved in maintaining them abound in externalities. Hence, urban planning is necessary. Cities in countries whose population is stationary can suffer from traffic and other forms of congestion. For example, Tokyo would probably be a highly congested city even if Japan's population had been stationary for the last decade: Technology and the urbanization that accompanies rapid income growth would be the basic cause. Here, too, the cure would appear to lie in our ability to master the economics of externalities, and in procedures that would regulate for the consequences of the externalities involved in the production of goods and services in urban areas. Population growth is the apparent but not the real cause of urban congestion. The basic point is that, while those who choose to have larger rather than smaller families should pay for the adverse external effects they impose on others, they should not have to pay for the adverse effects of externalities inherent in certain techniques of production.

FROM WHOSE VIEWPOINT?—THE DILEMMA OF WELFARE ECONOMICS IN CONNECTION WITH POPULATION GROWTH

It is frequently convenient to consider the population control problem in terms of imposing government determined (usually financial) deterrents. However, for most inducements and deterrents there is a basic dilemma. Inducements which are pronatalist help children and increase family size. The deterrents, while they may decrease family size, will in most cases worsen the conditions of existing children. For example, subsidies for not having a third child will make the children of families who do have three children relatively worse off. Similarly, schemes to tax those with a third child will make the children of parents who are not put off by the deterrent worse off. On the whole, this is probably not true for inducements which limit the proportions married or which increase the age of marriage. However, those that increase the age of marriage are not likely to be extremely effective when the choice is between the second or third child. A similar problem exists in assessing existing legislation whose initial intent was neither pronatalist or anti-natalist. Income tax exemptions for children fit this category. Removing such exemptions for lower income groups will worsen the lot of those children born into such groups, even if the net result is to reduce the total number of births.

However, it could be argued that, on the average, the current tax and subsidy structure is pronatalist for those in middle-income groups as well as low-income groups. The arguments presented so far do not support pronatalist policies. Thus, a case could be made for altering the tax and subsidy structure in such a way so as to eliminate the pronatalist bias for middle- and upper-income groups. The same argument cannot be made for low-income groups because of concern for the children of low-income groups.

The impact of population growth not only affects different groups differently, but it is likely that different answers might be obtained if we look at the problem from different potential viewpoints on the basis of different time horizons. Four distinct groups from whose viewpoint we might consider the problem follow: (1) present living adults, (2) children living in households, (3) those currently alive who will enter adult life later, and (4) unborn future generations. Most economic problems are looked at from the point of view of those currently alive. This is one of the basic assumptions of

welfare economics. However, the population growth problem cannot be viewed solely on this basis. A little reflection suggests that the interests of these different groups are not the same, and the impact of population growth on the different groups is quite distinct.

1. For present living adults time preference between different periods in the future plays a significant role. Present living adults would most likely put much more weight on a consequence that happens in the very near future, say next year, than one which would occur a century and a half from now. If the welfare of future generations is of no consequence, any impact in the far future, no matter how large, cannot have relevance for present living adults. If population growth reduces the income of the present adult generation (the interests of other groups excluded) in the future over what it would be without population growth, then their interest would be to limit those losses for their lifetime. Since the current adult generation is of different ages, the impact differs for people at different ages. Each cohort will evaluate the impact differently; but, we can, if we have some welfare function, combine the results of those impacts on different cohorts. *One significant result is that, if those who bear the children that contribute to that portion of population growth that has the adverse impact pay the full cost of the adverse impact to all those who suffer thereby, then others in the present adult generation can have no complaint.* Thus, from the point of view of the present adult generation, the significant question is not simply the impact of population growth but who bears the cost of that impact. To the extent that the cost is born by those who have the children, it had no adverse impact on the present adult generation.

2. The point of view of children now alive is a very different one. Even if their parents bear the cost of their nurture in such a way that it does not affect others who have fewer children, the welfare of children born into larger families may, nevertheless, be affected adversely. Consider the case of a single-child family versus, let us say, a five-child family. The welfare of the first child is very significantly affected depending on whether four other children are born into this household. The consequences for him or her exist irrespective of whether other households are in any way penalized by the fact that his own household happens to be a large one.

3. Once children leave the nurture stage and enter adult life they face "population problems" in addition to whatever problem they may have faced by the fact that the number of siblings they had was larger rather than smaller. The rate of population growth determines

whether they enter a world in which their own age group is large or small. Their career opportunities are likely to be different if they are from a larger cohort rather than a smaller one.

4. The size of future generations depends on the size of present generations apart from the impact of population growth on the present generation. Members of a large future generation will face different opportunities than those of smaller future generation cohorts.

It should also be clear that there is an important connection between the time horizon and the groups whose viewpoint we are considering. The shorter the time horizon, the less we need be concerned about the children who enter adult life and the future generations not yet born. If the time horizon is one year, then the main impact is on present living adults and on children living in households. A decade changes the picture: A considerable portion of children who enter adult life is now a significant group. Furthermore, children living in households become a significant variable rather than a constant. From the point of view of year zero, future generations enter the picture. Obviously, a time horizon of a century emphasizes future generations and reduces the relative importance of earlier groups.

A major distinction from the point of view of any time point is between those alive at the initial period and those that are born after the initial period. How do we assign relative weights to those presently alive as against the interests of those yet to be born? Should everyone be given an equal weight whether or not alive initially? If so, then the longer the period, the greater the weight assigned to future generations and the less significance attached to those who are present living adults.

The general problem of assigning weights to people alive at different points in time represents an essential unsolved problem in discussing the impact of population growth. The significance of this aspect of the problem cannot be understated. To assign the same importance to each group at a different point in time eliminates time preference. To include time preference means assigning greater weights to those currently alive. But the impact of population growth is likely to be a flow of consequences over time which extends indefinitely into the future.

By intentionally using income per worker as our index of economic growth, we avoid considering age structure effects. Age structure effects are fairly well understood. In general, the greater the rate of population growth, the lower the ratio of those who work as a proportion of the population, and hence the greater the burden of dependency. A higher rate of population growth for the same income per worker implies a lower

income per capita. But in this case, the lower income per capita does not imply that society is worse off than in the higher per capita income case if the children responsible for the higher population growth are wanted children. On the contrary, a forced reduction in the birth rate and a consequent higher income per capita would reflect less utility per family and a worse welfare situation in accordance with the usual principles of welfare economics.

CONCLUSIONS

As a result of some of the assumptions made about the relative rates of growth of population compared to human and physical capital, certain qualitative conclusions can be ventured. The conclusions that follow are from the viewpoint of the adults presently alive, and children living in households.

1. For the most part, the impact on output per worker will depend on a number of counterbalancing effects, some of which make a positive marginal contribution to the output and others, a negative marginal contribution.

2. In general, we should not expect the impact of population growth to decrease the real wage rate. In fact, there is every reason to expect that, apart from the unlikely possibility of extreme unemployment effects, real wages will rise throughout the period.

3. Even if the net marginal effect on output per worker is negative, we should expect the net impact to be less than the rate of population growth. For instance, if the rate of population growth is one percent per year, the net reduction on output per worker (compared to what it would be otherwise) should be less than one percent per year. The basic reason for this emerges from the considerations presented above to the effect that, to some degree, general capital accumulation depends on population growth.

4. The likely net impact of population growth on output per worker is small compared to other variables which are subject to governmental policies, actions, and influences. For example, increasing the current level of investment from the American level to, say, the Japanese level will have a much more significant impact on growth than lowering population increase. Reducing defense expenditures by two or three percentage points of national income (if possible) would work in the same way. It is conceivable that increased efforts in the area of consumer information and protection, and the elimination of agricultural price supports could possibly increase the value of consumer goods by more than one percent per year in the near future. Also, reducing the unemployment rate by two or three percentage points

(say from six percent to three percent) will have a greater impact on output per worker than reducing population growth to a zero level. Our aim is not to present an exhaustive list of alternative governmental activities, but to suggest that there are many policies and actions which would turn out to be more productive in increasing economic welfare in the next three decades than limiting population growth through the regulation of the number of children per family. Some of the possibilities mentioned above (such as increasing investment) affect the flows of inputs and will counteract the negative effect of population growth every year. Other possible changes affect stocks and their effect on income growth has an upper limit. But in the next three decades they probably can contribute to income growth to a considerable degree. None of this is to argue that we should exhaust all possibilities to achieve a maximum rate of growth. Growth has a price and what we want is an optimal growth rate somehow defined. The essence of what is being argued is that (1) minimizing population growth will only contribute marginally to achieving an optimum growth rate (probably significantly less than half a percentage point out of, say, five percent growth), and (2) in attempting to achieve an optimal growth rate, there are numerous substitute policies that would contribute as much as minimizing population growth would. Of course, in making such an assessment of alternative means of contributing to optimal growth, the political feasibility of alternative policies have to be taken into account.

We have ignored the welfare of children after their entry into the labor force, and the effects of reducing population growth on the welfare of generations unborn.

Two points have to be kept in mind:

1. Effective policies for population control need not be begun today. They can be deferred to the future when the net advantages of such policies appear much clearer than they do now. It may be argued that deferring such policies is detrimental to future generations because their population size will be greater if we do not institute such policies at present. But instituting such policies would occur at the expense of the satisfaction to those who want more children than necessary for replacement.

2. Future generations will have a higher per capita income than the present generation. The problem is similar to shifting income from a relatively poorer group to a relatively wealthier one. Is it rational to ask the poorer group to make sacrifices for the benefit of the wealthier one? Suppose that, if the American population a century ago had been forced to limit its family size (of

wanted children) and its rate of population growth (say by imposing a very late age of marriage), we would be 50 percent richer than we are today, and suppose also that this would have diminished the utility enjoyed by the families a century ago. Is it fair for us who enjoy a per capita income many times that of a century ago to ask of them to have made still further sacrifices in our behalf?

REFERENCES

1. Ansley Coale and Edgar Hoover, *Population Growth and Economic Development in Low Income Countries* (Princeton: Princeton University Press, 1958).

2. Ester Boserup in *The Conditions of Agricultural Growth* (Chicago: Aldine, 1965) developed a hypothesis of this sort for agricultural populations. In her view, historically agricultural populations shifted to superior available techniques only when population pressure rose sufficiently to induce them to do so.

3. This hypothesis derives in part from the author's X-efficiency ideas which claim that economies do not produce on their production frontier, and that actual output is well below the possible level. The amount of output and the rate of growth depends in part on the inducement provided by the motivational system inherent in the socio-economic organization of the economy. (See H. Leibenstein, "Organizational or Frictional Equilibria, X-Efficiency, and the Rate of Innovation," *Quarterly Journal of Economics*, November 1969.) It is not inconceivable that family size plays a role for some groups, say the self employed and middle and higher management, in the over-arching incentive system. The relation of effort to family size need not be monotonic to be effective. For instance, if the maximum effort level were for families that had between two and four children, there would most likely be a net positive effect. The article by Harold W. Guthrie, "Some Explanations of Moonlighting," Business and Economic Statistics Section, *Proceedings of the American Statistical Association*, 1966, pp. 460-67, supports the hypothesis that effort, supply, and family size are positively related.

4. See H. Leibenstein, "The Impact of Population Growth on Economic Welfare—Nontraditional Elements," in *Rapid Population Growth: Consequences and Policy Implications*, National Academy of Sciences (Baltimore: Johns Hopkins Press, 1971), pp. 188-193, for a statement of the replacement effect.

5. At the time of writing, a newspaper report has appeared that the U.S. Bureau of Mines--Coal Division's scientists have developed means of turning organic waste products in garbage into crude oil. (*International Herald Tribune*, September 8, 1971.)

6. For an analysis of the energy possibilities and its relation to vast increases in world population size, see Weinbert and Hammond, "Limits to the Use of Energy," *American Scientist*, July-August 1970, pp. 412-18.

7. Since there is a trade-off between pollution and other costs, the optimal amount of pollution is not necessarily the minimal amount technically feasible.

Part III
Economic Development
and Growth

[7]

WHAT CAN WE EXPECT FROM A
THEORY OF DEVELOPMENT?

I. The Romantic View of Economic Theory and the Predictability Test

Various kinds of knowledge are used in an economy. Most of the
knowledge employed does not involve ideas about how the economy
as a whole works. But some decisions, especially those taken at the
central governmental level, do or should involve conception about
the operation of the economy as a whole. This is an age when experts
are frequently asked to give advice on governmental policies. Economic development theories may, to some extent, influence the
advice given. It is therefore of interest to examine the nature of such
knowledge. In this paper I will discuss what we may expect from
economic growth theories as they are presently developed; and also
what, in principle, we may expect from the kinds of theories that are
likely to be created in the near future. For the most part, development
theories of an aggregative nature are under consideration.

A prejudice against methodological work is part of the tradition
in English speaking countries. As a consequence, many economists
do not write on the subject of knowledge or examine their own
methodological preconceptions in a rigorous fashion. Nevertheless,
there is some discussion of these matters on an informal basis and
certain views have been developed that, to the extent one can judge,
seem to have a fairly high degree of acceptance. I believe that these
views, many of which have developed informally, and some of which
have developed as a consequence of Professor FRIEDMAN's famous
essay[1], represent what might be called a 'romantic' approach to
economic theory. To be specific, we might look upon the following
assertions as part of the romantic view: (1) An economic theory
should be testable; (2) it should lead to prediction of at least a conditional character; (3) it should be conceivably falsifiable by events
in the outside world, if it is to be considered a meaningful theory;
(4) if it is true, then it should not have been falsified by events; and

1. M. FRIEDMAN, 'The Methodology of Positive Economics'; in: *Essays in
Positive Economics*, Chicago, University of Chicago Press, 1953, pp. 3–43.

1

HARVEY LEIBENSTEIN

(5) it should pass the same tests in principle, and possibly in practice, as theories in laboratory sciences.

I think that most of the above statements, or their equivalents, would be agreed upon by a great many economists. Yet I want to argue that all of the above statements are either wrong or inapplieable with respect to a very important class of economic theories, but in particular, with respect to economic development theories. The essence of the romantic view is that prediction is the only criterion of really meaningful 'scientific' knowledge.

Why should there be so much concern about prediction? The virtue of prediction as a test of a theory is that it can be a *sharp* test. That is to say, it is a test that is less subject to argument than other tests. This is especially true of laboratory prediction. If A claims that his theory produces a certain result and states the nature of his experiment to prove it, then B can replicate the experiment and determine whether or not the claim is justified. But as a *sharp* test, prediction functions most effectively as a rejection rule. That is to say, if the prediction does not work out, then the theory should be rejected. It shows that, within its sphere, the theory does not have universal predictive capacity. We cannot have a prediction test that is also an acceptance test since there is always the possibility that the next prediction will fail. Acceptance is always tentative.

It is also important to note that the importance of prediction as a scientific test is open to debate. However, it is not a matter that scholars will necessarily agree about, since it depends neither on logic nor on empirical matters. Although it may be true that the majority view in economics is that the purpose and test of scientific propositions is prediction, this is, nevertheless, simply a matter of faith or of taste. It is just as reasonable, in my view, to argue (indeed I believe it to be more reasonable) that the purpose of scientific theories is to obtain coherent explanations of phenomena and events. And it so happens that increased predictive power is often a by-product of having a *coherent explanation*[2]. It is from this point of view that prediction is sometimes used as a test. However, predictive capacity

2. Science creates bridges between facts. We integrate these bridges and facts with other experience. It is this awareness of 'bridges' and their integration that enables us to understand relationships. These 'bridges' are frequently facts arranged in precisely describable patterns—sometimes expressed in equations. These

WHAT CAN WE EXPECT FROM A THEORY OF DEVELOPMENT?

without explanatory capacity is really worthless. Mere clairvoyance, irrespective of its sharpness, does not itself have scientific standing. It is only predictive capacity, that arises out of having coherent and *communicable* explanations, that does have scientific standing. The power to predict is really subsidiary to the power to explain. In other words, explanation without prediction is sufficient, *but prediction without explanation is of no consequence from a scientific standpoint.*

The prediction test is frequently restricted to 'conditional prediction'. That is, the theory is supposed to work only under some specified set of conditions, and in some sciences these conditions can be established artificially in a laboratory. But where the specified conditions cannot be established artificially, or where the effects of changing conditions cannot be calculated exactly, then the prediction test ceases to be a sharp test. Aggregative economic theories fall into a category where conditional prediction cannot, strictly speaking, be applied.

Ideally, economic development theories are theories about unfolding segments of history in an environment that remains constant. But since we cannot stop one segment of the world while another segment of the same world is allowed to develop, conditional prediction cannot readily be applied as a sharp test that yields true or false answers to the questions of validity. The experience that such theories attempt to analyze is imbedded in an essential way in the matrix of general history. It is usually impossible to separate clearly from the total historical experience only those elements that we arbitrarily choose to study. Hence, if a prediction test is to apply generally[3], it must predict actual events.

II. The Prediction Engine and the Separability Hypothesis

Theories are more than simply prediction engines. Indeed even when they fail as prediction engines, they may still have many useful properties. This, in part, accounts for the fact that theories may be re-

patterns or sets of patterns sometimes have a time dimension, hence they make prediction possible. But prediction is a frequent, although not a necessary consequence of explanation.

3. Of course, a conditional prediction test may be possible in some instances for some individual development hypotheses.

3

HARVEY LEIBENSTEIN

tained even after they have clearly failed as predictive devices. What, then, are some of the other properties we may look for in a theory?

From a theory of development we expect at least a fruitful vocabulary—a set of concepts that enables us to reduce the multiplicity of detailed observations into a small enough bundle of general concepts that they may be discussed efficiently. But we also want something more—something that tells us how development works. The term development usually encompasses a number of events that occur and must be understood. Since development is an abstract term, we want to 'explain' its components at a somewhat lower level of abstraction; such as is evident in the growth in per capita income, the changing rate of investment, changes in labor productivity, the process of capital accumulation, the nature of population growth, and so on. We assume that many of these factors are related to each other and we want to understand, if possible, how they change, especially in their relations to each other.

I have suggested some minimal expectations from a theory: (1) a consistent vocabulary, and (2) some notions about the relations between the various components of 'development phenomena' to enable a partial understanding of how they operate simultaneously. But still we probably want something more. Let us now pause for a moment and see what we *cannot* expect from such a theory. *We cannot expect a theory that will tell us how history unfolds indefinitely, given certain data to begin with.* Although economic theories are often written so that they appear to do this, they in fact cannot, and we must keep this in mind at the outset in order to avoid misunderstanding. For example, some theories of the business cycle appear to suggest that if only we could determine the parameters underlying the difference or differential equations in which such theories are couched, we would be able to predict how the cycle will unfold, given certain initial data. Of course, we are usually not surprised when it does not quite work out in that way. But I believe that we should not blame our failures on our lack of ingenuity in measuring parameters. Rather, the difficulty lies in some intrinsic qualities of social phenomena that are frequently likely to make it impossible to succeed at such efforts; qualities that are frequently forgotten because we seek theories analogous to theories in physics.

4

WHAT CAN WE EXPECT FROM A THEORY OF DEVELOPMENT?

By the very nature of things our theories must be partial—they cannot take into account all human and social phenomena. But the unfolding of economic history is a consequence of the totality of the interactions of all human and social relationships. This, in itself, would not be crucial if the set of phenomena that economists choose to study were *separable* from other phenomena; i.e., if economic events were determined only by the economic relationships considered within our theories and not influenced by anything else. But since they are influenced by other matters, and since these are matters that cannot be accounted for on the basis of existing knowledge, we cannot determine the unfolding of economic history simply on the basis of economic theory.

Another way of looking at the matter is to distinguish between two types of parameters and to recognize that some parameters are likely to change, irrespective of our ingenuity in measurement. We may distinguish between *environmental parameters* and the *internal parameters* of the system. By the internal parameters we have in mind the values of the constants of the equations that describe the relations of the system. By the environmental parameters we have in mind the values of those elements that describe the environment under which the system operates. In fact, when economists elaborate their theories they assume the environment to remain constant but they do not specify the nature of the environment in detail. It is obvious that the environmental parameters change constantly and that the operation of the system is not empirically independent of the values of these parameters. Hence, a correct system in the predictive sense—a system that will, in fact, predict what will actually happen—is, in principle, impossible. Even if we knew all of the necessary initial data, as the system unfolds the environmental parameters would change; they would influence some of the variables within the system and the results would not be in accordance with what we would have predicted at the outset[4]. To see what is involved we note that this is

4. The French mathematician and physicist HENRI POINCARÉ developed this idea from a somewhat different viewpoint. 'I imagine a world in which the various parts can conduct heat so perfectly that they maintain a constant equilibrium of temperature...

Now let us imagine that this world cools slowly through radiation; the temperature will remain everywhere uniform, but will diminish with time. I imagine

precisely the sort of thing that the laboratory scientist is able to get
away from by creating an artificial environment in the laboratory
whose state he is able to control. Until the economist is able to obtain
laboratory controlled economic conditions, he will not be able to
test many of his theories in the same sense that the laboratory scientist
is often able to. This is not to suggest that the laboratory scientist
never runs into situations similar to those that face the economist, it
is to suggest that the economist cannot create the situation for his
work that the laboratory scientist is *often* able to create.

But the problem of predicting economic history is really deeper
than that. If a partial theory were correct it would still not be possible
to predict changes in the environmental parameters, because this
involves a knowledge of the total system that, in fact, the economist
does not even attempt to known. The problem is really more difficult,
since it is impossible to know *in principle*, as well as in fact, whether
the partial system is correct or not.

The system that the economist is interested in is really part of a
larger system of relations that is unknown in its totality. Thus he
is interested in part of a total system. Can we know the part without
knowing the system as a whole. To see what is involved consider the
simplified case in which the system as a whole is a three variable
system and the part is a two variable system. Let X, Y, and Z be the
variables in the larger system. The relations between X, Y, and Z
will form a surface in three dimensional space. Now suppose that we
could only observe X and Y without taking into account the relations
between X and Z, and Y and Z. Suppose our theory assumes that
X is a certain function of Y. We may, in fact, observe historical values

also that one of the inhabitants falls into a state of lethargy and awakens after a
few centuries. Let us grant, since we have already assumed so many things, that
he is able to live in a cooler world and that he can remember previous experiences.
He will notice that his descendants still write treatises on physics, that they still
make no mention of thermometry, but that the laws which they teach are very
different from those which he knew. For example, he had been told that water
boils at a pressure of 10 millimeters of mercury, and the new physicists observe that
in order for water to boil the pressure must be decreased to 5 millimeters. A body
which he had known in the liquid state will now be found only in the solid state,
and so forth. The mutual relations among the various parts of the universe all
depend on temperature, and as soon as the temperature changes, everything is
upset.' *Mathematics and Science: Last Essays*, Dover, 1912 ed., p. 11.

6

WHAT CAN WE EXPECT FROM A THEORY OF DEVELOPMENT?

of X and historical values of Y and attempt to draw a regression line from these two sets of values. However, an infinite number of such lines can occur because the value of X that happens depends not only on the value of Y that occurs, but also on the value of Z that occurs simultaneously. Hence, the regression line so obtained is not really a reflection of the relation between X and Y but may be much more a reflection of the way in which Z happens to change historically. Similarly, any set of relations of the partial system obtained while ignoring the rest of the system, are really *pseudo-relationships* that depend, to some extent, on historical circumstances.

This problem would not arise if the partial system could, in fact, be entirely *separated* from the total system. Suppose that all but one of the equations of the partial system did not involve any variables of the total system. And suppose further, that the one equation involving such a variable connecting the partial system to the total system, could for some reason be predicted in each instance on other grounds. In that case the degree of separability of the two systems would be virtually complete and it would clearly make sense to consider the partial system as a system in its own right. But, in fact, it is hardly likely that this is the case for that set of phenomena that involves economic development. The consequence of this condition is that if we work with the partial system and try to estimate its parameters on the basis of historical data, the estimates will have no relation to the parameters of the total system even in those equations that are the same in the two systems. These parameters are, in principle, of a type that will appear to change from time to time even if the parameters of the total system are in fact stable and fixed. Of course, we do not know whether the parameters of the total system are in some sense or other given for all time[5]. But even if they were, the subsystem that we work with would still be one that would appear to be

5. F.S.C. NORTHROP emphasizes the importance of the law of conservation in classical physics and the lack of a counterpart postulate in economics. His essential point seems to be that the specific properties of economic relations are not based on parameters that are fixed over time. In fact he argues that relations in economics are specified only in terms of their generic properties whereas, in the physical sciences, both the generic and the specific properties are specified. See his 'The Method and Limited Predictive Power of Classical Economic Science', in: *The Logic of the Sciences and Humanities*, Meridian ed., Cleveland, World Publishing Co., 1962, pp. 235–54.

HARVEY LEIBENSTEIN

changing all the time. On the basis of these considerations we could not expect our economic sub-system to be a theory that predicts the unfolding of economic history if the theory is really a partial system rather than a complete system.

III. Analytical Frameworks, Theories, and Models

Not all theoretical work ends in the creation of theories in the narrow sense. In what follows I will try to distinguish between various types of theoretical efforts, in order to help determine the sort of 'theoretical entities' we might expect in the development field. Unfortunately, there is no standardized vocabulary in this area. But it may be useful to distinguish three types of theoretical work.

(1) We want especially to distinguish an analytical framework from a theory proper. By a theory we have in mind a set of relations that are sufficiently specified so that some conceivably falsifiable conclusions can be reached. At least some of the conclusions resulting from the theory are, at least in principle, in a form that makes it possible for facts not in conformity with the theory to occur. In other words, such a theory does say something about the world of facts. Usually this requires that the parameters of at least some of the equations describing the relationships be sufficiently specified that the variables of the system can take on only some values and not *all* values. In sum, we might say that theories enable us to make assertions about the world of events. In laboratory situations these would often enable us to make predictions under controlled conditions.

(2) By an analytical framework I have in mind a set of relationships that do not lead to specific conclusions about the world of events. In other words, in an analytical framework the parameters are not sufficiently specified to lead to conceivably falsifiable conclusions. An example should illustrate the distinction between an analytical framework and a theory. Consider the relations usually employed in price theory, the simple demand and supply functions. If we say simply that price is determined by these two relations: (a) the quantity demanded as a function of price, and (b) the quantity supplied as a function of price, then we have an analytical framework. As long as the parameters are not specified, then specific events cannot possibly contradict the confluence of these two relationships. However,

8

WHAT CAN WE EXPECT FROM A THEORY OF DEVELOPMENT?

once we say that the relationships are of a certain specific type so that we can draw a conclusion as to what would happen in the event that there is, say, an increase in demand, then we have a theory rather than an analytical framework. The analytical framework may be looked upon as the mold out of which the specific types of theories are made. The sort of predictions that the theory has to yield in principle for it to be a theory need not be a specific numerical character. It may be sufficient that it predicts a specific direction of change and no more. If this direction could be falsified by the facts, then we have a theory that explains changes in direction. ·

It is worth noting that very often it may not be possible to tell when we have a theory and when an analytical framework. The distinction may often be very subtle. For example, price theory may be written in such a way, and so many forms of the basic relations may be considered and discussed, that all events could, with hindsight, be explained on the basis of shifts in some of the basic relationships. Textbooks in economics, from this point of view, usually provide us with analytical frameworks rather than theories. In other words, they may be looked upon as toolboxes from which we can fashion theories to explain events, but they are not themselves such theories.

(3) Another distinction often made is between a theory and a model. Here, especially, there is no standardized and well recognized usage. Sometimes the words are used interchangeably while at others they are meant to refer to different types of abstract entities. Sometimes models appear to be used in the sense of what we have described as an analytical framework. However, I wish to use the term in a somewhat different way. Roughly speaking, by a model I will have in mind a less rich form of a theory. For instance, let us assume that Keynesian theory should have, say, 14 equations and 14 unknowns. Now a theoretical construct that gives some of the same results as the Keynesian theory with fewer equations and fewer unknowns may be looked upon as a model of the Keynesian theory. Clearly, the model allows for a smaller range of possibilities and considers a narrower range of phenomena than the theory, but it reaches some of the same *qualitative* conclusions. As a consequence, models are especially useful for didactic and illustrative purposes. Another variant of a model would be to have the same set of relationships as the theory but

9

HARVEY LEIBENSTEIN

with the parameters restricted to a much greater degree to bring out some of the conclusions more clearly. Thus a theory may be said to have a large variety of models that are consistent with it. For example, if in the theory of price we assume that the demand relation is negatively inclined, then a model of the theory may assume that the demand relation is not only negatively inclined, but that it is also linear. It would be easy to think of many models of this kind. Very often we have exceedingly broad, and to some extent, unstated conceptions of our theories and to elucidate their nature we are forced to use models. It is easier to understand a model than a theory since it is either simpler or, by assuming simple specific relations, it is more sharply drawn.

IV. Notes on What We Can Expect from Development Theory

The main viewpoint I wish to propound is that knowledge is incomplete, and that the known and unknown aspects of social and economic phenomena are usually not completely separable, but are organically intertwined as part of entities larger than the entity being studied. I assume that this is an essential fact connected with the study of many aspects of economic development. My aim is to see how, in view of the nature of the knowledge involved, the 'known' elements can be used in a theory of economic development. Clearly, the idea of something being 'known' is different in this area than it is in areas where knowledge is *separable*.

In considering the previous argument about the difficulty of prediction in economics, a sharp distinction must be made between predictions that involve the operation of an economy as a whole, and those that involve only propositions about the operation of *some* economic entities under controlled conditions. For example, some economic propositions may turn out to be testable for the behavior of individuals or firms under controlled conditions. There is nothing in principle to eliminate this possibility. From this point of view it is conceivable that an economic theory as a whole may eventually contain parts that are based on 'tested propositions', just as in some of the biological sciences. However, at present economics is, at least in this respect, not as well developed as biology in which at least some of the propositions are based on laboratory tests.

10

WHAT CAN WE EXPECT FROM A THEORY OF DEVELOPMENT?

If we cannot count on the predictive test, then what conditions should we expect our theories to fulfill? There are some conditions that can be stated but ultimately they depend on a belief in the nature of the empirical world that is warranted by experience. Let me suggest three major conditions that a theory should fulfill: (1) Logical consistency, (2) sound behavior assumptions, and (3) consistency with *some* past experience. The meaning of these three conditions is far from obvious, although the meaning of logical consistency is probably the easiest to agree upon.

Consider the second condition. Theories usually have two types of assumptions: (1) those that indicate the area under which the theory is supposed to work, and (2) those that indicate how the various elements or entities in the theory are assumed to behave. For example, in the theory of price an assumption about the nature of the market falls into the former category, while the assumption of profit maximization falls into the latter. Assumptions about the area encompassed by the theory are in a sense arbitrary, but assumptions about behavior are not. The entities either do or do not behave as the theory says, and I suggest that these behavior assumptions should usually be consistent with experience, where comparisons with experience can be made.

The third criterion is the most difficult to interpret. Historical experience is determined by a larger system than the one under study. Hence, what can we mean by consistency with past experience? We mean that there may be events that are so clearly not suppressed or distorted by changes in the environmental parameters that we can suppose them to be determined largely by the economic system. In that case, theory should be consistent with the *possibility* of such events. Of course, whether or not the events are of the kind indicated may be a matter of dispute. Nevertheless, this does form a desirable condition, for the theory should have some contact with the world of experience and there are at least some experiences for which such contact exists.

But if we cannot expect theories to tell us the detailed sequence of events that will occur, then what degree of consistency between theory and fact can we expect? At the very least we should expect theory to throw light on the events that are not submerged by changes in the value of the environmental parameters. But we may inquire,

11

HARVEY LEIBENSTEIN

how can the theory tell us anything, if in principle we cannot obtain the correct values for the parameters of a model, because the model is really a part of a larger and unknown model? The situation, however, may at times be one in which the parameters obtained are for periods in which the other variables do not play too great a role in determining events. As a consequence, the sub-system that we used may, for the time being, give some degree of reasonable consistency with the events that occur. That is, the model has temporary predictive value.

But note that prediction in the strict sense is still out of the question. We cannot know whether in the future the environmental parameters will or will not be relatively stable. But we may be able to use the system for an assessment of events in the past. For with respect to past events we may be able to determine whether the general situation was one of tranquility or not, and whether the environmental parameters changed greatly or little. Even though we may not know this with respect to small changes, we may believe that there has been considerable stability so that the environment had little influence in determining large changes, i.e., we may reasonably expect the theory to help explain large changes.

Now, a theory of development and the estimates of its parameters should, in many situations, be able to at least explain some general trends. Hence, one thing we might expect of a theory of development is the explanation of trends that are not submerged by environmental influences. For example, the theory should not lead us to expect a long run decline in per capita income when in fact persistent increases are observed.

A more difficult matter arises with respect to turning points. Since a turning point is likely to be the consequence of opposing influences that to some extent balance each other out, and since close to the turning point such opposing influences are near to being balanced, we would expect the difference between them to be sufficiently small so that they in fact will be submerged by the environmental influences. However, if significant turning points are, in fact, observed then our theory must, at the very least, permit such turning points to occur in principle. In addition, there should be states on either side of the turning point, where the theory would suggest that prior to the turning point the trend direction is one way, and after it, another.

12

WHAT CAN WE EXPECT FROM A THEORY OF DEVELOPMENT?

V. Major Uses
of Development Theory—Diagnosis and Policy

Although a sharp test for a development theory may not exist, a theory may nevertheless be judged by its general effectiveness in the work that it is expected to do. Such judgments would not lead to definitive conclusions. But there are many scientific matters that cannot be settled beyond any shadow of doubt. There is really no reason to expect definitive judgments. Therefore, a theory's effectiveness can form the basis for some degree of judgment about its 'validity' given the evidence about its effectiveness.

The area in which a theory should prove its effectiveness needs to be clarified. The view taken here is that the two main jobs of a theory are: (1) as an engine of analysis of an existing situation, or as a means of explaining a historical situation, and (2) as an instrument for policy determination. These elements are closely related.

My basic underlying assumption is that *diagnosis should precede prescription.* In an economic system policies cannot be determined once and for all in such a way as to set the system right for ever after. As a consequence, there is a need for continuous diagnosis. Diagnostic tools should, if possible, be of an organized rather than of a random nature. Therefore, a theory that *in some way* (and to some degree) provides an organized set of diagnostic tools, is desirable from this viewpoint.

I have spoken previously about analytical frameworks. I have also suggested that the job of the theorist is, in part, to provide the frameworks that function as a mold for different kinds of models. This, it would seem to me, is one of the things we might expect from theoretical efforts in the development field. Now the models that result from such frameworks should be seen to contain *sample* propositions. These propositions are essentially relationships that in themselves are not necessarily true. They are samples in the sense that they suggest the form that the theory should take. After investigation, the actual relationships decided upon may be different from the initial samples. But obviously it is desirable to have samples at the outset.

Now some of the sample relations should involve propositions that in this initial form, or in some modified form, are likely to work

13

HARVEY LEIBENSTEIN

frequently. It is useful, in this context, to conceive a theory to be constructed from an integrated and organized system of sample relations, at least some of which are presumed to work 'frequently'.

I have suggested that although sharp prediction employed as a rejection rule is an inappropriate criterion, I have by no means eliminated some degree of prediction as a quality of some aspects of a theory. An example from medicine should help to clarify this idea. We may know, for example, that a given quantity of aspirin will frequently cure a headache. This type of knowledge contains some of the qualities that we might expect in a good economic development theory. (1) It is certainly a useful bit of information. (2) It is knowledge that does not pass the prediction test employed as a rejection rule. There are some headaches that aspirin does not cure. Nevertheless, we do not throw out the information because of this discovery. (3) It is the sort of knowledge that lacks precision but is nonetheless highly useful. The term 'headache' is not clearly defined. Nor for that matter is the term 'frequently' defined. Yet if this is all we know about the relation between aspirins and headaches, it would certainly be useful. Also, we can look upon it as a sample relation. We may, if we wish, get a more precise relation for some specific individual. Thus, we can take a sample and study its effectiveness with specific individuals and thereby improve upon the precision of the relation in this context. For some individuals we may find that a given dosage cures headaches all the time. For others, it may work but with certain undesirable side effects. And for some individuals it may not work at all. Nevertheless, it is quite obvious that as a sample relation it was certainly a useful one and further that it contained some degree of predictability.

Previously, we spoke about the prediction of trends. Trends may be predicted because a few relatively well understood elements that function in a given direction are seen to operate with sufficient magnitude in that direction that we believe this direction will continue for some indefinite time in the foreseeable future. Again, some degree of predictability is involved. There is also a relation between the magnitude of the independent variable and our feelings about the degree of predictability. In the previous example we may believe that very small dosages of aspirin are unlikely to cure the headaches. But that if we increase the dosage, the likelihood of cure might increase ac-

14

WHAT CAN WE EXPECT FROM A THEORY OF DEVELOPMENT?

cordingly, at least up to some point. Similarly, in driving an automobile it is unnecessary to know the exact relation between pressure on the accelerator and the speed that will be achieved. All we need know is that under given road conditions an increase in pressure will yield an increase in speed. Indeed, knowing this much about any automobile certainly operates as a useful sample relation despite the fact that the actual relation will differ in degree for different types of automobiles. Similarly, an economic theory may contain relations of a monotonic nature between increase in capital and increases in output. This relation may be a useful sample relation despite the fact that it lacks precision. Indeed, as with the aspirin example it would be useful even if, in fact, it did not work all the time but if it did work frequently.

Frequency is a matter of degree. However, we cannot say on *a priori* grounds what degree of frequency is adequate. Of course, on a *ceteris paribus* assumption, a theory whose relations work more frequently is superior to one that works less frequently. But the *ceteris paribus* assumption may not hold in different instances. In addition, some degrees of frequency may be so low as to make the theory uninteresting from an applied viewpoint. But the concept 'interesting' is admittedly a subjective notion. This means, in essence, that judgments on these matters cannot be mechanized.

But we do want theories that enable us to predict broad stable equilibrium paths for some time period with some reasonable degree of frequency, where 'reasonable' is a subjective, undefined term. The sample relations of the theory should suggest real relations so that prediction within some bounds may follow. The bounds will deal with time if the prediction is only of a directional character, and with the value of the variables that are predicted if the predictions are numerical. In other words, on the basis of some initial condition, there should be a time period such that within that time period we predict the values to fall within a certain broad path. This is illustrated in the figure below. Time is shown on the x axis and the predicted variable on the y axis. The area I is the area in which the initial conditions fall, and the area P is the area in which the predicted path should fall. At each time point the predicted path has a width W and the time dimension of the path is T.

Now, normally we would expect that the frequency with which

15

the prediction holds would depend on the variable width vector W and the time, T. Thus we would have a functional relation:

$$F = g\ (W,\ T)$$

To say that a theory works, in the sense that we have used the term, means that F is greater than zero for some values of W and T. Of course, to be interesting, the value of F would have to be greater than some minimum for a value of W less than some maximum, and a value of T greater than some minimum. While this introduces matters of judgment into what we mean by working, our concept is nevertheless meaningful, even if there are some subjective judgment elements involved.

How are these ideas related to the notion of theory as an engine of analysis? The sample relations suggest the areas we should investigate in an actual economy in order to see the extent to which any of them have worked frequently. The analytical framework would suggest additional sample relations and would operate as a means of organizing disparate relationships. To the extent that a number of the relations seem to have worked frequently we may, after study, come to understand some periods in that economy's development. Furthermore, we may come to understand enough of various elements in its development that we can point to the aspects of the economy that presented bottlenecks to further growth as well as those that were conducive to growth. It is clearly such knowledge that should enable us to diagnose current difficulties and the relation between current difficulties, current events, and the presumed aims that the analyst assumes exist for the economy. This is obviously the stage where some prescriptions could be attempted. I see this as a continuous process in which there is a continuous interaction between theory refinement, the analysis of a particular economy, and prescription.

Return now to the basic notion that although detailed prediction is out of the question in many cases, it may be possible to predict the direction of events. But even that may not be possible in all cases because the environmental parameters or variables may be more important at times than the forces considered in the theory. However, *some policy instruments may be of such a kind that they can be used in various sizes or to various degrees, and for some sizes or degrees their impact*

WHAT CAN WE EXPECT FROM A THEORY OF DEVELOPMENT?

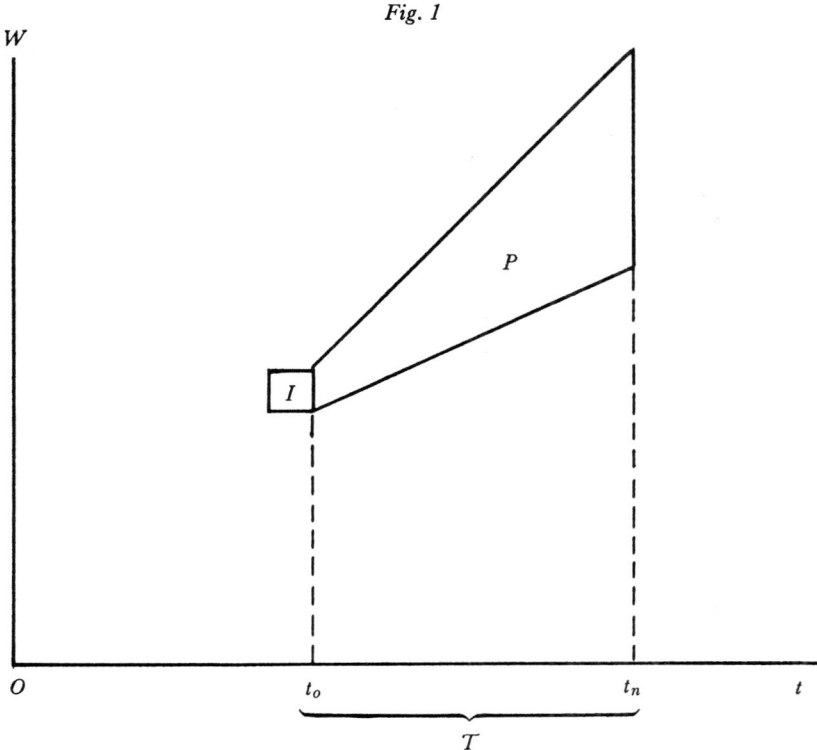

Fig. 1

will be larger than that of the environmental parameters. Under such circumstances it may be possible to determine the direction of change by using the policy instrument to a sufficient degree. Where this is done successfully it would surely prove the usefulness of a theory (even if it would not prove its 'correctness').

Consider a Keynesian type theory in a situation of underemployment. The theory may suggest that an increase in the rate of investment is necessary to increase the level of employment. It may not be possible, however, to determine the exact relation between a given increase in investment and a given increase in employment. The environmental parameters make such a determination impossible. But we would expect, if the theory is a good one, that an increase in investment would increase employment. Perhaps a small increase in investment would not do so. In that case we would increase the

17

HARVEY LEIBENSTEIN

investment rate still further and see what happens. If the theory about the direction of change is correct, then we would expect that under normal circumstances a sufficiently large increase in investment would overcome any environmental forces operating in the opposite direction. Thus, each increase in investment would result in a change that would tell us whether we have gone in the right direction. If not, then we could correct the situation by increasing the dose. In such a way we should eventually be able to approach a full employment state. A theory that would lend itself to procedures of this sort would clearly be more persuasive than one that would not. It is similar to a capacity to drive a car on unknown and unmarked roads in order to reach a certain destination with the aid of only a compass, and with only a knowledge of the initial point and the end point. We cannot determine the optimum way of getting to the destination. Nor can we always be sure that we will get on to a road that will always go in the right direction. But the compass enables us, every so often, to check our progress with respect to direction, to correct errors, and eventually to reach the destination. Clearly, some predictive power is necessary in such cases. But it need not be a power that is universally correct and the quality of the prediction is of a much lower order than that required by the strict prediction-rejection test.

Now what should we expect from a development theory? Briefly put, we should expect a conceptual framework that would facilitate the creation of theories or models that contain manipulable variables whose dosages can be raised sufficiently to swamp the environmental effects and sufficiently to obtain accurate directional predictions for a limited period of time. This leaves room for many unsettled issues.

In this connection a special problem might arise with respect to manipulable variables whose impact appears at remote periods of time. For example, suppose that investment in education has a ten year lag in perceptible impact on output, while investment in capital has only a one year lag. Here a heroic decision may have to be made as to whether or not to use investment in education on the basis of partial data, but not on the basis of a strict test of the model. A sharp test of the kind used in the exact sciences is out of the question. The decision would have to be made with judgments based on bits of data here and there, as well as with general impressions. This approach

18

WHAT CAN WE EXPECT FROM A THEORY OF DEVELOPMENT?

clearly differs from that of the exact sciences, but we simply have to face the fact that the nature of the problems we deal with do not lend themselves to the methods of the exact sciences, and there is no point in seeking 'pseudo-tests' based on imitation.

VI. Summary and Conclusions

Although many of the points I have made are well known, the general viewpoint I end up with is radically different from that currently accepted. I have dealt with both negative and positive aspects of the problem. On the negative side I have argued against the prediction test as a rejection rule. On the positive side I have put forth a view of theory as a set of sample relations that are helpful in the discovery of specific relations in specific contexts and that we hope will work frequently in a loosely fitting servomechanism type of arrangement.

We cannot really determine whether or not an aggregative development theory is correct in the strict sense. There are no strictly true theories in this area that we would expect to work on the basis of precise prediction. In the same sense, we should not expect any universally true statements about the direction of change or about turning points. The denial of the expectation of finding *universal* truths in this area certainly differs from the contemporary view of the matter.

The views presented also have implications for economic planning. If exact numerical relations are out of the question, then precise planning cannot be based on 'true' relations. In addition it would appear that planning schemes that require optimization procedures must be based on illusory relations or what we have called pseudo-relations, given the inseparability of the highly abstracted submodel that we have to handle and the larger model whose real nature is beyond our understanding. If 'planning' is to take place without being illusory, it must be of a rather loose fitting type consistent with the nature of our knowledge.

What we can hope to do is to say something about the adequacy of certain theories within given contexts. But such assessments are to a considerable extent separate from the theory itself, or from the accuracy with which it reflects the phenomena it deals with. Rather, it may depend on the factors that happen to be socially manipulable (i.e., on available policy instruments) and on the degree to which the

19

HARVEY LEIBENSTEIN

environmental variables happen to be stable during the historical period in question. Thus, theory *A* may be more adequate than theory *B* in one period and less adequate in another. In this connection some current arguments about the desirability of having an all-embracing economic growth theory that would apply equally well to both developed and underdeveloped countries strikes me as ill conceived, since the environmental variables are likely to operate differently during different stages. There is no reason why a different theory should not apply to each stage.

Finally, what is the job of the development theorist? It is twofold: (1) to create analytical frameworks, and (2) to create *sample* theories consistent with the analytical framework. But in the absence of specific historical studies, or in the absence of specific policy situations, the sample theories are not to be looked upon as working theories but simply as illustrations of the kinds of working theories or working models that could be created. Furthermore, a working model should not be expected to work indefinitely. From time to time we would expect that old working models would have to be retired and replaced by new ones.

This view of the matter also means that our sample hypotheses or relations need to be based on fact. The view that looked upon theories as entities that are to be subjected to a rejection rule did not need to concern itself with the manner in which the hypotheses were arrived at. All that mattered was whether they passed the prediction test time after time. But if we no longer expect our theories to work in a precise predictive sense, but view them only as samples, then it is important that our sample hypotheses have some degree of credibility. And credibility would depend in part on experience. We would expect hypotheses that consistently flout experience to be poorer samples than those that frequently agree with experience in some sense.

In essence, this view is based on what appears to be a realistic judgment of the nature of economic hypotheses. There is a variety of types of scientific information. Some of it fits the categories utilized in such laboratory sciences as chemistry and physics. But not all scientific information is of this type. I have suggested a view of theory that is more complex, apparently more realistic, and one that also seems to fit the contemporary notion of cybernetic devices of a

20

WHAT CAN WE EXPECT FROM A THEORY OF DEVELOPMENT?

loosely fitting sort that is probably more applicable to social organization, than an interpretation based on a stricter, more mechanistic viewpoint.

University of California,   HARVEY LEIBENSTEIN
Berkeley

SUMMARY

Prediction as a rejection test for theories is limited and unnecessarily severe. Useful knowledge frequently does not fall into this mold. Also the prediction test does not follow from the view that science provides coherent explanations of experience. The inapplicability of prediction as a sharp test is especially likely to be true for macro-economic development theories. Thus it may not be meaningful to say that a given theory is correct or incorrect in a strict sense. Where the phenomena that a theory covers is inseparable from a large system in which it is imbedded then it may be impossible in principle to discover the true relations between variables. Although no single simple test may exist for a class of theories there may be a number of considerations that help us judge the adequacy of some theories.

Development theories may be looked upon as sets of partially connected *sample* relations that operate within a changing environment. Such relations should be credible. Sample relations based on hypotheses that constantly flout experience are likely to be poor samples. Thus the realism of assumptions matter. Theories of the type considered may be useful in that the sample relations are helpful in the discovery of specific relations in specific contexts that we hope will work frequently in a loose fitting servo-mechanistic type of arrangement so that (1) diagnoses of existing difficulties can be made, and (2) corrective policies fashioned which, while they cannot be expected to work universally, do work sufficiently frequently in terms of directional changes to be of interest.

ZUSAMMENFASSUNG

Theorien danach zu bewerten, ob sie Prognosen ermöglichen, ist nur von begrenztem Nutzen und überdies eine unnötig strenge Bedingung; auch wenn sie diese Bedingung nicht erfüllen, können ökonomische Theorien durchaus brauchbar sein. Ebenso lässt sich die Berechtigung dieses Tests auch nicht daraus ableiten, dass es die Wissenschaft uns ermöglicht, Ereignisse und Erscheinungen der ökonomischen Wirklichkeit logisch zu erklären. Vor allem auf makro-ökonomische Entwicklungstheorien kann dieser Test nicht rigoros angewendet werden. Es ist deshalb auch nicht unbedingt sinnvoll, unter Anwendung dieses Kriteriums eine Theorie als «richtig» oder «falsch» zu bezeichnen. Sobald der Vorgang, den

HARVEY LEIBENSTEIN

eine Theorie zu erklären sucht, überdies nur Teil eines grösseren Systems ist, kann es ja auch a priori unmöglich sein, die genauen Relationen zwischen den einzelnen Variablen zu bestimmen. Obschon es somit für eine bestimmte Kategorie von Theorien keinen rigorosen «Richtigkeits»-Test gibt, können wir dennoch mit Hilfe verschiedener Methoden die Adäquanz dieser Theorien prüfen.

Entwicklungstheorien können aufgefasst werden als Systeme partiell interdependenter hypothetischer Relationen innerhalb eines sich ändernden Rahmens. Solche Relationen sollten an sich zuverlässig sein; wichtig ist, dass sie realistisch sind und nicht auf wirklichkeitsfremden Hypothesen basieren. Diese Relationen sollten uns helfen, bestimmte Beziehungen bestimmter Problemkreise aufzuzeigen; wir können gleichzeitig hoffen, dass sie wenigstens soweit zusammenhängen, dass wir 1. in der Lage sind, Diagnosen bestimmter Probleme zu stellen, und 2. auch korrigierende Massnahmen formulieren können. Wir dürfen zwar nicht erwarten, dass sie universell gültig sind, doch können sie immerhin soweit operationell sein, dass sie uns darüber Auskunft geben können, in welcher Richtung eine Korrektur zu erfolgen hat.

RÉSUMÉ

L'appréciation des théories selon leur aptitude à permettre des pronostics semble inutilement sévère. Des théories utiles sont souvent dépourvues de cette qualité. De même la justification de ce test ne dérive pas du fait, que la science nous donne des explications cohérentes de l'expérience. Spécialement pour les théories de développement macro-économiques, ce test est inapplicable. Pour cette raison, ce n'est pas nécessairement sensé de juger une théorie comme correcte ou incorrecte en se basant sur ce critère. Dès que le phénomène, qu'une théorie essaie d'expliquer, n'est qu'une partie d'un grand système, il est impossible de déterminer les vraies relations entre les variables. Bien qu'il n'existe pas un seul test compétant pour une certaine catégorie de théories, nous pouvons quand-même juger la validité de quelques théories à l'aide d'un nombre de considérations.

Les théories de développement peuvent être considérées comme des systèmes de relations *d'exemples* partiellement liées opérant dans un environnement changeant. De telles relations devraient être croyables; il est important, qu'elles soient réalistes et ne se basent pas sur des hypothèses non vérifiables. Ces relations d'exemples devraient nous aider à découvrir des relations spécifiques dans des contextes spécifiques; nous pouvons en même temps espérer qu'elles soient liées de telle façon, à ce que nous puissions 1. être capables de poser des diagnostics sur des difficultés existantes et 2. de formuler des mesures correctives. Nous ne pouvons supposer que ces relations aient une portée universelle, mais qu'elles opèrent suffisamment pour pouvoir nous indiquer frequemment la direction de la correction.

22

[8]

WHY DO WE DISAGREE ON INVESTMENT POLICIES FOR DEVELOPMENT ?

I. Introduction

THE question of investment policy for the economic development of underdeveloped areas is still, at least in my opinion, a very much unsettled matter.[1] That this should be the case is hardly surprising since the " correct policy, " if such exists, depends on the solution of a number of intellectual problems that have as yet not been solved. It is *not* my purpose, in this paper, to set forth and argue for the " correct " investment allocation policy. On the contrary I hope to show that given the present imperfect state of our knowledge with respect to the factors that are significant in economic development it is impossible to come to a definitive conclusion on this matter. Different scholars may be warranted in holding different positions with respect to investment policies. If this be so then it follows that the " orthodox position, " i.e., the position that emphasizes the *usual* interpretation of the marginal productivity criterion, has not been demonstrated to be the correct one, nor, by the same token, has any alternative position been proven to be correct beyond any shadow of doubt. Perhaps this is platitudinous and obvious. I hope so. But some of the recent, and not so recent literature on the subject, as well as both casual and serious conversations with a number of economists, has suggested to me that this is not quite the case. Many appear to hold very strong views on the matter—often very much stronger than our present knowledge would seem to warrant. It is this feeling that prompts the present attempt to analyze why different investigators may logically and reasonably reach different conclusions on this question.

II. Alternative Decision Environments

Apart from errors in logic there are two main reasons why people come to, or appear to come to, different conclusions with respect to the same problem ; different interpretations of

---

[1] The literature on this subject is now quite large and seems to be growing without abatement. For a review of some of the issue see Gerald M. Mejer and Robert. E. Baldwin, **Economic Development,** John Wiley and Sons, New York, 1957, pp. 354 ff. Also, cf. A. E. Kahn, " Investment Criteria in Development," **Quarterly Journal of Economics,** February 1951, W. Galeson and H. Leibenstein, "Investment Criteria, Productivity and economic Development," **Quarterly Journal of Economics,** August, 1955, as well as the articles by Otto Eckstein, and F. M. Bator in the August 1957 issue of the **Quarterly Journal of Economics,** and the article by A. K. Sen in the November 1957 issue of that Journal.

significant concepts, or because they start from different premises. We shall leave until later the matter of semantics. The matter of premises or assumptions is far from simple in this connection. What is involved, often implicitly, is not a difference in a single assumption, or a single set of assumptions of the *same* kind, but different premises and views of the problem that come under a variety of headings. Indeed, the word assumptions or premises may be misleading in this connection, and therefore I shall use the notion of a "decision environment" to indicate what I have in mind. The following schematic outline indicates what I mean by a decision environment, and the discussion that follows suggests its relevance to the investment decision problem.

> *Schematic Outline of the Problem*
> A. *The Situation or Situation Class.*
> B. *The Decision Environment.*

Normative
Aspect

1. Social objective or objectives
   (a) General statement of the objective(s),
   (b) Side conditions or constrains on the objective or its components,
   (c) Means of evaluating components of the objective(s).
2. Values, resraints, and views, regarding the use of instruments to achieve the objectives(s).
3. Time commitment and conditions connected with the time elements.

Economic
Aspects

1. Target variables through which one judges the object ive and its furtherance.
2. Target variables through which one judges the object-
   (a) Equation system,
   (b) Characteristics of the behavior equations,
   (c) Assessment of the value of the parameters.
3. Costs, benefits, and effects of direct (and permissable) instruments.

> C. *Policy.*

The outline suggests the main elements that may be involved in an investment policy. The specific economic situation that the country finds itself in is, of course, a crucial factor. That is to say, it would be foolish to make a specific investment allocation without taking into account the specific facts at the time the decision is made. On a higher level of abstraction we would consider a class of situations that a country might find itself in, and attempt to establish investment criteria for that class. But the point of this paper is that a knowledge of the situation is not enough to determine an investment decision, nor is a knowledge of the characteristics of the situation class sufficient to determine investment criteria. Other matters are vitally involved, and it is these other matters that I refer to as the decision environment. In a short paper one cannot be exhaustive. The points listed in the outline above are intended only to be suggestive. However, they are probably sufficient to show why reasonable and logical men who agree on the situation class might very well disagree on investment policies. But we should not jump to any conclusions at this stage. There is more to the problem than simply the fact that different individuals may differ with respect to the decision environment.

The decision environment can be devided into two parts : A normation aspect, and an economic one. The division is far from perfect, and we may argue about its exact boundary, but it will do for our purposes. One aspect of the decision environment depends on norms, aims, values, and so on. It depends on the social goals and values of the society. To that extent it is normative rather than objective or scientific. On the other hand, the economic aspect depends on our view of how the economy operates. If economics were a completed science, and all the necessary facts were available, then we might all agree on the economic aspect, although we might still differ on the normative aspect.

1. Consider the problem of choosing the development objective. There are a large number of possible objectives. But the problem is also complicated by the fact that the statement of such objectives will have a number of dimensions. For example we may consider maximizing the aggregate output stream, or the aggregate *per capita* income stream or the aggregate *per capita* consumption stream, or the average length of life, etc. But statements such as these are usually incomplete. One problem is the treatment of time. In other words, if we consider the maximization of the aggregate output stream, the question arises over what period of time it is to be maximized. Usually, we conceive of some discounting procedure and attempt to maximize the present value of the output stream. In any event something has to be said in the statement of the objective as to how the time dimension is to be handled.

Another complicating feature lies in the fact that the variable to be maximized is rarely to be considered by itself in the absence of all

372   THE INDIAN ECONOMIC JOURNAL

other considerations. In other words, what we usually ask to do is to maximize some variable subject to a number of stated constrains. Thus we might attempt to maximize the present value of the output stream subject to the constraint that the income distribution is not worsened in the process.

The objective may have more than one component (or variable) that is to be optimized. In that event some way of assessing the relative importance of different components has to be determined. Clearly, economists, as well as citizens, might differ on the appropriate objectives for development.

2.   Development is not an ultimate objective that supercedes all other considerations. Not all possible means to achieve given ends are legitimate. We shall see that the constraints that we impose on the means that we can employ may affect our investment policy.

What is involved here is in part the age old question between 'agenda and non-agenda. That is to say, with respect to what variaables are we to assume that the government or the state can interfere and control and what variables are we to assume are determined by the freely chosen actions and activities of the individuals involved. We shall also see that these sets of questions are in part related to our view of the development processes.

This point may perhaps best be indicated by a few examples. We may assume, for example, that the size of the population is determined entirely from within the system. Or we may assume that the population size can somehow be controlled by governmental action and that therefore it is a variable whose value is determined exogenously. Another possibility is that the level of consumption of population is determined within the system. Or we may assume that it is determined in part socially through a system of taxes and subsidies. Similarly we may perhaps argue that the rate of saving is determined by individual action or that it is determined by government interference. In general we can see that with respect to many variables we can make either an assumption of control or an assumption of lack of control. It will turn out that in some instances, *but not all,* we get different results depending on which set of assumptions we make.

3.   The time element enters the problem in a variety of ways. At the extremes we might consider a single, once and for all investment decision apart from any other decision, as against an investment policy to cover an infinite series of investment decisions. We shall see that there are cases where it does make a distinct difference whether the decision or criterion to be applied is with respect to an isolated case, or part of a series of decisions.

INVESTMENT POLICIES   373

4. If the social objective is stated in broad terms then there arises the problem of interpreting the objective in terms of one or more economic variables. For example, if our objective is to maximize the " standard of living " of the populace, how is this to be interpreted in economic terms. For example, how is leisure to be valued in such circumstances. We shall not go into detail in this matter, but clearly there are great possibilities for differences of opinion in this regard.

5. Really significant differences may arise with respect to our view of the development process. What will be the train of consequences that will result from a given investment allocation ? The theory of economic growth is not at present in such a state that all would readily agree on this matter. The number of possible dynamical systems that we could invent is certainly very large. Given different views of economic development processes we may (but need not always) arrive at different investment criteria. We will see that whether or not different development theories lead to different criteria will depend, in part, on the other components of the decision environment.

6. The employment of direct instruments, for example, the attempt by the state to determine directly the rate of savings, or the birth rate, is usually not costless, although such costs are often ignored in discussions. Economists may legitimately differ on the costs and consequences of direct instruments, even in those cases where the normative aspects of the decision environment permits their use. The importance of this aspect will become clearer as we proceed.

There are an infinite number of decision environments that are possible. Obviously, it would be too tedious and time consuming to consider one by one all the possible decision environments that can be obtained by varying slightly its components. As a result we shall limit ourselves to examining only a few possibilities, picked in part because they help to illustrate some interesting points.

We will find that there does not exist a one-to-one correspondance between the alternative combinations of objectives, theories, socially determined parameters, etc., and the allocation criteria that can be deduced from them. Rather, we shall see that there are many-to-one correspondences. Namely, there are sets of combinations which lead to different criteria. That is to say we can outline a set of objectives, theories, and socially constraints, and so on, for which a given allocation criteria may be correct for each of the combinations within the set. But there is more than one such set, and as a consequences there is more than one " reasonable " allocation criterion. However, the fact that there are often a number of decision environments consistent with a given criterion may sometimes have given the impression that the criterion is universally (or almost universally) applicable.

III. The Investment Allocation Problem

Before we proceed any further it is well to indicate the exact nature of the problem we have in mind. We begin with a given decision environment. Next, we assume that there is a given investment fund available, and that some central agency is in a position to influence or determine the allocation strategy. We differentiate between the allocation strategy and the mechanism of allocation. These are really two separate matters, although they are in some cases related to each other. For present purposes we are concerned only with allocation strategies and not with the question of the optimal mechanism under which to carry out the appropriate strategy. Thus we are not concerned with whether the government actually makes the allocations, or whether these are made through the mechanism of private enterprisers operating on their own, or operating under a system of subsidies and taxes, etc.

The given investment fund available at the outset can be allocated among a number of industries or uses. The two main aspects of the allocation problem solved simultaneously, in practice, are (1) the allocation between industries and (2) the allocation among techniques. Any concrete allocation must involve choosing the technique while one chooses simultaneously the industry. But to simplify the discussion we shall assume, except where we specifically indicate otherwise, that the allocation is to be made among industries. That is, we assume that for each indutry the technique of production is given, unless otherwise stated.[2]

Now we have to distinguish between an " allocation plan " and an " allocation ". By an allocation plan we have in mind any specific allocation of the investment fund among the industries. Thus if A is an allocation plan, we may write $a_1,...,a_k$ as the details of this allocation plan. In other words, a_i denotes the amount of the investment fund that is to be used for the addition of capital in the ith industry. We view a_i as a specific allocation and A as an allocation Plan. There are, of course, innumerable allocation plans that are possible and our problem is to pick that allocation plan which most meets the objective contained in the decision environment. The general allocation problem is to find a criterion or principle (i.e., a startegy) by which to order or rank alternative allocation plans. Usually the allocation plans are in themselves of so complex a nature, or their consequences taken as a whole are so complex, that it is not possible to rank alternative

---

[2] We can get around this problem by defining " industry " in such a way so that the production of a commodity with a different technique implies as different industry. The reader may substitute this interpretation for the one in the text if he wishes.

plans directly. An alternative (and usual) procedure is to find a means of evaluating the consequences; for example, the income stream, of a specific allocation. By comparing the consequences of alternative allocations, and by shifting units of investment from one allocation to another until the consequences are equated at the margin an optimum is obtained. In this manner the ranking of allocation plans is achieved indirectly.

More specifically, the usual scheme is to assume that there is a specific consequence that follows from a specific allocation. Let us write c_i for the consequence that follows from the allocation a_i. Once we know the set of consequences c_i, for all i, and once we are able to tell what happens when we shift a small amount of investment from industry i to industry, j, or *vice versa*, we are then able to apply the well known equi-marginal principle in order to obtain a maximum.[3] But it is important to observe that this really does not tell us very much about the solution of the problem in any concrete situation. What it does do is merely suggest some of the questions that have to be answered in order to approach a solution. For example, (1) What are the consequences to be considered for any specific allocation ? (2) How are these consequences generated by the economic system as a whole ? That is to say, how do we visualize the process that generates the stream of consequences resulting from a specific allocation ? (3) Are the consequences unique and unalterable by social action or can they be changed, to some extent, by interference of a social agency ? (4) For any given allocation what is the variety and range of consequences and how are these consequences related to each other ? etc.

The time element enters the problem in several significant ways. We have already alluded to the fact that the time factor may enter implicitly or explicitly in the determination of the development objective. One consequence of this is that we have to devise means by which to judge alternate output streams ; for example, through a discounting technique, that enables us to evaluate alternate streams in terms of their present values.

But the time element enters the picture in a more fundamental sense. There is a time aspect to our view of the allocation problem.

---

[3] At no point should we argue against the applicability of the equi-marginal principle, or some variant thereof. The appropriateness of the calculus to maximum problems is not in question. Even in those case where it appears that the marginal productivity criterion is not applicable, we should not argue against the " marginal " aspect of the criterion. The argument rather is always to be understood to be with respect to the content of the criterion and not the application of the marginal concept as such. The marginal concept may be said to be contentless. Economists' arguments, should not be about the mathematics of maximization.

Namely, are we to be concerned with a single allocation plan or a sequence of them. That is, the determination of the allocation plan for one year may be very different, if we determine it as a once-and-for-all matter, apart from future plans, or if we determine it in connection with a series of future plans. In other words, the strategy for a single year need not be the same as the strategy for that year when we are simultaneously considering the strategy for n years.

Now, the time elements probably determine the extent to which the indirect effects of an allocation plan should be taken into account. It is likely that the greater the time period that is considered the more significant are the indirect aspects of the problem, and the less applicable are the *ceteris paribus* assumptions. But the longer the series of allocation decisions to be made, the greater the possibility of taking into account and influencing some of the indirect effects.

We now state in a few words the crux of our analysis. We distinguish between the *direct* and *indirect* consequences that we attribute to specific allocations. By a direct consequence we have in mind the increase in the output stream in a given industry that results from the allocation of investment to that industry. The indirect consequences are all of the other effects that may be attributed to this allocation, either by itself or in connection with the rest of a specified allocation plan, or series of plans. The hearth of the matter is whether the indirect consequences are significant for development purposes. The differences between the few models that we shall elaborate, and the allocation criteria appropriate to them, and between a host of other possible models, will rest almost entirely on the extent to which the indirect consequences of given allocation are taken into account.

To elaborate this idea, we might specify briefly some of the indirect consequences that come to mind. The allocation plan may affect (1) the future investment as well as the future output stream. (2) It may affect the propensities to consume and the propensities to save. (3) The allocation plan and the accumulation of capital that results thereby, may change the environment in which work takes place and in this way may possibly affect, (a) intensity of effort, (b) the energy of the work force, (c) the degree to which the labour force is willing to adhere to work displine, (d) the degree to which they develop feather bedding and innovation-retarding practices, (e) the nature of work morale, (f) the degree of economic and social mobility, and a host of other similar factors. (4) The allocation, by affecting the structure of capital, will affect the productivity of the labour force from the point of view of establishing a new relationship between the capital structure and the skill structure of the work force. (5) Finally, the allocation plan, and its consequent capital accumulation, may affect the social and cultural environment under which the economy operates, and in turn affect various aspects of the quality of the population. We shall elaborate on some of these matters as we proceed.

INVESTMENT POLICIES   377

IV. *Some Alternative Models Considered*

If there were no space and time limitations, then we might consider, one by one, a large number of decision environments. But in view of such limitations a rather brief characterization and comparison of only a few decision environments will have to suffice. We shall consider two for which the social marginal productivity criterion is correct, and then sketch one environment for which the social marginal productivity criterion does not apply. Finally we shall discuss some of the critical elements that would determine the applicability of social marginal productivity or other criteria.

Model 1—A neo-classical type model

For our first decision environment we shall assume : (1) that the objective of development is to maximize the present value of the *aggregate* output stream ; and (2) that there exists some acceptable discounting procedure, and discount rate.

The theory we have in mind for this particular decision environment is that which comes closest to the static, conventional, microeconomic (text-book variety) model of the economic process. We assume the existence of factors of production, human and non-human, which form the stock of potential inputs. These inputs are combined in the production process in order to yield the stream of outputs. Investment, in this model, is defined as the net addition to the stock of non-human inputs. It is further assumed that during the time period involved the quality, size, and nature of the work force remains constant.

The consequence of investment, in this case, is simply, and only, to add to the stock of capital goods. The allocation problem here is reduced to a comparison of those income streams that result as a consequence of alternate allocation plans, and to the choice of a startegy that leads to that allocation plan whose output stream has a present value that is equal to or greater than that of all alternative allocation plans. The conventional marginal productivity principles is clearly effective here. The allocation of funds to a given industry results in an increase in the present value of that output stream. At the margin one can determine the present value of the output stream that results from the marginal input of investment in that industry. By comparing the marginal productivities thus defined, that is, the addition to the present value of the output stream that results from the application of a marginal increment to the capital stock, and allocating the capital fund so that the marginal productivities are equal for all industries, we maximize the addition to the output stream.

In this case only the *direct* consequences of any specific allocation are taken into account. Note the assumption that the total consequences of an allocation plan are no larger than the sum of direct

378   THE INDIAN ECONOMIC JOURNAL

consequences of each of the specific allocations. That is to say, there are no social economies or social diseconomies that enter the picture. The marginal productivity of an allocation and the *social* marginal productivity of that allocation are one and the same thing in this particular case. However, this is not always the situation, and we must allow for those instances.

It is not altogether clear from the literature how the word " social " in " social marginal productivity " is to be intepreted. There are at least two meanings that we could attach to the adjective " social ". (1) We can assume that the marginal product of an allocation has a different social valuation than its individual private valuation. This may be because of effects of the production activity which are not taken into account in determining private costs and prices. The usual examples are such things as smoke nuisances, noise, etc. There exist in production processes costs which, because of their nature, are not borne privately. Likewise there may be social benefits of the same nature.

The other meaning that may be attached to the adjective " social," in this context, is that the output of the allocation plan is not the same as the sum of the outputs of each of the individual allocations, when they are considered apart from the other allocations that make up the allocation plan. This involves the well-known complementarities of production between industries.

Assuming that we add into our evaluation of the marginal product the differences between the social valuation and the private valuation we then obtain the application of the well-known social marginal producivity criterion. It is to be observed that in the first case it is quite simple to add the difference between the social and the private values of the marginal product since these are applied to the specific allocation themselves, apart from the other allocations that occur within the investment plan, while, in the second case, it is much more difficult because we cannot know the social valuation for a given allocation without knowing the rest of the investment plan. That is to say, for every alternative investment plan, here exists an alternative social valuation of the particular allocation under consideration.

The important consideration for our purposes is that it is assumed that the social valuation of a specific allocation depends only on differences between social and private costs, social and private benefits, and on the complementaries of production. Notice that the social valuations of the results of investment do not depend, in this model, on the effects of the allocation plan on the size, nature, quality, or desires of the work force, and populace as such. It is this last aspect that will differentiate, in great part, this decision environment from the one that we shall consider below under model 3.

Model 2—Neo-classical model—per capita output maximized.

The decision environment we now consider is exactly the same as the one above with the sole exception that the objective of development is to maximize the present value of the *per capita output stream* rather than the present value of the aggregate output stream. It turns out that the result in this case is exactly the same as in the decision environment considered above. This is due to the fact that changes in population and the work force are independent of the allocation plan. Similarly, it follows that any objective involving the population, or some property, characteristic, or a quality of the population, will lead to the same allocation criterion as above as long as such characteristics and properties are assumed to be independent of the allocation plan.

Model 3—The strong interdependence model

Under this heading we outline a decision environment very different from the ones considered previously.

The objective is the same as in model 2—namely, the maximization of the present value of the *per capita* output stream. However, the vision of the economic process is very different in this case.

The crucial difference here is that we assume that the allocation plan in the first period will affect a number of variables that were assumed to be independent in the previous models. To be specific we assume that the allocation plan in period one affects in a significant way the following aspects in subsequent periods:

(1)   The propensity to consume in subsequent periods.

(2)   The inducement to invest in subsequent periods.

(3)   The size of the population and labour force in subsequent periods.

(4)   The quality of the work force in subsequent periods. To be specific, the energy level of the work force, its morale, its responsiveness to discipline, etc. Last but not least, the educational and skill level of the work force.

Once we insert into our decision environment the interdependence of the investment plan in one period and the nature of the inputs in subsequent periods then we have a completely different situation from that in the models considered above. To see this consider for a moment the possibility that arises from the fact that population growth is no longer exogenously determined. For example, allocation plan *A* may maximize the present value of the aggregate output stream but induce a large rate of population growth, while allocation plan *B* may lead to a smaller increase in the aggregate output stream but induce a more than proportionately smaller increase in population growth. Allocation

380   THE INDIAN ECONOMIC JOURNAL

plan *B* will then be preferred to *A* if our objective is to maximize *per capita* output. The marginal productivity criterion, as this is usually defined, no longer suffice under such circumstances.

At this juncture a semantic note is in order. The concept of productivity is rarely, if ever, considered to be identical with the totality of consequences that follows from a given allocation plan. Rather, by the productivity of a given set of inputs we usually mean the flow of outputs that results directly from the combination of the inputs. It does not take into account other consequences that are not directly related to the flow of outputs. That is to say, it is rarely, if ever, suggested that the concept of producivity should also include the behaviour of the factors of production in their capacities as consumers, investors, procreators, and so on. Clearly this is in accordance with the ordinary and common sense usage of the word " product " and " prductivity ". Thus it follows that when the aggregate product stream, in the sense just indicated, is not the sole consideration then an allocation criterion that involves only the product stream, (or productivity), such as the marginal productivity criterion, cannot be universally applicable.

The correct allocation criterion under decision environment 3 is much more difficult to determine and state than under the others. Here we have to look for that allocation plan that leads to a time pattern of capital growth *per capita,* and of growth in the quality of the population, again *per capita,* so that the present value of the output stream *per capita* is maximized. There are two streams that are of primary importance. First, we have to consider the regular re-investment stream. That is to say, we have to take into account the extent to which the allocation plan affects the investment rates and amounts, on a *per capita* basis, in the future. Second, we have to consider what might be called the human re-investment stream. That is to say, we have to take into account the extent to which the consumption patterns, as well as the investment patterns, that are consequences of the allocation plan, affect the quality of the population, and in turn, the productive capacity of the population—all of these in *per capita* terms. For present purposes we need not attempt to spell out the exact criterion applicable to this decision environment. It should be clear from the foregoing that many more considerations are involved here than are usually taken into account in the application of the marginal productivity criterion. Certainly the marginal productivity criterion, as defined here, will not always give the correct result under these circumstances.

However, the semantic aspect of the debate must not be lost sight of. That is to say, part of the argument may have to do with differences in the way we use words. For example, a great deal depends on how we interpret the word " social " in the social marginal productivity criterion. If by social rather than private marginal producivity valuations we are to understand the inclusion of all of the factors that we have considered in the last decision environment then, of course, the social marginal productivity criterion will always give the right result. But in this case are we not stretching the meaning and interpretation of the word "social"? It seems to me that the only thing that "social" suggests is the fact that there may be some valuations which for society as a whole are different from the valuations as determined by private decision making entities. All that the adjective "social" really tells us is to be on guard and not accept the private valuations of productivity. It does not tell us, nor does it spell out, what are the factors to be taken into account in the determination of social valuations rather than the private valuations. Clearly, on this latter aspect, there may be legitimate differences of opinion. Problems arise because such differences are often not made explicit.

V. Review of Critical Elements

Semantic illusions may lead us to believe that we differ on allocation criteria when in fact we are merely using words differently. But apart from such semantic tangles the differences may be real ones when they are based on different decision environments. However, we have seen that different decision environments are in themselves not always sufficient to lead to different investment criteria. In other words, there is not a one-to-one correspondance between decision environments and appropriate allocation criteria. Rather, there are many decision environments for which the same allocation criterion may be applicable. (It is this feature that may be responsible, in part, for the belief in the near universality of some criteria). For example, decision models 1 and 2 considered above implied the same allocation criterion and policy although the objectives in these decision environments were different. The reason for this was that the difference in the objectives was connected with a variable (population) that was assumed to be exogenous to the system and hence could not be affected by the investment plan.

Whether or not different decision environments lead to different allocation criteria and policies will depend, in great part, on the interaction between four broad factors: (1) the significance of the indirect consequences of the allocation plan (or plans), (2) the possibilities and costs of using direct social instruments (e.g., government action) to determine the values of variables or parameters, (3) the differences in the view of the economic development process (i.e., in different development theories), and (4) differences in objectives.

(a) *Indirect consequences of allocations and direct social instruments.* Items (1) and (2) above are very closely connected because the operation of the second may nullify the significance of the first. That is, if the indirect consequences of an allocation plan is important, but if the values of the variables or parameters so affected can be altered by the use of direct social instruments which are costless, then the indirect consequences can always be counteracted. For example, compare models 2 and 3 in the previous section. The objectives in both models are the same, but in model 3 some of the indirect consequences of the allocation plan are assumed to be important, and to affect variables (population size, investment rate, etc.,) that are assumed to be exogenous to the system in model 2. The two models do imply different investment criteria and policies. But if we had assumed (as part of the decision environment) with respect to model 3 that the government could by direct action determine the size of the population, the quality of the labour force, the rate of investment, and so on, and if the costs of doing so were trivial, then the same investment criteria and policies would have been applicable in both cases. But, of course, some may believe that the use of direct social instruments for some of these purposes may not be possible, or that they should not be used for ideological reasons, or if possible and permissible they may be costlier than taking into account the indirect consequences of the allocation plan. In any event we see that different views about the possibility and efficacy of various types of potential government activities, and their costs, may logically lead to different views about appropriate allocation policies.

(b) *The time aspects of the decision environment.* Whether or not the indirect consequences of an allocation plan (or series of plans) are significant may depend on the time horizon and time committment aspects of the decision environment. Once again compare models 2 and 3. If the time horizon is very short, say only five years rather than several generations, then the indirect consequences considered in model 3 may be trivial, and the appropriate investment policies may be the same for the two models. That is, it may take some time for the indirect consequences to take hold, so to speak.

Even more important is likely to be the question of the time committment of the investment policy. For example, consider the possible difference between a one-shot-only investment policy versus one for a whole series of potential investment plans, for, say, twenty years. The indirect consequences of a single plan may turn out to be trivial, and may perhaps best be ignored. In this case the policies for models 2 and 3 can be the same. But the indirect consequences of a series of investment plans over a twenty year period may be considerable. In this latter case the investment criteria and policies applicable for the two models may be very different indeed. Also, the appropriate investment plan for a given year that is looked upon as a one-shot-only affair, without reference to future investment plans, may be very different than the appropriate investment plan that is part of an integrated series

The imporance of the indirect consequences of an allocation plan is determined, in part, by our views of the development process, which, in turn, is distinguished by the nature and importance of the variables that we assume to be endogenous to such a process. We now consider briefly the treatment of some of these matters.

(c) *Population.* The question of how to treat the population aspect in our decision environment enters in at least two different important respects. If the objective is to maximize some *per capita* variable then the growth of population enters in a significant sense since it determines the denominator of the ratio that determines the *per capita* value. The second sense in which population may enter the problem is that the qualities of the population (in the sense of acquired qualities such as learned skills, education, health, and so on) may change over time and affect some of the target variables. For example, the energy and skills of the population may change over time as a consequence of the pattern of investment, and as a result change the productive capacity of the population.

With respect to population size the usual argument revolves around the fact that fertility patterns of various groups in a population may depend on the roles, especially social, familial, and economic roles, that the individuals composing these groups generally play. For example, urban populations often have different fertility rates than rural populations, white collar groups often have different fertility rates than either rural agricultural groups, or urban manual labourers, and so on. Since the pattern of investment allocation is likely to involve both the demand and supply of the labour, and in turn influence the economic and social role patterns, and the distribution of role patterns, it may in this way also influence the consequent fertility rates of the population. It is through such indirect means that the allocation plan may have an effect on population size and population growth.

More directly the allocation plan may determine both the aggregate output and the level of consumption which in turn may, to a certain extent, influence mortality rates, and therefore the rates of population growth. The main point to be considered here is that there is little question but that we can visualize circumstances in which a connection exists between the allocation plan (or series of plans) and the rate of population growth.

(d) *Investment and reinvestment rates.* In considering the effects of an allocation plan (or plans) we must take into account not only the addition to the output stream that results from the allocation plan (or plans) but also their possible influence on the rates of savings and investment in the future periods. As before the importance of this element depends on whether we look upon the rate of savings and investment as determined exogenously or whether it is determined in part

384   THE INDIAN ECONOMIC JOURNAL

by the social and economic environment created by the sequence of allocation plans. If it is the latter, then we arrive at a different conclusion about investment policy, one that is closer to that considered under model 3 than if it is the former. On *a priori* grounds it would appear that rates of savings and investment depends on income distribution and perhaps on the role composition of the population, and on the social and cultural environment in which the population finds itself. To think of it in terms of extremes the pattern of savings of peasants is likely to be very different from that of socially mobile white collar workers. Also, we might expect that the environment and the role composition of the population may be determined by the allocation plans that take place. As before a lot depends on whether or not we believe the savings and investment rates can be determined by direct governmental action, or the use of other social instruments, and also whether such determination is or is not costless.

(e) *The possible relation of social objectives to the development theory.* A point well worth commenting upon, but one which is quite different from our previous considerations, is the possibility that the objective of development may depend on both the development theory we have in mind and the possibilities of development given the investment fund available. For example, if we believe in the *critical minimum effort thesis* that the author has developed elsewhere,[4] then we might take the view that if an investment fund is too small then there may not be any allocation that will lead to sustained development. In this case the objective may be made to depend on whether or not sustained development is possible If the investment fund is such that a sustained development is a possibility then we might allocate the investment fund in accordance with policies that lead to high rate of reinvestment in the near future, and as a consequence not raise the consumption of the population in the early periods to the level that it might have achieved without the higher investment rate. On the other hand, if the investment fund is too small to generate sustained development, then we may decide that since development is not of the question in any event, that we should concentrate our efforts on maximizing the consumption level of the population even if in the long run this leads eventually to a return to the previous rate of consumption. We shall not elaborate on this aspect of the problem but merely point to the fact that appropriate investment policies may depend, under some circumstances, on criteria other than the maximization of the output stream.

(f) *Population and lobour force qualities.* A second variable (or set of variables) of significance that is usually not considered in static or short run economic analysis is the changes in the quality of

[4] H. Leibenstein, **Economic Backwardness and Economic Growth,** John Wiley and Sons, New York, Chapter 8.

the population, in the resulting labour force, and in all of the characteristics and properties that we may associate with the notion of acquired population qualities. We cannot take up every aspect that might come under this global concept, but an enumeration of a few might indicate what we have in mind. Some of the qualities that may be of significance for productive purposes are the energy of the population, the acquired skills of the population, the flexibility of the labour force, the economic and social mobility of the population, and the general responsiveness of the population to economic incentives, and so on. The question that arises is whether changes in these properties are independnt of the allocation plans that occur, and hence of the investment policies that determine them. It must be clear that we can think of some possibilities under which the allocation plans would affect the qualities of the population. For example, the nature and variety of consumption goods, which are, in part, determined by the allocation plans, will in turn have their influence on the energy level of the population. Also, expenditures on such things as education and educational facilities will in part determine the acquired skills of the population, and their productive capacities. Similarly, the invironment created by a series of allocation plans, may, in part, determine the psychological attitudes of the population as well as their flexibility, mobility, and responsiveness to economic incentives.

A central aspect of the view just presented is that the qualities considered are entirely acquired rather than innate. They are characteristics that are determined by the social and economic environment under which the population lives, and in part, determined by the expenditure patterns of the population as such. But the expenditure patterns, both of an investment and consumption kind, may be determined in part by the nature of the allocation plans that take place. Thus we see that an obvious relationship between these elements and investment policy exists. Whether this relationship is really significant or not may be a debatable matter. But clearly our view of what investment policy is appropriate will depend on whether the elements that we have just considered are looked upon as endogenous or exogenous variables within our theory.

In this general connection we may look at model 3 as one that is consistent with the view that economic development involves not only growth in the capital stock, looked at in terms of the aggregate valuation of the physical non-human assets of the economy, but also that it depends on the transformation of the labour force and population as such. That is to say, the nature of an industrial populations, the stimuli to which they respond, their energy, the motivations that lie behind their behaviour, as well as the things that they value and the skills that they possess, are very different from that of the typical peasant population that form so large a part of the population in the typical underdeveloped area. If this type of transformation is looked

386   THE INDIAN ECONOMIC JOURNAL

upon as the paramount phenomenon of development then it would seem to follow that model   is more appropriate than the others considered.

On the other hand, if we view the process of development as some thing that does not affect in any marked degree the population as such, then of course models 1 and 2 may be adequate. It is to be noted, of course, that we may accept the view about the importance of the transformation of the population as part of the process of develop-ment and yet not accept the appropriateness of model 3. This would be correct if we believed that such a transformation occurs independ-ently of the allocation plans in the initial and subsequent periods. In other words even, if we accept the view that the transformation of the acquired qualities of the population is of paramount importance, we may believe that such a transformation is entirely socially (or government-ally) determinable. That is to say, it can be achieved directly without in any way involving the investment plans within any period, or it may be achieved through exogenous factors or influences that are pri-marily functions of time but which in no way are related to the invest-ment plans period by period. Which view is correct is the subject for another occasion. Here we merely suggest that these are some of the issues that may be at the heart of the debate over appropriate invest-ment allocation policies.

Berkeley, California.   H. Leibenstein

[9]

INVESTMENT CRITERIA, PRODUCTIVITY, AND ECONOMIC DEVELOPMENT*

By Walter Galenson and Harvey Leibenstein

I. A Suggested Criterion for Investment Allocation

In recent years there has been increased attention to the problem of establishing criteria for allocating investment in programs for economic development. A general rule has emerged, from which practical policies are inferred. A. E. Kahn, in an article that appeared in 1951, set forth the "rule of social marginal productivity" as a guide to investment, and deduced, among other things, that as a consequence of this "rule," underdeveloped areas should choose industries and techniques requiring a lower capital/labor ratio than that prevailing in developed countries.[1] Hollis B. Chenery accepts the criterion of social marginal productivity, and attempts to demonstrate its application to a number of empirical situations.[2]

We propose in this paper to examine the conclusions that have been reached, and to suggest a line of reasoning that appears to us to be more in consonance with the peculiar problems raised by economic development. We do not intend to advance a complete model for investment allocation; that would obviously be impossible within the confines of a brief paper. Our object is primarily to call attention to the shortcomings occasioned by the failure of economic theory in dealing with economic growth, to relax some of the assumptions that are relevant in treating static problems. We shall also indicate briefly some of the institutions and practices characteristic of back-

* Several friends were kind enough to read an initial draft of this paper. We are grateful to them and especially to Professor Gottfried Haberler of Harvard University for many valuable suggestions. The responsibility for the paper itself remains, of course, entirely our own.

1. Alfred E. Kahn, "Investment Criteria in Development," this *Journal*, LXV, 38.
2. Hollis B. Chenery, "The Application of Investment Criteria," this *Journal*, LXVII, 76.

343

344

ward areas which we believe must enter into the framework of a theoretical formulation suitable as a guide for successful economic development.

Chenery voices the general proposition that "Economic theory tells us that an efficient allocation of investment resources is achieved by equating the social marginal productivity of capital in its various uses."[3] With this bald statement we can have no quarrel. However, it is open to the same general objection that Friedman raised with respect to Lerner's famous "Rule": standing by itself, it provides no guide to policy.[4] The real question arises when one attempts to make precise the notion of "efficient allocation" in this context.

In economic statics when we consider allocation of resources, we can attach a clear-cut test to the idea of efficiency. The test is the maximization of the value of the national product. That allocation which maximizes the value of national product is the efficient one — and equating marginal productivity in different uses is the rule for achieving such an allocation. But even here some ambiguity arises in the case of capital goods, and this may have something to do with the imperfect state in which capital theory finds itself. The difficulty arises because of the *ceteris paribus* assumption[5] necessary in comparative statics, e.g., we do not know of what value these capital goods will be to generations yet unborn. With respect to the production of consumer goods the situation appears to be fairly clear, since the valuation of the goods depends on their worth to the population in the current period, rendering the *ceteris paribus* assumption reasonable. But the valuation of capital goods depends on the value of the output stream generated by an increment of capital projected into the indefinite future. Apart from difficulties of predicting the output stream, there is also the problem of knowing what meaning to give to the *ceteris paribus* assumption in situations involving the indefinite future, as well as the practical consideration as to the value of the assumption under conditions in which technology, tastes, and population will most certainly change.

The question that immediately arises in applying conventional theory to problems of economic development is whether the goal of

3. Chenery, *op. cit.*, p. 76.
4. Milton Friedman, "Lerner on the Economics of Control," *Journal of Political Economy*, Oct. 1947, p. 405.
5. I.e., tastes, size and composition of the population, the state of the arts and expectations remain the same. Or, another way of looking at it is that an "efficient" allocation requires an accurate forecast of tastes, population, and the state of the arts in the future. See also Lionel Robbins, "On a Certain Ambiguity in the Conception of Stationary Equilibrium," *Economic Journal*, June 1930, pp. 159–79, esp. p. 168.

maximization of the national product necessarily leads to "development." Suppose that in every period 110 per cent of the GNP is consumed, would we then say that development is taking place even if in period after period the GNP is the maximum it could possibly be under the circumstances? As soon as we leave the theoretical world of statics, maximizing output is no longer a sufficient criterion, nor does "efficiency" have the same meaning.

To get at the correct criterion, we must determine the appropriate goal of the economy during the process of development. Unfortunately, this cannot be done on the basis of economic analysis alone; a social welfare function of some sort is necessary. The goal must depend ultimately on values that come from outside economic analysis, and these are arbitrary to some extent. Nevertheless, a good case can be made for the proposition that the appropriate economic goal should be the maximization of *per capita* output, or *average* income, either over time, or at some time in the future.[6] This is hardly a startling position: it appears to be quite widely accepted. But it should be noted that maximizing per capita income is not at all the same as maximizing the national product once the *ceteris paribus* assumption is dropped.

For a closed economy, *per capita* income and *per capita* output are identical, but there may be considerable deviation between *per capita* output and the *per capita* level of consumption. If we are interested in alleviating the mass poverty that prevails in backward areas, then ultimately we must be interested in their *per capita* level of consumption. However, in the short run raising *per capita* output and raising *per capita* consumption may be antithetical, for the rate of capital accumulation will depend on the extent to which increases in output are not followed by equal increases in consumption. Thus, while the raising of *per capita* consumption levels may be, and perhaps must be, an ultimate goal of development, if we concentrate on consumption as an immediate goal, it may be impossible of achievement as an ultimate goal. It is therefore *per capita* output that must be looked upon as an appropriate index of economic development.

We turn now to a consideration of the extent to which the practi-

6. It should be noted that there are numerous and difficult problems involving the element of time that we do not consider in this paper. For example, the ordering of income magnitudes over time is a matter fraught with most important considerations of economic welfare; and so is the precise future time at which it is desired to achieve maximum output. Unless the time path or the time horizon is given, there is no meaning to the concept of maximization in the future. As we shall see below, however, the time element is intimately related to specific variables, of which the rate of population change is perhaps the most important.

346

cal corollaries which have been deduced from the social marginal productivity rule (SMP) focus on this goal. Although the literature is far from clear on this point it seems to us that three general corollaries of SMP have been advanced as valid policy guides. They are: (1) to maximize the current output/investment ratio; (2) to maximize the labor/investment ratio; and (3) to maximize the export goods/investment ratio.

The discussion is often needlessly complicated by attempting to consider simultaneously development problems and balance-of-payments problems. Where investment funds or capital goods are obtained from abroad, a balance-of-payments problem *may* develop. The extent of the problem will depend, in part, on the allocation of the investment. But since the extent of the balance-of-payments problem will also depend on numerous other monetary conditions, both internal and external to the underdeveloped country, it is best, initially, to treat the two questions separately, and to leave the balance-of-payments problem for another occasion. We shall therefore omit corollary (3) in this paper, and consider only corollaries (1) and (2), and their relationship to the SMP criterion.

Kahn tells us that "The SMP of capital is not correlated with the rate of turnover."[7] The rate of turnover is of course the output/investment ratio. Yet later he concludes that ". . . general adherence to the capital-turnover criterion . . . is particularly desirable (a) where capital is relatively scarce and labor extremely plentiful. . . . With respect to the first circumstance (a), the rule of thumb of employing the minimum amount of capital necessary to absorb excess labor does indeed approximate the SMP criterion."[8] But there is no clear-cut explanation why this should be the case. There are, however, good reasons to believe that the rate-of-turnover criterion is not likely to be consistent with the proper interpretation of SMP from the point of view of development.

It is obvious that in computing social marginal productivity, we must consider the effect of an increment of capital on the output stream in the indefinite future, and not only on the magnitude of the output during the initial period. If the income stream is the same period after period, then the capital-turnover corollary would appear to favor, as Kahn correctly says in a footnote,[9] short-lived over long-

7. Kahn, *op. cit.*, p. 39.
8. *Ibid.*, p. 51.
9. The notion of short-lived vs. long-lived capital may need some amplification. For this purpose it may help if we reproduce the example given by Kahn (p. 39). "Compare the following financial data for investments *A* and *B*, which differ only in that equipment in *A* lasts only two years, in *B* ten years:

lived capital. But if national capital is to be maintained, and the total effect on the income stream is to be considered, then the length of life of any individual capital good is an irrelevant consideration. If the income stream increases over time, then the application of the capital-turnover criterion *can* quite clearly result in the allocation of investment to uses that have a lower SMP than the alternatives. For example, between two alternatives, *A* and *B*, the following might be the case: Equipment in *A* lasts five years while in *B* it lasts ten years. Assume that in both cases the income streams over the life of the equipment is twice the investment cost. Clearly the rate of capital-turnover is twice as great for *A* as for *B*. But if replacements are made so that capital is maintained intact indefinitely, then with a rising output stream for *B* and a constant output stream for *A* it is certainly possible that the SMP for *B* would be larger than the SMP for *A*. Where industries of increasing returns with respect to scale are among the possible alternatives, it is likely that the capital-turnover criterion will result in the wrong choice. A constant or decreasing returns industry may have a higher capital turnover ratio than an alternative increasing returns industry, but the increasing returns industry may in the long run make a greater contribution to national product.

If SMP is to be interpreted in this context to take account of the addition to the income stream in the indefinite future (no matter how discounted), then we cannot assume, as a static interpretation of SMP would have us, that other things remain constant during this process; we must take into account the time pattern of possible changes as a consequence of the addition to capital. Thus, with respect to many investment alternatives, we have to account for such dynamic factors as the development of skills, the development of markets, overcoming production bottlenecks, etc., and the effect of these factors on the time pattern of output — circumstances under which the capital turnover rule is likely to come up with the wrong answer. In the short run, the capital turnover ratio could be highest in those endeavors that required few new skills, that depended on

Investment..............	$100,000	$100,000
Annual Data:		
Output...............	60,000	20,000
Depreciation.........	50,000	10,000
All other Costs......	20,000	10,000
Capital Turnover......	60 per cent	20 per cent

In a long range investment program, in which real national capital must presumably be kept intact, there would appear to be no advantage in choosing the shorter- over the longer-lived investment, since both yield the same annual output net of depreciation." However, as we will argue, there is an advantage in longer-lived investment because of the lower replacement cost in a growing economy.

348

existing markets, and in which there were no production bottlenecks to overcome; but over the longer period it might be those investment alternatives that involved the learning of new ways of doing things that would make the greatest contribution to the social product.

We now turn to corollary (2), under which the labor/investment ratio is to be maximized. The extent to which labor can be absorbed in any economic process depends on the flexibility and adaptability of the other factors of production (i.e., capital). One can easily visualize situations in which the maximum labor absorption criterion would not maximize the addition to total output. Figure I illustrates

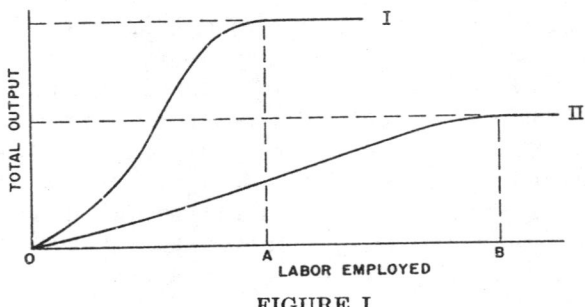

FIGURE I

such a situation. The investment in alternatives *I* and *II* are the same. The maximum absorption of labor in either case is up to the point where the marginal productivity of labor is zero, if we assume that the marginal productivity of labor on the land is zero. In Figure I, investment alternative *I* would absorb *less* labor but add more to total output than would investment alternative *II*. As a consequence alternative *I* rather than *II* is consistent with SMP. Nor is there any reason to believe that highly productive capital is necessarily related to highly flexible and adaptable capital. Indeed, there is good reason to believe that quite the reverse is true. With respect to machinery it is likely that the more productive the machine, the more specialized it is, and as a consequence the less adaptable and flexible with respect to changes in other factors.

A second set of difficulties has to do with the time element. Corollary (2) does not tell us in any clear way when the labor is to be absorbed. If the labor employed as a result of the investment is the same period after period, then there is no problem, but suppose the time pattern of labor absorption varies from period to period, as it may with developing skills in the use of capital; then, of course, there is a problem similar to the one previously considered in our discussion of the capital turnover rule. We need not go through the difficulties involved on this point, since the analysis parallels that considered under the capital turnover rule. It would follow from such an analysis, even in those cases where over the initial life of the capital good, the labor absorption rule and SMP are consistent, that they need not be consistent in the long run when all the dynamic considerations are taken into account.

Corollary (2), if taken literally, would imply that labor displacing investment would almost never be accepted no matter how high its contribution to national product.[1] For example, the United Nations experts on development tell us that:

" . . . labour-saving technology is not of great value to an economy which is over populated. There the search should be rather for technologies which increase the yield of land per acre, or which enable large numbers of persons to be employed in secondary industries for a small expenditure of capital."[2]

Investment in agricultural machinery would scarcely pass corollary (2), since it would increase the actual or disguised unemployment on the land. This is, of course, one of the implicit issues in the by now celebrated dispute between Professor Viner and his draftsman,[3] namely, that excess capacity is not an economic sin, but can be an economic virtue. Under conditions of decreasing costs the creation of excess capacity can lead to lower costs or greater output per unit of the variable factor regardless of what the fixed factor happens to be. Similarly, increasing the amount of excess labor by the introduction of labor displacing capital can result in a greater addition to output than the use of labor absorbing capital. In such a case corollaries (1) and (2) are also likely to be inconsistent with each other. The highest capital turnover rates may come about through the use of labor displacing rather than labor absorbing investment.

Finally, we may note that there is also a practical difficulty with the labor absorption rule. The extent to which the rule is useful depends on its greater ease of application than the general SMP criterion. Of what use is corollary (2), and what constitutes absorption, if the investment is to take place in an industry in which disguised unemployment exists? In order to measure the alternate points with respect to alternate investment possibilities the marginal

1. This is not to imply that any of the writers previously mentioned would suggest that the labor absorption rule be applied apart from any other considerations.

2. United Nations, *Measures for the Economic Development of Underdeveloped Countries* (New York, 1951), p. 7.

3. Jacob Viner, "Cost Curves and Supply Curves," *Zeitschrift für Nationalökonomie*, 1933.

350

productivity of labor in the industry (or sector) becomes zero. Surely, it would be difficult to show that this is any easier to measure than the SMP itself.[4]

It is a likely consequence of corollaries (1) and (2) that low labor productivity will be perpetuated. Wherever the SMP criterion or rules dictate the application of capital to agriculture, where there is likely to be a great deal of disguised unemployment, and where the potentialities for further population growth are usually very high, then it is highly probable that low labor productivity will be perpetuated. To begin with, the marginal productivity of labor on the land is likely to be extremely low. To the extent that investment increases productivity it will increase population and subsequently the labor force, and as a consequence *tend* to reduce average product to its former low level.[5]

The application of investment to capital-light industries such as handicrafts, corollary (1), is also likely to lead to the maintenance of low labor productivity. Since corollary (1) seeks to maximize output per unit of capital, it also implies, other things equal, using as much labor as possible with the existing capital.

We can summarize briefly why the practical corollaries that have been drawn from the SMP criterion are not appropriate for economic development. (1) The emphasis of these corollaries is on the productivity of capital not on the productivity of labor. In the long run, given the inevitable population increases that accompany industrialization, it is quite possible to raise output per unit of capital without raising output per unit of labor (labor productivity) to any extent. But it is high labor productivity that makes possible high levels of living. Put differently, corollaries (1) and (2) may yield a maximum aggre-

---

4. See Wilbert E. Moore, *The Economic Demography of Eastern and Southern Europe*, chap. III, and Appendix II, for the difficulties involved in attempts to measure "surplus" labor.

5. It may be argued that on ethical grounds, corollary (2) is sound in that it leads to lower mortality rates in agricultural areas. But this will only be a temporary gain that will be wiped out as soon as the consequent population increase reduces productivity *per capita* to its former level. Two sorts of welfare questions are involved. First, what sector should be favored with the initial increase in productivity and income? Second, is it ethical to sacrifice a temporary gain in living standards in order to insure long-run permanent gains? These are very serious questions, and welfare questions so fundamental in significance can scarcely be dealt with in a footnote. However, it may be pertinent to point out that (1) there is almost universally a direct correlation between industrialization, broadly defined, and standards of living, and (2) there is probably no case of "painless" industrialization on record, as any reader of *The Town Labourer* will recognize. Even in the United States, where an optimum situation for development prevailed, the immediate consequences were not always pleasant.

gate national product but not a maximum product *per capita*. The last two magnitudes can conceivably go in opposite directions. (2) The corollaries emphasize aggregate output and not the rate of investment, whereas it is precisely this rate that determines the extent of capital accumulation and as a consequence the capacity of the economy to produce goods and services in the future. The formal rules do not take into account what happens to the final product during any period, but it is just this that determines the rate of investment. (3) The rules enumerated above do not take into account changes in the factors other than capital. For example, no account is taken of the population growth that may be a consequence of investing in a certain manner and achieving a certain product mix. It is population and labor force growth that tend to reduce capital *per capita* and hence reduce output *per capita*. The crux of this argument is that the allocation of capital, the consequent allocation of the final product, and population growth are not independent factors.

If it be granted that the object of development is to attain a level of economic capacity which maximizes output *per capita* at a determined future time, then the correct criterion for allocating investment must be to choose for each unit of investment that alternative that will give each worker greater productive power than any other alternative. To achieve, this result we must maximize (a) the amount of capital per worker, and (b) the quality of the labor force, i.e., its skill, knowledge, energy, and adaptability.

Apart from the human factors, it is the capital/labor ratio that determines output *per capita*. From this point of view the criterion to be adopted is the one that leads ultimately to the maximum capital/labor ratio. The amount of capital per worker that is created in the long run depends on two broad factors: (1) the amount of investment year by year stemming from the product of the initial investment; and (2) the increase in the size of the labor force. We must therefore take into account the initial investment plus the sum of all subsequent reinvestments divided by the size of the labor force at the end of the stipulated time horizon.

The marginal principle applies here as it does elsewhere — but not marginal *productivity* in the usual sense. The criterion we suggest might be called the *marginal per capita reinvestment quotient*. The best allocation of investment resources is achieved by equating the marginal *per capita* reinvestment quotient of capital in its various alternative uses. The result of such a policy would be to maximize the *per capita* output potential at some future point in time.

352

To secure a clear notion of what is meant by the marginal *per capita* reinvestment quotient we must consider the basic factors involved in its determination. Briefly stated, the seven basic factors are as follows: (1) gross productivity per worker; (2) "wage" goods consumed per worker; (3) replacement and repair of capital; (4) increments in output as a result of noncapital using innovations, such as improvements in skills, health, energy, discipline, and malleability of the labor force; (5) declines in mortality; (6) declines in fertility; and (7) direction of reinvestment. The first six factors determine the *per capita* reinvestment available period after period, and the last one deals with its allocation.

The gross productivity per worker minus the consumption per worker determines the gross amount available for reinvestment per worker.[6] Deducting replacement and repairs per worker yields the net amount (per worker) available for reinvestment during any period. Over a succession of periods there may be increases in productivity that arise *not* out of additions to capital but rather because of increases in skill, organizational innovations, or improvement in health, energy, or discipline of the labor force that have to be taken into account. Capital per worker declines if the labor force grows at a more rapid rate than capital accumulates. But the rate of growth of the labor force will depend, for the most part, on the rates of mortality and fertility of the population, leaving aside the question of labor force participation.

It is a common experience in all underdeveloped areas that mortality declines at a faster rate and earlier than fertility as levels of consumption increase. Therefore, the greater the gap between output and consumption, the less the rate of population growth and the less the dilution of capital. The extent of fertility decline will also depend on the allocation of investment, since the type of investment that stimulates urbanization will create a more favorable environment for fertility decline than the type of investment that perpetuates the rural agricultural environment.

---

6. We abstract here from the very difficult problem of ensuring that this Ricardian "surplus" is indeed reinvested, which involves either the creation of a Schumpeterian ideology among entreprenuers, government control, or outright government investment. Which of these alternatives is adopted depends, of course, upon the specific institutional situation of the country undergoing development.

II. The Case for High Labor Productivity in Underdeveloped Areas

1. The level of labor productivity in underdeveloped areas.

We consider first such empirical data as are available with respect to the differences in labor productivity between developed and underdeveloped areas.

(a) An excellent statistical analysis has been made of the productivity of labor in underdeveloped areas relating to the cotton textile industry of five Latin-American countries — Brazil, Chile, Mexico, Ecuador, and Peru.[7] It was determined that for the so-called "old" mills, which comprised 90 per cent of the entire industry in these countries, "labor consumption per kilogramme of fabric (taking into account the process of spinning and weaving) is five times greater . . . than that which could be expected under the best conditions — within practical limits — of modernity of equipment, size, organization and administration."[8] The standards against which labor inputs were measured were models, to which were attributed the "best possible process and labor organization, and it was supposed that they would operate with the best efficiencies attainable without impairing the quality of the product."[9] These standards were undoubtedly above the average efficiency of cotton mills in the United States, but since they were constructed by a U. S. engineering firm, it may be assumed that good U. S. practice served as a guide. It should also be noted that cotton textile manufacturing is one of the best developed and relatively most efficient industries in Latin America.

(b) The accompanying table purports to compare productivity in

Industry	Output per Operative, in Pounds Sterling					
	United Kingdom, 1935		Egypt, 1937		United States, 1937	
	Net value of output	Index of output	Net value of output	Index of output	Net value of output	Index of output
Chemicals.......	617	100	69	11	1,145	186
Textiles.........	159	100	39	25	318	200
Clothing.........	168	100	61	36	356	212
Leather.........	237	100	45	19	417	176
Clay and stone...	238	100	28	13	588	247
Paper...........	332	100	68	21	867	261
Food...........	487	100	82	17	760	156
All manufacturing	264	100	56	21	595	225

Source: Gamal Eldin Said, "Productivity of Labour in Egyptian Industry," *L'Egypte Contemporaine*, Nos. 259–60, May–June, 1950.

7. United Nations, Department of Economic Affairs, *Labor Productivity of the Cotton Textile Industry in Five Latin-American Countries* (New York, 1951).
8. *Ibid.*, p. 5.
9. *Ibid.*, p. 127.

354

various Egyptian manufactures with that in the United States and Great Britain.

These figures indicate that for the years in question, productivity in Egyptian manufacturing as a whole was about 10 per cent of the U. S. level, though for the clothing industry, which is labor-intensive in the United States, the disparity was smaller.[1]

(c) Comparative productivity data for the Soviet Union in 1928, at the commencement of the industrialization program, and the United States in 1939, are shown in the following table:

SOVIET PRODUCTIVITY IN 1928 AS A
PERCENTAGE OF U. S. PRODUCTIVITY IN 1939

Coal mining	20
Iron ore mining	11
Crude oil and gas extraction	24
Iron and steel	17
Cotton cloth	16
Shoes	38
Beet sugar	14
Manufacturing and mining	22

Source: Walter Galenson, "Industrial Labor Productivity," in Abram Bergson (ed.), *Soviet Economic Growth* (Evanston, 1953), p. 190.

Soviet industry was considerably more advanced in 1928 than that of Egypt in 1937, and the difference is reflected in the comparative productivity data. Yet the Soviet 1928 level is seen to have been far below that of the United States, reflecting the great relative backwardness of the preplanning Soviet economy.

(d) A comparison of manufacturing labor productivity in China (1936) and the United States (1935) yielded the conclusion that Chinese productivity was about 5 per cent of the U. S. level.

"The difference is appalling. Yet this is not the whole picture. When the comparison is made between the output produced by an American worker and a Chinese handicraft worker, the result is almost unbelievable . . . one day's work of an American worker will be equivalent to fifty days' work of a Chinese handicraft worker. This low productivity is, of course, only partly due to the inefficiency of labor, and partly, perhaps mainly, due to the meagerness of capital investment."[2]

1. Though the data appear to have been prepared carefully on the basis of censuses of manufacturing, they are subject to the limitation of more or less arbitrary exchange rates. The author converted at the rate of 97½ piastres to the pound sterling, which prevailed in 1944, adjusted for the decline in the internal purchasing power of the piastre from 1937 to 1944. The British and U. S. data were taken from L. Rostas, "Industrial Production, Productivity and Distribution in Britain, Germany and United States," *Economic Journal*, April 1943.

2. Pao-San Ou and Foh-Shen Wang, "Industrial Production and Employment in Pre-War China," *Economic Journal*, LVI, 433.

(e) Labor productivity in Ceylon *circa* 1950 is reported to have been from 20 to 30 per cent below the level prevailing in India.[3] So far as the authors are aware, there is not available a comparison of labor productivity in India and the United States, though observers are agreed that Indian productivity is low indeed.[4]

The foregoing data are not sufficiently homogeneous to support any precise generalization as to the level of industrial labor productivity that may be expected to obtain in an underdeveloped area. For one thing, there are likely to be sharp interindustry variations. It is quite possible for single plants or industries within an industrially backward country to measure up to the levels of efficiency prevailing in advanced nations. However, the evidence that is available indicates that for manufacturing as a whole, a level of labor productivity above, say, 40 per cent of that of the United States is characteristic of a developed nation,[5] with substantially lower levels, perhaps 20 per cent and less, prevailing in underdeveloped areas. In other words, in a typically underdeveloped area, it will require at least five, and perhaps ten or even more workers to produce the same amount of goods as a single American worker.

2. *Labor productivity and capital allocation.*

From the policy interpretations of SMP that we have discussed above it would appear that India, for example, would be deviating from the prescribed course if in allocating capital to an industry, or to a process within an industry, it attempted to attain the U. S. (or British) labor productivity level unless such result were the unavoidable result of fixed technical coefficients, since the marginal product of the capital invested would undoubtedly be greater diluted than concentrated.[6] Labor productivity should presumably rise at a relatively slow rate as capital trickles into the defiles marked by marginal productivity.

In fact, actual development programs have often run counter to these prescriptions. In the case of a group of Mediterranean countries, the major share of recent investment of industrial capital

3. International Bank for Reconstruction and Development (IBRD), *The Economic Development of Ceylon* (Baltimore, 1953), p. 523.
4. See Wilbert E. Moore, *Industrialization and Labor* (Ithaca, 1951), p. 108.
5. Just before World War II, Great Britain, Germany, Russia, Sweden, and Holland were said to be within a range of 40–50 per cent of the U. S. productivity level. L. Rostas, *Comparative Productivity in British and American Industry* (Cambridge, 1948), p. 40.
6. We assume that there is a direct correlation between capital intensity and labor productivity. This proposition cannot be proved on the basis of data presently available. It has been asserted of Europe that "there is a close rela-

356

has gone into high capital-intensity producer services.[7] A similar allocation of capital in Mexico caused some disquiet to an apparently orthodox-minded International Bank mission.[8] A disproportionately large share of Soviet capital resources have been diverted into capital-intensive heavy industry rather than into more labor-intensive light industry, and into capital-intensive processes within industry.[9]

Some arguments in favor of the goal that we have advanced, i.e., maximization of the capital/labor ratio through application of the criterion of the marginal *per-capita* reinvestment quotient, and against the practical corollaries of SMP follow:

(a) It may be well to dispose first of the popular argument that allocation of investment to labor-intensive industry is a social desideratum where surplus population exists. For the very short run, it is incontrovertible that the maximum number of persons can be put to work with the minimum amount of capital investment if the capital is simple in form and widespread in its distribution. For example, the WPA program in the United States, the purpose of which was employment regardless of output, represented a logical application of this principle. In the longer run, however, there is considerable doubt of the general validity of the proposition.

The point may best be illustrated by a simple model. Let us assume that a product can be manufactured under alternative combinations of labor and machinery, e.g., with an automatic machine requiring little labor or with a semiautomatic machine requiring more labor. For any year, the employment provided by any combination

tionship between horse-power per head and output per head." United Nations, *Economic Bulletin for Europe*, Vol. 3, No. 1, p. 24. However, Rostas found "no correlation between horse-power per unit of output and output per worker, i.e., industries where horse-power per unit of output is higher in the United States are not identical with industries where United States output per worker is also relatively high." L. Rostas, *op. cit.*, p. 54. We should judge that the relationship between capital intensity and labor productivity is closer at lower than at higher states in industrial development, i.e., that the capital factor plays a more important role as a determinant of productivity where there is little capital than where industry is already heavily capitalized.

7. Chenery, *op. cit.*, p. 76.

8. The mission noted in its report: "In Mexico, the principal capital goods industries require a much higher investment of capital per unit of value added and per worker employed than the major consumer goods industries. It is this factor which makes the orientation of industrial investment toward capital goods industries a matter of especial concern in a country where capital resources are scarce and the potential market for capital goods smaller than for consumer goods." IBRD, *The Economic Development of Mexico* (Baltimore, 1953), p. 65.

9. See Norman M. Kaplan, "Capital Formation and Allocation," in Abram Bergson, *op. cit.*, p. 37, and the comments of Alexander Erlich, *ibid.*, pp. 92–97.

of men and machines, can be represented by the following equation:[1]

$$(1) \qquad E_{t+1} = E_1 \left(1 + \frac{p - ew}{c}\right)^t$$

1. The variables may be defined as follows:

I = total investment in any period
P = gross value added in any period
W = total real compensation of labor in any period
w = real wage rate
N = number of machines
p = output per machine, i.e., $P = Np$
E = total employment
e = number of workers per machine, i.e., $E = eN$
c = cost per machine
v = wage cost per machine, i.e., $v = ew$

It is assumed that $I = P - W$, i.e., that the total amount invested in any period is the difference between total gross value added and the real compensation of labor. Then:

(1.1) $I = P - Ew$
(1.2) $I = Np - Ew$
(1.3) $I = Np - eNw = N(p - ew)$
(1.4) $c\Delta N = N(p - ew)$

$$\Delta N = \frac{N(p - ew)}{c}$$

(1.5) $\dfrac{\Delta E}{e} = \dfrac{N(p - ew)}{c}$, from the relationship $\Delta E = e\Delta N$

(1.6) $\Delta E = \dfrac{eN(p - ew)}{c}$

(1.7) $\Delta E = \dfrac{E(p - ew)}{c}$, and substituting $v = ew$,

(1.8) $\Delta E = \dfrac{E(p - v)}{c}$

This yields the basic equation: $\Delta E_t = E_t \left(\dfrac{p - v}{c}\right)$

(2.1) $E_{t+1} = E_t + \Delta E_t = E_t \left(1 + \dfrac{p - v}{c}\right)$

(2.2) $\dfrac{E_{t+1}}{E_t} = 1 + \dfrac{p - v}{c}$ for all t

(2.3) $E_t = E_1 \dfrac{E_2}{E_1} \dfrac{E_3}{E_2} \cdots \dfrac{E_{t-2}}{E_{t-3}} \dfrac{E_{t-1}}{E_{t-2}} \dfrac{E_t}{E_{t-1}}$

(2.4) $E_t = E_1 \left(1 + \dfrac{p - v}{c}\right)^{t-1}$

This may be rewritten

(2.5) $E_{t+1} = E_1 \left(1 + \dfrac{p - v}{c}\right)^t$, and in our original symbols

(2.6) $E_{t+1} = E_1 \left(1 + \dfrac{p - ew}{c}\right)^t$

358

where E_{t+1} represents employment in the $t + 1$ year, E_1 employment in the initial year, p the output per machine, e the number of workers per machine, w the wage rate, and c the cost per machine. If E_1, p, and e are assumed to be parameters, then the value of E_{t+1} will depend upon the relationship of c and w.

Essentially, all this formula does is to state formally a simple notion that can be grasped intuitively: that the larger the portion of the output of an industry, or a society, which is reinvested rather than consumed, the more rapid will be the process of capital accumulation, and *pari passu*, the growth of employment opportunities in industry. Conversely, the greater the share of output that is consumed, the slower will be the rate of expansion of capital and employment.

The following data for the Indian textile industry *circa* 1943, may be used to illustrate the application of the formula:[2]

	Capital investment per worker (rupees)	Value added per worker (rupees)	Annual earnings per worker (rupees)
1. Power machinery, large scale .	1200	650	80
2. Power machinery, small scale .	300	200	80
3. Automatic loom, cottage industry..........	90	80	80
4. Hand loom, cottage industry .	35	45	80

So, for example, if we apply the data for a small scale power loom to formula (1), we have, for year $t + 1 = 5$, the following:[3]

$$E_5 = 4\left(1 + \frac{200 - (1)(80)}{300}\right)^4 = 15.3$$

Similarly, the formula may be applied to the above data for other types of mills, and for other time periods, the results being as follows:

2. The source of the capital and value added data is *The Eastern Economist*, July 23, 1943, p. 340. The figure of 80 rupees used in the illustration was purely hypothetical, chosen for purposes of illustration. In fact, annual earnings in the non-cottage sector of the Indian textile industry were considerably higher in 1943, varying from 204 rupees in Bihar to 832 rupees in Bombay. A. N. Agarwala, *Indian Labor Problems* (Allahabad, 1947), pp. 49–50. However, the capital data in the example may well refer to an earlier year, and since there was a severe wartime inflation, a realistic wage figure is difficult to determine. Moreover, the wage should be differentiated among the various sectors of the industry.

3. In applying this formula, it is assumed that total investment in each case is 1200 rupees, so that in the case of the small scale power loom, an initial investment of 1200 rupees would make $E_1 = 4$. In each case e is taken to equal one, and therefore p is equal to the value added per worker.

359

HYPOTHETICAL EMPLOYMENT PROVIDED BY INITIAL
INVESTMENT OF 1200 RUPEES IN VARIOUS TYPES OF COTTON
TEXTILE MACHINERY

Year (t + 1)	Modern mill, large scale	Power loom, small scale	Automatic loom, cottage industry	Hand loom, cottage industry
5	5	15	13	35
10	34	83	13	35
15	242	444	13	35
20	1,718	2,390	13	35
25	12,200	12,860	13	35

It is assumed in the above example that the total product, less labor cost, is reinvested each year. No allowance is made for capital replacement, although this could be accomplished by reducing the product available for reinvestment by a depreciation factor, thus slowing up the process of capital accumulation. As we shall see, however, it may be quite appropriate to disregard the depreciation factor in an economic development model of this character.

It is clear from the above example that the wage rate (w) is the critical variable; that the amount of employment provided in any future year by a unit of investment depends largely upon the wage deduction from the product of industry. If, for example, an annual wage of 150 rather than 80 rupees had been used,[4] employment provided by the large scale modern mill would have been 24 in ten years, as against only 16 in the small scale power mills. The higher the real wage level, the greater is the advantage in terms of potential employment accruing from the use of capital-intensive machinery.[5]

(b) Failure to introduce capital intensive techniques at the outset of the industrialization process may create insurmountable institutional barriers to modernization. This is true particularly in democratic communities, where labor/capital coefficients cannot be altered by fiat. The case of Cuba is very much in point:

"Cuban industrial development has been greatly retarded by labor's resistance to new machinery, modern methods, or virtually anything that will increase the efficiency of production. . . . When improved methods or machinery are introduced into a factory with permission of the workers, it is generally under the stipulation that the same number of workers be employed as were used under the older, inefficient methods. The workers also commonly see to it that the new equipment turns out no more products than the old."[6]

4. See *supra*, n. 2, p. 358.
5. Thus in Surinam, where wages are relatively high, it was suggested that "the development of the country must rather be in the direction of relatively high capitalized production, where the productivity of the workers can be great enough to justify their level of wages." IBRD, *Surinam* (Baltimore, 1952), p. 26.
6. IBRD, *Report on Cuba* (Washington, 1951), pp. 143–44.

360

In neighboring Puerto Rico, "the legislative branch of the Insular government, which is highly responsive to the representations of the electorate, has shown considerable interest in creating and protecting job opportunities, although these sometimes involve make-work practices for a class of firms which might otherwise be unnecessary."[7] Low productivity in Mexican textile manufacturing was attributed in large measure to "present contract legislation for the industry, which stipulates the number of workers to be employed in relation to the capacity of the mills, and establishes an inflexible basis for the proportion between production and wages."[8]

In all of these countries it was observed that newly established factories had considerable latitude in determining their labor/capital ratios; it was in the older, established plants that the problem was acute. This suggests that the failure to adopt the correct criterion at the very outset of a development program may render infinitely more difficult the attainment of high output per worker, which must be the eventual goal of a development program.

(c) Industrialization almost inevitably means urbanization, and urbanization entails charges upon the production surplus available for capital accumulation. In some countries, e.g., Turkey, an industrial labor force must be recruited from the farm and brought to the city, entailing a considerable investment in such urban facilities as housing, sanitation, water and canteens. But even where large cities with surplus manpower already exist, as in India or China, the social costs involved in bringing newly recruited industrial workers up to a minimum efficiency level may be very considerable. The Colombo Plan, for example, allocated 18 per cent of projected capital investment to "social capital," compared with only 10 per cent to "industry and mining."[9] In the case of Egypt, it has been pointed out that many workers are living below the subsistence level, in completely inadequate houses, leading to chronic undernourishment, and high disease rates, which in turn result in a high rate of absenteeism and low productivity. Where an efficient labor force is to be maintained, the social capital costs may be very high. Such costs are often neglected when the criterion of SMP, and particularly its accompanying corollaries, are advocated.

The establishment of the highest initial productivity of labor will

7. Simon Rottenberg, "Labor Cost in the Puerto Rican Economy," *Revista Juridica of the University of Puerto Rico*, Vol. XX, No. 2, Nov.-Dec. 1950, p. 59.
8. *Labor Productivity of the Cotton Textile Industry in Five Latin-American Countries, op. cit.*, p. 84.
9. Chiang Hsieh, "Underemployment in Asia," *International Labor Review*, July 1952, p. 32.

minimize urbanization cost by bringing into the industrial labor force a minimum of workers. One may question the wisdom of *minimizing* the transfer of manpower from agricultural employment to industrial and urban pursuits, but the optimal transfer rate would probably be significantly lower than the maximum rate of labor absorption. The establishment of a high initial productivity of labor, following our criterion for allocating capital, will yield a lower ratio of urbanization cost to output per worker than under the orthodox criterion, and thus contribute to maximizing the rate of capital formation.

(d) Too little attention has been paid to the *pattern* of industry which will facilitate, or indeed, make possible, industrial development. It is not a matter of indifference whether capital is allocated, say, to the manufacture of iron and steel, or to the manufacture of textiles. Development mission recommendations are all too prone to assume that funds invested in light industries based, for example, on local raw materials, will in some unexplained manner lead eventually to economic development.

Properly speaking, neither the criterion of SMP in its orthodox interpretation nor our SMP criterion will lead automatically to the establishment of an industrial pattern which will maximize industrial development. This is a subject as yet largely unexplored, and it can probably best be tackled in terms of a model investment grid, based upon the specific conditions of each underdeveloped area. However, the above-cited corollaries of SMP are likely to lead in a direction other than industrialization, for the average productivity of capital tends to be greatest in light industries, where a considerable amount of labor may be used, and least in heavy industries, where the substitutability of labor for capital is less.[1] Conversely, our criterion of maximizing the capital/labor ratio tends to favor those industries which are essential to the development of modern industry.

(e) As we have pointed out, the usual prescriptions for capital allocation favor short-lived over long-lived capital goods. From the point of view of our suggested criterion a strong case can be made for the obverse rule; viz., that there are considerable advantages to be

1. This is an empirical statement for which factual proof is largely lacking. However, 1947 U. S. Census of Manufactures data indicated that capital investment per worker in American industry clearly tended to be greater in the heavy capital goods industries than in the light consumer goods industries. For example, capital investment per worker in the industrial chemicals industry was $15,868; in iron and steel, $7,309; in machinery (excluding electrical), $6,993; compared with $4,673 per worker in textile mill products; $2,954 in apparel; $3,376 in leather and its products. There were exceptions to the rule, such as canning and preserving, with $10,036 invested per worker, but in general the data appear to support the statement in the text.

362

gained from longer-lived rather than shorter-lived capital goods. Domar has demonstrated that under conditions of growth, replacement/gross investment ratios can be considerably lower for longer-lived than for shorter-lived capital goods.[2]

At the outset it should be made clear that it is replacement and not depreciation that is the significant variable for purposes of development. Depreciation cost, as usually conceived, is an accounting matter,[3] and is not directly connected with the productive power of a capital good at any point in time. Thus, for our purposes the important variable is not net investment, as usually defined, but gross investment less replacement cost. (For ease in communication we shall refer to gross investment less replacement as GIR.)

Initially there are three advantages to longer-lived capital under conditions of capital growth. (1) The longer the life of the capital, the longer the period of time during which no replacements have to be made, and hence the greater the available output per man during this period than with capital of a shorter life. (2) Out of a greater output per man there is the possibility of greater reinvestment per man. (3) With greater output and reinvestment per man there is a greater chance of overcoming the critical minimum effort[4] hurdle than otherwise.

If the capital stock is to be maintained intact, then eventually replacements must be made. But even after the advantage of the early no-replacement period has passed, there is still an advantage in a capital stock that is on the average longer-lived than shorter-lived under conditions of growth. This is because the longer the average life of the capital, the smaller is the proportion of gross investment needed for replacement, and therefor the larger is the GIR period after period. For example, suppose that the rate of gross investment growth is 5 per cent per year, then, according to Domar's figures,[5] if the average length of life of capital is four years, the ratio of replacement to gross investment will be 82 per cent per year; if the average length of life of capital is ten years the replacement/gross investment ratio drops to 61 per cent; and if the average length of life of capital is thirty years, the replacement/gross investment ratio drops as low as 22 per cent. Clearly, the greater the life span of

2. E. D. Domar, "Depreciation Replacement and Growth," *Economic Journal*, LXIII (March 1953), 1–32.

3. Strictly speaking, physical depreciation interpreted as user cost is an economic variable that does have to be accounted for. In order not to complicate the argument we assume that user cost is an insignificant portion of accounting depreciation. In any event, user cost is a short-run cost consideration since it varies with output.

4. See below, p. 366, for a discussion of this term.

5. Domar, *op. cit.*, p. 8.

investment goods, other things equal, the greater the possibility for economic growth.

3. *Population growth and development.*

(a) To a considerable extent our arguments in the previous sections were based on the notion that there is a dependent relationship between the allocation of investment, the consequent allocation of the labor force, and the growth and quality of the population. Although this is hardly a novel idea it is customary for economists to argue as though these were independent matters.[6] Solutions that may appear to be appropriate in instances where the population problem is disregarded often cease to be appropriate when it is recognized that the population aspect is an integral and inseparable part of the problem. Although we cannot go into detail at this juncture, we shall indicate something of the nature and significance of this point.

In considering the population factor there are three things about which we can be fairly certain on the basis of past experience: (1) that economic development, if it takes place, will be accompanied by rapid population growth; (2) that the only way to reduce population growth is to reduce the birth rate; and (3) that declines in birth rates, if they take place, will follow rather than precede declines in death rates. This implies that in order to avoid the Malthusian dilemma, and at some point to achieve a slackening of population growth, it is necessary to create an environment that is conducive to a reduction in birth rates. From past evidence it would appear that the urban, industrially and commercially developing sectors rather than the rural agricultural areas provide the environment conducive to falling birth rates.

Reference to the vital statistics of most underdeveloped areas suggests that economic development will be accompanied by rapid population growth. On the average the underdeveloped countries of the world are increasing their population at a rate of 1.4 per cent per year.[7] Improved nutrition and public health measures that often accompany economic development can reduce death rates so that the average rate of growth may rise to 2 or 2.5 per cent per year. The last rate will yield an increase in population for the underdeveloped

---

6. For example, Professor Viner, in observing that population increases will tend to worsen a country's terms of trade, argues that " . . . this will apply equally, as a tendency, to countries whether they are predominantly agricultural or predominantly industrial, and the appropriate remedy in either case would be to check the rate of population growth." (Viner, *op. cit.*, p. 142.)

7. This generalization is based upon a study of the United Nations, *Demographic Yearbook*, 1953.

364

two-thirds of the world of some two *billion* people by 1984. So much
for the magnitude of the problem.

The reasons behind the other assertions have been investigated
and long studied by demographers and ably summarized by Professor
Notestein:

> "The more rapid response of mortality than of fertility to the forces of
> modernization is probably inevitable. The reduction of mortality is a universally
> acceptable goal and faces no substantial social obstacles. But the reduction of
> fertility requires a shift in social goals from those directed toward the survival
> of the group to those directed toward the welfare and development of the indi-
> vidual. This change, both of goals and of the social equipment by which they
> are achieved, is at best a slow process. As a result, the period of modernization is
> virtually certain to yield rapid population increase."[8]

On the factors that were and are responsible for the eventual reduction in birth rates Notestein writes that they

> " . . . center around the growing individualism and rising levels of popular aspira-
> tion developed in urban industrial living. With the growth of huge and mobile
> city populations, the individual came to depend less and less on the status of his
> family for his place among his fellows. The station to which he was born gave
> place to his accomplishments and possessions as the measure of his importance.
> Meanwhile, the family lost many of its functions to the factory, the school, and
> commercial enterprises. All these developments made large families a pro-
> gressively difficult and expensive undertaking; expensive and difficult for a popu-
> lation increasingly freed from older taboos and increasingly willing to solve its
> problems rather than to accept them. In short, under the impact of urban life,
> the social aim of perpetuating the family gave way progressively to that of pro-
> moting the health, education, and material welfare of the individual child; family
> limitation became widespread; and the end of the period of growth came in
> sight."[9]

If Notestein's view is correct, and it is certainly true for the past,
then the allocation of investment funds can be important in determining the point at which the rate of population growth declines. Certainly, investment in agricultural-rural pursuits will have much less
effect (if not a negative effect) in fostering fertility declines than the
creation of an urban industrial-commercial environment where the
factors mentioned by Notestein can take root, grow, spread, and have
their effect on the birth rate.

At first blush there may appear to be an apparent contradiction
between the point just made and our previous recognition of the
problem of the social cost of transferring workers from agriculture to
urban pursuits. We cannot suggest that on the one hand, city-ward
migration should be reduced in order to minimize the social costs of

8. Frank W. Notestein, "Population — The Long View," in Theodore W.
Schultz (ed.), *Food for the World*, pp. 40–41.
9. *Ibid.*, p. 41.

urbanization, and at the same time that rural-urban migration be maximized in order to facilitate the reduction of fertility rates. But this is only an apparent dilemma. Both the fertility effect and the social transfer costs effect must be taken into account and balanced against one another in terms of their combined effect on the eventual capital/labor ratio. These two factors are not entirely antithetical, for it is rising standards of living as a consequence of increasing wages and productivity in the urban environment that creates the proper atmosphere for fertility decline. If wages in the new industries are permitted to decline through the substitution of labor for capital, this will not only reduce the rate of reinvestment but also diminish the creation of those social conditions that lead to the economic and social mobility conducive to fertility decline. Thus, an optimum rate of urbanization should not be confused with the short-run maximum rate; it is rather the highest rate consistent with the maintenance of increasing wages and productivity under general social conditions conducive to fertility decline.

There is another viewpoint from which the two factors are not contradictory. The net social transfer cost is the opportunity foregone of adding to the stock of producers goods. But that part of the social transfer cost that aids in fertility reduction makes an indirect contribution toward increasing the capital/labor ratio. Thus, expenditures on educational facilities, birth control clinics, or other facilities that change attitudes or dispense information conducive to fertility decline contribute toward increasing capital per worker in the future. Much more can be said on this aspect of our problem but we would certainly go beyond the bounds of this paper if we attempted to derive a theory of the optimal rate of urbanization.

Our interest in the possibility of achieving varying rates of population growth as a result of different investment patterns arises out of the consequences of varying rates of population growth on the *per capita* output potential. First, population growth reduces the capital/labor ratio and as a consequence reduces the *per capita* output potential. Second, population growth, through its adverse effect on *per capita* output and savings, tends to reduce the rate of reinvestment as a consequence of any initial investment. Thus, the lower the rate of population growth, or the earlier the decline in the rate of population growth sets in, the greater the *per capita* reinvestment quotient. In sum, the allocation of investment will affect not only total output but also the distribution of the labor force, the growth of the urban sector of the community, the social and cultural conditions under which people live, and the consequent attitudes towards early mar-

366

riage, family size, and the resultant population growth. Therefore, the allocation that maximizes current output may be quite different from the allocation that maximizes the ultimate capital/labor ratio or the ultimate output potential per man.

(b) If an underdeveloped country is to develop successfully, it is necessary for that country to make a large initial effort to increase output and to do so very early in the development attempt. If the initial or early effort does not reach a critical minimum, then it is likely that the country will revert back to its former underdeveloped stage. The reasons for the need of an initial or early minimum effort follow:

(1) The potential growth of population makes it necessary to have initially a sufficiently large increase in capital, which induces successive increases in capital, so that it is not possible for the population increases to reduce the average amount of capital per worker.

(2) A minimum effort is necessary in order to create the economic environment where external economies are possible. For example, railroads, communication systems, and irrigation works all may require large-scale initial efforts.

(3) The initial effort must be sufficient to raise incomes per head so that savings can be achieved, to continue the rate of capital accumulation. For once the rate of capital accumulation declines, there is always the challenge of population increases reducing the amount of capital per head.[1]

The critical minimum investment necessary will depend, in part, on the allocation of the investment funds. The SMP corollary allocation may or may not minimize the critical minimum investment necessary, while the allocation under our criterion, which directly takes into account the population factor, will tend to maximize the chances of overcoming the critical minimum. For that allocation that yields a lower rate of population growth, or leads to an earlier decline in the rate of population growth, reduces the critical minimum investment necessary, other things equal.

We may note that the critical minimum effort thesis implies the desirability of rapid capital accumulation early in the process of development not only in order to overcome the population hurdle,

---

1. For an elaboration of this idea see H. Leibenstein, *A Theory of Economic-Demographic Development* (Princeton University Press, 1954), chaps. IV and V. H. W. Singer appears to suggest the same idea, in somewhat different words, when he argues that the underdeveloped economies are faced with a series of interlocking vicious circles that only an able, significant, and sustained effort can break. "Economic Progress in Underdeveloped Countries," *Social Research* (Mar. 1949), pp. 5 ff.

but also because there may be a connection between the tempo of change, the rate of urbanization, and the creation of an environment conducive to the lowering of the birth rate. This last point, while not an established fact, would appear to be a reasonable speculation since growing individualism, economic and social mobility, loosening of family function, and lesser dependence on family status and traditional values generally go hand in hand with a quickening economic tempo.

4. *Some obstacles to high labor productivity in backward areas.*

The determination of a correct general criterion for capital allocation is not tantamount to its application. It may well be that environmental and institutional factors dictate extensive modifications in practice.[2] For example, even if it were determined that an indigenous iron and steel industry was basic to rapid development, the lack of iron ore and fuel might prevent its establishment. There may be a hundred reasons why a high initial level of labor productivity is impossible of achievement.[3]

It is our belief that the criterion of the marginal per capita reinvestment quotient and the corollary of a high capital/labor ratio are appropriate general guides in programs for economic development. In this section we shall consider some of the factors which stand in the way of the indicated solution for allocating available investment resources.

(a) The surplus of manpower, and the consequently low wage level, that characterize the major underdeveloped areas of the world, are serious stumbling blocks in the path of economic growth. The surplus may be hidden in the form of underemployment in agriculture, where the marginal productivity of labor must often approach zero; or it may be all too evident in the form of chronic urban unemployment. In extreme cases, low quality labor may be virtually a free good; in Ecuador, for example, it was estimated that a cotton mill could have ten times as many workers as an American mill without any difference in the relation of the labor cost to the value of the finished product.[4] "Because of keen competition in the employment market, the levels of wages earned in these occupations are kept extremely low, and because of low wages the management has little

2. Also moral or religious considerations may require modifications of the criterion.
3. See Wilbert E. Moore, *op. cit.*, chap. V.
4. *Labor Productivity in the Cotton Textile Industry in Five Latin-American Countries, op. cit.*, p. 67.

368

incentive to raise its standards of efficiency."[5] In such situations the
employment of as large a number of workers as possible appears not
only to make good economic common sense, but to be socially desirable as well.

One possible solution under these circumstances is to alter conditions to conform with our criterion by making labor scarce artificially.
This can be done in a number of ways: by legislation establishing
relatively high minimum wages and working conditions;[6] by direct
governmental control of manpower; or, in the case of state industry,
by imposing high labor productivity targets upon management. None
of these prescriptions is an easy one to follow. The islands of favored
employment will have to be protected by the government in some
manner, for individual entrepreneurs will find it difficult to resist the
constant temptation of cheap labor. Yet there is ample precedent
for such a policy; one may cite the oil refineries in the Near East,
where foreign management polices the barriers, and a modern Egyptian textile mill where native entrepreneurial policy is effective in
this regard.[7]

(b) The shortage of skilled labor is almost invariably cited as an
obstacle to high productivity,[8] and undoubtedly it is. Yet there is
reason to believe that the difficulties in this respect are exaggerated.
Looking to the Russian industrialization experience, it was necessary
to train for the semiskilled trades millions of raw farm hands within
the space of a few years. During the First Five Year Plan the Soviet
industrial labor force roughly doubled in size. Of the 12.5 million
new workers who entered industry for the first time between 1928 and
1932, 8.5 million had been peasants.[9] The training they received was
certainly not thorough; most of it was done directly on the job. True

5. Chiang Hsieh, "Underemployment in Asia," *International Labor Review*,
June 1952, p. 703.
6. It is quite true that higher wages by themselves reduce the amount of
production available for reinvestment. The point is that higher wages, by restrict-
ing the use of manpower, may lead to a lower *total* wage bill, depending upon the
elasticity of the demand for labor and the absolute magnitudes involved. Furthermore, by developing a socio-economic setting in which we can overcome the institutional barriers to rising productivity we can get a larger surplus for reinvestment.
7.. Gamal Eldin Said, *op. cit.*, p. 506.
8. E.g.: "Even more serious, there will in all likelihood be severe shortages
of skilled labor for jobs which require technical knowledge, or which involve the
exercise of organizational or supervisory talent." IBRD, *Surinam*, p. 89. "Other
difficulties may well emerge in the supply of foremen, skilled and semi-skilled
workers." IBRD, *The Economic Development of Iraq*, p. 83. " . . . the acute
shortage of trained personnel . . . is one of the main obstacles to rapid progress."
IBRD, *The Economic Development of Ceylon*, p. 55.
9. Solomon Schwarz, *Labor in the Soviet Union* (New York, 1951), pp. 9,
31–32.

vocational schools were virtually nonexistent. Yet though the process was wasteful, it sufficed, and permitted the Russians to take greater pains with subsequent generations of labor inductees. The training of technical personnel was a longer-range problem, and here the cadres of well-trained pre-Soviet engineers were of great importance. By 1940, however, technical schools were turning out large numbers of qualified engineers and technicians.

(c) Under contemporary conditions of economic development in the democratic countries, a strong labor movement is likely to arise at the inception of industrialization, rather than at a fairly advanced stage as in the past. Moreover, the unionism of backward areas is apt to be radical in its orientation, in view of poor labor conditions and the impatience of workers with the seeming inability of the method of collective bargaining to secure for them immediate betterment. There is therefore ever present the danger that resources will be diverted from investment to consumption, that the seeds of industrial development will not be permitted to mature.

High productivity, with its implication of fewer and better paid workers, will tend to mitigate the upsurge of labor protest, to moderate the extremism of the labor movement, and to provide a climate of worker opinion favorable to technological change.[1] This is by no means a complete answer to what will undoubtedly be one of the crucial problems in industrialization, but at least it can be said that the high productivity solution appears to provide the labor conditions which are most propitious for success.

III. Conclusion

We have endeavored to show in the foregoing pages that the criterion of allocating investment on the basis of the marginal productivity of each unit of capital invested is not suitable for contemporary underdeveloped areas because of the invalidity of what we have termed the *ceteris paribus* assumption. When the facts of rapid population growth, political instability, and institutional obstacles to technological change, all of which are generally typical of underdeveloped areas today, are taken into account, it becomes clear that time is of the essence in developmental programs. The process of development must be sufficiently rapid to satisfy the swiftly burgeoning aspirations of people suddenly released from a Malthusian world and endowed with political power. The alterna-

---

1. We assume that the low productivity solution will yield such small results in terms of higher standards for the larger number of workers affected as to have little mollifying effect upon the degree of labor protest.

370

tive is the constant encroachment of consumption upon the national product; falling rather than rising *per capita* incomes as a consequence of explosive population growth; and eventual chaos as the mass organizations called into being by industrialization in "width," rather than in "depth," are forced to exploit their power by pressure from below.

Our thesis, baldly, is that successful economic development under present conditions, particularly in the face of gross backwardness, hinges largely upon the introduction of modern technology upon as large a scale as possible. Professor Gerschenkron has pointed out that in the past,

> "to the extent that industrialization took place, it was largely by application of the most modern and efficient techniques that backward countries could hope to achieve success, particularly if their industrialization proceeded in the face of competition from the advanced country. . . . This seems to explain the tendency on the part of backward countries to concentrate at a relatively early point in their industrialization on promotion of such branches of industrial activities in which recent technological progress has been particularly rapid. . . . In viewing the economic history of Europe in the nineteenth century, the impression is very strong that only when industrial development could commence on a large scale did the tension between the pre-industrialization conditions and the benefit that may be expected from industrialization became sufficiently strong to overcome the existing obstacles and to liberate the forces that made for industrial progress."[1]

This applies with even greater force to twentieth century Asia and Africa, with their far greater relative and absolute backwardness. These areas can best hope to see the completion of successful programs of economic development within the reasonable future, and (what is critical) under the auspices of political democracy, if in allocating available capital resources, the twin desiderata of up-to-date equipment and relatively high initial capital/labor ratios are kept to the fore.

UNIVERSITY OF CALIFORNIA
BERKELEY

WALTER GALENSON.
HARVEY LEIBENSTEIN.

2. Alexander Gerschenkron, "Economic Backwardness in Historical Perspective," in Bert F. Hoselitz (ed.), *The Progress of Underdeveloped Areas* (Chicago, 1952), pp. 7–9.

THE THEORY OF UNDEREMPLOYMENT
IN BACKWARD ECONOMIES[1]

HARVEY LEIBENSTEIN

University of California, Berkeley

IN THE literature on "underdeveloped areas" there are frequent assertions that such areas have a great deal of "disguised" or visible underemployment.[2] Indeed, it has become commonplace to argue, as Professor Nurkse does, that a means of developing these economies is to employ the "surplus labor" on the construction of capital. In some studies we find attempts to measure the extent of the surplus labor in agriculture;[3] in others we find attempts to measure the capital needed to absorb the surplus labor in non-agricultural pursuits.[4] In all such studies there is the clear implication that the marginal product of labor in agriculture is really zero.[5] It is observed that agricultural workers in underdeveloped areas do receive a positive wage, yet the notion of surplus labor receiving a positive wage or income is a contradiction in the light of received theory. There is clearly some need to reconcile what are presumed to be the broad facts and our theory on the matter.

I. INTRODUCTION

In the case in which all land is owned by those who work it there is no problem of explaining the simultaneous existence of surplus labor and of positive incomes received by those who work the land. But where this is not the case the problem is rather complex.

First consider the case in which the entire economy is made up of smallholders. Everyone owns his own land. The return to every small-holder is a combination of rent and wages. It makes

---

[1] I am indebted to Professors C. M. Li, Peter Steiner, and A. G. Papandreou and to Dr. Margaret Gordon for helpful comments.

[2] See R. Nurkse, *Problems of Capital Formation in Underdeveloped Countries* (Oxford, 1953), pp. 33 ff.; P. N. Rosenstein-Rodan, "Problems of Industrialization of Eastern and Southeastern Europe," *Economic Journal*, June, 1953, pp. 202 ff.; W. E. Moore, *Economic Demography of Eastern and Southern Europe* (Geneva, 1945), chap. iii; Doreen Warriner, *The Economics of Peasant Farming* (London, 1939), pp. 68 ff.; and many others.

[3] Moore, *op. cit.*

[4] See K. Mandelbaum, *The Industrialization of Backward Areas* (Oxford, 1945).

[5] Of course, these studies do not *prove* that the marginal product of labor is zero in such areas. By the same token, no one has shown that this is not or cannot be the case.

91

no difference how we divide the small-holders' income between rent and wages. If we attribute it all to rent, we can square the theory with the presumed facts. Marginal productivity is zero, and therefore the imputed wage is zero. Each small-holder will work his little piece of land to the point at which there is some marginal return just above zero. This will require less labor than he has available. No small-holder will want to hire any labor, since each has more time than he can use on his piece of land. There is, therefore, no demand or price for labor, and we, indeed, have disguised unemployment and a surplus of labor.

Once we leave this hypothetical world of small-holders, it becomes more difficult to work out a neat explanation. Suppose that the agricultural community is made up of landlords who do not work the land and of tenants or sharecroppers who do. In this case the rent goes to the landlord. The sharecropper gets only the return from his labor; this return depends on the competitively determined share of the crop. Now, suppose each sharecropper has a small plot for which the rent is, say, 50 per cent. In keeping with the nature of our problem, let us assume that it takes him only half his time to work his plot. The rest of his labor time is a free good to him. It is therefore in the interest of each sharecropper to seek an additional piece of land even if he has to pay a higher rent for it. Thus the competition for additional land must reduce tenant shares. How far can such a reduction go? On the one hand, no matter how small the share becomes, there is always an incentive for an individual sharecropper to get more land at an even smaller share. The tenants' share cannot fall to zero, since tenants have to subsist. But it would appear that the tenants' share cannot remain positive, because competition for land will force it down to zero.

Finally, consider the case in which the agricultural labor force is made up of landless laborers rather than tenants or small-holders. The analysis of this case is very similar to that of tenants or sharecroppers, except that now the unemployment will be visible rather than disguised. If we assume perfect markets then, as usual, competition will force wages down toward zero. That is to say, if there is a labor surplus, then some members of the work force must be unemployed, and the unemployed will be willing to work at less than the going wage. This will certainly depress the wage level. But can this process go on indefinitely? Obviously, the possibility of a zero wage cannot be seriously entertained. What is the way out of this dilemma?

Some writers have suggested that the "unemployment difficulties of underdeveloped areas . . . stem from . . . limited opportunities for technical substitution of factors and inappropriate factor endowments."[6] While this may be true, it is not difficult to show that it can explain only a part of our problem.

Consider the possibilities illustrated in Figures 1 and 2. These figures show a two-product (or two-sector), two-factor economy. Product A is the agricultural commodity, and product N is the non-agricultural commodity. The two factors of production are L, labor, and K, the non-labor factor. I shall refer to the owners of factor K in the non-agricultural sector as employers and to the owners of factor K in the agricultural sector as landlords. Figures 1 and 2 show the case of fixed coefficients of production. The line $N_K A_K$ is the locus of all combi-

[6] R. S. Eckaus, "Factor Proportions in Underdeveloped Areas," *American Economic Review*, September, 1955, pp. 540 ff.; see also Masao Fukuoka, "Full Employment and Constant Coefficients of Production," *Quarterly Journal of Economics*, February, 1955, pp. 23–44.

nations of products A and N that it is possible to produce with the fixed available quantity of factor K if the necessary amounts of L are available. Similarly, $N_L A_L$ is the locus of all combinations of the two products that can be produced with the fixed available quantity of L if the necessary amounts of K are available. In each figure the heavy line is the production possibility locus, which shows the combinations of outputs that can be produced given the fixed available quantities of both factors. In the situation shown in Figure 1 there is always some excess labor regardless of the distribution of output between products A and N.

In Figure 2 either factor can be in surplus depending on the allocation of out-

factors are involved, and labor will be underemployed regardless of its price.

The situation shown in Figure 2 is the more interesting. Suppose that the initial position is point D, which represents an output bundle for which there is excess labor. (The relative price of the two commodities can be read from the slope of the relevant segment of the production possibility curve.) Can the output bundle at

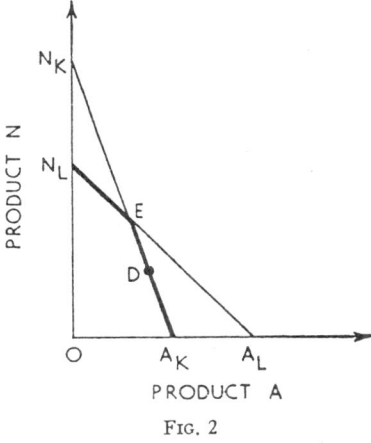

FIG. 2

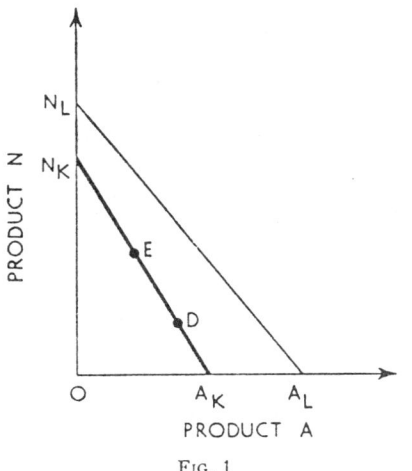

FIG. 1

put between products A and N. If most of the output is agricultural, then L is in surplus; if most of the output is non-agricultural, then K is in surplus. Point E is the output bundle that allows for the full employment of both factors. The broken line $N_L A_K$ is the production possibility curve.

In the case illustrated by Figure 1, underemployment is purely and entirely technologically determined. No economic

D really be a stable one? If there is competition in the labor market, the excess labor will force a reduction in the wage rate, which in turn will induce a fall in the relative price of product N. If product A (the agricultural commodity) is a wage good and product N is not, then a shift in the relative demand for the two commodities toward point E is certainly a possibility. By far the largest part of labor's income in a backward economy is spent on food. As wages decline, a point will be reached at which the entire labor income is spent on the wage good. Beyond some point, as wages fall, the demand for product A must fall almost proportionately, since the price of A must include the price of factor K, the scarce factor, whose price relative to L does not fall as the price of labor falls in terms of the wage good.[7] Moreover, the reduction in the demand for A by workers cannot usually be fully made up by an increase in demand by landlords and employers, since these groups are usually small in proportion to the total population. Therefore, we may expect that the demand for product N will increase as wages fall. It is thus possible that, as wages continue to fall, the relative demand for N increases to such an extent that the full-employment point is eventally reached.

But in a competitive labor market, as long as there is an excess supply of labor, wages will continue to fall until the excess disappears. Therefore, another possibility is that, no matter how low the wage rate, the relative elasticities of demand are such that the increase in the demand for N can never be large enough for the full-employment point to be reached. In other words, the alternative is that at all wage rates, including zero, the output bundle chosen will lie on the segment EA_K below the point E. But in this case there is always an excess labor supply, and we therefore expect the wage rate to fall to zero. We seem to end up with two alternatives: full employment and a zero wage rate. But neither of these alternatives seems to occur. Hence our dilemma.

II. THE WAGE-PRODUCTIVITY RELATIONSHIP

The clue that leads us out of our dilemma is the often-neglected relationship between the wage level and productivity. Simply put, the extent to which laborers are maintained will determine to some degree the amount of effort (or the number of units of work) that will be forth-coming. The amount of work that the representative laborer can be expected to perform depends on his energy level, his health, and his vitality, which in turn depend on his consumption level and most directly on the nutritive value of his food intake. That such a relation exists for some income levels may appear to be intuitively obvious, but the importance of the relationship can be illustrated by considering briefly some of the relevant facts stressed by the literature in the fields of nutrition and public health. Of course, I cannot review this body of literature in a critical and exhaustive fashion in this article, but it is nevertheless worthwhile to point out some of the highlights in order to show that there is a substantial empirical underpinning to the basic relation that I shall employ in my analysis.

The wage-productivity relationship can best be examined if it is broken up into two parts: (1) the relation between income (wages) and nutrition and (2) the relation between nutrition and productivity. A 1936 study by Lord Boyd Orr shows clearly that in England the value of the nutritive components of diet (such as calories, proteins, fats, calcium, and iron) are monotonic increasing functions of income.[8] Studies reported by the League of Nations' Committee on Nutrition give similar results for a number of other countries.[9] It is also evident from the estimates of calorie consumption in various countries made by the Food and Agriculture Organization of the United

---

[7] The relative price of K will probably rise. The price of K is mostly rent, and rent theory suggests that, as wages fall, rents rise relatively.

[8] *Food, Health, and Income: A Survey of Adequacy of Diet in Relation to Income* (London, 1936), pp. 34–35.

[9] *Nutrition: Final Report of the Mixed Committee of the League of Nations on the Relation of Nutrition to Health, Agriculture and Economic Policy* (Geneva, 1937), pp. 247 ff. See also International Labour Organisation, *Workers' Nutrition and Social Policy* (Geneva, 1936), chap. iii, "Facts on Workers' Diets," esp. p. 68.

THE THEORY OF UNDEREMPLOYMENT IN BACKWARD ECONOMIES   95

Nations (FAO) that, generally speaking, calorie consumption is directly correlated with per capita national income.[10] A number of detailed studies of workers in various underdeveloped countries show that for the groups studied the calorie intake per man per day was considerably below that designated by nutrition authorities as adequate for the maintenance of health and normal body weight and for the carrying-out of a full day's work at "normal" speed.[11] In general, it is believed that, when countries are divided into three groups according to per capita national income, in the underdeveloped areas the calorie intake per day is about 2,100; in the middle group of countries it is between 2,200 and 2,800; and only in the advanced countries is it above 3,000.[12] These figures may be compared with the intake of between 2,800 and 4,500 calories per day usually considered to be required for many types of work.

On the relation between calorie intake and productivity there are two types of evidence to be considered. The first comes from numerous physiological experiments whose results enable one to calculate the calories needed for various types of activities.[13] Of course, the number of calories required depends on the

size of the man and on the nature and strenuousness of his activities. A five-foot, six-inch man weighing 130 pounds requires about 1,400 calories for his resting metabolism alone, while a six-foot man of normal weight will usually require over 1,700 calories for this purpose. For every activity additional calories are needed. Thus for simply sitting an additional intake of 15–20 calories per hour will usually be needed; for moderate work between 80 and 240 additional calories per hour will probably be required. For example, walking requires 130–240 additional calories per hour, while activities that involve climbing may require 400–900 calories per hour.[14]

The significance of these figures can be seen from a few calculations. Let us assume that a day is made up of eight sleeping and sixteen waking hours and that 1,500 calories are needed for resting metabolism. Adding approximately 100 calories per hour for moderate work for a period of four hours and about 20 calories per hour for the remaining twelve hours of relaxation, we get a total of 2,140 calories needed to support a four-hour work day. We may observe that an addition of 320 calories, or a total of 2,460 calories, will support an eight-hour work day of the same degree of strenuousness. This implies that, if at the outset an employer pays a wage that permits his workers to buy a diet of no more than 2,140 calories, then he can approximately double his effective work force by paying a wage that would permit the workers to buy a diet of 2,460 calories. Of course, in actual practice the workers will, in both

[10] Food and Agriculture Organization, *The State of Food and Agriculture* (Washington, D.C., 1948). See also FAO, Committee on Calories Requirements, *Calorie Requirements: Report of the Committee . . .* (Washington, D.C., 1950).

[11] On this see, among others, V. Ramalingaswami and V. N. Patwardhan, "Diet and Health of South Indian Plantation Labor," *Indian Journal of Medical Research*, XXXVII (1949), 51–60. On the plantations studied over 3,000 calories per day were required to carry out the work well, but over 50 per cent of the workers consumed less than 2,000 calories per day. See also E. R. DeMello *et al.*, "A Nutritional Survey among Factory Workers in Bombay," *Indian Journal of Medical Science*, IV (1950), 337–60.

[12] FAO, *The State of Food and Agriculture.*

[13] See Henry C. Sherman, *Chemistry of Food and Nutrition* (New York: Macmillan Co., 1941), chaps. viii–xi; cf. Magnus Pyke, *Industrial Nutrition* (London, 1950), chap. ii.

[14] Pyke, *op. cit.* There are many standard works in this field that yield similar calculations.

cases, be working what appears to be a full day, but under the 2,140-calorie regime they will work much more slowly, with less energy and enthusiasm, and in a more lethargic fashion. There will probably also be more absenteeism under the less adequate diet.[15]

The direct connection between calorie intake and productivity is shown very clearly in a number of studies by Kraut and Muller made in Germany between 1942 and 1945.[16] Twenty men building earth embankments shifted 1.5 tons of earth per hour per man when they consumed 2,400 calories; but, when the calorie intake was raised to 2,900, the output rose to 2.2 tons per man, and at the same time body weight increased by about 9 pounds per man. Allowing 1,600–1,800 calories for metabolism and relaxation, we see that an increase of approximately 60 per cent in "working" calories leads to an increase of almost 50 per cent in output. But of greater interest for our purposes is that a 21 per cent increase in total calorie intake results in an increase of almost 50 per cent in output. Another study of thirty-one miners found that an increase of from 1,200 to 1,600 work calories led to an increase in output from 7 to 9.6 tons per day. The experience of miners in the Ruhr district, also reported by Kraut and Muller, confirmed these

general results. On the average the mining of a ton of coal required about 1,200 calories. When, during the war period, the calorie intake of the miners was reduced, output fell proportionally, and, when at a later stage the diet was increased, production rose proportionally. Even more spectacular results are reported in a study of construction workers in Central America, where it was found that the efficiency of workers increased threefold when they were provided with an adequate calorie allowance. Since the original calorie intake of the workers is not reported, it is not possible to compare the relative change in calorie intake with the relative increase in output, but the report nevertheless suggests the sort of results that can be obtained by increasing the calorie intake of workers.[17]

It would be easy to continue to pile up additional experimental and empirical evidence relating not only calorie intake, but also other nutritive elements to output, either directly or indirectly through their effect on such things as debilitating diseases, absenteeism, and lethargy. But enough has been said to suggest my main point. There is an obvious relationship between income and output, and, furthermore, it is clear that up to some point the amount of effective work is increased as wages are increased.

It follows from the preceding discussion that we must distinguish between the supply of labor time (man-hours or man-years) and the supply of work (or effort) and between wages per man and wages per work unit. In the short run the supply of labor time may be said to be fixed, and Figure 3 therefore shows the supply curve of labor as a vertical line *SS*.

[15] See R. K. Mukerjee, "Food and Food Requirements of the Indian Labourers," *Indian Journal of Economics*, XII (1932), 263. The inverse relation between quality of diet and absenteeism seems to be fairly well established. On this point see also C. E. A. Winslow, *The Cost of Sickness and the Price of Health* (Geneva: World Health Organization, 1951), pp. 35 ff.

[16] "Calorie Intake and Industrial Output," *Science*, CIV (1946), 495–97. See also the more recent studies by G. Lehman, E. A. Muller, and H. Spitzer (*Arbeitsphysiologie*, XIV [1949–50], 166 ff.). They determine the extent of the deterioration in work output resulting from different levels of calorie feeding and develop prediction tables for workers of different weights for various occupations.

[17] Winslow, *op. cit.*, p. 33.

The supply of labor time starts at the minimum sustenance wage OA. However, the number of units of work supplied by the whole labor force will increase gradually as wage rates and consumption rise. Therefore, the curve $S'S'$, the supply of work, in the left half of Figure 3 slopes gradually upward to the left. Each point on $S'S'$ indicates the number of units of work that would be forthcoming in response to a given wage rate. Above some wage the supply-of-

much work, as he will at a high wage, the *average* product of labor time will be high. Therefore, at each wage rate there are a separate average productivity of labor-time curve and a related *separate* marginal product of labor-time curve (MP_1 and MP_2 in Fig. 3). We expect the average curve at a high wage to be wholly above one for a lower wage, because at the high wage more work is put forth, and therefore we expect a larger product per man. As usual, we assume that be-

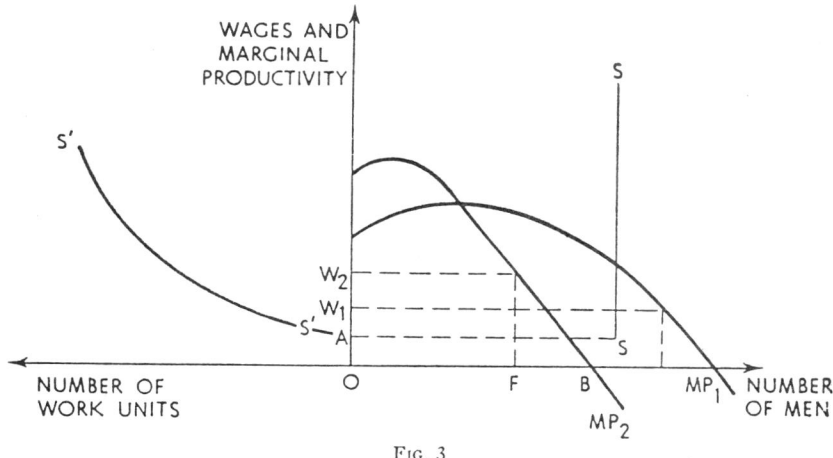

Fɪɢ. 3

work curve will have the same shape as the supply of labor time. In other words, beyond some point increases in consumption are unlikely to add appreciably to the health, vigor, and vitality of the average worker, so that the work performed per unit of time is no greater than at a lower wage.

The average and marginal products of labor time are related, of course, to the average and marginal products per unit of work, but the two sets of products must be clearly separated from each other. Where each man supplies little work, as he will at a very low wage, the *average* product of labor time will be rather low; where each man supplies

yond some point there are diminishing returns and that the average productivity curves are negatively inclined.

But the marginal product of labor-time curves (MP_1 and MP_2) are not so simply related. Consider the curves MP_1 and MP_2 in the right half of Figure 3. The marginal product of labor time (MP_1) for the low wage rate w_1 falls much more slowly than does the marginal product of labor time (MP_2) for the high wage rate w_2. At some point the marginal productivity curve for the high wage rate will fall below the one for the low rate. To see why this may be the case, we must observe that there are two forces in operation working in opposite directions:

(1) On the one hand, the higher the wage, the more work is performed by each man per unit of time. (2) On the other hand (beyond some point), as more work is performed, the marginal product per *unit of work* declines. Now it is entirely possible that the marginal product per unit of work eventually begins to decline quite rapidly. The rate of decline may be so rapid that for the higher curve (representing more work per man) the rate of decline in the marginal product per man (as men are added) is greater than it is for the lower curve (MP_1). Therefore, the higher-wage curve (MP_2) will cross the lower-wage curve (MP_1) and fall below it. In other words, beyond some point we expect the declining marginal productivity of work to become more important than the fact that each man does more work.

Let us look again at the possibility shown in Figure 3 and see what it implies for the problem under consideration. The curve MP_1 is drawn in such a way that at its related wage (w_1) there is actually a scarcity of labor. This implies that so few work units are put forth at this low wage that the existing non-human resources could be combined advantageously with many more units of work. Hence at the low wage w_1 more men could be hired before the marginal product would be equal to the wage. As the curve marked MP_2 is drawn, the reverse is true of it and the related wage w_2. At the wage w_2 the supply of labor on SS is greater than the amount demanded, OF—assuming that the amount demanded is determined at the point where the marginal product is equal to the wage.

All this implies that at very low wages there may be a labor deficit, because so little work is done by each man. But at higher wages the work done per man increases so rapidly that a labor surplus is created. For the underdeveloped areas this may mean that the allegedly observed manpower surpluses in agriculture do not really exist when wages are very low but that they do indeed become a fact when wages rise sufficiently.

In addition, it is worth observing in Figure 3 that at the low wage (w_1), the marginal product of the fully employed labor force is above zero but that at the higher wage the marginal product per man may fall to zero (as at point B) or even below zero.

III. INSTITUTIONAL RIGIDITIES, WAGE RATES, AND MARGINAL PRODUCTIVITY THEORY

An interesting consequence of the wage-productivity relation discussed in the last section is that it can be shown that there are circumstances under which it is to the benefit of landowners to pay a wage above the competitive level. This also implies that it may pay landlords as a group to pay a wage greater than the marginal product of labor. Indeed, it may be to their interest to pay a positive wage even if the marginal product of labor is zero. Specifically, we shall see that under circumstances in which competition among the visibly unemployed forces wage rates toward zero, it may be to the benefit of landlords as a group to operate under institutional arrangements (or traditions) that do not permit wages to fall to their competitive level. That is, they may operate under a system of disguised unemployment at higher than competitive wage rates.

I shall not examine in detail the specific types of institutional arrangements that would enable landlords to employ the entire labor force at a wage in excess of its marginal product, but it is not difficult to think of some possibilities. The appropriate institutional arrangements will usually arise out of the historical situation of the backward economy. A system of serfdom, under which landlords have to utilize all the serfs born on and tied to the land, is essentially of this nature. Rules, mores, or conventions by which people born into certain castes are permitted to carry out only a limited range of tasks are also of this nature. Other institutional arrangements of this type are found in various backward economies. The point of the discussion that follows is that such institutions need not be irrational. Indeed, we shall see that such institutional arrangements may lead to a greater total product than would otherwise be possible.

Let us continue our analysis from the point at which it was left in the previous section. Starting with the marginal productivity curves in Figure 3, I shall build up through diagrammatic illustrations a comparison of the possible outcomes for landlords as a group under two alternative situations: (1) a situation in which landlords can ignore the effects of unemployment and (2) a situation in which unemployment has a depressing effect on the wage rate and in which this effect on the wage rate also affects landlords' incomes.

Figure 4 shows a family of marginal productivity curves similar to those in Figure 3. Each curve is related to a specific wage rate. As before, the curve MP_1 indicates the marginal product per man for different numbers of men if the wage rate is w_1; the curve MP_2 indicates the marginal product, if the wage is w_2; and so on. Suppose that landlords as a group can hire any number of men they wish without regard to whether this will result in a labor deficit or a labor surplus or to the possible consequences of such a deficit or surplus. How many men will they hire? In other words, we shall examine

the demand side first without regard to supply conditions. (Later, of course, supply will be taken into account.) For each wage rate and its related marginal productivity curve there is an optimal number of men that landlords as a group will hire if they are to maximize their group income. The "optimal" number of men to be hired is determined, as usual, at the point at which the wage is equal to the marginal product of labor time. In Fig-

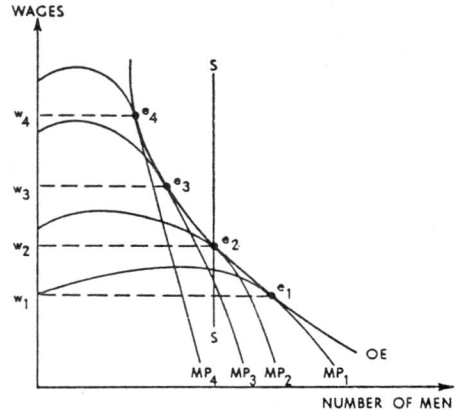

Fig. 4

ure 4 for the curve MP_1 this optimal point is e_1, where the marginal product is equal to w_1. Similarly, we obtain e_2 and e_3 for the curves MP_2 and MP_3, and so on. The locus of such optimal employment points is indicated by the curve OE in Figure 4. This curve is, *in a sense*, a demand curve for labor. At each wage it tells us the number of workers that landlords as a group would hire if they could hire the number that would maximize their group income, without regard to the consequences of any labor deficit or surplus that might be involved.

Figure 5 combines the curve *OE* and the inelastic supply curve for labor *SS*. In this illustration at high wage rates the optimum number of men employed is less than the supply, and at low wage rates the reverse is true. We may ask whether the *OE* curve need cross the *SS* curve at any point. Generally speaking, it is probable that there is always some wage rate so low that the optimum employment exceeds the supply. But we need not worry about this general point at present. For present purposes it is sufficient to concentrate on the possibilities shown in the graphs.

The next step in the argument is to relate the points on the optimal employ-

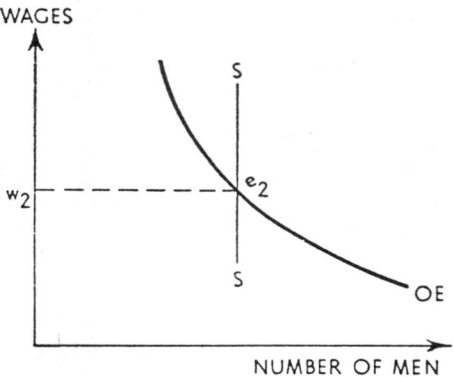

WAGES

NUMBER OF MEN

FIG. 5

ment curve to the net revenues obtained by landlords at various wage rates. Associated with every wage rate and every optimal number of men employed there is a particular net revenue of landlords as a group. This relationship is illustrated by the curve *OR* in Figure 6. (For each *MP* curve shown in Figure 5 the net revenue is equal to the area under the marginal productivity curve and above the "wage line." For example, for the curve MP_1 in Figure 5 it is the area under the curve and above the line w_1e_1. Roughly put, it is the sum for all workers of the marginal product of each "additional" worker less his wage.) For every wage rate and related point on the *OE* curve,

a corresponding net revenue is shown in the left half of Figure 6. The locus of these points may be called the *optimal-employment* revenue curve, *OR*.

Next, suppose that the *entire* labor force is employed. Then, in a similar fashion, we can obtain the *full-employment* revenue curve, *FR*. That is, for every wage some particular net revenue will accrue to the landlords if the whole labor force *SS* is employed. Of course, in some cases this will involve employing a greater number of workers than landlords wish to employ, and in other cases a number smaller than that which would maximize their group income.

The shapes of the curves *OR* and *FR* and their relationship to each other are of special interest. Consider first *OR*. As usual, it is assumed that beyond some point there are diminishing returns (in the physical sense) per unit of work. It should be clear that at very low wage rates the amount of effort per man is also very low, and hence the marginal product per man is likely to be low. In this case many men are each doing very little work. The per capita costs of co-ordinating the work force, and other overhead costs, are likely to be high in relation to output. It seems reasonable to believe that there is some very low wage rate at which the net revenue of landlords will be just slightly above zero. As wages increase, effort per man grows and the optimal number of men declines, and overhead costs per *unit of work* decline accordingly. As a consequence net revenue may be expected to rise. At least two general factors are responsible for increases in net revenue as wages rise: (1) As wages rise, the amount of work done by each man may increase more than proportionately. (2) With the greater total amount of work done, it may be possible to combine non-human resources and labor so that the combination of factors is more nearly optimal, and as a result the output per unit of work may increase. Thus up to some wage rate, net revenue is likely to increase as wages increase. However, beyond some wage rate there must certainly be a reversal of this tendency. At some point an increase in wages will bring with it no increase in the amount of work supplied per man. Even before this point is reached, as wages rise, the amount of work done per man will in-

are identical. In Figure 6 this is shown at point L, where the FR curve touches the OR curve.

It should be clear that the full-employment revenue curve need not be at a maximum at the wage w_2, where the labor supply and the optimum employment are equal. It is true that at wages above w_2 the full-employment revenue must always be less than the optimum-employment revenue, since the optimum-employment revenue must be re-

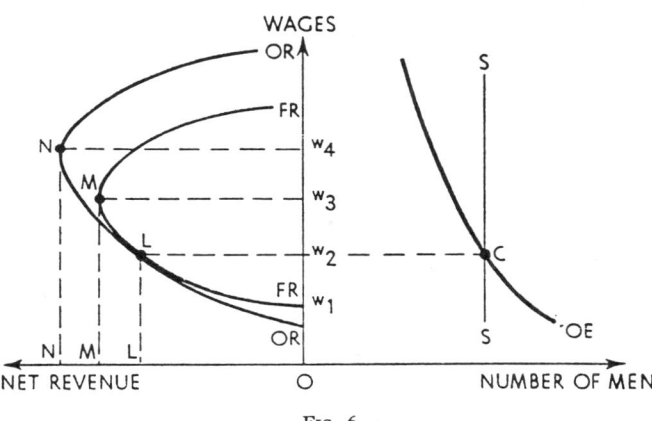

FIG. 6

crease less than proportionately. Hence beyond some point, the higher the wage rate, the lower the net revenue. Of course, at some very high wage rate the net revenue will be zero, since there is obviously a wage that is greater than the maximum possible output per man. For these reasons the OR curve is illustrated in Figure 6 in the shape of a U on its side.

The main thing to observe about the full-employment revenue curve is that at every wage rate except one the full-employment revenue is less than the optimal employment revenue. Of course, at the wage at which the optimum employment curve, OE, crosses the labor supply curve, SS, the optimal employment revenue and the full employment revenue

duced by the employment of excess men whose wages are below their marginal product. But the full-employment revenue may nevertheless be higher than it would be at a lower wage. The explanation for this is similar to the explanation of the increase in optimal revenue as wages rise. Above the wage w_2 the amount of work done per man may still increase more rapidly than wages, and this effect may, up to some point, be more significant than the depressing effect of the greater wage bill on net revenue.

Three points in Figure 6, N, M, and L on the curves OR and FR, are especially worthy of attention. If landlords can pay any wage they please and hire any number of workers, they will pay a wage of w_4 and achieve the maximum possible net revenue, ON. But at this wage there will be an excess supply of labor. If there is some means of getting rid of the excess labor in a costless fashion, then this is the optimum solution from the landlords' point of view. But if there is nowhere for "surplus" labor to go, and competition among the unemployed and the employed depresses wages, then the wage rate will fall below the level w_4. The wage decline will continue as long as there is an excess supply of labor, and wages will eventually drop to w_2, the wage at which the optimum-employment curve crosses the labor-supply curve. *But at this point net revenue drops to OL.* It is clear that in the situation illustrated in Figure 6 employers can improve their position by employing the entire labor force and simultaneously raising wages to w_3. They will then enjoy a net revenue of OM, which, of course, is greater than OL. This is the best solution under the circumstances. For, as long as they leave some of the excess labor unemployed, there is a danger that wage rates will be driven down to a level at which revenue is less than OM. Hence landlords as a group are better off if institutional arrangements permit them to employ the entire labor force, pay a wage of w_3, and yet not utilize the entire labor force. Possibilities and institutional arrangements of this sort *can* account for the phenomenon of disguised unemployment.[18]

Let us examine some of the character-

istics of this solution. First, we may note that this solution (a wage of w_3 and a net revenue of OM) can account for the existence of surplus labor and of disguised unemployment. At this wage the labor force could cultivate more land with the same auxiliary resources if there were more land available. Second, we see that under the postulated conditions the wage can be above the marginal product of labor. Indeed, it is in the interests of both landlords and workers that this be the case. It also follows easily from the foregoing that it is logically possible to have a marginal product of labor of zero and a positive wage.

The essential aspect of the argument is that, where the amount of work put forth is related to the wage, landlords can improve their position by employing excess labor rather than by employing the "optimum" amount of labor and permitting the unemployed to drive wages down. If wages are driven down, they may reach a level at which the amount of work done is so reduced that the landlords' net revenue decreases.

Now consider the extreme case in which M and L of Figure 6 coincide; that is, where the maximum full-employment revenue is at the wage at which the optimum-employment curve and the supply-of-labor curve cross. In this case, the landlords' optimum solution is to pay the wage w_2 and to hire the entire labor supply. Labor's marginal product will be equal to the wage. It may appear that these circumstances are not quite consistent with the notion of an excess labor supply and disguised unemployment. This depends on how we interpret the notion of excess labor. It is true that in this case at the optimum wage w_2 there is no surplus of labor and that the marginal product of labor is above zero. But if our criterion is that there is excess

[18] Indeed, it has been shown that such institutional arrangements may lead to a greater total product than would otherwise be possible. Thus we come to the rather curious conclusion that, far from necessarily being a vice, institutional arrangements that permit a degree of disguised unemployment may actually enable the economy to be more productive.

labor where the existing labor supply could cultivate more land without loss of efficiency, then we may have excess labor even in this extreme case. For under these circumstances the existing labor force could cultivate more land if it received some portion of the produce of the additional land cultivatêd. A greater output would probably lead to some increase in wages, which in turn would lead to more work done per man, thus enabling the fixed labor force to cultivate more land. However, it is of interest to note that, should the economy undergo industrialization and try to shift some of the labor force off the land without increasing wages per man, there would be a shortage of labor. This may perhaps shed some light on the experiences of some of the countries in the Soviet orbit where a shortage of labor appeared in the agricultural sector after attempts at forced industrialization were made. Prior to this it had been believed that there was a considerable amount of disguised unemployment.

[11]

Harvey Leibenstein
Harvard University

Some Notes on
Economic Development Planning
and the Rate of Interest
under Multiple Sovereignties*

The motivating idea behind this foray into the theory of planning is that economic planning is likely to involve multiple sovereignties and multiple

* This is a revised version of an unpublished paper written a decade ago. Special note should be taken of the paper by Jan Drewnowski, "The Economic Theory of Socialism: A Suggestion for Reconsideration," *Journal of Political Economy*, August 1961. Although there are some similarities between our papers, there are also significant differences. The emphasis here is on the significant difficulties involved in interpretation and consistent implementation of the dominant preference function under multiple sovereignties.

86

behavioral systems. The special case of socialist planning in which most of the productive units are publicly owned, and the multiplicity of behavioral systems involved, is likely to be a major aspect of the planning problem. Such systems involve technical problems that for the most part have neither been recognized nor solved. It is the purpose of this essay to examine in part the nature of these problems.

The approach to this aspect of planning will be considered on a highly abstract level. Although there is no space to go into details, it should be evident as we proceed that the examination is applicable to two basic issues: (1) the interpretation and analysis of the operation of existing planning systems, and (2) the design of economic planning. As a shorthand way of expressing things symbols are used but no basic mathematics is involved.

Special attention will be given to the role and meaning of the interest rate in determining resource allocation under conditions of economic growth and at least in part *dictatorially determined* economic decisions. The word *dictatorial* is used in a general and formal sense and is not intended to imply anything about the political structure of the country. By *dictatorial* we refer to any method of making economic decisions other than on the basis of consumers' sovereignty. Economies in which decisions are made in this manner may or may not be political dictatorships.

*J. The Allocation Problem
and Dictatorial Values*

In conventional static theory the interest rate, in part, serves the same function in the time dimension as transportation cost does in the space dimension. Just as in the latter case transport costs enable us to evaluate all activities as though they occurred at one point in space, so an interest rate enables us to consider all events, and decisions regarding such events, as though they occurred at one point in time. Rational calculation is facilitated by utilizing the interest rate to reduce all values to present values. Capital goods are transformed into value equivalents of consumer goods through discounting the future stream of services that the capital good yields.

A convenient way of looking at the problem is to note that in the pure-competition–consumers' sovereignty model the interest rate plays a part in three of the following four steps for achieving a rational allocation: (1) The interest rate transforms the value of future flows in terms of current flows, (2) The interest rate and the marginal efficiency of investment transforms capital goods into consumer goods value-equivalents, (3) Proper allocation involves allocating inputs to equalize the value of various current flows at the margin, and (4) Consumers' preferences determine the relative values of current flows, and they also determine the interest rate that enables us to obtain an equivalence between current and future flows. It is important to note that steps (1), (2), and (3) are independent of the system of valuation between present and future goods and between different present goods. Any scheme of relative valuations obtained from and consistent with any set of preferences can lead to a proper allocation. Conversely, every allocation implies one (or more) relative valuation schemes. These notions and their implications may be clarified if we treat the matter more formally and illustrate these ideas for specific dictatorial objectives.

We define *rational allocation* as one that is consistent with a stated objective. The objective may be the maximization of consumer satisfaction given certain constraints, or some other. Consider the following sequence: (a) Every objective implies a rule of choice between alternatives, or a set of such rules consistent with the attainment of the objective, (b) The rule(s) of choice plus the relevant preference maps of the decision-making entities determine the specific choices that are actually made, (c) For given factor availabilities the application of the preference maps and the rule(s) of choice yield sets of relative valuations for the factor flows in their various uses and for the commodities produced by the factor flows, and (d) Given the relative valuation among commodities there is usually one (or more) allocation(s) of factors among alternative uses consistent with the attainment of the objective. Although the initial preference map and the relative valuations between commodities may be related to the objective, they are not necessarily determined by it. Therefore, we may say that the objective and its implied rules of choice operating on the valuation scheme lead to a certain allocation, and if all these elements are consistent it is rational allocation.

For our purposes we shall assume that the rules of choice are correct for the objectives considered *if information was complete and accurate*— that is, they are rules that when applied do lead to the objective. For want of a better term we shall call such rules of choice *optimizing rules*. Given the alternatives open to the decision-making units in the economy and some other data, the application of the optimizing rules leads to a set of choices one of whose results, in the aggregate, is the allocation of resources. Of course, a knowledge of the optimizing rules alone is not sufficient to make a choice. It is commonplace that a set of relative valuations of some entities that can enable one to determine, directly or indirectly, the relative valuations of the alternatives are needed, in addition to a knowledge of the optimizing rules, in order to make an intelligent choice. In actuality, the decision processes and the other elements of the economic processes that determine the resource allocation are a much more complicated affair. But for our purposes it is convenient to concentrate on the essentials and omit the intervening elements that may be involved. With this in mind let us write O_a for the set of rules consistent with object a.[1] V_a is a vector of values whose elements are prices of factors and commodities including the interest rate(s); and A_a represents the final allocation whose elements are those quantities of capital goods and consumer goods that result as a consequence of the operation of O_a on V_a, given the resources. We write this relationship as follows:

$$O_a(V_a) = A_a$$

For purposes of discussion it is simpler to speak of an objective in the singular. We shall do so throughout this paper since this simplification is unlikely to affect the points we have in mind, although we recognize the possibility that the discussion can also be carried forward in terms of *objective functions*—that is, sets of multiple objectives that can be reconciled in some fashion.

With respect to our equation, we expect the following relationships to hold. Every objective (and related optimizing rules) combined with a set of relative valuations implies a resource allocation, which may not be unique. Further, every set of optimizing rules and consequent allocation implies a related set of values, although there may be more than one set of valuations that fits these conditions. Finally, and most important for our purposes, every allocation (assuming it to be a rational one) and set of values implies a set of optimizing rules and an objective, although the latter need not be unique.

We consider two such relationships:

(1) $O_a(V_a) = A_a$
(2) $O_b(V_b) = A_b$

where (1) represents the situation under consumers' sovereignty, and (2) represents the situation under some dictatorial objective function and dictatorial values. Now, suppose the rules O_a are permitted to operate. Then the dictator's problem is to find a set of values V_c so that

(3) $O_a(V_c) = A_b$

From this we obtain $V_c - V_a = T_c$, which is a vector whose elements are the necessary taxes and subsidies that give the dictator his desired allocation.

The point of this is that from the dictator's view the entire scheme as visualized in equation (3) is perfectly rational, but from an outside observer's view none of it would seem to make any sense. The operation of O_a may give the impression that the objective is maximum consumers' satisfaction. Not knowing O_b, V_c certainly seems to make no sense to the observer. But even if O_b could be guessed at on the basis of other evidence V_c would still not make any sense since V_b is not known.

An observer's attempt to understand the rationale of the allocation process would be confounded if the rules of choice O_a were not of the type to which competitive conditions have accustomed him. The problem for both the observer and the dictator is really somewhat more complicated than we have just indicated. The reason is that the economy is likely to be subject to dual or multiple sovereignties. Consumers' choice may be permitted in the consumer goods market, but the firms may have to operate on another basis. Let us see what happens if the dictator tries to use the price system as an allocative mechanism under such circumstances.

We divide O_a into two parts. Let O_a' represent the behavior rules of consumers and O_a'' the rules for the firms. Commodities are of two kinds, producer goods $\mathcal{K}$ and consumer goods C, so that the final allocation flow $A = C + \mathcal{K}$. The relationship that determines the dictator's allocation reads $O_b(V_b) = C_b + \mathcal{K}_b$, or for each sector separately we have $O_b'(V_b') = C_b$, and $O_b''(V_b'') = \mathcal{K}_b$. The dictator's problem is to find V_c' so that $O_a'(V_c') = C_b$, that is, a set of prices that results in the consumption of exactly C_b. This last yields $\mathcal{T}_c'$, the vector of taxes and subsidies on consumer goods that permits C_b. Once C_b is determined, finding V_c presents no special conceptual difficulties since it is the set of prices that clears the market for the given quantities. But the problem in the other sector is more complicated.

The dictator would like to see the result $\mathcal{K}_b$ in accordance with his objective and values relationship $O_b''(V_b'') = \mathcal{K}_b$. But finding a V_c'' so that $O_a''(V_c'') = \mathcal{K}_b$ becomes a very difficult matter if the price mechanism alone is used, since calculations for investment choice by the firms depend on prices of consumer goods (V_c') that do not reflect the valuations of the consumers or of the dictator. It is not a matter of setting prices that will clear markets to final consumers. To choose between investment alternatives, firms have to calculate the value of the output stream of different types of producer goods. If the firms use current prices they would use either V_c' or $V_c' - \mathcal{T}_c'$, but neither of these would yield the result $\mathcal{K}_b$ and hence would not fit in with the dictator's objective. Similarly, the dictator cannot instruct firms to use V_b' since this would not give the right result because the firm's objective is O_a'' and not O_b''. One way out is simply to instruct firms to produce $\mathcal{K}_b$. Considerations of this sort may explain the use of output targets in an economy like the Soviet rather than reliance on the pricing mechanism. Another solution is to instruct firms to make economic choices in accordance with O_b, and to give firms planning prices V_b to work with.

The major implication of this discussion from our point of view is that the degree of rationality of dictatorial decisions cannot be determined unless we know the dictator's objective and the dictator's values. The reason for this is that there is a degree of freedom between interest rate(s), factor prices, and commodity prices. Where prices (or values) are arbitrarily determined, there is some set of prices combined with a zero interest rate that will yield the same allocation as some other set of prices and a positive interest rate.[2] Or, conversely, the interest rate is meaningful only in relation to other prices but not apart from them. Whatever allocation can be achieved by a positive interest rate can also be achieved by a zero interest rate if we are permitted to manipulate all other prices including future prices.

It may be argued that when we speak of a zero interest rate in this context we are not really talking about a zero interest rate as we usually understand that term, but only of a hidden interest rate that is disguised by the freedom to manipulate all other prices. But this is consistent with our main point. Under dictatorial values the interest rate need not have any meaning in the usual sense. The interest rate has meaning only in relation to known objectives, related optimizing rules, and a known scheme of price determination.

Let us stop for a moment and reinterpret some of our ideas. The first equation may be looked upon as representing actual operating rules and people's actual objectives. In any economic system some of the units are likely to operate in terms of the motivations developed for these units. The dictator has to realize that he cannot dictate behavior in every respect. There are essentially three basic choices that exist: (1) The dictatorial planning agency may try to issue specific commands, that is, to indicate in detail the inputs and outputs and activities of every operating unit, (2) Another scheme is that which parallels the operation of a free enterprise system in which the working units pursue their own ends but their objectives are deflected through the introduction of a system of taxes and subsidies, resulting in different allocations than would occur without taxes and subsidies, or (3) the dictator can issue rules of behavior to operating units as well as necessary parameters, such as shadow prices, and have the operating units follow these rules. Of course, combinations of all three procedures are possible.

The first approach, using dictatorial command, is either technically impossible in detail or highly inefficient. The second approach is especially interesting since it is the one most likely to be recommended by economists.

Here we return to the problem mentioned earlier. The dictator wants an output of capital goods different from that produced on the basis of the derived demand of the expected output of consumer goods. (We need not consider why the dictator wants a unique output of capital goods. One possibility is that he has in mind a future stream of con-

91

sumption goods quite different from that which would be produced under consumers' sovereignty.) The basic question is whether a set of prices exists consistent with the equation

$$(4) \quad O_a''(V_c'') = K_b$$

First, we should note certain differences between this and the consumer goods case. In the consumer goods case, a set of subsidies and taxes clear the market for the quantities desired by the dictator. In the capital goods case this does not work. A set of subsidies and taxes can possibly induce firms to produce the dictatorially desired output of capital goods, given producers' motivations. However, these prices inclusive of subsidies and taxes are not the prices at which the output is wanted by the firms that purchase capital goods since their demand is determined by the costs and subsidies for the production of consumer goods. Thus we need another set of subsidies and taxes to determine the purchase of the capital goods produced for each *use*. A given commodity could sometimes be used either as a consumption good or a capital good. Hence, buyers who have multiple uses for such goods will have to be policed to make sure that the goods they buy at a given price inclusive of a subsidy are put to the appropriate use.

Additional difficulties enter when decreasing cost industries are involved. In such circumstances taxes have to be imposed that increase with the quantity of capital goods produced so that the dictatorially desired amount is realized. To do this correctly would require a knowledge of the details of the production functions of all plants. A similar problem arises if the dictator has different trade-offs between the present and different dates in the future. In this instance firms should take different interest rates into account in determining the output of capital goods of different durabilities. It is possible that a complex set of taxes and subsidies would induce firms to produce that output of capital goods of durabilities desired by the dictator. The point to be stressed is that to calculate the appropriate taxes and subsidies requires much more knowledge than is likely to be available. Since the appropriateness of the decisions is likely to be known only to the dictator in the future, there is no present test (such as clearing the market) for the levels of taxes and subsidies employed.

Two more basic difficulties enter the picture. First, taxes and subsidies produce incentives for the creation of black markets. Obviously tax avoidance leads to the possibility of personal gain by some members of producing firms. It is likely that the output of capital goods that does not go through the tax system is more profitable for both sellers and buyers than one that does. For example, some firms would buy some capital goods produced by others without taxes, but they might find it profitable to produce these goods themselves if in this way they could avoid taxes. Once again the problem and costs of policing the system enter the picture.

A second difficulty is that the level of *directed* effort by workers and managers may be very different under a system of publicly owned firms than under private ownership. This may also hold true for various systems of taxes and subsidies in the sense that they divert efforts either toward black market activities or toward record-keeping and other administrative techniques necessary to police the system.[3]

Finally, we must consider the possibility that the dictator will not use only taxes and subsidies but may wish to impose rules of operation on firms. This is most likely to occur where the firms are publicly owned and where the motivation system is not really understood. However, it involves the problem that the rules of behavior imposed on operating units will probably not be those they will want to follow. It is one thing to legislate rules of choice, but it is quite a different matter to have the units themselves follow such criteria. The degree to which rules are followed will depend on the motivating system, and if the rules do not follow the self-interest of the agents to a great degree there is likely to be considerable deviation from these rules. The main point is that we visualize a difference between actual behavior and prescribed behavior. Of course, it is recognized that prescribed behavior will influence actual behavior. Using our previous notation we can visualize the following relations:

$$(5) \quad O_a(\mathcal{V}_b) \neq A_b$$
$$(6) \quad O_{ab}(\mathcal{V}_b) \neq A_b$$

The interpretation of these expressions is that the actual objective a under the given set of valuations dictatorially desired $\mathcal{V}_b$ will not yield the desired allocation A_b. Furthermore, firms pursuing objective a but told to operate under prescribed rules b will also *not* yield the desired allocation A_b. Thus, the dictator has to guess which new set of valuations will yield the desired allocation, if such a set is available. If not, then the next stratagem may be to impose a set of *pseudorules* and/or a set of *pseudovalues*. By *pseudorules* we mean those that, combined with normal incentives, will lead to the results that the planners desire. But this stratagem probably goes too far. It is most unlikely that the planners know enough about the motivations of organizations and individuals to determine the correct set of pseudorules and pseudoprices. In fact, planners are frequently unaware that this problem exists. Hence, it is not surprising that the targets that planners have in mind are frequently not realized and that their aims are frequently frustrated. This aspect of the problem has been ignored in the discussion of the Lange-Lerner prescription for socialist economies since in that discussion it was implicitly assumed that any prescribed set of rules would be followed. Experience with actual organizational behavior would indicate that this is a false premise on which to operate.

II. Allocation Criteria and the Interest Rate under an Aggrandizing Dictator

For purposes of this essay we shall consider two extreme types of dictatorial objectives. For want of better names, we shall refer to one as that of the *aggrandizing* dictator and to the other as that of the *benevolent* dictator.

In the aggrandizing dictator we visualize one who attempts to maximize the *growth* of the productive capacity of the economy, that is, he attempts to maximize the growth of *all* productive factors. He wants as large an economic domain as possible. This objective would appear to be reasonable for the power-seeking dictator. The value of any factor other than inventories of final goods is imputed from their productivity, but the value of final goods is determined by dictatorial values. The dictator may permit some consumer goods to be valued in accordance with consumers' preferences, but others, for example military goods, would be valued on the basis of other priorities.

In the benevolent dictator we visualize one who wants to maximize *per capita* consumption. His focus is on the productivity of labor and its relationship to per capita consumption. The valuation of current consumption goods may be on the basis of consumers' preferences, but the valuation of future outputs of consumers' goods would not be.

We shall see that the allocations under these two types of dictatorial decision functions are quite different, and consequently the role of the interest rate is also quite different.

Maximizing the rate of capital accumulation will not yield the desired solution for the aggrandizing dictator if the allocation of resources is in any way a determinant of the rate of growth of any resources other than capital. Since this is the case, it follows that increases in capital accumulation, given the full employment of all resources, will be at the expense of the rate of growth of some other factor.

Consider the example where there are only two factors and two commodities: labor and capital, consumer goods and capital goods. In this situation, under the assumed dictatorial objective, the nature of consumption goods differs from that in the nondictatorial case. They now become a factor in the production of the resource labor. To the extent that an increase in consumption affects fertility rates, mortality rates, or current health (and hence the productive efficiency of the labor force), consumption goods may be looked upon as investment in labor. Thus, the opportunity cost of a unit of capital is measured by the extent to which it decreases the total labor force. The interest rate may be measured in terms of the marginal productivity of consumption goods. Maximization of all resources is achieved by an allocation of current output in such a way as to equalize the marginal productivity of all goods produced.

At this point something must be said about the meaning of the marginal productivity of consumption goods. We assume that there is a determinable relationship between a dollar expenditure on consumption goods and an increase in the labor force. A unit increase in the labor force will yield an increase in the stream of goods in the future, and the discounted net revenue of this stream represents the marginal productivity of consumption goods. In computing the discounted net revenue it is necessary to maintain this additional unit of labor in perpetuity, that is, the labor equivalent of repair, maintenance, and replacement of capital.

Under these circumstances, to determine the allocation between current consumption and investment the appropriate interest rate is the marginal productivity of consumption goods as it has been defined in this context. Equating the marginal productivity of capital with this interest rate will yield the optimum rate of accumulation of capital for the aggrandizing dictator. The next problem is to find the appropriate discount rate in obtaining the present value of the stream of goods attributable to any factor. Under consumers' sovereignty the interest rate that determines the allocation between capital goods and consumer goods is also the appropriate rate to be used as the discount rate of the future stream of goods. In both cases it measures simultaneously consumers' sacrifice and hence the rate of substitution between present goods and future goods. Under the aggrandizing dictator's objective the interest rate determined by the marginal productivity of consumption goods becomes, in a similar fashion, the appropriate discount rate in determining the present value of the output stream. Here too the interest rate so defined measures the rate of substitution between present consumption goods and future consumption goods. Labor, in this context, may be looked upon as stored up consumption goods that have the power of producing other consumption goods. Adding to the capital stock is essentially a means of increasing the future flow of consumption goods at the expense of the current flow. The extent to which these two flows are substituted for each other at the margin is measured, of course, by the marginal productivity of consumption goods. In a sense, we substitute the marginal productivity of consumption goods under this objective for their marginal utility under consumers' sovereignty. However, the two interest rates implied by these two alternate objectives are by no means likely to be the same.

It is of interest to note that our *simplified* model of the aggrandizing dictator is the same as the von Neumann model of an expanding econ-

omy.[4] Two characteristics of the von Neumann model and of our model
are of interest. First, in equilibrium the allocation will yield the greatest
rate of expansion of all possible allocations. Second, in equilibrium the
rate of interest is equal to the rate of expansion. Neither of these properties holds for the consumers' sovereignty model or for the Lange-Lerner
type of socialist economy model. Thus, employing the interest rate implied in either of those models will not yield a maximum rate of economic expansion. We may note also that once an economy of this kind
gets into equilibrium the standard of consumption is constant over time
if the technological parameters, as well as the parameters determining
mortality and fertility rates, remain the same.[5]

For some, the interesting case from the point of view of economic
growth may not be the equilibrium position but rather the course of development prior to the achievement of the equilibrium expansion path.
If we consider the nonequilibrium case and drop the assumptions of no
fixed factors and of all goods entering into all production processes, then
we must modify our conclusions. Under such circumstances we would not
expect all factors to expand at the same rate. We are given a dictatorially
determined system of values for all stocks (that is, for both human and
nonhuman assets) and the commodities in all *investment* uses (using investment in the broad sense of adding to both human and nonhuman
stocks). Under the optimum allocation a dollar's worth of any commodity
adds a dollar's worth of value to some stock. The rate of interest, viewed
as the opportunity cost of capital, will therefore be equal to the momentary
rate of expansion in the *value* of total assets. But in this nonequilibrium and
less restrictive case, the interest rate will not be one that will maintain
itself through time. It would be noteworthy for some purposes to work
out all the implications of the nonequilibrium case, but for present purposes it is sufficient to observe that in this instance the interest rate is
equal to the momentary rate of expansion in the value of total assets,
whereas under other objectives the interest rate varies inversely, or is
unrelated, to the rate of expansion.

In the previous two-commodity example we assumed that consumers' goods were productive in the sense that they added to the productive capacity of the economy. We now expand our considerations to
include nonproductive consumers' goods. We shall refer to these nonproductive consumer goods as *luxury goods*—although they need not be
luxuries as the term is commonly understood. They may be civilian
goods that do not add to longevity or work capacity; or they may be
military goods, memorials to the dictator, and so forth. What properties
does the rate of interest have in this case? The answer to this question
depends on whether or not, with respect to changes in investment, luxury
goods are produced in a given proportion to consumers' goods. That is,
if there is a 10 percent decrease in the output of capital goods will this

result—given the dictator's demand schedule or preference schedule for luxury goods—in a proportional increase in both luxury goods and productive consumer goods or not? Consider the situation in which changes in output in consumer goods and luxuries are proportional. The opportunity cost of a unit of capital is a set mix of consumer goods and luxuries. Luxuries may be looked upon as a cost to entities that can be used in the expansion of the economy. Luxuries bear an opportunity cost but are of no value from the point of view of expansion. The new rate of substitution between present goods and future goods is the expansive power of a unit of a consumer goods mix (including luxuries), which is lower than it was when there were no luxury goods by the amount of expansive power foregone in producing luxury goods instead of productive consumer goods. Thus, the interest rate is lower than it was in the previous case. In equilibrium the interest rate is still equal to the rate of expansion of the economy, but it is lower than the rate of expansion of all resources in the no luxury goods case. If we think of luxury goods as military goods, this analysis implies that in the expanding equilibrium one of the properties of this solution would be a constant ratio of military goods to manpower.

If the proportion of productive consumer goods in the consumer goods mix changes over time, there is little reason to expect the rate of interest to be equal to the rate of expansion of all factors. Suppose that, given the dictator's demand function for luxuries, the proportion of productive consumer goods in the mix decreases with increases in the labor/capital ratio. In this situation maximizing the rate of expansion would call for substituting capital for labor, and we would expect the capital stock to grow at a faster rate than the labor stock. Conversely, if the proportion of productive consumer goods in the mix increased with increases in the labor/capital ratio, we would expect labor to increase more rapidly than capital. Although the interest rate would not be equal to the rate of expansion in the productive capacity of all resources, in equilibrium the interest rate is equal to the rate of growth of stocks if stocks are measured by the extent to which they contribute to expansion. Consider the situation in which the ratio of productive consumer goods in the mix decreases as labor increases. Therefore every unit of labor is less effective as a growth-contributing factor as labor is added. Labor, or what is the same thing, the productive consumer goods that produce labor, must not be permitted to grow to the point at which their growth-contributing power falls below that of the capital that could be produced by the same amount of resources. Therefore, labor grows less rapidly than capital but at the margin, in equilibrium, the growth-contributing power of labor and capital is equal, but the rate of increase of the quantities of these two factors is not.

Thus far, in referring to the rate of interest we considered only the *real* rate of interest that is consistent with the dictator's objective and values. In other words, we assumed that $O_b(V_b) = A_b$. But now suppose that consumers' preferences are permitted to operate in the consumer goods market. In this instance prices of consumer goods would not be equal to what they would be under V_b. It is unlikely that consumer demand would be in proportion to what the "demanded" commodity adds to the expansibility of the economy. A dollar expenditure by a consumer need not add one dollar's worth of labor force. Thus, the prices necessary to clear consumer goods markets (part of V_c) would not be equal to the productivity of consumer goods. The *operating* interest rates employed would depend on the prices that firms and planners use in making their calculations. Therefore, the operating interest rate need not reflect the rate of expansion. In other words, we have to distinguish between the *real* interest rate that depends on the dictator's objective and relative valuations and the *operating* interest rate imposed on various decision-making entities, because these entities calculate on the basis of valuations determined by consumers' preferences rather than by the dictator's preferences. If any interest rate is observable it will be the operating interest rate. Of course, the operating interest rate will appear to be irrational from the point of view of consumers' sovereignty. Also, the observed operating interest rate may seem irrational if it is examined *only* in the light of the dictator's objective.

III. Allocation and Interest under the Benevolent Dictator

What the problem looks like for the benevolent dictator will be sketched only briefly.

There is a variety of related entities that the benevolent dictator can choose to maximize. We assume that the dictator wants to maximize the rate of growth in per capita consumption, subject to certain constraints, such as setting certain minimum standards for the present population.

The basic decision for the economy is to choose between present consumption per capita and future consumption per capita. From the point of view of the benevolent dictator the value of capital depends on the extent to which it can increase consumption per capita which, in turn, depends on the effect of investment on (a) increasing the future flow of goods, (b) increasing or decreasing the size of the population, and (c) the consequences of the interaction of these flows. This will depend on the extent to which labor and capital are subject to decreasing or increasing returns. Suppose labor is subject to decreasing returns and capital is not. In this instance an additional unit of investment increases future per capita consumption in several ways. First, investment decreases current consumption and leads to a higher mortality rate and therefore a slower rate of population growth. Second, if the rate of investment is larger than the rate of population growth the stock of capital per individual increases, and as a consequence we would expect that normally output per capita would increase accordingly. On the other hand, if the rate of investment is too small to overcome the rate of population growth, the choice is between present consumption and preventing declines in future consumption per capita. The opportunity cost of capital lies in the loss in current per capita consumption, just as the gain from capital lies in potential future gains in per capita consumption. The rate at which the current loss and future gain are substituted for each other depends on the dictatorially determined rate of sacrifice of current for future gains. Thus the interest rate is arbitrarily picked by the dictator, and it represents that rate of discount at which the future consumption standard is substituted for the present one.

How does this differ from the consumers' sovereignty case? First, the dictator picks the rate of substitution; it is not based on the consumers' desire to save. Second, the revenue stream of investment that is to be discounted is the net addition to *per capita* consumption and not the net value of the stream of outputs attributed to this unit of investment. This implies that the effects of investment decisions on population growth are considered. It is clear that the investment decisions on this basis would be different from those under a regime of consumers' sovereignty.

In this instance the interest rate is not equal to the rate of expansion of the economy. Indeed, the real interest rate varies inversely with the rate of expansion of per capita output.

Here too we are faced with the problem of dual sovereignties, depending on the latitude given consumers and firms in the determination of economic decisions and on the objectives firm managers are presumed to pursue. We would therefore expect the operating rate of interest to be quite different from the real rate consistent with the dictator's objective.

IV. Conclusions and Summary

Under the dictatorial objectives assumed above, the criterion for the allocation of resources and the allocation of investment turned out to be quite different from the marginal productivity criterion under consumers' sovereignty as that term is usually defined.

Suppose that the dictator is interested in "forcing" the development of the economy. In that situation an allocation on the basis of the conventional marginal productivity criterion will not maximize what the

dictator may want to maximize. Maximizing the value of the future output stream as it is valued under consumers' sovereignty (where the discount rate equals the interest rate that reflects consumers' time preference) is not what the aggrandizing dictator or the benevolent dictator
wants. For the aggrandizing dictator, maximizing the future output stream
as valued under consumers' sovereignty will not maximize the rate of
growth of the capital and labor stocks, and hence of the output capacity
of the economy. Nor for the benevolent dictator will maximizing the
future output stream maximize the rate of growth in per capita consumption if the rate of population growth is a function of the rate of investment
and its allocation.

Once we leave the familiar and well-trodden precincts of static
analysis under consumers' sovereignty, the variable we knew as the interest rate can take on meanings and values that we had not considered
sensible in their former habitat. Allocations and interest rates that are
rational in the context of static analysis and consumers' sovereignty may
be irrational in others, and vice versa. In our efforts to analyze the role
of the interest rate in such unfamiliar contexts, we found that a distinction
has to be made between the *real* and the *operating* interest rate. The real
interest rate is the interest rate that is consistent with the dictatorial
objective and dictatorial values. The operating interest rate, which differs
from the real interest rate, is the interest rate consistent with the fact
that decentralized decision-making bodies make decisions in accordance
with objectives and values that differ from the dictatorial objective. The
real interest rate is a measure of the opportunity cost of capital *in terms
of the dictatorial objective and values*. The operating interest rate reflects
neither the dictatorial objective, consumers' preferences, nor any other
single set of objectives and values. Rather, it is that rate necessitated
by the dominance of the dictatorial objective and values over those permitted to operate in some sectors of the economy so that the net outcome
of all economic activities yields an allocation approximating the dictatorially desired allocation.

To illustrate our general notions we examined the allocation problem for two dictatorial objectives. We saw that in our first example, that
of an aggrandizing dictator, the real rate of interest reflects the expansibility of the economy. In the special equilibrium case where no "luxuries"
are produced, the real rate of interest is equal to the rate of expansion of
all factors. This equilibrium case is described by the von Neumann model
of an expanding economy. In our second example, under a benevolent
dictator, the real rate of interest reflects the dictatorially determined rate
at which consumers sacrifice their present consumption standard for their
future standard.

On the basis of such ideas it would appear that the Lange-Lerner
solution for the socialist economy is, at best, incomplete. The problem

100

does not end with the socialist state simulating the economist's idealized state of perfect competition. The Lange-Lerner simulated competitive solution misses the point that a real competitive system is not only a de-centralized system but it is also a motivational system. By reproducing in some sense the decentralized part of the system, one is not reproducing the same motivation scheme. In other words, a system that possesses the informational processing capacities of a competitive system does not necessarily have its identical motivational properties. Firms with different ownership relations and different interests in the proceeds of the firms' outputs are likely to have different motivational properties. Thus a system of decentralized units plus rules imposed from above will not yield the same results as in the case where the procedural rules arise as a conse-quence of internally determined motivations. Also, the *raison d'être of* some types of socialism may imply objectives different from that of con-sumers' sovereignty, in which case the meaning of opportunity costs and interest rates change considerably. Multiple sovereignties are almost in-evitable under many kinds of planning, and as a consequence special problems of pricing and interest rate determination, problems absent from the state of perfect competition, enter the picture.

This paper probably raises more questions than it answers. The bits of analyses presented should be looked upon as nothing more than primi-tive conjectures which, hopefully, may stimulate further research in this area.

Footnotes

[1] The optimizing rules may be (but need not be) unique for the objective. But when we write O_a we specify both the optimizing rules (O) and the objec-tive (a). Note that by O_a we do not necessarily have in mind a single rule. O_a may be a set of rules of choice followed by the various decision-making units involved. Also, the objective may be complex in the sense that it need not involve the maximization of a single variable but may involve the finding of an optimum among variables that move in opposite directions. Although we need not belabor this point and attempt to spell out all the possibilities, it may be well to remember that O_a can be a highly complex operator involving more than a single rule that is uniformly applied.

[2] Compare E. Malinvaud: "Capital Accumulation and Efficient Allocation of Resources," *Econometrica* (April, 1953), pp. 252ff. This point can be seen in-tuitively if we consider the analogous rate of the transportation cost in the space dimension. Consider a country where the only significant transportation cost is along the east-west axis. Suppose that including transportation costs an even spatial distribution of production is optimal. Suppose that weight is a major distinguishing feature between the various commodities. Apart from transportation

cost, at existing prices, production of all commodities can be carried on most efficiently either at the east or the west boundaries of the countries. But if prices can be set by the dictator, it is possible for him to set factor prices so that an even spatial distribution of production is obtained even if transportation cost is formally priced at zero.

[3] On the possible significance of this point see the author's "Allocative Efficiency vs. X-Efficiency," *American Economic Review*, June, 1966.

[4] "A Model of General Economic Equilibrium," *The Review of Economic Studies*, XIII (1945–46), 1–9. See also Robert M. Solow and Paul A. Samuelson, "Balanced Growth and Constant Returns to Scale," *Econometrica*, XXI (1953), 412ff.; and T. C. Koopmans, *Activity Analysis of Production and Allocation*, pp. 98ff.

[5] It may be worth noting that in the von Neumann model the system of prices and outputs is not uniquely determined as is the equilibrium rate of interest. There may be a number of possible systems of prices and outputs consistent with the maximum rate of expansion. Cf. D. G. Champernowne, *The Review of Economic Studies*, XIII (1945–46), 13–18.

[12]
The Kibbutz: Motivations, Hierarchy and Efficiency

I Introduction

The remarkable thing about the Israeli kibbutz is that it exists at all. The philosopher Martin Buber stated, 'The kibbutz is an idea that has not yet failed'. Yet, even if it should fail tomorrow, which is most unlikely, it would be amazing that it has lasted this long.

The earliest kibbutzim were started about eight decades ago and by the 1920s the kibbutz system was well established. Until recently, it has out-performed the Israeli economy as measured by various indices of efficiency and growth. Recent data, however, support arguments that the kibbutzim may not now be doing quite as well as the general economy. Regardless of how it compares with the general Israeli economy, the main point is that on the basis of standard economic theory the kibbutz should not exist at all.

II The Nature of the Kibbutz and Kibbutz Philosophy

The kibbutz started and still exists as an organizational form based on socialist principles. In theory consumption is carried out in common while production activities depend on the capacities of members. The philosophical prescription is presumed to be, 'To each according to their needs and from each according to their capacity'. In practice what it comes down to is a strong egalitarian principle with respect to consumption. Three-quarters to four-fifths of consumption is carried out in common and the residual available for consumption is given to members in the form of money which they can spend according to their desires. Simply put, the consumption standard does not depend in any way on an individual's contribution to production.

While consumption is clearly equal it is worth noting that if we think of income as it is conceived outside of the kibbutz system, then it is not equal for all. In the kibbutz a family's income rises as the family has children. In other words these children are supported by the kibbutz in the form of increased income to their families. Then, later in life family income falls as children support themselves in or outside the kibbutz system. Visualize a rising income level as individuals enter the kibbutz

231

workforce and as the number of family members increase. If the first child is born when parents are in their mid-twenties, and the peak consumption level of children is when they receive a university education (for those who do), then on average, family income may rise until the parents are about 45 or 50 years old, and then fall thereafter. The income profile of kibbutz families does not differ much from that of the Japanese, where seniority is the major determinant of income, making it likely that it will rise to the point of retirement from the firm, say at age 55.

How production is carried out in the kibbutz is somewhat more complicated. As a general rule individuals are allowed to choose their jobs. Jobs needing to be done for which there are an insufficient number of applicants are filled on the basis of rotation. In other words, those jobs perceived as being less desirable are shared approximately equally by all members.

When necessary, people are appointed to leadership positions for short periods of time. These leadership roles, such as manager of a factory or general secretary of the kibbutz, are assumed for a fixed period, say three years, and then rotated to another member irrespective of performance. It is of interest to note that people in these leadership roles enjoy exactly the same consumption as everyone else.

Kibbutzim vary in size from 300 to about 1,500 people, usually made up up of somewhere between 200 to 1,000 adults. All adult members vote in the general meeting of the kibbutz. And it is at these general meetings that policies and plans are determined and people elected to the most important leadership roles.

Although members are always free to leave, not everyone is free to enter. All individuals born on the kibbutz or into kibbutz families almost automatically become members around age 22, or 23, after their military service. There is a *pro forma* year of candidacy, but all those born into the kibbutz are usually admitted. The same is true for those who marry into the kibbutz. However, all others wishing to join must apply to the kibbutz system as a whole. The upper limit for admission is usually age 35, and only about one in ten applicants are accepted.

While the overall size of the kibbutz membership has held up over the years (indeed it appears to have grown slightly though not as rapidly as the general Israeli population), it is most important to note that the kibbutz system is small compared to the general population. Only about three percent of Israeli adults are kibbutz members.

Initially the kibbutzim began as strictly agricultural organizations. Over time it became clear that the system could not be maintained entirely on this basis since the mechanization of agriculture meant fewer and fewer individuals were needed to grow both food and other products. It soon became evident that with such mechanization other jobs had to be found for members. There was soon too little to do and too much 'capacity' to do it. Because kibbutz philosophy values productive work many kibbutzim were forced to find other economic activities for their members. Some built small factories on kibbutz land. Other kibbutzim diversified into the tourist service industry. A number of those built large guest houses catering to tourists. These facilities have proven very successful as measured by their equal or superior occupancy rates compared to Israeli hotels in general.

In order to continue our analysis in the following sections it is not necessary, however, to believe that the kibbutzim have outperformed the Israeli economy. We need only assume that it has, on average, been at least as good as the overall Israeli economy through the years.

III The Lack of Economic Incentives

Since in theory and in practice there is almost a complete absence of differential economic incentives in the kibbutz, it is surprising that the system has done so well. The lack of normal incentives which are available either in private enterprise in capitalist economies or in government service should mitigate against the success of the system. The history of most kibbutz-like societies attempted in North America in the 19th century does not record great success. In fact, most such experiments failed quickly — frequently lasting less than a few years. Even in communist countries some kinds of economic incentive systems usually exist. Frequently there are considerable differentials in pay for people in different positions. Yet for the most part, the kibbutz system has succeeded in eliminating the need for these types of incentives.

Let us now, therefore, examine briefly this absence of economic incentives. The most clear-cut manifestation is the lack of differential pay for differential contributions. Thus people who do very different types of work, which in the private sector would receive highly differential wages, receive exactly the same real income under the kibbutz system. Since, most of kibbutz income is provided in kind rather than money, members take most of their meals in a common dining room, are allocated housing in accordance with family size, and receive equal small amounts of money for the sort of goods and services that the kibbutz cannot provide. Despite this, there is no hiding the fact that contributions of various members differ greatly both on similar and different types of jobs.

Given the equal consumption principle there is perceived to be no need for a promotion system. And since hierarchy is repressed it is impossible for individuals to receive promotions even for unusual contributions. Certainly this clearly distinguishes the kibbutz from the general Israeli society. Unquestionably, outside of the kibbutz system promotions and career structures are major incentives.

It is also important to note that within the kibbutz system there is no possibility for individuals to build up wealth. While the overall standard of living may rise as the kibbutz invests in its production facilities, all members share equally in the increased productive capacity. Individuals cannot accumulate more wealth from the kibbutz than other individuals within the system. However, in some cases monies and property inherited from family members outside of the kibbutz are not included in the wealth of the kibbutz community.

If an individual leaves the kibbutz there is no severance pay, and rights to severance pay cannot be accumulated. There are also no retirement funds or retirement provisions within the system. Finally, individuals cannot accumulate shares in the kibbutz which they can appropriate to themselves. Thus, on the whole, almost all pecuniary or economic incentives that exist outside the kibbutz system can be seen to be absent within it, and yet the system appears to work well.

IV Non-Monetary Incentives

Why should kibbutzniks work hard on their jobs? Why shouldn't they maximize the amount of effort free-riding that may be possible in the situation? All the evidence appears to be that, in fact, they do on average work quite hard. Furthermore, by most reports, they work harder than workers in the non-kibbutz sector. Usually the answer given by kibbutzniks is 'social pressure from peers'. While in general this response is correct it is perhaps too simplistic to lend much meaning to what in reality goes on. Who are these peers and in what form is this social pressure exerted? Are the peers the kibbutz as a whole, are they specific peers on the job, friends or family members, or other entities? The answer usually given is some or all of the above, yet there seems to be general agreement that peers on the job exercise the most influence. In order to understand how this pressure is exerted, we have to consider the system of job allocation.

The kibbutz is generally divided into 'branches'. Each branch represents a unit of economic activity, which may or may not produce a physical product. For instance, in the agricultural sector of the kibbutz the cowshed will be one branch while the banana grove will be another. The number of people in a branch may vary anywhere from half a dozen to several dozen depending on the activity. A small factory may constitute a single branch, while a larger factory may contain several branches.

Thus, branches are locally defined work units to which people are 'assigned'. Assignments to desirable jobs are usually *pro forma* since enough people volunteeer for these jobs and there is, therefore, no need to allocate people against their will. Some individuals develop a sense of seniority on certain jobs, and therefore feel they almost have a right to work in certain branches. This does not imply that a branch is a lifetime commitment, but it can become a very long-term one for an individual who chooses it. Normally an individual will want to find a branch to work in where his or her workmates will be compatible and from whom he or she can earn group 'membership' and approval.

Older branch members are usually more familiar with the necessary tasks of the branch, and it is believed, correctly or not, that performance of these necessary tasks involves a zero-sum game. In other words, if somebody works less hard then this imples that somebody else must work harder. Shirking is viewed as being at the expense of other branch members. There is even the risk that a less than average effort worker may be viewed as 'a parasite'. Hence it is thought to be in the interest of all branch members to assure that others pull their own weight. The social pressure structure involves four components: (a) free choice of jobs, (b) peer pressure within the branch, (c) the spread of peer approval or disapproval via the gossip system, and (d) the threat of sanctions through hints and sometimes outright requests that the errant individual should seek to join another branch.

Individuals are likely to be informally judged as to whether they are good workers or not. Since the kibbutz is a relatively small organization in which people see each other almost every day and in which 'living' and 'work' are not clearly separated, it is likely to have a very active gossip pipeline. Hence anyone who is clearly known for being either a good worker or a non-good worker will find this knowledge has spread throughout the community. Intra-branch judgements are likely to lead to judgements beyond the branch.

Sometimes there is use of direct negative peer pressure. Those whose performance is deemed inadequate are likely, at least informally, to be asked to 'try their luck' in another branch where 'they might be happier'. Thus the social pressure system is aided and abetted by the existence of relatively free choice of jobs. It is through these informal means, and as a last resort through formal means, that the branch work-approval and social pressure system is likely to lead to relatively high effort levels.

Another motivating force pointed to by kibbutzniks, is a sense of belonging to the unit fostered by the specific branch in which they work and the kibbutz as a whole. Members believe in a common destiny determined, to some degree, by each individual's contribution. Individuals are aware that others in the system are providing their food, housing, childcare, education, and various other services. As a consequence it is believed that a majority of members (but alas not all) feel obliged to perform well in return for what is provided for them. In other words the sense of belonging as well as the sense of common destiny create a society in which the desire for effort free-riding is either blunted or repressed. Nevertheless there are usually some free-riders who, while rare, exist, are recognized, and are referred to as 'lazy'.

A point sometimes made is that the system of informal work evaluation also leads to some sense of a work standard. Thus individuals need not put forth the maximum effort of which they are capable. The more talented individuals may get along by simply meeting the informal work standard. However, since there is recognition of especially good workers, and frequently a desire by workers to achieve that recognition, this leads to rising effort standards rather than constant ones. While this argument is put forth by kibbutz members to explain high effort levels it is not believed to be as influential as other aspects of the social pressure system.

V The Choice-of-Job Problem

A surplus of member volunteers for some jobs and a scarcity for others is the result of approximate but not complete free choice of jobs. A frequently heard complaint is that some types of work are boring. For example, a great number of factory jobs are considered boring, and as a consequence there is frequently a scarcity of worker volunteers for them. This, in part explains the fact that a number of kibbutz factories are manned by hired labor. In some extreme cases the entire factory is manned by hired labor and kibbutz members are only in management positions. This latter situation is seen to create a number of incentive problems. It is generally believed that hired labor is not motivated to work as well as kibbutz members, since hired labor is not expected to be influenced by the 'social pressures' of the kibbutz. It is of interest to observe that where there is a mixture of kibbutz members and hired labor, the hired workers appear to work more effectively than when kibbutz members only hold managerial positions.

The job preference practices which result in the necessity for hired labor also create conflicts with basic kibbutz principles. This is due, in part, to the socialist belief that hired labor is, of necessity or by definition, exploited. For example the more leftist kibbutz, Kibbutz Artzi, feels very strongly that all hired labor should be eliminated, yet they have not succeeded in doing so. It was reported to me by a member of that kibbutz that this failure is a source of much soul searching and discussion on the part of its members. In other kibbutzim the problem may not be seen as stemming as much from strongly held philosophical views as from the fact that hired labor is scarce. It is clear that the younger kibbutz members are less concerned with doctrine than some older and 'more participatory' members, yet having to rely on hired workers still poses a problem for them. Regardless of how strongly kibbutzniks adhere to or have strayed from the philosophy of the movement, they almost all recognize that the need for hired labor results from the practice of free job choice.

Relatively free job choice is also central to the question of motivation on the kibbutz. People are unlikely to work as effectively in jobs imposed on them as in those they choose freely. Hence, maintaining free job choice is seen as an efficiency consideration. In addition there is the fear that a lack of interesting jobs will cause members to leave the kibbutz and the movement. As a consequence, in order to maintain the kibbutz and especially the basic principles, managers must somehow find factories or additional services which provide the kind of job mix that fit the demand of members. When one stops to think about it, it becomes evident that this poses unusually difficult problems. In most work situations there is likely to be a mixture of interesting and boring elements. Very few occupations have eliminated all boring aspects. In the non-kibbutz sector boring jobs may be compensated for by higher monetary rewards. But this last is not an option available to the kibbutz since they cannot offer the equivalent of pay differentials. Many types of managerial posts are more interesting than non-managerial jobs, but this option is also not available to the kibbutz. The reason is that the attempt to repress hierarchy is likely to contribute to a system of rotation which does not permit managerial or, for that matter, other skilled jobs to become permanent vocations. As a consequence, the kibbutz must face the difficult problem of finding new activities to invest in that are profitable for the kibbutz, have interesting job mixes for its members, and do not violate the minimum hierarchy principle.

Some kibbutz members suggested to me that the period of rotation for undesirable jobs has not been carefully assessed and is not of an optimal nature. It would appear, therefore, that further research into better rotation periods for undesirable jobs might help to resolve the boredom problem. Another possible solution might entail giving individuals some mix of interesting and boring jobs, say, eight months at an interesting job and four months at a boring one, or morning 'boring' and afternoon 'interesting'. Or perhaps offering trade-offs between 'boring' and 'interesting' might help to solve the problem. In other words, the individual who is given a more interesting job might be required to spend some more time on a boring one and vice versa. On the surface these options do not appear to go counter to basic kibbutz philosophy.

Boredom is not the only reason for rejecting specific jobs, however. Other reasons are given, though they are not necessarily consistent with each other. Different people are likely to reject the same job for quite different reasons. But certain categories of jobs are almost universally seen to have inherent problems. If a position is one to which members can make requests or register complaints, that job is likely to be rejected by most kibbutz members. For example, it is frequently difficult to find members willing to take on the job of Executive Secretary. While this is unquestionably a prestigious job, it requires dealing with a great many issues about which many members may feel strongly. The person holding the job can be expected to hear from those individuals and to receive numerous requests and complaints from other members. The position of construction engineer is another interesting case in point. I was informed that if construction engineers were more readily available the kibbutz could effect considerable savings by doing their own building rather than having to hire a Histadruth construction company. Yet very few kibbutz members apply for training as construction engineers, the explanation being that such an individual would be flooded with conflicting requests from members asking to have repairs and or additions to various buildings made. This makes the position of construction engineer an undesirable one.

In general, jobs are said to have more prestige, a desirable quality, if they are more profitable to the kibbutz. This is especially true of activities that lead to exportable products. Hence some jobs will be refused because they are not 'prestigious' in this sense. Factory jobs, however, although contributing to profits are frequently refused because, as was indicated earlier, they are 'boring'. Thus, a job that fails by some specific criterion may be rejected even though it has other desirable qualities.

Of special interest is the role of women in the kibbutz. In general there appears to be a consensus of what constitutes 'women's work'. On average, men do not volunteer to do it. Thus for the most part only women work in and run the daycare centers and teach the elementary school classes. There is usually little difficulty in getting volunteers who have some qualifications to teach, but obtaining volunteers to run the daycare centers presents great difficulties. Caring for and keeping sometimes as many as

thirty preschool children busy for the better part of a day, is character-
ized as both physically and emotionally draining, and is therefore avoided
when possible. Frequently women are appealed to in terms of making a lasting
contribution to the kibbutz in order to have them volunteer for service in
the daycare centers.

Very few kibbutz members volunteer for sustained work in the kitchen or
in the dining room. Most of this work is handled on a rotation basis, and
some of it is done by short-term volunteers from overseas.

The point must be made that while there appears to be something truly
akin to what might be described as a 'kibbutz spirit' and a willingness to
work hard on the job, the spirit wanes when it comes to what are perceived
to be undesirable jobs.

VI The Hierarchy Problem

The question of hierarchy poses another difficult and unique problem for the
kibbutz system. The strong egalitarian bias in the system dictates that
nobody should be singled out as being superior to anyone else. Nevertheless
it is recognized that work done by a large group of individuals requires
somebody to be in charge, at least temporarily. Thus, for functional
purposes a superior–subordinate relationship is likely to be necessary. The
kibbutz ethos is to minimize the inequality of that relationship. Thus the
principle used is that all managerial or supervisory jobs should be strictly
temporary and preferably rotated. Ideally every individual should have the
capacity and opportunity to take on these jobs. An individual should be
selected from time to time for a managerial post and then after his or her
period of duty is over, say after two or three years, the individual should
go back to being an ordinary working member.

In practice rotation is, indeed, carried out. However, some managerial
posts are held for more than the 'normal' three year period. Furthermore, it
has recently been discovered that while rotation takes place, it is often
'horizontal'. That is, individuals with managerial skills are shifted from
one upper level job to another with occasional brief periods at the lower
levels. In view of the fact that there are differences in innate managerial
skills as well as knowledge, a rigid rotation system (one that permits
everyone to be a manager for equal amounts of time) would have to exist at
the expense of efficiency. Thus the question arises, does rotation, as it is
actually practised, eliminate hierarchy? Kibbutz members frequently express
the belief that it does. In fact, however, for those who serve only in subordinate roles, rotation does not eliminate hierarchy though their managers
or supervisors may change from time to time.

Since the availability of interesting jobs in factories is limited
and since many of the more interesting factory jobs are likely to have
managerial components, it may be necessary to relax the anti-hierarchy
principle in order to maintain the factories as integral parts of the
kibbutz. In addition some members want jobs that have career paths of some

sort. Some people desire professional or managerial jobs, or jobs outside the kibbutz which require high level skills they may have or would be able to obtain. Such jobs clearly involve a violation of the anti-hierarchy principle. It therefore seems clear that there is bound to be conflict between reality on the one hand and the anti-hierarchical principles on the other as the kibbutz moves more and more towards industrial and service activities.

As implied above not all jobs held by members are performed within the confines of the kibbutz. This is especially true of professional or near professional jobs. Thus, kibbutz members will serve on faculties of nearby universities, or in the case of physicians and dentists, they will serve in nearby hospitals or cities. It is not at all unusual for a member who is a physician to work outside the kibbutz (and live inside) and for the kibbutz to hire a physician from the outside. This phenomenon is often explained as a parallel to physicians not treating members of their own family. When members work outside the kibbutz, their salaries revert to the kibbutz while they enjoy the same consumption standard (but no higher) than those who work inside the kibbutz. Thus we see that there are, in fact, career opportunities for members beyond the possibilities available on the kibbutz, but such careers do not carry with them pecuniary advantages.

VII Ideological Biases Have Economic Consequences

For reasons of ideology, and in part because of special circumstances, the kibbutz will usually have a bias in favor of production of physical objects. In part, the initial socialist philosophy that inspired the original kibbutz experiment was based on the classical economists' (and Marxists') distinction between productive and unproductive labor. Generally speaking productive labor produces physical goods. This leads to a bias against services. In addition the kibbutz is usually located on a fixed piece of rural land and defines itself, in part, in terms of its rural location. Hence, services which are normally carried out in cities are outside of the purview of the kibbutz. Nevertheless, a number of kibbutzim (especially those located near recreational areas) have gone into the tourist hotel business on their land. Still, for the most part, the bias against services exists, so that non-agricultural kibbutz activity has been primarily directed towards manufacturing.

A bias related to that against services is that against activities connected only with internal consumption. Thus a kibbutz barbershop would not be looked upon as a productive activity since it does not earn money for the kibbutz. Hence a great variety of activities normally accounted for in national income statistics as productive because households purchase them from each other, would not be looked upon by kibbutz leaders as valued activities. This bias means that economic opportunities connected with internal consumption, which may be of high utility, are ignored or under-invested, whereas production of physical commodities may be overinvested. An example which we frequently encountered during our visit was that of the kibbutzim that were delighted to grow flowers for sale in Europe which they considered a worthwhile and profitable activity, but chose not to do so for their own tables.

Probably the bias that is the greatest source of inefficiency is the bias against sales and marketing activities. On the one hand there is the grudging recognition that such activities are necessary if certain kibbutz factory products are to be sold. On the other hand there is considerable underinvestment in these activities because they are not defined as physical products. Sales and marketing activities are often viewed grudgingly as a necessary expense rather than a form of investment in desirable services. Yet if the kibbutz system is to further expand outside of agriculture then such investments are probably absolutely necessary.

VIII Entrepreneurship

The most significant motivational deficiency in the kibbutz system appears to be the absence of rewards for entrepreneurial activities. Entrepreneurship is a subject hardly touched on in the kibbutz literature I have seen. On the whole, it seems to occur either by accident, or by some process involving committees or general meetings of the kibbutz. On the whole there is no system that rewards individual entrepreneurial talents and no encouragement of these talents which may be put at the service of the kibbutz. Yet is is likely that among the 100,000 plus kibbutz members there is a latent reserve of considerable entrepreneurial talent which is hardly tapped by the kibbutz movement.

It is clear that direct pecuniary advantages for successful entrepreneurial acts cannot be offered. Thus, the entrepreneur cannot become a residual claimant within the kibbutz system. Nevertheless, indirect advantages which are not offered at present might be considered. Most importantly the kibbutz might offer unusual job opportunities (such as a managerial role in the new enterprise) to a successful entrepreneur. Second, attempts might be made to give the successful entrepreneur prestige, or special praise or satisfaction in helping the kibbutz grow. At the same time, efforts could be made to repress negative criticisms which might readily extinguish enthusiasm for new ideas. There is nothing in the overall kibbutz ideology against giving people such non-pecuniary rewards.

Perhaps the most important encouragement to entrepreneurship would be specific entrepreneurial training. This could be a mix of general business and marketing training and the kind of motivational training suggested by McClelland.[1]

IX 'Retirement' and Old Age Services

Where the kibbutz really shines compared to almost all other organizational forms is in the provision of opportunities for senior citizens. Retirement as such does not exist in the kibbutz system. Clearly it is unnecessary because of the 'equal consumption standard' philosophy. As kibbutz members get older, and beyond some point, the number of hours of work are reduced, but there is usually no abrupt cut-off between a working and non-working life. Frequently the kibbutz will provide work situations for older kibbutz members that are not as physically demanding as those done by younger members. Such arrangements might even be at the expense of economic considerations. Yet the kibbutz will gladly bear the cost of such projects for what they term 'social' reasons. However, where possible, individuals work on products which are sold in the marketplace not only in order to earn for the kibbutz, but also to give the older employees the sense that they can continue to contribute to the generation of kibbutz income.[2]

X Summary and Conclusions

We must conclude from the kibbutz experiment that people are clearly responsive to non-pecuniary incentives. Peer approval, general approval, and a sense of belonging are important motivational elements. These are similar in part, to those that exist in the Japanese firm. (Of course, sharp contrasts also exist between the kibbutz and the Japanese firm.) In general this suggests that for economic analysis it is important to at least consider a mix of non-pecuniary and pecuniary elements. However, lessons from the kibbutz experiment, apart from those just stated, are difficult to apply elsewhere since they entail unique elements of history, culture and the system.

Non-monetary work incentives appear to inhibit shirking and elicit high effort levels. These incentives consist of a system of social pressure, the incentive for a person to establish him/herself in a desirable branch, a sense of belonging to the branch work unit, and a sense of the common destiny of the kibbutz. The desire for recognition as an above average worker may lead to a rising informal effort standard.

On the negative side there are motivational problems that could affect efficiency. There is a scarcity of volunteers for undesirable jobs (e.g., boring work, work lacking prestige, the worker being subject to members' demands, 'women's work'). There is a bias against services, and under-investment in sales and marketing despite their importance for efficiency. There is also a bias against production solely for internal consumption, regardless of utility.

Furthermore, the fundamental egalitarian philosophy resists hierarchy despite its advantages for motivation and efficiency (e.g., many interesting jobs entail managerial components, large enterprises require some hierarchy, some people prefer jobs with career paths, etc.). To a considerable degree a horizontal rotation of 'managers' occurs, and hence hierarchy is not really eliminated. Nevertheless, the degree of actual hierarchy, and felt hierarchy, is probably considerably less in the kibbutz sector than in the non-kibbutz sector.

Kibbutz managers have the difficult problem of finding profitable ventures that have an interesting job mix and a minimum of hierarchy. This difficulty might be eased by finding the optimal rotation on boring jobs, or by giving individuals a mix of boring and interesting jobs.

The most important consideration impacting on efficiency in the kibbutz is a lack of rewards for entrepreneurship. It might be possible for the kibbutz to encourage enterpreneurs by offering interesting jobs or prestige as rewards for success, and in addition by offering entrepreneurial training.

On the positive side the kibbutz eliminates many of the uncertainties faced by individuals outside the system. This forms a sufficiently strong attraction so that the system still has considerable choice in the selection of new members and faces few risks of not maintaining membership. The handling of the problems of the aged stands out as one of the major and unique achievements of the kibbutz system.

Notes

[1] McClelland, David C. and Winter, David, G., *Motivating Economic Achievement*, 1971, Free Press, N.Y.; and McClelland, David, *The Achieving Society*, 1961, Von Nostrand, N.Y.

[2] In Kibbutz Afikim there is a plywood lampshade factory where older kibbutz members work at their own pace and time. So, for example, if a worker finds he or she cannot sleep a full night (a problem many older people have), they can go to the factory and work. This factory is not only a source of productive work for older members, but also for pregnant women, and people recovering from medical problems requiring reduced activity. Since it is important to workers to know that they are contributing to the income of the kibbutz the factory's sales figures are posted so that they can see the consequences of their efforts. Concrete proof of their continued value.

Sources of Information

In addition to the literature mentioned below, this paper is based on interviews with a number of scholars and kibbutz members conducted during a visit to Israel in February and March 1986. I am indebted to the following: Chaim Barchai, Joseph Blasi, Yehuda Don, Chaim Ginzburg, Amir Helman, Joe Kreidin, David Mittelberg, Michal Palgi, Dov Peleg, C. Peretz, Yakov Roll, Menachem Rosner, Ehud Satt, Reuven Shapira, Joseph Yassour, Nira Yetlin, and others whose names unfortunately I did not record.

Among the literature perused are the following:

Don, Yehuda, 1985, 'Industrialization in the Israeli Kibbutz: An Economic Appraisal', unpublished paper, Department of Economics, Bar Ilan University, Israel.

Eden, Dov, and Leviatan, Uri, 1974, 'Farm and Factory in the Kibbutz: A Study in Agrico-Industrial Psychology', *Journal of Applied Psychology*, 59, No.5: 596 – 602.

Helman, Amir, 1986, 'Development and Trends in the Economic Planning of the Kibbutz', unpublished paper, Ruppin Institute, Haifa University, Israel.

Helman, Amir, 1985, 'The Inclination to Give Up Kibbutz' Values in Favor of Economic Efficiency', unpublished paper.

Helman, Amir, 1980, 'Income Consumption Relationship within the Kibbutz-System', in Bartolke, *et al.*, (eds) *Integrated Cooperatives in the Industrial Society*, Assen, The Netherlands, Van Gorcum: 131 – 141.

Helman, Amir, 1979, 'The Contradiction Between Cooperation and Individualism (The Israeli Kibbutz)', *Journal of Rural Cooperation*, 7, No.1 – 2: 35 – 39.

Helman, Amir, 1979, 'Lecture given at Hotel Hilton, Jerusalem, September 1979', Ruppin Institute, Haifa University, Israel.

Helman, Amir, 'Kibbutz Distribution and Welfare Economics', unpublished paper.

Helman, Amir, and Sonis, Michael, 1977, 'The Position of Agriculture in Kibbutz Economy – An Attempt at Quantitative Projection', *Socio-Econ. Plan. Sci.*, 11: 319 – 321.

Magid, Joel, *Kibbutz: The Way We Live*, booklet, The Federation of the Kibbutz Movements/ Documentation and Information, Israel.

Peleg, Dov, 1986, 'The Kibbutz Economic Model', unpublished paper, Kibbutz Sa'ar, Israel.

Rosner, Menachem, 'Emancipatory Use of New Technologies as Seen in Kubbitzim', unpublished paper.

Rosner, Menachem, 'The Factory of the Future and the Typical Kibbutz Factory', unpublished paper, The Institute for Research on the Kibbutz and the Cooperative Idea, Haifa University, Israel.

Satt, Ehud, 'On the Value of Labor and Economic Democracy in the Kibbutz', revised version of a paper presented at the International Conference on 'Kibbutz and Communes – Past and Future', Yad-Tabenkin, Efal, Israel, May 1985.

Sharipa, Reuven, 1982, 'Managers, Workers and Expertness: Trust and Market Relations in an Automatic Process Plant', Ph.D. Dissertation, Tel Aviv University, Israel.

Valency, Aharon and Evans, Martin G., 1983, 'Intrinsic Motivation and Extrinsic Rewards', Ruppin Institute Discussion Paper, Haifa University, Israel.

Part IV
Entrepreneurship in Developing Countries

[13]

ENTREPRENEURSHIP AND DEVELOPMENT*

By HARVEY LEIBENSTEIN
Harvard University

I

The received theory of competition gives the impression that there is no need for entrepreneurship. If all inputs are marketed and their prices are known, and if all outputs are marketed and their prices are known, and if there is a definite production function that relates inputs to outputs in a determinate way, then we can always predict the profit for any activity that transforms inputs into outputs. If net profits are positive, then this should serve as a signal for entry into this market. The problem of marshaling resources and turning them into outputs appears to be a trivial activity. From this point of view it is hard to see why there should ever be a deficiency of entrepreneurship. But there is frequently a lack of entrepreneurship. The answer is that the standard competitive model hides the vital function of the entrepreneur.[1]

My aim in what follows is twofold: to suggest a theory of the economy and of entrepreneurship in which entrepreneurship has a unique and critical role and to use this theory to indicate why entrepreneurship is a significant variable in the development process.

In a paper published in 1966 [9] I argued that there does not exist a one-to-one correspondence between sets of inputs and outputs.[2] There are three main reasons for this: contracts for labor are incomplete, the production function is not completely specified or known, and not all factors of production are marketed. I will argue that these are the basic postulates for an economy in which entrepreneurship has a distinct and critical role.

We may distinguish two broad types of entrepreneurial activity: at one pole there is routine entrepreneurship, which is really a type of management, and for the rest of the spectrum we have Schumpeterian or "new type" entrepreneurship. (We shall refer to the latter as N-

* The author would like to thank his colleagues Sam Bowles, Albert O. Hirschman, Gustav Papanek, Nathan Rosenberg, and Ray Vernon for helpful comments that led to some revisions of an earlier version. They are not responsible for the deficiencies that remain.

[1] This point is elaborated in detail in Professor Baumol's paper [3]. His quotation from Veblen is especially apt. Professor Hirschman makes similar points in [8a, pp. 2–5].

[2] See [9] for evidence of specific cases. Econometric evidence on production functions is hard to interpret. Production functions fitted for specific industries frequently have very low values for R^2. While this is consistent with the notion that there is no one-to-one correspondence between inputs and putputs, there are also many other reasons why the fits may be poor. See Marc Nerlove, "Recent Empirical Studies on the CES and Related Production Functions," in *The Theory and Empirical Analysis of Production* (N.B.E.R., 1967), p. 78.

entrepreneurship.) By routine entrepreneurship we mean the activities involved in coordinating and carrying on a well-established, going concern in which the parts of the production function in use (and likely alternatives to current use) are well known and which operates in well-established and clearly defined markets. By N-entrepreneurship we mean the activities necessary to create or carry on an enterprise where not all the markets are well established or clearly defined and/or in which the relevant parts of the production function are not completely known. In both cases the entrepreneur coordinates activities that involve different markets; he is an intermarket operator. But in the case of N-entrepreneurship not all of the markets exist or operate perfectly and the entrepreneur, if he is to be successful, must fill in for the market deficiencies. To my mind one of the main obstacles to our understanding of the entrepreneurial role lies in the conventional theory of the production function. This theory seems so reasonable at first blush that we are likely not to notice the subtle assumptions it makes. The basic culprits are the following assumptions: that the complete set of inputs are specified and known to all actual or potential firms in the industry, and that there is a fixed relation between inputs and outputs. The first assumption is implicit. To my knowledge, it is never stated explicitly, but I have not made an exhaustive search of the literature to check this. The second assumption is explicit, but it is rarely challenged.

In its usual conception the production function is considered to be clearly defined, fully specified, and completely known. Where and to whom in the firm this knowledge is supposed to be available is never stated. In fact, there are great gaps of knowledge about the production function. Points on the production function refer to well-defined inputs. To the extent that they are not completely defined in actuality, the entrepreneur must in some way make up the deficiency. Suppose that to produce a certain commodity, a certain type of machine has to be employed. If no one in the country produces such a machine and if imports are barred, only entrepreneurs who have access to information on how to construct the machine can enter the industry. The potential entrepreneur has to make up for a market deficiency. But that is not his only major function.

Important inputs not well marketed are types of management and market knowledge. Even managers of the more routine type may not be available in well-organized markets in many developing countries. Where available, their capacities may be very difficult to assess. One of the important capacities of management is the ability to obtain and use factors of production that are not well marketed. In some countries the capacity to obtain finance may depend on family connections rather than on the willingness to pay a certain interest rate. A successful entrepreneur may, at times, have to have the capacity to operate well in the political arena connected with his economic activities.

The usual characteristics attributed to entrepreneurs involve gap-filling as one of their essential underlying qualities. For example, it may be thought desirable that entrepreneurs possess at least some of the capacities to: search and discover economic opportunities, evaluate economic opportunities, marshal the financial resources necessary for the enterprise, make time-binding arrangements, take ultimate responsibility for management, be the ultimate uncertainty and/or risk bearer,[3] provide and be responsible for the motivational system within the firm, search and discover new economic information, translate new information into new markets, techniques, and goods, and provide leadership for the work group. In a world of perfect markets, if such a world were possible, each of these characteristics would be marketed as a specific service. Thus, some firms might specialize in the discovery of economic opportunities and sell this information to others. A similar remark could be made of each of the capacities mentioned above. The reason that this is not the case is because some inputs are inherently unmarketable, and some are difficult to market and are frequently unmarketed. For example, we cannot have a perfect market in risk-taking since, among other reasons, there is a "moral risk" problem in profit insurance. (The entrepreneur can intentionally do poorly and cash in on the policy.) Similarly, if the motivational system is the sum of all the human elements and their relations to each other within the firm rather than something specifically provided from outside the firm, then this element cannot be marketed. One of our basic points is that the conditions for perfect markets and the nature of some commodities are inconsistent with each other.

It is important to stress that entrepreneurial activities do not arise only because of market structure imperfections. This view gives too shallow an interpretation of the entrepreneurial role.[4] First, some gaps in markets are inherent in all cases. Second, and what is perhaps less apparent, is that the entrepreneur has to employ some inputs that are somewhat vague in their nature (but nevertheless necessary for production), and whose output is indeterminate. The provision of leadership, motivation, and the availability of the entrepreneur to solve po-

---

[3] Schumpeter [12, p. 137] is very firm on the point that the entrepreneur is not a risk bearer or uncertainty bearer: "The one who gives credit comes to grief if the undertaking fails." Furthermore, in countries with highly developed stock markets some entrepreneurs can shift the risk by selling shares.

[4] A narrow "imperfect market" interpretation of the entrepreneurial role gives the impression that markets are perfectable, say by the elimination of monopolistic influences, and that by doing so, the significant aspects of the entrepreneurial role can be eliminated thereby. This is not the view taken in this paper. The ideas of this paper are not brought out fully by thinking that the entrepreneurs' role depends only on market imperfections.

tential crisis situations, the capacity to carry ultimate responsibility for the organizational structure and the major time-binding (implicit or explicit) contractual arrangements are of this sort. Third, and most important, the entrepreneur has to possess what might be called, for want of a better term, an "input completing" capacity. If six inputs are needed to bring to fruition a firm that produces a marketable product, it does no good to be able to marshal easily five of them. The gap-filling and the "input-completing" capacities are the unique characteristics of the entrepreneur.

As we have defined the entrepreneur he is an individual or group of individuals with four major characteristics: he connects different markets, he is capable of making up for market deficiencies (gap-filling), he is an "input-completer," and he creates or expands time-binding, input-transforming entities (i.e., firms).

Entrepreneurship is frequently a scarce resource because entrepreneurs are gap-fillers and input-completers and these are scarce talents. Other things equal, the amount of gap-filling and input-completing required determines the degree of scarcity. Gap-filling is necessary because information about some inputs are unmarketable; and because private information about markets cannot always be proven and made public information. Of course, gap-filling will also be necessary where universalistic markets have not been developed, or where the inputs are, in principle, marketable but for some reason such markets have not arisen. For any given economic activity there is a minimum quantum of various inputs that must be marshaled. If less than this minimum variety is universalistically available, the entrepreneur has the job of stepping into the breech to fill the lack of marketable inputs; i.e., he must be an input-completer.

In my "X-efficiency" paper [9] I argued that neither individuals nor groups (say, firms) work as hard or as effectively or search for new information and techniques as diligently as they could, nor is effort maintained at a constant level. The nature and degree of directed human effort of a given individual is not invariable in the sense in which the characteristics of some physical inputs and their capacities may be said to be invariable. The degree of directed effort depends on a variety of factors that determine the internal motivational state of the firm and the external motivational state of the appropriate segment of the economy. Thus, under some circumstances the level of directed effort of the human inputs may be low and, as a consequence, some firms operate under a considerable degree of slack [5] [9]. Persistant slack implies the existence of entrepreneurial opportunities.

The motivational state is likely to be composed of the following elements: (1) The system of financial rewards for effort, some of which may be directly related to the quantity of output but some of the rewards may not be clearly related to output. (2) There may also be a system of rewards and "punishments" related to aspects of behavior other than the productive ones. For example, promotion within a firm may be related to personality traits or kinship or personal ties unconnected to the direct pursuit of the aims of the firm. (3) Finally, there is an interpersonal mechanism of group approval and disapproval, as well as approval-disapproval relations between individuals in different relative hierarchical statuses that normally influence productive behavior. The sum of these relationships is essentially the motivational state of the system. It seems clear that the degree and nature of directed effort will depend on the motivational state. This is especially likely to be true for nonroutine aspects of directed effort such as those involved in the introduction of technological change.

There is a significant relation between the entrepreneur's perceptive capacity and the fact that firms operate under some degree of slack [9]. The existence of slack and the fact that not all inputs are marketed means that the market signals for profit opportunities are blurred. Since there is no one-to-one correspondence between inputs and outputs, a knowledge of output price and input prices can no longer yield the necessary signals. On the other hand, an error in perception can be partially counterbalanced by increased effort in marshaling resources and in operating the plant.

It is noteworthy that the traditional theory does not explain the existence of firms as time-binding entities. The theory presented here suggests that since the production function is incomplete, firms become valuable storehouses of detailed experience and knowledge. In part, this means that successful firms are entities that house successful motivational systems that can be retained only through a scheme of renewable contractual arrangements of different time durations. It is in this way that the firm captures some of the long-term benefits of previous gap-filling and input-completing conquests.

A way of looking at the essential elements is to visualize the economy as a net made up of nodes and pathways. The nodes represent industries or households that receive inputs (or consumer goods) along the pathway and send outputs (final goods and inputs for the other commodities) to other nodes. The perfect competition model would be represented by a net that is complete, that has pathways that are well marked and well defined, that has well-marked and well-defined nodes, and one in which each element (i.e., firm or household) of each node deals with every other node along the pathways on equal terms for the same commodity. In the realistic model we have in mind there are holes and tears in the net, obstructions (knots) along the pathways, and some nodes and pathways, where they exist, are poorly defined and poorly marked or entirely unmarked from the viewpoint of elements of other nodes. We may refer to this net as impeded, incomplete, and "dark" in contrast to the unimpeded and "well-lit" net that represents the competitive model. Of course, a portion of the real economy net may very loosely approximate the "unimpeded" net of the perfect competition model. Entrepreneurs working in the well-defined, non-hole, non-obstruction part of the net carry out routine entrepreneurial-managerial activities, while those that operate on the impeded, incomplete, and dark parts carry out N-entrepreneurial activities. Entrepreneurial activities will make some portions of the net less impeded through extending markets (i.e., creating new pathways) but may make others more so through the creation of monpolies, or the creation of other obstacles (e.g., high entry costs) where they previously did not exist. Inventions and the creation of new knowledge will to some extent extend the net to vague and incomplete areas, but other inventions may substitute relatively well-defined pathways and nodes for those which were ill-defined and obstruction-laden previously.

II

Although there is no universally accepted theory of development we can point to two important elements in the process: (1) Per capita income growth requires shifts from less productive to more productive techniques per worker, the creation or adopton of new commodities, new materials, new markets, new organizational forms, the creation of new skills, and the accumulation of new knowledge. (2) Part of the process is the interaction between the creation of economic capacity and the related creation of demand so that some rough balance between capacity growth and demand growth takes place. The entrepreneur as a gap-filler and input-completer is probably the prime mover of the capacity creation part of these elements of the growth process.[5]

We now know that development is not simply a process of physical and human capital accumulation in the usual sense. If that were all that were involved, then development would simply be a function of the willingness to save. Experience has shown that this is not the case. The work of Solow and others [1] [2] [13] have shown that growth cannot be explained by the contributions of the increase in standard inputs. The work of Chenery and Strout [4] emphasizes that the degree of capital absorption can be a significant constraint to growth in developing

---

[5] The basic idea is that firms do not operate on their production possibilities frontier. In part, the internal motivational state of the firm determines the degree to which actual output is less than the production possibilities frontier output. Thus, costs per unit of output are not minimized. The size of the difference between actual costs and true minimum costs offers opportunities for those entrepreneurs who think they can produce at lower costs.

countries. The existence of and need for gap-filling and input-completing capacities could explain why standard inputs do not account for all outputs and why capital absorption should be a problem. Economic planning experience in many countries reveals that there is frequently a considerable divergence between plan targets and results. This divergence may be partly explained by the fact that enterpreneurship is not a normal input whose contribution can be readily determined, predicted, planned for, or controlled.

We now sketch briefly some of the basic strands of a theory from which the concept of the entrepreneur as a gap-filler and input-completer derives.

The demand side is determined by the following: (1) The maximal production possibilities set in the sense of maximum knowledge. By maximum knowledge we mean that the techniques are known somewhere in the world—knowledge that is conceivably obtainable although it may be at an exceptionally high cost. (2) We deduct from the large maximal possibilities set the subset of techniques in use and those techniques that contain the following basic characteristics: they are actually known in detail without anything more than routine search activities and the inputs required for production are marketed on a routine basis. (3) What is left is that portion of the maximal production possibilities set which forms the potential opportunities for gap-fillers. Now, gap-filling and input-completing activities are usually costly. Taking these costs into account and calculating the expected prices of marketed inputs and potential outputs, each element in the gap-filling opportunity set can be associated with a set of potential profits or losses (depending on who does the gap-filling). We reduce the gap-filling opportunity set to those possibilities that are associated with expected yields of positive net profits. This set is likely to be very much larger than what will actually be pursued by entrepreneurs. The gap-filling opportunity set is likely to be non-unique since the costs associated with gap-filling depend on the specific entrepreneur that attempts to take advantage of the opportunity. The sequence in which gap-fillers choose opportunities will determine the degree to which any one turns out to be profitable. In addition, the degree of effort put forth by different enterpreneurs and the same entrepreneur at different times will vary, depending on the personality, circumstances, and the motivating influences that exist at the time. Thus, the association between gap-filling opportunities and profitable opportunities is not likely to be a unique one-to-one correspondence.

The supply side is determined by the following: the set of individuals with gap-filling and input-completing capacities, the sociocultural and political constraints which influence the extent to which entrepreneurs take advantage of their capacities, and the degree to which potential entrepreneurs respond to different motivational states, especially where nontraditional activities are involved. Clearly, the personality characteristics of entrepreneurs are important. Apart from gap-filling and input-completing capacities, the potential entrepreneurs' response to opportunities will depend on their preference for certain modes of behavior as opposed to others. Thus, the entrepreneurial personality theories developed by Hagen [6] and McClelland [10] which connect nurture to the creation of entrepreneurial drives are significant elements on the supply side. Last, but not least, the alternatives open to individuals are important, since we must take into account opportunity costs of entrepreneurial acts.

In such a theory growth would depend, in part, on the degree of routine entrepreneurship, the degree to which gaps and impediments in markets exist, and the quality, motivations, and opportunity costs of the potential gap-fillers and input-completers available.

It is not possible at this stage to develop a complete and detailed model of economic development and entrepreneurship. One reason for this is that we do not have, at present, a theory of obstructed, incomplete, and "relatively dark" economic systems. However, it may be useful to sketch briefly the broad outlines of what such a model might contain if further research proved successful.

The model, if it were successfully developed, should enable us to describe the the motivational state that arises from any given state of the impeded system and the reactions to the motivational state. That is, the model should show the links between the maximal opportunity set and those opportunities that are actually perceived and pursued by entrepreneurs. We now attempt to specify the links that are likely to be involved: (1) The input gaps are in part determined exogenously. (2) Given the input gaps, and the opportunity set, the interfirm motivational state should determine the degree to which firms expand in response to the pull of profit opportunities and the push of the fear of falling behind competitive firms. The interfirm motivational state itself is determined by the number of firms in the industry, the nature of the market structure, and the energy and aims of the entrepreneurs within these firms, which in turn determines the degree of competition between firms. The interfirm motivational state is unlikely to be sufficient to determine how any specific firm behaves. Among the intervening elements is the perceptive mechanism of the firm which determines the way in which firms receive, filter, and process market information and the degree to which firms become aware of changes of relative competitive status. (3) Thus, the intrafirm motivational state, whose constituents we have described above, determines how firms react to the activities of competitors, and to changes in the opportunities the firm faces. The intrafirm motivational state depends in part on the organizational structure of the firm and in part on the rate of change of manpower (especially managerial personnel) within the firm. The basic notion here is that as new individuals enter the firm, the existing equilibrium between decision-makers and their reactions to each other and to external opportunities may change so that the intrafirm motivational state changes accordingly. Of course, this last depends also on the degree to which new management personnel are similar or different in their capabilities and attitudes from those that they replace. (4) Finally, the input-completing and gap-filling capacities of the potential entrepreneurial pool determines the response of members of this pool to changes in opportunities and motivational states. An important aspect of the abilities involved is both the perception of economic opportunities and the capacity to assess such opportunities. These are presumably determined in part by factors exogenous to the system such as those involved in nurture, informal training, experience, as well as formal education of individuals. In sum, the model should in some way enable us to specify the relations of the links mentioned to the nature of economic states so that we can determine entrepreneurial reactions to changes in the economic state.

It might be helpful to classify N-entrepreneurs into different categories and determine each category's responsiveness to a given motivational state. Probably a significant part of such a model would be the interaction of different types of entrepreneurs to each other's activities (i.e., imitation, linkages, followers on "cleared" pathways, knowledge spread, etc.). Each period the response of the N-entrepreneurs to the motivational state creates a new state of the system and changes the motivational states in subsequent periods. At the same time it changes the supply of N-entrepreneurs in subsequent periods since some of those that enter foreclose their availability on subsequent occasions. Thus, the impulses created by entrepreneurial acts lead to sequences of entrepreneurial activities and changing opportunities which influence the pattern and rate of growth.[6] In addition, basic secular factors would have to be taken into account, since each year some potential entrepreneurs retire and others enter, while, at the same time, inventions lead to changes in the technical frontier and add new elements to the impeded and incomplete part of the market net.

III

To be of interest a theory needs some conjectures to tell us how some basic elements in the theory behave. Hence, to add some interest to this

---

[6] It would be interesting to see under what assumptions we could derive from such a model the growth promoting backward linkages suggested by Professor Hirschman [7] [8].

paper, I will hazard the following, all of which are on an "other things equal" basis: (1) The greater the rate of growth desired, the greater the quantum of gap-filling and input-completing capacities required. (2) The supply of active gap-fillers depends on opportunity costs. (3) The greater the assets of the group related to the gap-filler by kinship or friendship ties, the greater the gap-filling capacity of the entrepreneur involved. (4) Differential gap-filling and input-completing capacities are a critical element in explaining the differential rewards of entrepreneurs. (5) The routinization of gap-filling activities reduces the rewards of entrepreneurs.

There are a set of theories about entrepreneurship which revolve around the notions that in underdeveloped countries entrepreneurs prefer traditional industries, that their behavior is tradition-bound, and that they face overriding institutional obstacles. Yet, developing countries have periods of low growth and other periods of rapid growth. My conjecture in this connection is that in fact traditionalism is not the critical element but that the motivations present—e.g., the profit rates —are such that those with gap-filling capacities are willing and able to exert themselves under some motivational circumstances and reduce the degree of exertion under others. Thus, the ebb and flow of low and high growth rates can be explained without positing institutional rigidities that would appear to be almost impossible to overcome.

Two related elements that come to mind are the facts that entrepreneurs frequently come from groups which have fairly large extended families who are often engaged in trade and that they are disproportionately recruited from elements of the population that in some sense or other are looked upon as "outsiders." The extended family aspect can be explained by the fact that gap-filling capacities depend in part on kinship relations in which there is a much higher degree of trust and through which one can draw on more diverse capacities than exist on a universalistic basis. While there are many aspects to the outsider part of the phenomena, part of it, perhaps, can be explained by the fact that to the extent that outsiders are restricted from some economic opportunities, their opportunity costs as entrepreneurs are likely to be lower than other portions of the population, and hence they more readily engage in entrepreneurial activities compared to "insiders" whose opportunity costs are higher. However, not all outsiders become entrepreneurs since low opportunity costs can only be a facilitating and not a sufficient condition for entrepreneurship.

I realize that I run the risk of being charged, to use Professor Baumol's phrase, with offering nothing more than a taxonomy. I want to suggest that this is not the case—that the characteristics of the world described in this paper and the specified nature of the entrepreneurial role is such that it does lead to potentially interesting conclusions for development problems.

Our basic assumptions are as follows: (1) Motivation internal to the firm is a basic input that is not marketed. (2) There always exists some degree of slack (or excess capacity) due to low X-efficiency. (3) To bring any enterprise into fruition requires the marshaling of a minimum quantum of inputs. (4) Some inputs are "nonexhaustible" in the usual sense; that is, they do not necessarily decrease with use. Indeed, in some cases the opposite may be the case. Knowledge and motivation are two inputs of this type.

Some possible conclusions derivable from our assumptions are as follows:

1. While entrepreneurship may be scarce because of a lack of input-completing capacities, some entrepreneurial characteristics may in fact be in surplus supply; that is, they are unused simply because of the lack of the input completing capacity. In addition, some may be unused because the motivational state does not bring forth an adequate entrepreneurial response. As a consequence, it is possible that in some cases, small changes in the motivational state or in the reduction of market impediments may turn entrepreneurial scarcity into an abundant supply.

2. Our analysis of entrepreneurship requires us to reconsider the literature on investment criteria. Since investment can alter the market impediments and hence alter the supply of entrepreneurship, we must consider such possible side effects in our investment criteria. Thus, a lower profit investment that releases entrepreneurial energies and capacities may be more fruitful in the long run than a higher profit investment, if profit is calculated apart from the side effects we have just mentioned.

3. Some types of input creation which would normally appear to be functional may in fact be dysfunctional when the side effects are taken into account. For example, some types of higher education provided to potential entrepreneurs may be dysfunctional in that it increases the opportunity costs of potential entrepreneurs and may as a consequence decrease the supply of entrepreneurship.[7]

4. The theory suggests that training can do something to increase the supply of entrepreneurship. Obviously, not all characteristics of entrepreneurs are trainable. However, since entrepreneurship requires a combination of capacities, some of which may be vital gaps in carrying out the input-completing aspect of the entrepreneurial role, training can eliminate some of these gaps. For example, it may be difficult to train people to spot economic opportunities, but it is possible to train them to

---

[7] Somerset Maugham's story of the illiterate verger is an illustration of this possibility.

assess such opportunities once perceived. Similarly, certain managerial skills are trainable, but without them new firms might not survive because of their inability to overcome initial managerial difficulties.

For policy purposes, the theory suggests that development economists focus their attention when concerned with specific countries on studying the gaps, obstructions, and impediments in the market network of the economy in question and on the gap-filling and input-completing capacities and responsiveness to different motivational states of the potential entrepreneurs in the population.

REFERENCES

1. M. Abramovitz, "Resources and Output Trends in the United States Since 1870," *A.E.R.*, May, 1956.
2. O. Aukrust, "Investment and Economic Growth," *Prod. Meas. Rev.*, Feb., 1959.
3. W. Baumol, "The Entrepreneurship in Economic Theory," *A.E.R.*, May, 1968.
4. H. B. Chenery and A. M. Strout, "Foreign Assistance and Economic Development," *A.E.R.*, Sept., 1966, p. 686.
5. R. M. Cyert and J. G. March, *A Behaviorial Theory of the Firm* (Prentice-Hall, 1963).
6. E. E. Hagen, *On the Theory of Social Change* (Irwin, 1962).
7. Albert O. Hirschman, *The Strategy of Economic Development* (Harvard Univ. Press, 1951).
8. ———, *Development Projects Observed* (1967).
8a. ———, *Journeys Through Progress* (1963).
9. H. Leibenstein, "Allocative Efficiency vs. X-Efficiency," *A.E.R.*, June, 1966.
10. D. McClelland, *The Achieving Society* (Princeton, 1961).
11. G. F. Papanek, *Pakistan's Development* (Cambridge, 1967).
12. J. A. Schumpeter, *The Theory of Economic Development* (Harvard Univ. Press, 1951).
13. R. Solow, "Technical Change and the Aggregate Production Function," *Rev. of Econ. and Statis.*, Aug., 1957

[14]
International Business Format Franchising and Retail Entrepreneurship: A Possible Source of Retail Know-How for Developing Countries

Patrick J. Kaufmann
Harvard Business School

Harvey Leibenstein[1]
Harvard University

We wish to thank Louis T. Wells, Thomas K. McCraw, and Dennis M. Ray for their suggestions and comments.

Introduction

Manufacturers of branded products have used franchising as a method of controlled distribution since the German and British brewers introduced the concept in the eighteenth century (Stamworth and Curran, 1978; Hackett, 1976). By the middle of the twentieth century, a number of large manufacturers (e.g. automobiles, soft drinks) from the industrialized nations had found this form of licensed distribution to be an efficient method for entering foreign markets, including those of developing nations. Today, because of companies such as Coca Cola, product franchising - as it is known - is familiar throughout most of the world.

Another form of franchising, business format franchising, is a more recent phenomenon, originating with the fast food restaurant formats of the 1950s. Although relatively much less familiar in developing countries than product franchising, business format franchising is an important part of the retail distribution systems of many industrial nations. In fact, in the United States although business format franchising currently accounts for a lower percentage of total franchise sales than does product franchising, there are nearly twice as many business format outlets, and total business format franchising sales are growing twice as fast (US Dept. of Commerce, 1987). Moreover, because it arguably provides an efficient way to import marketing and retail know-how while creating opportunities for prospective local entrepreneurs, business format franchising might prove to have a significant impact on the economies of developing countries, as well.

In this paper, we explore the potential for international business format franchising in developing countries. We focus on the adaptability of foreign franchises to developing countries, and the ability of international business format franchisors to provide local franchisees with the same efficiency producing retail concept, business format, and ongoing support available to home country franchisees. In doing so, we examine some of the expected economic and social effects of business format franchising and retail franchise entrepreneurship in developing countries. Our purpose is to begin to assess some of the benefits and costs of international business format franchising from the perspectives of three constituencies; the local franchisee, the international franchisor, and the host country government.

International Business Format Franchising

Although *product franchising* is essentially a method of distribution, *business format franchising* more closely resembles a joint venture between an established retailer and a local entrepreneur. In product franchising, the franchisor is typically a manufacturer seeking outlets for its branded goods. The manufacturer/franchisor may provide some advertising and management assistance and training, but the franchisee generally conducts business as an independent distributor.

The business format franchisor, on the other hand, is typically an operating retailer who has experienced a level of success sufficient to suggest that if other retailer franchisees were to reproduce the franchisor's business formula and systems in other similar locations, they would also succeed. The franchisees, therefore, not only receive the right to use the franchisor's trademark, but also operate under specific guidelines covering all aspects of the business, including marketing, operations, finance, accounting, and often even the design of the premises and the color of employee uniforms. By following those guidelines, the franchisees' businesses are distinguishable only by location from those of other franchisees and the franchisor's prototype business. Because the franchisor's revenue is dependent on the continuing success of each franchisee, this similarity is not only permitted, but enforced through franchisor monitoring of the franchisees' operations. Therefore, typically in return for a one-time franchise fee and a royalty on all franchisee sales, the business format franchisor agrees to provide the means necessary for each franchisee entrepreneur to become the perfect imitator of a successful retail operation.

The support provided by the franchisor goes hand in hand with control over many of the franchisee's decisions. Acceptance of this control may require personality characteristics not always found in completely independent entrepreneurs.[2] Some researchers have suggested that business format franchisees cannot be considered true entrepreneurs[3]: 'Franchisees are not entrepreneurs. If they were, they could never take the regimentation and rules imposed on them. [Franchising] is for people who value security more than risk.' Alfred Modica (O'Donnell, 1984).

Since this article focuses on entrepreneur-like behavior, and since there is little consensus as to the criteria for 'true' entrepreneurship, how franchisees are labeled is not critical. It seems clear, however, that business format franchising offers an intermediate level of risk, cost, and return which appears to appeal to a large number of persons interested in owning their own business. The innovative spark is provided by the franchisor in formulating a novel business concept and format, and the franchisee provides the energetic on-site implementation of the business plan and the acceptance of the ultimate risk of failure (however limited). Business format franchising, therefore, joins two different types of 'entrepreneur', the innovator/coordinator and the imitator/implementer, in a quasi-hierarchical structure which has proven efficient in a significant variety of business environments (Williamson, 1979).

Business format franchisors have become increasingly attracted to the growth potential of foreign markets (Hackett, 1976). To date, US franchisors have been the most active participants in international business format franchising, but a growing number of European firms have begun opening foreign outlets, as well. Although approximately 15 per cent of their franchised outlets are in developing countries, US business format franchisors have concentrated primarily on franchising outlets in industrialized nations with developed economies (US Dept. of Commerce, 1987). Table 1 shows the worldwide distribution of franchised outlets of US business format franchisors.

In 1985 the types of US-based business format franchises most prevalent in less developed countries were auto rentals and restaurants, but there were also significant numbers of franchised convenience stores and other retail food stores; as well as some auto service centers, non-food retailers, and business services (US Dept. of Commerce, 1987).

French franchisors, very active in Europe, the United States, and Canada, have also franchised outlets in less developed countries throughout the world. Of the 88 members of the French franchising association, Federation Francaise de la Franchise, 16 are currently operating franchised outlets in Africa, and 10 have outlets in South America or Mexico. Twenty of the members are doing business in the Middle East, and 6 have franchisees operating in the South Pacific islands (Federation Francaise de La Franchise, 1987).

Table 1
US International Business Format Franchising (1985)

Location	Outlets	Franchisors
Canada	9,054	239
Japan	7,124	66
Australia	2,511	75
United Kingdom	2,291	68
Mexico	542	36
New Zealand	402	22
Continental Europe (excluding UK)	4,398	73
Asia (excluding Japan)	1,755	74
Caribbean	803	88
Africa	626	28
South America	515	35
Central America	167	27

(US Dept. of Commerce, 1987)

Business Format Franchising and Economic Development

Because business format franchising focuses on the transfer of retail know-how rather than on product distribution, it is the form of international franchising which would be most likely to have a direct effect on the economic development of developing countries.

Porter (1985) has argued that efficiency at the distribution level in the value chain not only reduces consumer prices, but also fuels manufacturer innovation. In other words, the existence of powerful rationalized retailers may pressure suppliers to improve price/quality ratios through rationalization of their own procedures. To the extent that franchising provides would-be entrepreneurs with access to specialized retail know-how and sophisticated operational systems, therefore, it should encourage not only retail efficiency, but manufacturing efficiency as well.

There is some supporting evidence for Porter's view in the context of international business format franchising. Because business format franchisors typically do not receive a significant part of their revenues from the supply of products to their franchisees, local sourcing is preferred. However, when McDonald's entered the British market, there were no local suppliers of rolls and other processed foods capable of meeting their demand. The franchisees initially sourced those requirements externally while assisting local suppliers in their efforts to develop the necessary production expertise. Eventually, local suppliers developed more advanced manufacturing processes, increased the quality and quantity of their own offering, and competed effectively for the franchise system's local business (Love, 1986, pp. 442 - 5). If business format franchising could be expected to have a similar effect in developing countries, therefore, it could prove not only to be a valuable source of retail know-how, but may also have a positive impact on general economic development.

Delivery of Risk-Reducing Benefits to International Franchisees

In the United States and other industrialized nations, by providing proven concepts, viable business formats, and ongoing support to franchisee entrepreneurs, franchisors have created highly efficient retailing systems. A spokesperson for the US Commerce Department has been quoted as saying that less than 4 per cent of US franchisees closed in 1985 (Schlender, 1986). The fact that franchisors have created efficient systems in their home countries, however, does not necessarily mean they can be successfully transplanted internationally. Whether franchisors can provide international franchisees with the same efficiency-producing and risk-reducing benefits depends on the additional costs occasioned by crossing geographic, legal, and cultural boundaries. When the franchisees reside in less developed countries, those costs may be even more severe. Although an assessment of the potential for a particular international franchisor's format varies from country to country, the analysis must focus on the three primary areas mentioned above; the concept, the format, and the ongoing support.

A proven retail concept

Business format franchise concepts are predominantly niche strategies. They are designed to provide a limited segment of the market with a retail concept particularly suited to their preferences. This kind of demand segmentation of the retail market allows the franchisor to design a concept that perfectly matches the preferences of the target segment, and to serve that segment better than other retailers who are less focused. The franchisor's innovation, therefore, first requires the identification of a segment large enough to support a successful business, and the design of a retail concept that satisfies the unmet needs of that segment.

Given the vast differences among cultures, however, it does not seem reasonable to expect that a concept that has proven itself acceptable to consumers in a particular culture would *necessarily* be appropriate to another. In fact, franchisors have been sued for misrepresentation for claiming that a franchise concept was transferable 'as is' to a foreign market (Rudnick and Brennan, 1987).

Nevertheless, at least among the industrialized nations, this may be changing. Some researchers have argued that markets are becoming essentially the same worldwide. Levitt (1983) suggests that national differences in tastes and modes of doing business are rapidly disappearing as we move toward global markets, and cites numerous examples, including McDonald's success from the Champs Elysees to the Ginza, as evidence. Levitt acknowledges that the international marketer or franchisor must be ready to make some modifications in the product or service concept to conform to local demand patterns, but argues that the basic underlying needs and preferences of the world community are converging (albeit at differential rates). The relatively low ranking which franchisors give to 'concept transferability' as a problem in international franchising seems to indicate that many franchisors agree with that argument (Trankiem, 1979; Hackett, 1976; Walker and Etzel, 1973). It should be noted, however, that the franchisors surveyed in those studies were operating predominantly in other industrialized economies, not in developing countries.

Nor, of course, does this address the question of whether those factors which promote this homogenization of tastes are culturally acceptable and/or facilitators of development processes. Foreign franchise systems bring concepts and products which could replace traditional retailing methods and products, and thereby destroy an element of local culture. Similar criticisms of franchising have been made even within the industrialized countries (Fishwick, 1983). Although beyond the scope of this discussion, those criticisms raise important social and political questions which must be addressed by host country policymakers. Perhaps an equally important empirical question would be whether such homogenization of tastes, in and of itself, affects economic development.

The differences between home country and host country markets present both difficulties and opportunities. It is becoming increasingly difficult for franchisors to differentiate themselves from other franchisors in their home markets. However, in foreign markets their unusual formats and offerings are often much more distinctive, and their outlets achieve a high degree of visibility. In fact, the uniqueness of franchising, in general, may encourage trial by the more innovative local consumers. For franchisor and local franchisee, therefore, the benefits of uniqueness could offset some of the costs of unfamiliarity and reduce the changes required to ensure consumer acceptance of the concept.

Even simple modifications to a franchise concept can significantly increase costs. One of the major strengths of franchising is the uniformity of the system. Monitoring costs are minimized because standards are constant. This allows data to be collected from the various outlets and compared to system averages. Deviations signal implementation variance. When the concept must be changed to comply with local tastes, these standards no longer apply and monitoring becomes customized to each market with the commensurate increase in cost.

In addition to differences in taste, differences in the economic environment may radically alter the way a franchise system functions in a foreign market. Franchising typically focuses on serving the needs of a particular market segment. If a franchise concept is introduced into a foreign market, it might attract an entirely different consumer segment. For example, a concept which relies on relatively high levels of disposable income might attract consumers from the middle class of an industrialized nation, but attract more upper class consumers in a developing economy. From a public policy perspective, a concept which focuses on a select group of privileged consumers may not be as attractive as one which has more universal appeal.

As part of the franchise concept, the franchisor must be able to provide the franchisee with a protected trademark. The trademark is valuable to the franchisee because it embodies the franchisor's reputation for quality. It is valuable to the consumer because it provides information about the particular outlet, that is, that it will provide a level of quality similar to other outlets with the same trademark. The trademark, therefore, is gradually developed through a history of customer experience and (possibly) advertising.

In a foreign market, few home country trademarks have any initial recognition value, and the franchisor must be committed to developing the trademark locally. Even if that is the franchisor's intent, however, there can be serious impediments to doing so. For example, with respect to advertising, television advertising could be unavailable because of government restrictions or lack of media development. Moreover, the relatively small size of each foreign market and the initial small number of outlets, could preclude the realization of economies of scale and make advertising significantly more expensive. The most important aspect of trademark development, however, is the constant monitoring of system outlets to ensure that they are delivering a standard level of quality service. The enforced standardization of customer experience creates a trademark which conveys information to the market and is a valued asset for all franchisees, as well as for the franchisor.

An even more serious deterrent to a franchisor introducing or developing a trademark in a foreign market concerns local trademark law. When operating in the home market, trademark registration will protect the franchisor's interests and those of all of his or her franchisees. The results of trademark infringement litigation are reasonably predictable, and the risk and cost of infringement are incorporated into the general business plan of the franchisor. In international franchising, local law must be researched in each jurisdiction and the trademark must be registered separately. Moreover, the level of protection given to the franchisor's trademark can be significantly less predictable. In countries with high levels of variability in the outcome of trademark cases, either over time or across localities, the risk to the franchisor and to the local franchisee (who has paid for the benefits of the trademark as part of the franchise fee) is heightened. In fact, franchisors report that insufficient trademark protection is one of the more serious difficulties in entering foreign markets (Trankiem, 1979; Hackett, 1976; Walker and Etzel, 1973).

A proven franchise concept with demonstrated consumer acceptance, protected by a trademark, is an important feature of a successful franchise system. Cultural and legal differences can increase the costs and risks associated with transferring the concept and trademark into foreign markets. Cultural differences sometimes can be accommodated through careful modification of the franchise concept. Institutional impediments such as inadequate trademark protection, however, may effectively deter international franchisors from permitting local entrepreneurs to join their system.

An efficient and transferable business format

A good retailing concept must be supported by an efficient business format for it to be turned into a profitable enterprise. It is through the business format that the franchise concept becomes industrialized, and the idiosyncratic retailer is replaced by a standardized service producing assembly line (Levitt, 1972). From procurement to production to marketing to delivery of the service, the business is rationalized and documented so that the franchisee need only learn and follow. The attention given to optimizing each element of the business format, and the relationships between them, accounts for the franchisor's successful differentiation from other retailers (Porter, 1985). It is the unique way in which the franchisor organizes all retailing activities so that the prototype operation can be efficiently reproduced that is the core of the franchisor's innovation, and an important source of risk reduction for the franchisee.[4]

When a finely tuned business format is exported to a foreign market, however, many of the assumptions on which it was based no longer apply. For example, one of the most important elements in a franchise system is the relationship the system has with its suppliers. The franchisor's business format was created to be consistent with the home country's supply infrastructure. In the new foreign market, local sources of supply must be found (if possible) and relationships formed. Differences in those relationships may radically affect the operation of the franchisee's business (Love, 1986). Likewise, marketing procedures inherent in the franchisor's format often reflect expectations concerning access to media and other methods of consumer communication.

These assumptions can extend to the level of automation built into the system. The optimal relative levels of capital and labor in the design of the production or service delivery system for the home market may not be appropriate in some foreign markets. High priced, sophisticated machinery designed to reduce labor expenses in the United States or Europe could be poorly suited to the relatively cheap labor markets found in less developed countries. If the machines are unavailable in the host country, tariffs could increase their cost relative to the cost of labor, creating an even less efficient capital to labor ratio. Moreover, even if the cost of the machines was not excessive, their maintenance might require skills unavailable in the host country.

Just as the product or service offering must be modified to reflect local consumer preferences, so the operational systems and procedures contained in the business format must also be examined and modified to reflect the environment. These modifications may be as simple as translating the operations manual into another language, or as complex as changing job descriptions to match the peculiarities of local labour relations. Determining the extent to which the system must be modified will typically require a company-owned and operated prototype outlet in each new market (Adlers and Arthur Young, 1987). A local prototype allows the franchisor to test the format's overall adaptability to local conditions. Without a local prototype, the operational feasibility of the format in the local market is not fully tested, and the franchisee bears the risk of an unproven system.

Operation of a local prototype outlet, therefore, signals a level of franchisor commitment to the market greater than merely licensing a local franchisee.

The franchisor's format also assumes a specific legal environment. When operating within one jurisdiction, the franchisor and franchisee realize economies of scale in the system's legal expenses. In international franchising, the law of each market must be examined separately for peculiarities which will affect the rights of the franchisor and franchisee and the overall operation of the system. For example, in some jurisdictions the franchisor may be prevented from retaining 100 per cent ownership of a prototype outlet, and may have to involve a local franchisee prior to firmly establishing the viability of the concept in the host country environment. Likewise, the granting of exclusive territories to franchisees is a common provision in franchise agreements while, in some jurisdictions, it is a violation of antitrust law (Mendelsohn, 1987).

Another area in which the assumptions of the business format franchise must be challenged when crossing international boundaries is training. In a study of Canadian franchisees, Knight (1984) found that 72 per cent had little or no experience in management prior to joining the franchise system, and relied not only on the franchisor's documented business formula, but also on the training program and other support services. It is possible that those individuals in developing nations capable of amassing sufficient capital to buy a franchise may be more likely to have managerial experience. Nevertheless, even significant experience in related areas does not always prepare the entrepreneur for the peculiarities of the new business as well as a carefully designed franchisor training program (Hunt, 1973). Experience is general; franchisor training focuses directly on the particulars of the relevant business and is a key element in most successful franchise systems.

Typical franchisor training programs provide free training at the franchisor's headquarters. The franchisee is required to pay for his or her travel expenses and, sometimes, also for room and board. Within the franchisor's home country, this requirement normally is insignificant. However, in international franchising the franchisee's additional costs due to necessary training may be substantial. More importantly initial on-site training and opening support are often key components of the training program for home country franchisees. Both require franchisor personnel to spend time at the franchise location. Unless the franchisor is prepared to provide those benefits to international franchisees as well, their training will be deficient, and their risk of failure will increase.

Continuing franchisor support and monitoring

The final risk-reducing element of franchising is the continuing support the franchisor provides the franchisee. This support can take many forms including periodic system-wide programs (e.g. special marketing promotions), research and development, or advice on the specific problems faced by a particular franchisee. International franchising poses unique challenges to franchisee support. The major impediments to providing equivalent support to international franchisees, are nontransferable experience, distance, and communication difficulties.

Because the franchisor acts as a clearinghouse for problems and opportunities, franchise systems can economize on devising solutions. International franchise systems are capable of realizing the same scale and learning effects. However, to the extent that problems and opportunities faced by international franchisees differ in kind from those of home country franchisees, home country experience will be nontransferable. Some functional areas will be more affected by differences than others. Production issues are likely to be somewhat more consistent across national and cultural boundaries than marketing issues. For the same reasons that the concept could need adjustment to adapt to local consumer preferences, the evolving marketing problems and opportunities facing home country and foreign franchisees will require different responses.

Within a particular foreign market, local franchisees will face similar problems and opportunities. The franchisee base typically will be smaller, however, and the cost of developing an appropriate plan of action will be spread over fewer individuals. Moreover, the chances are greater for each individual franchisee that he or she will experience the costs of a problem before the system has devised a solution.

The most obvious problem franchisors face when entering foreign markets is that they are generally less accessible. Continuous franchisee support typically includes first hand observation of the franchisee's business. In international franchising the cost of providing such support will be substantially higher. Initially, this will involve travel expenses. Then, when some critical mass is achieved in the foreign market, the franchisor will incur the expense of a local office. If the franchisor resists investing sufficient funds to provide local support, a significant risk reducing element of franchising will be unavailable to the local franchisee.

Although direct relationships between franchisors and franchisee owner/operators dominate international franchising (Trankiem, 1979; Hackett, 1976; Walker and Etzel, 1973), some international franchisors enter foreign markets by granting a master or area development franchise.[5] By using these forms of franchise arrangements, the franchisor reduces the number of costly contacts with the foreign market. Moreover, master or area development franchisees generally provide the franchise system with more locally specialized marketing and advertising expertise. Multiple languages and culture present serious difficulties in coordinating system-wide marketing programs. The local input from master or area franchisee, concerned with performance of the entire local system and not just one outlet, can be invaluable.

Both area and master franchising agreements, however, diminish some of the basic benefits of franchising. In area franchising, the system loses the efficiency of owner-operated outlets. Outlets are run by employees with incentives to shirk, instead of profit minded owners. Perhaps more importantly from a developing country's perspective, this form of franchising promotes the development of a few large companies rather than many small local entrepreneurs. Concentration is not a problem with master franchising, where individual owner/operator entrepreneurs are subfranchised by a local master franchisee. However, the subfranchise system is only as good as the local master franchisee. The franchisor is cut off from direct supervision of the local system, and must train the master franchisee to be a stand-in franchisor with recruiting, training, and support responsibilities. These are skills which the franchisor's organization has acquired through experience, and transferring them to the master franchisee risks loss of efficiency. Although master and area development franchises reduce the number of required contacts and increase local marketing input, therefore, they introduce inefficiencies which may be ultimately more costly to the system.

From the franchisor's perspective, monitoring and controlling foreign franchisees is as difficult as providing them with ongoing support. The franchisor has a duty to all franchisees to protect their investment by policing the system and maintaining the quality standards the consumer expects. Distance insulates the foreign franchisee from much of the control the franchisor typically exerts over the decisions of home country franchisees. Consequently, foreign franchisees have greater freedom from interference. Because franchisee entrepreneurs generally perceive franchisor control over their business as a cost of franchising, foreign franchisees might value their relative independence more than they value the corresponding reduction in franchisor support. The efficiency implications of this reduced control will be idiosyncratic to the particular franchisee and franchise system. If the relative lack of control allows a resourceful franchisee to respond more quickly to the needs of his or her local market, the result could be beneficial to both franchisee and franchisor. However, many standards are unrelated to consumer preference (for example, bookkeeping methods which allow for effective estimation of royalties). In those instances where the interests of the franchisor and franchisee diverge, the transaction costs may be significant.

The ability to offer continuing support to foreign franchisees also assumes an effective mode of communication between the parties. Because of cultural differences, the literal interpretation of communications is often misleading. In a culture where it is inappropriate to say no to a superior, the franchisor must understand what it means when a franchisee is only giving the franchisor's recommendation 'serious consideration' (Love, 1986, p. 435).

Royalty payments are closely related to the franchisor's commitment to ongoing franchisee support. Among the most serious disincentives to international franchising identified by surveyed franchisors were the monetary policies of host countries which precluded or interfered with the expatriation of royalties (Hackett, 1976). Without the ability to receive royalties from the foreign franchisee, the franchisor has no interest in the ongoing success of the franchisee. A significant amount of economic analysis has been done which suggests that the royalty fee is an important feature of franchising. Caves and Murphy (1976), Rubin (1978), and Blair and Kaserman (1982) all found that a mixed fixed-fee/output-royalty strategy was necessary to ensure the optimal franchise relationship. Host country interference in the free contracting between the parties and/or the expatriation of royalties will at a minumum serve to distort incentives and create inefficient franchise relationships. In the extreme, it will discourage international franchisors from transferring valuable operational and marketing know-how to prospective local entrepreneurs.

Conclusions and Implications

Business format franchisors in the industrialized nations have responded to the competitive pressures of their retail environment by creating highly efficient franchise systems. In their home countries those systems provide previously unavailable economic opportunity for a new group of 'imitator entrepreneurs'. If those systems prove to be adaptable to the various cultural, economic, and legal environments of developing countries, they may be valuable sources of retail know-how, and may also have significant impact on development processes. In this paper we have explored some of the general impediments to that adaptation. Of course, each separate franchise system will also face its own individual difficulties in adapting to foreign markets, and among developing nations there will be vast differences as to the appropriateness of the various retail concepts and the viability of the business formats.

If adaptation is possible, however, the cost of adapting the system to its new environment will be a critical concern for all the constituencies (that is, franchisor, franchisee, and host government). Clearly, the dominant economic power of the franchisor will permit the pass-through of many of the adaptation costs to the local franchisee in the form of higher franchise fees and royalty rates. On the margin, however, higher investment requirements will reduce (or eliminate) the willingness of franchisees to join the system, and/or increase the cost of recruitment. Moreover, as the investment necessary to become a franchisee increases, the group of prospective entrepreneurs capable of taking advantage of the opportunity will be increasingly limited to only wealthy individuals. Policymakers interested in expanding economic opportunity to a wider cross-section of society by encouraging this form of retail entrepreneurship, therefore, will also be interested in minimizing the costs of adaptation.

Each successful franchise system represents a careful balance between the inclusion of risk-reducing franchisor support features (such as concept testing and development and franchisee training) and the franchise fee and royalty rate necessary to sustain them. In an effort to minimize adaptation costs, and thereby control the increase of franchise fees and royalties, the franchisor may be tempted to reduce the protection generally offered home country franchisees. For example, the franchisor may avoid opening and running a company-owned prototype outlet in the new environment even though such a prototype may be necesasry to test the local viability of the concept and business format. If this occurs, the franchisee's investment may be lowered, but the risk of failure will significantly increase.

As discussed above, royalties are an integral part of the franchise relationship. They link the franchisor's incentives to franchisee success and motivate continued franchisor support. Regulations which interfere in the free flow of royalties will drastically reduce the efficiency of franchise systems or, more likely, remove the country from the consideration of reputable franchisors.

In this paper we have implicitly assumed a reputable franchisor with a proven concept, viable format, and history of support for his or her franchisee. Clearly, some fringe franchisors are interested only in the income derived from selling the franchise, and do not offer any continuing support to the franchisee. Prohibitions against, or interference with, royalty distribution will compel reputable franchisors to obtain the full value of their business format through the initial franchise fee, and the franchisee will have no assurance of continued support. Institutional restrictions on royalty expatriation, therefore, discourage reputable franchisors whose business format includes the continued support of their franchisees, and thereby lessen the efficiency gain achievable through franchising.

Unfortunately, a favorable royalty expatriation policy does not prevent fringe franchisors from taking advantage of unwary local franchisees, and each franchisee must carefully research prospective franchisors (a task not easily accomplished from . afar). Disclosure statements are required of all franchisors operating in the US and for all members of the British Franchise Association. It should not discourage most international franchisors if the same information or document is required to be provided to franchisees in the host country. However, if local regulations require filing unfamiliar disclosure documents, the increased legal expenses could be a significant disincentive to an international franchisor.

Although most of the discussion has focused on the adaptability of those elements of the franchise system which reduce the franchisee entrepreneur's risk, franchising also raises some serious social issues for developing countries. For example, we have mentioned the possible deterioration of local culture occasioned by increased exposure to westernized retailing methods and products. It should also be noted that local franchisees would have significant ongoing economic ties to foreign businesses which might be difficult for the host country to control. Finally, the gains in allocative efficiency might be concentrated in distribution systems most closely associated with wealthier members of society. It will be necessary for the governments of the developing nations to address these and other social issues, as well as the economic costs and benefits of business format franchising, in setting their policies so as to encourage or reject this source of retail know-how.

Footnotes

1 Because Professor Leibenstein has not had the opportunity to review the final draft of this paper prior to submission, all errors of commission and omission are mine. Patrick J. Kaufmann.

2 This can be complicated by the fact that there can be significantly different perceptions as to where the locus of control actually resides for particular operational decisions. Hunt (1975) found that although fast food franchisees believed that they were in control of five major elements of their businesses, approximately half of their franchisors thought that they were in control of those same activities.

3 It has been suggested that the degree of independence (that is, the locus of control in self or other) is the key distinguishing feature on the continuum of entrepreneurship which runs from solo independent business persons to franchisees to profit center managers to large corporate managers (Vesper, 1980; Brockhaus, 1982).

4 For example, there is evidence that the systematization of routine administrative tasks provided by a detailed operations manual allows franchisees to specialize on the revenue producing tasks for which they are better suited (Etgar, 1976).

5 The terms master franchise and area development franchise are used to refer to various types of franchising arrangements (Peters and Schneider, 1986). As used here, in a master franchise agreement the franchisor grants the master franchisee the right to subfranchise the franchisor's concept to others within an exclusive territory, thereby creating a three level franchise relationship. In an area development franchise agreement a franchisor grants an area development franchisee exclusive rights to a territory and requires the franchisee to open and own a specified number of outlets in that territory according to a detailed development schedule. Trankiem (1979), Hackett (1976), and Walker and Etzel (1973) have examined the type of ownership employed by samples of US franchisors when expanding into foreign markets. Franchisee ownership of individual outlets dominated, but many franchisors also grant master or area development franchisees. A number of franchisors operated company owned outlets in markets outside the United States. Although some franchisors employ different ownership strategies in their foreign markets, in the aggregate franchisors had approximately the same proportion of company owned to franchised stores abroad as in the United States (5 per cent company owned) (Trankiem, 1979, p. 28). Joint ventures, where franchisor and franchisee are both part owners of the local outlet, were much less common. It should be noted that in each study there was a strong sampling bias toward international franchising in developed nations. Current ownership patterns of franchised outlets in less developed countries could be quite different.

References

Franchising in the U.K., (1987), (London: Adlers and Arthur Young).

Localisation des Franchises F.F.F. (Hors France), (1987), Paris: Federation Francaise de la Franchise).

Blair, Roger D. and David L. Kaserman, 'Optimal Franchising', *Southern Economic Journal*, (1982), 49(2), 494 - 505.

Brockhaus, Robert H. (1982), 'The Psychology of the Entrepreneur', in *Encyclopedia of Entrepreneurship*, Calvin A. Kent, Donald L. Saxton, and Karl H. Vesper eds., 36 - 56.

Caves, Richard E. and William F. Murphy (1976), 'Firms, Markets and Intangible Assets', *Southern Economic Journal* , 42(4), 572 - 86.

Etgar, Michael (1976), 'The Economic Rationale for Becoming a Franchisee in a Service Industry', *Journal of Business Research*, 4(3), 239 - 54.

Fishwick, Marshall (1983), *Ronald Revisited: The World of Ronald McDonald*, (Bowling Green: Bowling Green University).

Hackett, Donald W. (1976), 'The International Expansion of U.S. Franchise Systems - Status and Strategies', *Journal of International Business Studies*, 7(1), 65 - 75.

Hunt, Shelby D. (1973), 'Experimental Determinants of Franchise Success', *Journal of Economics and Business*, 26(1), 81 - 3.

Hunt, Shelby D. (1975), 'An Evaluation of Franchise Independence', *Marquette Business Review*, 19(1), 9 - 16.

Knight, Russel M. (1984), 'The Independence of the Franchise Entrepreneur', *Journal of Small Business Management*, 22(2), 53 - 61.

Levitt, Theodore (1972), 'Production Line Approaches to Service), *Harvard Business Review*, Sept./Oct., 41 - 52.

Levitt, Theodore (1983), 'The Globalization of Markets', *Harvard Business Review*, May/June, 92 - 102.

Love, John F. (1986), *McDonald's: Behind the Arches*, (New York: Bantam Books, Inc.).

Mendelsohn, Martin (1987), 'The European Commission Moves Toward a Block Exemption Regulation', *Journal of International Franchising and Distribution Law*, 1(4), 180 - 85.

O'Donnell, Thomas (1984), 'No Entrepreneurs Need Apply', *Forbes*, 134 (13), 124 - 30.

Peters, Lena and Marina Schneider (1986), *The Franchising Contract*, Study No. 68, Doc 1, (Rome: Unidroit).

Porter, Michael E. (1985), *Competitive Advantage* (New York: Free Press).

Rubin, Paul H. (1978), 'Theory of the Firm and Structure of the Franchise Contract', *Journal of Law and Economics*, 22(1), 223 - 33.

Rudnick, Lewis G. and Michael G. Brennan (1987), 'Protection of Foreign Franchisees under American Franchise Registration and Disclosure Regulations', *Journal of International Franchising and Distribution Law*, 1(3), 113 - 17.

Schendler, Breton R. (1986), 'Working on the Chain Gang', *Wall Street Journal*, Monday, May 19, 14D.

Stamworth, John and James Curran (1978), 'Franchising at a Major Crossroads', *Marketing*, April, 22 - 6.

Trankiem, Luu (1979), 'International Franchising: A Way to Capture Foreign Markets', *Los Angeles Business and Economics*, 4(4), 26 - 30.

US Department of Commerce (1987), *Franchising in the Economy*, (Washington, D.C.: U.S. Government Printing Office).

Vesper, Karl H. (1980), *New Venture Strategies*, (Englewood Cliffs, N.J.: Prentice Hall).

Walker, Bruce J. and Michale J. Etzel (1973), 'The Internationalization of U.S. Franchise Systems: Progress and Procedures', *Journal of Marketing*, 37(April), 38 - 46.

Williamson, Oliver E. (1979), 'Transaction Cost Economics: The Governance of Contractual Relations', *Journal of Law and Economics*, 22(Oct.), 233 - 61.

Part V
Production Theory

[15]

INCREMENTAL CAPITAL–OUTPUT RATIOS AND GROWTH RATES IN THE SHORT RUN

Harvey Leibenstein

ONE of the attractive aspects of the Harrod-Domar model is the magnificent simplicity of its variables. This is especially true of the incremental capital-output ratio (ICOR). It has served as a magnet for economists (including the present writer). Many have been unable to resist employing it as a major element in their attempts to understand economic growth. But are ICORs really helpful in understanding growth? How are ICORs[1] and growth rates really related?

In a recent paper, Ohkawa and Rosovsky[2] presented a graph that showed growth rates and ICORs for Japan from 1890 to 1931 (seven-year moving averages were employed). The remarkable thing immediately apparent from the graph is the inverse relation between the growth rates and the ICORs. In the few cases where this relation does not hold, the changes in

growth rates are very small. Is this relation a curiosity that holds only for Japan, or is it likely to hold for other countries? I want to show both on the basis of theory and of empirical evidence that the latter is what we should normally expect.

We should expect an inverse relationship between observable ICORs and growth rates, in most cases, for the following reasons: (1) the investment rate is a more stable variable than are other variables affecting growth; (2) the significance of non-capital inputs is greater than that of capital inputs; (3) changes in the level of employment of all inputs affect growth more than investment; and (4) some outputs are related "probablistically" to inputs.

On purely *a priori* grounds, we can say nothing about these relationships. It is possible to invent hypotheses that would lead to the conclusion that ICORs and growth rates are *not* inversely related. However, it is also possible to reason plausibly, but *not* necessarily, that ICORS and growth rates *are* inversely related. It is this type of plausible reasoning that I wish to undertake.

We know on the basis of studies by Solow, Aukrust, Fabricant, and others,[3] that increases in capital contribute only a small proportion to total growth. The proportion is probably somewhere between ten and 20 per cent. As a consequence, most of the growth rate is accounted for by non-capital inputs. The main burden of the argument is that investment is a much more stable variable than the non-capital inputs. First we will examine the consequences of this assumption, and then argue why it is likely to be so.

Consider the case in which output is explained by the Cobb-Douglas production func-

---

[1] On *a priori* grounds one can distinguish three types of ICORs. Elsewhere, I have made the distinction between the *net* incremental capital-output ratio and the adjusted incremental capital-output ratio. By the net incremental capital-output ratios (NICORs) I mean the incremental capital-output ratios as they would be on the assumption that the supplies of all other factors are held constant. By the adjusted incremental capital-output ratio (AICOR) I mean the capital-output ratio as it would be if it were adjusted to a *given* increase in the supply of other factors — for example, a one per cent increase in the labor force. In practice, however, neither of these concepts are actually employed. Instead, we use the actual increase in the capital stock as a ratio of the actual increase in income. In principle, we should not expect that the actual or observable ICOR would behave similarly to the somewhat purer and more restrictive NICOR and AICOR concepts. But the actual ICORs are much easier to employ statistically and have been used to a great extent. Therefore, their behavior is of great interest to us. In the case of both the NICORs and the AICORs we should expect a clear-cut positive relationship between capital and output. That is, as capital increases we should expect output to increase also. In addition, in both these cases we should not expect the capital-output ratio to vary in any special way with the growth rate. However, for practical work we use actual ICORs and it is these that are under consideration in this paper. See the author's *Economic Backwardness and Economic Growth*, 178. See also the excellent discussion in Gerald M. Meier, *Leading Issues in Development Economics* (Oxford University Press, 1964), 101 ff.

[2] Ohkawa and Rosovsky, "Economic Fluctuations in Prewar Japan," *Hitotsubashi Journal of Economics* (Oct. 1962), 24.

[3] R. Solow, "Technical Progress and the Aggregate Production Function," this REVIEW XXXIII (Aug. 1951). See also R. Solow, "Investment and Economic Growth," *Productivity Measurement Review*, No. 19 (Nov. 1959); Odd Aukrust, "Investment and Economic Growth," *Productivity Measurement Review*, No. 16 (Feb. 1959); and S. Fabricant, *Basic Facts on Productivity* (New York: National Bureau of Economic Research, 1959).

[20]

tion. Growth and the ICOR will then be given by the following equations:

$$G = a + bN + cC \tag{1}$$

$$\text{ICOR} = \frac{C}{G} = \frac{C}{a + bN + cC} \tag{2}$$

where G is the growth rate, and N and C are the rates of change in the non-capital and capital inputs respectively. As usual, coefficients $\underline{b} + \underline{c} = 1$, and $\underline{a}$ is a shift factor representing "technical progress" not taken into account in the improvement of the quality of non-capital inputs.

If N varies much more than C, then it can readily be seen that in the most likely cases, G and $\frac{C}{G}$ will vary in opposite directions. For instance, if C is constant then (if we examine our two equations) we see that, as N varies, the growth rate and the ICOR will vary in opposite directions. If both N and C vary and they move in the same direction, but if N varies much more than C, and $b \geqq c$, then once again the growth rate and the ICOR will vary in opposite directions. A similar argument holds if N and C move in opposite directions. As long as the contribution of the change in N to growth is more significant than the change in C, then G and the ICOR will vary in opposite directions. For example, the range of growth rates may be from zero to ten per cent. If the change in N contributes most of the variation, and N itself varies a great deal (i.e., N is as much as tenfold on some occasions that which it is on other occasions), and C contributes relatively little to change (C varies from about eight per cent to 25 per cent of NNP, but usually considerably less than that), then it seems clear that the growth rate and the ICOR will vary in opposite directions. Of course, in those instances in which the change in N is small and the change in C large (so that the change in C determines the change in G), then the growth rate and the ICOR will vary in the same direction. But for reasons we shall suggest below this last is likely to occur infrequently.

We may note also that the value of $\underline{a}$ is likely to vary, and as $\underline{a}$ varies G and $\frac{C}{G}$ vary in opposite directions. Thus, to the extent that techni-cal progress is not accounted for by changes in the value of N, it also will lead to the type of inverse relation under consideration.

Let $G = f(N,C)$ and let $\frac{C}{G} = \frac{C}{f(N,C)}$. In general, as N varies, G will vary in the same direction and C will vary relatively little compared to N, and have a much smaller impact on the value of G than the variation in N does. Thus, if N varies considerably, G will vary considerably, and in the same direction, and C will vary little and have little impact on G. Under such circumstances it follows that G and $\frac{C}{G}$ will vary in opposite directions. While we may usually expect these relationships, we cannot expect them invariably. It is possible that in some instances N will vary a little and C will change quite a bit.

What are some of the elements that frequently keep the investment rate fairly stable? Government investment is likely to change slowly. The government investment decision is likely to be made prior to knowledge about what the growth rate is going to be. To a considerable extent, government investment depends on tax revenues, and on an assessment of "necessary" social overhead construction through the political process. A zero growth rate will not reduce government investment to zero. Contrariwise, government investment will not determine the growth rate. It seems likely that there is very little "complementarity" between government investment and the use of other "growth inputs." Roads, bridges, dams, public buildings, and military structures are likely to be highly durable, non-income producing in the short run, and not related to the growth of other inputs in the short run.

Some of the components of private investment may operate similarly. For example, the private construction component of investment may be highly durable and unrelated to growth. The value of all construction is likely to be unrelated to the growth rate of output contributed by construction, since a number of factors such as (1) the changing capacity to which construction is utilized, (2) the lengthy and variable period of gestation during construction, and (3) the political character of many of the decisions affecting construction, are all unlikely to be related to growth in any special way. For example, the recent E.C.E. study on *Factors in the Economic Growth of Europe During the 1950's* shows a lack of correlation on a cross-sectional basis between construction rates and growth rates.[4] Even if, as Mr. Hill [5] argues, investment in machinery and equipment is well correlated with the growth rate, it is a small and variable component of the other elements of investment.

Another stabilizing influence is that private investment may be carried out for defensive purposes as well as for expansion. This idea has been developed by Lamfalussy.[6] When growth rates are low and many firms are operating under reduced profits or enduring losses, they may nevertheless be stimulated to invest in order to renovate or modernize some aspects of their operations for the purpose of defending their relative position, even if the absolute position of the industry as a whole does not make improvements.

In contrast, it seems that many of the non-capital inputs are likely to be highly variable from year to year. Such factors as technological progress, organizational and managerial changes, and changes due to increases in knowledge do not occur as a steady progression. Indeed, a great deal of evidence suggests that both the locus and impact of such changes on output are likely to be highly variable. It would take us too far afield to review all of the evidence, but the very nature of some of these factors suggests that they are frequently not systematic or within the control of the firm. Usually a firm cannot choose to have a brilliant idea, to invent a new product, or even to manage itself a great deal better. While improvements in innovation or management may, in some cases and to some degree, be matters of choice, they are normally less subject to control by the firm than are investment and replacement decisions.

[4] United Nations, Economic Commission for Europe, *Factors in the Economic Growth of Europe During the 1950's*, part 2 of *Economic Survey of Europe in 1961* (Geneva, 1964), U.N. Sales No. 64.IIE.1, Chap. III, 10.
    [5] T. P. Hill, "Growth and Investment According to International Comparisons," *Economic Journal*, 54 (June 1964), 287–304.
    [6] A. Lamfalussy, *Investment and Growth in Mature Economies, the Case of Belgium* (London: Macmillan, 1961), Chap. VII, 79–94.

The studies previously cited suggest that N is likely to be large compared to C, and that b is likely to be greater than c. If $b + c = 1$ then an increase in b will imply a decrease in c. Thus if b rises G will rise and the ICOR will fall, and vice versa. Hence we have another element that helps to explain the inverse relation between ICORs and growth rates. In this case the relative sizes of N and C are significant apart from their relative stability.

There is another element that works in the same direction. All inputs are probably subject to some degree of excess capacity. Let us refer to the amount of excess capacity as slack. When slack is decreased the growth rate rises, and vice versa. Clearly, the amount of slack need not be related to the investment rate. Therefore, as slack declines the capital output ratio falls and growth rises, and as slack rises the capital-output ratio rises and growth declines.

There are three main constituents in capacity usage: (1) the degree to which physical plant is utilized, (2) the degree to which labor is employed, and (3) the degree of effort that people put into their work. It is fairly clear that there are great variations in the degree to which plant is used. The ECE study has some interesting estimates in this connection. The rate of growth of actual output varies significantly more than the rate of growth of full-capacity output. For example, in western Germany in the two quinquenia, 1950–1954 and 1955–1959, the investment ratios were about the same, and the rates of growth of full-capacity output rose from 7.4 to 8.8 per cent, but the actual output rate of growth fell from 12.5 to 8.2 per cent. The main difference between the two periods may be explained by reduced utilization of capacity. In the case where growth rates are compared with degree of capacity utilization in different branches of industry, it seems clear that the growth rates were usually highest in those industries in which capacity utilization rose most. For instance, in oil refining, capacity utilization rose from 46 to 79 per cent and the growth rate was 24 per cent, while in sawmills and timber, capacity utilization fell from 95 to 77 per cent and the growth rate was only 1.9 per cent. In many industries, at least 30

INCREMENTAL CAPITAL-OUTPUT RATIOS   23

per cent or more of the growth rate seems to be accounted for by changes in capacity utilization. When we add to this a changed utilization of the labor force, as well as increases or decreases in effort, then the importance of capacity changes seems to be especially significant.[7]

It is readily apparent that capacity changes support the inverse relation between growth rates and ICORs. An increase in capacity will increase G but it will have no effect on C in the ratio $\frac{C}{G}$. It is, obviously, an element that helps to maintain the inverse relation. We can add capacity components to our Cobb-Douglas function if we wish to elaborate that approach to our analysis. For instance, let:

$$G = a + bN + bN' + cC + cC' \qquad (3)$$

$$\frac{C}{G} = \frac{C}{a + bN + bN' + cC + cC'} \qquad (4)$$

where N' and C' stand for the rates of increase in the utilization of the non-capital inputs and the capital inputs, respectively. Since C is not affected by changes in capacity, it can readily be seen that the greater the importance of the variation in capacity utilization, the greater the influence of capacity on the inverse relation between growth rates and ICORs. That is, the larger the values of N' and C', the more likely it will be that G and $\frac{C}{G}$ will be inversely related.

The existence of excess capacity does raise a problem for theory which has not been completely solved. Do entrepreneurs readjust their capital stock toward an optimal amount as a consequence of excess capacity? While it may be reasonable to believe that they try to do this, it has yet to be demonstrated that they succeed. While entrepreneurs sometimes may readjust their capital stocks *toward* an optimum, they do not necessarily readjust during the year in which the excess capacity exists, or sufficiently to eliminate all excess capacity. Furthermore, the readjustments are likely to have a less important effect on the stock of capital than will the other factors that may affect the growth rate. There are limits to which an economy can retire capital from use

[7] United Nations, Economic Commission for Europe, *op. cit.*, Chap. IV, 19–20.

during any year in which excess capacity exists. On the upswing, readjustments must be very much related to expectations. That is, firms will have little desire to expand their capital stock if they visualize a temporary increase in demand, but will do so only if they believe the increase in demand is persistent. Thus, there is still room for considerable variation in the utilization of capital without increasing the capital stock, or for increases in capital stock without a proportionate increase in utilization, while the rate of output may change as a consequence of the degree of utilization of inputs.

Frequently we assume that the relation between inputs and outputs is non-probabilistic, but there is no reason to believe that this is the case for all inputs. Many inputs, especially those of an indirect or residual nature, may be probabilistically related to output. We need not go into the causes of why this might be the case. It may be that from year to year the output obtained from a given quantity of a "probabilistic" input varies considerably, but that in the long run the output approximates a given average. The consequences of this for our problem are interesting. In years when the yield from probabilistic inputs is high, the ICOR will be low, and vice versa. This will obviously be in conformity with our hypothesis. Even if the variation in yield is small, since the yield comes from all probabilistic inputs, it could have a significant effect on such marginal magnitudes as growth rates and ICORs.[8]

Now let us look at the evidence. The growth rates and ICORs for 18 countries, chosen more or less at random, were investigated. The results for five of these countries have been graphed and are illustrated in figure 1. The

[8] Another possibility is the effect of errors. Errors in estimating GDP are likely to have a greater impact on the growth rate than on the ICOR. Suppose the error in estimating investment is the same, and is in the same direction as the error in GDP. Suppose the growth rate is six per cent and the investment rate is 15 per cent; then a three per cent error in GDP will change the growth rate by 50 per cent, but the investment rate by only 20 per cent. Obviously, such errors would bias the observed rates toward an inverse relation between ICORs and growth rate. However, I have been informed by one of the readers that errors in changes are less common than errors in absolute magnitude, and that such errors would effect capital formation more than output. I do not know how to assess the relative likelihood of different types of errors and leave it to the reader to draw his own conclusions.

FIGURE 1

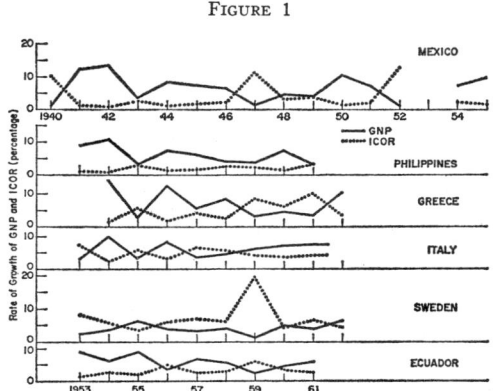

other results are presented in table 1. Where data were not available in constant prices, the consumer price index for each country was used to deflate current values. The surprising thing about the results is the persistence with which the inverse relation holds. It holds true in 129 out of 134 observations. We would normally expect that it might not hold in some of the cases in which the variation in output is small. These cases could occur by accident either because of statistical bias in the initial calculation, or because the consumer price index is only an approximate deflater. Indeed, we find that of the five cases where the inverse relation does not hold, in four, the range of variation in the growth rate is exceedingly small.

The inverse relation between growth rates and ICORs holds to some extent also for cross-sectional data. For different countries we must expect that the relation would exist where the differences in the growth rates are large, but not where they are small. Where the differences in the growth rates are small, we would expect that the different effects of other variables (which differ from country to country) would not result in any particular relationship. The ECE growth study supports this expectation. The ICORs are very much higher for countries with low growth rates than for those with high growth rates. For example, West Germany,

Austria, and Greece, which have the highest growth rates for the decade of the fifties, have ICORs of 3.3, 3.9, and 3.0, respectively, while Belgium, the United Kingdom, and Ireland, which have the lowest rates for the decade, have ICORs of 5.6, 6.7, and 13.7, respectively. This report provides ICORs and growth rates for sectors, and to some degree the same results hold for most sectors, but not for all. For instance, the inverse relation holds pretty well for the agricultural sector, manufacturing, mining, and services. But there seems to be no special relation between growth rates and ICORs in public utilities and dwellings. It is quite likely that in these sectors the non-capital inputs are not significant. (See table 2 for some of the data involved.)

There are several implications of these findings. First, it would appear that the ICOR is really a function of growth, rather than the other way around. A low ICOR implies that growth has been rapid, and vice versa. Second, it casts grave doubt on the appropriateness of the acceleration principle as a tool of analysis. Third, it casts doubt on the incremental capital-output ratio as a planning instrument. It suggests that it is the consequences of economic behavior and, to some extent, the consequences of other aspects of the planning machinery, which determine the incremental capital-output ratio, rather than the other way around.

I have restricted my comments to the short run. Whether the average capital-output ratio in the long run has economic significance as an independent variable is still an open question. The seeming long-run stability of such ratios may be a consequence of the averaging process, and in part it may be a consequence of substituting capital for labor when capital-output ratios fall, and vice versa. Or it may be that there is some technological *limited* variability in the long run which does not exist in the short run. At present, we seem to be on more solid ground if we restrict ourselves to the short-run relation.

TABLE 1. — INCREMENTAL CAPITAL-OUTPUT RATIOS (ICORS) AND RATES OF GROWTH OF GNP OR GDP IN PERCENTAGE TERMS FOR VARIOUS COUNTRIES

(1)	(2)	(3)	(4)	(5)	(6)	(7)	(8)	(9)	(10)	(11)	(12)	(13)	(14)	(15)	(16)
	Sweden			Greece			Italy			Portugal			Ireland		
Year	Rate of Growth of GNP	ICOR	Direction of Change in Cols. (2) & (3)	Rate of Growth of GDP	ICOR	Direction of Change in Cols. (5) & (6)	Rate of Growth of GDP	ICOR	Direction of Change in Cols. (8) & (9)	Rate of Growth of GDP	ICOR	Direction of Change in Cols. (11) & (12)	Rate of Growth of GNP	ICOR	Direction of Change in Cols. (14) & (15)
1951															
1952	2.65	8.05													
1953	3.48	5.55	+ −				3.02	7.39		5.41	3.45				
1954	6.30	3.55	+ −	14.33	1.36		10.0	2.38	+ −	5.67	3.10	+ −			
1955	3.94	5.83	− +	3.06	5.30	− +	3.40	6.91	− +	2.13	7.60	− +	1.94	9.51	
1956	3.20	6.86	− +	12.94	1.58	+ −	8.26	3.20	+ −	negative			negative		
1957	3.75	6.07	+ −	5.44	4.01	− +	3.95	6.48	− +	4.43	3.74		0.46	26.03	
1958	1.09	19.59	− +	8.52	2.69	+ −	4.60	5.77	+ −	4.38	4.44	− +	negative		
1959	4.89	4.63	+ −	3.02	8.43	− +	6.12	4.23	+ −	1.36	13.50	− +	4.60	3.94	
1960	4.03	6.41	− +	4.68	6.10	+ −	7.05	3.86	+ −	5.80	3.32	+ −	5.42	2.93	+ −
1961	6.27	4.15	+ −	3.59	10.08	− +	7.40	4.10	+ +	7.99	2.70	+ −	4.79	3.33	− +
1962				10.99	3.35	+ −	7.50	4.16	+ +	6.98	3.56	− +	3.27	5.50	− +

(1)	(2)	(3)	(4)	(5)	(6)	(7)	(8)	(9)	(10)	(11)	(12)	(13)	(14)	(15)	(16)
	Cyprus			Austria			Kenya			Ghana			Rhodesia & Nyasaland		
Year	Rate of Growth of GNP	ICOR	Direction of Change in Cols. (2) & (3)	Rate of Growth of GNP	ICOR	Direction of Change in Cols. (5) & (6)	Rate of Growth of GDP	ICOR	Direction of Change in Cols. (8) & (9)	Rate of Growth of GNP	ICOR	Direction of Change in Cols. (11) & (12)	Rate of Growth of GNP	ICOR	Direction of Change in Cols. (14) & (15)
1953	8.82	2.18													
1954	0.4	64.0	− +												
1955	2.07	15.3	+ −				8.53	3.07							
1956	5.68	5.89	+ −	5.11	4.81		3.79	6.46	− +	negative					
1957	12.28	2.67	+ −	5.88	4.36	+ −	3.39	6.75	− +	3.9	3.68		10.93	4.12	
1958	negative			3.64	6.86	− +	negative			5.83	2.57	+ −	4.97	5.93	− +
1959	negative			2.34	10.89	− +	3.36	5.75		11.11	1.97	+ −	7.93	3.50	+ −
1960	negative			8.91	3.56	+ −	3.93	4.85	+ −	6.31	3.88	− +	4.60	5.48	− +
1961	10.3	2.33		5.26	5.67	− +	negative			negative			4.35	5.24	− −
1962	6.23	5.41	− +	2.28	11.41	− +	3.25	4.34		negative			negative		

TABLE 1 — *continued*

INCREMENTAL CAPITAL-OUTPUT RATIOS (ICORS) AND RATES OF GROWTH OF GNP OR GDP IN PERCENTAGE TERMS FOR VARIOUS COUNTRIES

(1)	(2) Ecuador Rate of Growth of GNP	(3) ICOR	(4) Direction of Change in Cols. (2) & (3)	(5) Argentina Rate of Growth of GDP	(6) ICOR	(7) Direction of Change in Cols. (5) & (6)	(8) Honduras Rate of Growth of GDP	(9) ICOR	(10) Direction of Change in Cols. (8) & (9)	(11) Burma Rate of Growth of GNP	(12) ICOR	(13) Direction of Change in Cols. (11) & (12)	(14) Philippines Rate of Growth of GNP	(15) ICOR	(16) Direction of Change in Cols. (14) & (15)
1952	9.00	1.29		negative	3.66		7.28	2.86		18.39	1.17		8.98	.889	
1953	6.02	2.45	− +	5.61	6.96		negative			15.63	1.40	− +	10.73	.845	− −
1954	8.89	1.96	+ −	3.35	4.52	− +	2.99	5.97		4.52	5.08	− +	3.12	2.90	+ +
1955	3.60	4.83	+ −	5.31		+ −	8.63	2.11		0.6	35.1	− +	7.38	1.32	− −
1956	6.57	2.64	− +	negative	5.57		6.21	2.96		negative			6.15	1.60	− +
1957	5.66	2.90	+ −	4.68	9.18		3.31	4.42	+ −	0.1	161.3		4.09	2.63	+ −
1958	2.58	5.82	+ +	2.69		− +	4.24	3.27	− +	1.95	11.5	+ −	3.889	2.40	− +
1959	4.73	3.36	+ −	negative	6.42		1.22	12.03	+ −	16.60	1.37	+ −	7.42	1.29	+ −
1960	5.82	2.77	+ −	4.23		+ −	4.29	3.16	− +	negative			3.20	3.27	− +
1961				5.68	4.76		6.43	2.56	+ −						
1962															

Mexico

(1) Year	(2) Rate of Growth of GNP	(3) ICOR	(4) Direction of Change in Cols. (2) & (3)
1940	1.1	10.2	
1941	12.4	1.0	+ −
1942	13.2	0.8	− +
1943	3.7	2.6	− +
1944	8.5	1.2	+ −
1945	7.6	1.6	− +
1946	6.6	2.0	− +
1947	1.3	11.3	− +
1948	4.5	3.3	+ −
1949	4.3	3.5	+ −
1950	11.3	1.5	+ −
1951	7.2	2.0	− +
1952	1.1	12.6	− +
1953	negative		
1954	7.7	2.0	+ −
1955	9.8	1.6	+ −
1956	6.7	2.3	− +
1957	3.6	4.4	− +
1958	4.4	3.3	+ −
1959	4.6	3.1	+ −

Japan

(5) Year	(6) Rate of Growth of GDP	(7) ICOR	Direction of Change in Cols. (6) & (7)
1888	1.15	4.24	
1889	negative		
1890	21.41	0.52	
1891	negative		
1892	4.31	2.51	
1893	2.76	4.58	− +
1894	18.66	0.38	+ −
1895	negative		
1896	negative		
1897	3.63	3.28	
1898	29.01	0.38	+ −
1899	negative		
1900	2.18	5.27	+ −
1901	6.15	1.28	
1902	negative		− +
1903	13.41	0.61	
1904	0.6	15.48	
1905	negative		− +
1906	16.48	0.66	
1907	6.06	1.48	− +

Japan

(10) Year	(11) Rate of Growth of GNP	(11) ICOR	Direction of Change in Cols. (10) & (11)
1908	5.52	1.93	− +
1909	negative		
1910	negative		
1911	14.20	1.10	− +
1912	8.09	1.42	
1913	negative		
1914	1.49	7.18	+ −
1915	1.81	4.70	+ −
1916	10.28	.76	− +
1917	3.15	2.27	+ −
1918	14.13	.67	− +
1919	18.81	.83	− +
1920	negative		
1921	1.26	12.15	+ −
1922	1.52	9.86	+ −
1923	10.5	1.14	− +
1924	10.5	1.42	0
1925	8.06	1.73	− +
1926	0.9	14.94	+ −
1927	0.7	22.94	− +

Japan

Year	(15) ICOR	(14) Rate of Growth of GDP	(16) Direction of Change in Cols. (14) & (15)
1928	3.27	4.35	+ −
1929	7.45	2.00	− +
1930		negative	
1931	12.16	1.1	
1932	1.34	10.95	+ −
1933	1.43	10.31	− +
1934	6.42	2.51	+ −
1935	2.16	8.36	− +
1936	2.45	7.68	+ +
1937	3.60	5.66	− −
1938	3.79	6.68	+ −

SOURCES: For all countries other than Japan and Mexico the basic statistics are taken from the United Nations, *Statistical Yearbook* for various years and the United Nations, *Yearbook of National Accounts Statistics* for various years. The source of the statistics for Mexico is J. M. M. de Costa, *Occupational Distribution and Economic Development in Mexico* (Unpublished Master's Thesis, University of California at Berkeley, 1964) and the source of the Japanese statistics is K. Ohkawa and H. Rosovsky, *op. cit.*

INCREMENTAL CAPITAL-OUTPUT RATIOS   27

TABLE 2. — GROWTH RATES OF OUTPUT IN WESTERN COUNTRIES AND INCREMENTAL CAPITAL-OUTPUT RATIOS (ICORs) FOR ALL SECTORS AND VARIOUS SELECTED SECTORS, 1949–1959 [g]

Country	All Sectors		Agriculture			Mining			Manufacturing			Public Utilities			Dwellings			Services		
	Growth Rate	ICOR	Country	Growth Rate	ICOR	Country	Growth Rate	ICOR	Country	Growth Rate	ICOR	Country	Growth Rate	ICOR	Country	Growth Rate	ICOR	Country	Growth Rate	ICOR
West Germany (W.G.)	7.4	3.3	Gr.	5.7	0.9	Fin.	18.6[a]	3.0[a]	W.G.	10.1	1.5	Sp.	15.1	2.8[f]	Yug.	13.4	21.6	Tur.	6.4	0.9
Austria (Au.)	6.0	3.9	Tur.	4.3	1.8	It.	15.3	2.8	It.	9.0	1.5[c]	Tur.	13.6	17.2	Tur.	11.1	6.8	W.G.	6.3	2.2
Greece (Gr.)	5.9	3.0	Sp.	3.7	1.7	Ire.	14.4	1.5	Yug.	7.9	3.0	Yug.	13.5	15.9	Gr.	9.1	11.8	Au.	6.1	1.8
Italy (It.)	5.9	3.7	It.	3.5	3.2	Can.	9.7	3.1	Gr.	7.1	1.6[c]	Gr.	12.8	10.0	W.G.	7.4	32.5	Por.	4.9	2.2
Turkey (Tur.)	5.9	2.6	Den.	3.0	2.4	Tur.	8.0	1.6	Ne.	7.1	2.9	Por.	11.6	7.5	Can.	5.7	25.0	Fin.	4.3	5.2
Yugoslavia (Yug.)	5.5	4.2	Yug.	3.0	2.5	Au.	5.6	4.6	Fin.	6.3	3.0[d]	Au.	11.1	8.9	U.S.	4.6	23.6	Can.	4.1	3.3
Iceland (Ice.)	5.4	5.7	W.G.	2.7	8.5	Sp.	5.2	2.8[b]	Au.	6.0	1.7[c]	Can.	10.4	1.7	Ire.	3.6	29.2	Gr.	3.9	2.1
Spain (Sp.)	5.2	3.1	Fin.	2.4	6.8	Yug.	5.0	8.0	Por.	6.0	1.6[c]	U.S.	9.4	6.9	Por.	3.5	30.1	It.	3.6	2.7
Switzerland (Sw.)	5.2	4.5	U.K.	2.0	7.0	Sw.	3.1	4.0	Tur.	5.9	2.7[c]	Den.	9.2	5.8	Nor.	3.2	84.1	Ne.	3.6	2.6
Netherlands (Ne.)	4.8	5.2	Por.	1.9	3.7	Nor.	2.4	8.4	Sp.	5.4	2.8[e]	W.G.	8.6	9.7	Den.	3.1	19.7	Nor.	3.4	3.8
France (Fr.)	4.5	4.6	Ne.	1.8	6.6	W.G.	2.3	10.8	Sw.	4.4	2.9	Fin.	8.3	11.6	Ne.	2.6	65.8	Bel.	3.1	3.3
Canada (Can.)	4.2	6.0	Au.	1.1	18.7	Ne.	2.0	6.7	Can.	4.1	3.6	It.	8.2	6.7	Au.	2.2	163.7	Ire.	2.0	7.1
Finland (Fin.)	4.2	7.2	U.S.	0.9	17.6	U.S.	1.3	23.0	Bel.	4.1	3.0	Ne.	7.8	10.0	U.K.	2.0	42.9	U.K.	1.7	5.1
Portugal (Por.)	4.1	4.0	Bel.	0.9	9.2				U.S.	4.0	2.9	Nor.	7.5	18.0	It.	1.8	88.3			
Luxembourg (Lux.)	3.8	6.2	Nor.	0.6	31.4				Nor.	3.9	5.0	Sw.	7.3	11.7	Bel.	1.3	46.1			
Norway (Nor.)	3.4	9.5	Ire.	0.1	118.1				Den.	3.6	2.5	Ire.	7.1	12.4						
Sweden (Sw.)	3.4	6.3							U.K.	3.3	3.4	U.K.	5.0	17.4						
United States (U.S.)	3.3	5.5							Ire.	3.2	4.7	Bel.	4.8	6.4						
Denmark (Den.)	3.2	5.5																		
Belgium (Bel.)	3.0	5.6																		
United Kingdom (U.K.)	2.4	6.7																		
Ireland (Ire.)	1.3	13.7																		

SOURCE: Compiled from United Nations, Economic Commission for Europe, *Some Factors in Economic Growth in Europe During the 1950's*, part 2 of *Economic Survey of Europe in 1961* (Geneva, 1964), U.N. Sales No. 64. IIE. 1, Chapter II, 17 (table 6), Chapter III, 52, 58.

[a] Includes manufacturing.
[b] Includes manufacturing, construction, and public utilities.
[c] Includes construction.
[d] Includes mining.
[e] Includes mining, construction, and public utilities.
[f] Includes mining, manufacturing, and construction.
[g] Compound annual percentage rates of growth of GDP, and of contribution of each sector to GDP.

[16]

Chapter 11

TECHNICAL PROGRESS, THE PRODUC- TION FUNCTION, AND DEVELOPMENT

BY

HARVEY LEIBENSTEIN
University of California

I. INTRODUCTION

THE neo-classical theory of price, production, and output did not lead to the development of a theory of innovations. Apart from Schumpeter's work, inventions and innovations have been matters left outside of economic theory. In recent years there have been some attempts to develop investment functions that incorporate 'technical progress', but for the most part, these have *not* been widely accepted. The situation is still very much up in the air. But, if we are to have a take-off type theory of development this implies that at some point the induced rate of investment must be accelerated and that this higher rate of investment must sustain itself. But why should the rate of investment at a somewhat higher level of *per capita* income be higher than at a lower level? Temporary exogenous events could explain occasional high investment rates, but this would be just as true for backward as for less backward and growing economies.

A major argument that is often put forward is connected with the rate of savings. It is argued that at higher levels of *per capita* income the subsistence requirements for most of the population are met, and a higher rate of savings out of non-subsistence income naturally occurs. While this may not be unreasonable and may be a contributing factor, it is really a theory that depends on the savings bottleneck as a deterrent to high rates of investment. In other words, if this were the only factor involved, it would then imply that sufficient investment inducements always exist irrespective of the stage of development that the country is in, and that the problem would be solved if only there were enough savings. In this paper I want to take the opposite viewpoint. I want to consider part of a model in which the inducement to invest is the crucial bottleneck to overcome. In particular, I want to suggest a type of production

185

The Economics of Take-off into Sustained Growth

function and some generalizations about inventions and innovations which support the argument that at some stage in the development process there will exist effective inducements for relatively high levels of investment that do not exist in the pre-take-off stage.

There is very much more to the problem of investment determination than the points made in this paper. What follows does not pretend to be a theory of investment. It is only part of the picture. I simply want to sketch some notions about the nature of the production function and the nature of technical progress that would support the type of investment functions under which low rates of investment would exist in the pre-take-off stage and high rates afterwards.[1]

At the outset it may be well to begin with a few general statements that could be made about economic development with which very few would quarrel. For instance: (1) the technological inventions of the last few centuries are the prime factors that make it possible for a country to shift from low levels of income *per capita* to high levels of income per head. (2) Capital accumulation is not enough. At low levels of technical knowledge there are severe limits to the extent to which output per man could be increased by mere capital accumulation. (3) It is only because of the vast increases in technical knowledge, especially with respect to the utilization of non-animal energy sources, that we are able to increase output per man considerably. The question to be answered is this: In view of the possibilities available today via the utilization of modern production techniques, why do low income countries in many of their production processes employ such primitive techniques of production? The obvious and perhaps somewhat superficial answer that we have all learned to give to this question is a lack of capital accumulation, or at least a lack of capital accumulation at a sufficient rate so as to increase, considerably, capital per worker. While this may be true, I believe that it is a somewhat unsatisfactory answer.

The argument appears to depend very much (indeed, too much) on changes in the propensity to save within a *rather narrow range*. Suppose that the rate of population growth is 2 per cent and the capital output ratio is 3:1. It is quite common for an economy with a low rate of *per capita* income to have a net savings rate of around 6 per cent. If its net savings are $7\frac{1}{2}$ per cent then *per capita* income will grow at $\frac{1}{2}$ per cent rate per year. Does the answer

---

[1] Whether my theory is correct or not is an empirical question which remains to be considered at a later time. But there may, nevertheless, be some value in trying to present such a theory at this juncture in a bold and simplified fashion, if only perhaps to enable us to focus our attention and discussion on the relation between technical progress, the production function, and economic development.

Leibenstein — Technical Progress and Development

really lie in the belief that such economies can manage to save 6 per cent but simply cannot handle $7\frac{1}{2}$ per cent? It depends too much on arithmetic — too much on the propensity to consume. In other words, I feel that a greater part of the burden of the answer should lie on the inducement to invest rather than on the propensity to save. There is, of course, much more to the inducement to invest than those elements of it connected with technical progress. However, I suspect that a part of the argument may lie in the nature of technical progress and the impact of technical progress on production functions. What follows is a sketch of the type of production function that is somewhat different from that commonly found in the literature, but which is consistent with the take-off hypothesis.

II. THE SHAPE OF THE PRODUCTION FUNCTION

The conventional textbook version of the production function has at least these three characteristics: (1) continuity, (2) the assumption that the firm knows all of the alternative production processes available, and (3) a sharp distinction between a shift of the production function and a movement along a given production function. This last distinction often appears to be all that conventional theory has to say about technical progress. Namely, technical progress involves a shift in the production function. Thus, if we use isoquants to denote our production function then technical progress will involve a shift to the left from one set of isoquants to another. All that is usually said about the nature of the shifts is that it is of such a kind that some combinations of the factors will produce a greater output than was produced by these same combinations before the shift took place. But almost nothing is suggested about the nature and locus of such shifts. The basic hypothesis of the argument that follows is with respect to the locus of such shifts. In addition, I want to argue that discontinuities are also likely to play an important part in the production functions of many, although not necessarily all, commodities.

The type of production function that I want to propose is depicted by the isoquant in the figure below.

In Fig. 1 the curve marked Q is an isoquant depicting alternate combinations of capital and labour necessary to produce a given quantity of output Q. The line marked E_1 is a given expenditure (or budget) line assuming that the prices for capital and labour units are given. E_2 is another such expenditure line that reflects the fact that the wage rate is here considerably higher than it is at E_1.

The Economics of Take-off into Sustained Growth

Consider the shape of the isoquant. There are two facts to be observed. First, it is drawn in such a way as to reflect discontinuous rather than a continuous range of alternatives. Only the points *a*, *b*, *c*, *d*, and *e* represent different distinct techniques, while points in between *a* and *b* simply reflect the fact that a certain proportion of the output will be produced by the use of technique *a* and another proportion will employ technique *b*. The second fact to observe is that technological alternatives are available when the capital-labour ratio is low, and relatively many are available when the capital-labour ratio is high. That is to say, as we move upward along the isoquant in the direction of the arrow the new alternative

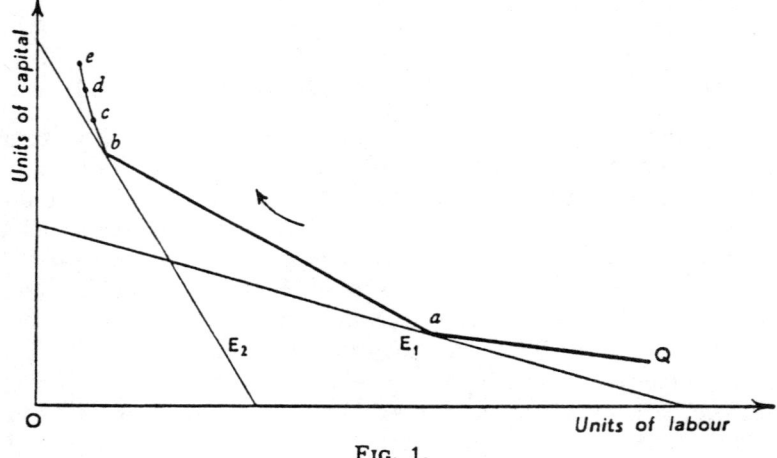

FIG. 1.

techniques available are closer and closer together. Another way of looking at it is to say that the greatest discontinuities in production exist where the amount of capital per man is least.

To see what is involved in our diagram let us examine its implications. If the wage is low, let us say at W_1, and the expenditure line is E_1, then the technique used will be technique *a*, as shown in the figure — the technique determined by the point of tangency between the isoquant and the expenditure line. Suppose now that the wage were slightly higher. This will mean a slight shift in the slope of the line E_1. However, the point of tangency will still be exactly the same as it was before. In other words, small changes in wages do not imply any change in technique. Only a very large change in the wage of the kind that is reflected by a shift from the slope of E_1 to the slope of E_2 will lead to a shift in technique from *a* to *b*. In general, where discontinuities in technique are considerable, it will take a

Leibenstein — Technical Progress and Development

considerable change in the relative wage to capital costs before we can induce firms to shift from one production technique to another. On the other hand, suppose we begin with a relatively high wage rate. Then the point of tangency of the isoquant will, let us say, be at point *c*. We will then be operating within an area on the isoquant for which slight changes in wages will lead to shifts in technique.[1]

What are the overall implications of all this ? Increases in wage rates can only be sustained, in the long run, if there are increases in *per capita* output. But increases in *per capita* output require increases in productivity per man, which in turn implies shifting from lower techniques to higher ones. But the extent to which such shifts take place will depend on the sensitivity of entrepreneurs to changing economic conditions. And this last in turn depends, in part, on the nature of the production function. If the production function is as illustrated, then we see that small anticipated changes in wages will not lead to changes in technique necessary to sustain the support of these higher wages, if the initial level of *per capita* output is low. On the other hand, small anticipated changes in wages will induce the adoption of new techniques when the level of output per man is relatively high. Thus, in the pre-take-off stage small stimulants to growth will not stimulate permanent shifts in technique and hence, will not stimulate development. Only a relatively large and fairly sustained stimulant can get entrepreneurs to a point on their production functions where they are quite ready to shift from lower techniques to higher ones.

We can also connect this particular type of production function with another characteristic of economic backwardness — namely that of structural underemployment. In recent years several writers have argued that structural underemployment (and disguised unemployment) of the kind usually found in low income countries can be explained by discontinuities in the production function. Now, it is usually observed that this type of unemployment exists in a much lesser degree in advanced economies than in backward ones. Furthermore, within a given economy it is usually more typical of the more backward sectors such as the agricultural sector. If the discontinuity argument is correct, then this would suggest that such discontinuities occur to a lesser extent and are less important in well advanced economies. But it is precisely such more advanced economies which operate on points on their production function at which the capital-labour ratio is higher.

[1] All wages and capital input prices are assumed to be relative to each other and do not reflect only absolute money wages or capital input money prices.

The Economics of Take-off into Sustained Growth

III. THE FIRM, WAGE INCREASES, AND RELATIVE
FACTOR PRICES

In discussing the diagram in the previous section of the paper it may have appeared that I assumed that the wage increase takes place exogenously. This is not quite what I have in mind. Rather, what I do have in mind is a dynamic process in which entrepreneurs anticipate increases in output if such increases are warranted by past experience. Now, the main point is that such increases will be warranted if the subsequent events following the increase are of a type that the increase can be fulfilled. Indirectly, such anticipated increases in output will also result in increases in real wages. In other words, we raise the question whether the initial anticipations are consistent with other possibilities in the economy. They will be consistent if production functions are such so that output can be increased. To be somewhat more specific, in the successful case, individual firms will anticipate an increase in output, this in turn will imply an increase in demand for labour. But this increased demand for labour will raise the wage rate, which in turn will lead to the inducement to increase capital per man (i.e. substitute capital for labour) and hence, productivity per man. This, in turn, leads to the greater output out of which the higher wage rate can be paid. In such a dynamic process, at whatever point we break into it, the anticipated increase in output (based on past experience of such increases in output) will turn out to be self-fulfilling. The main point of the argument attempted in the previous section is that where there do not exist any more capital intensive techniques in the neighbourhood of the existing technique the sequence breaks down because it becomes impossible to increase the productivity per man out of which increased wages must come in the long run.

If there is underemployment, then, of course, additional difficulties may arise. Namely, for some types of labour the increase in output and the subsequent increased demand in the labour force will not result in an increased wage. In such industries we have another reason why the successful sequence suggested in the last paragraph would break down. However, the labour that is unemployed is not likely to be substitutable for all types of labour, and hence, while this may be true for some industries, it would not be true for all industries. Even in the same industry it need not be true for all types of labour. Thus, while we recognize the underemployment deterrent to capital accumulation, it is, of course, not the only deterrent, and the present paper attempts to emphasize

Leibenstein — *Technical Progress and Development*

those deterrents that may exist in view of the nature of the production function.

It is important to observe that in considering the consequence of a wage rise I am not concerned with absolute increases in the wage rate, but rather with a change in the relative price between labour inputs and capital inputs. Now, it has been argued that an increase in wages will not necessarily change the relative price of labour and capital. The point made is that both capital goods and consumption goods require labour inputs, and hence, when wages rise, the price of capital will rise proportionately to the increase in labour if we assume a two-factor world in which capital goods are made entirely out of labour, and in which we consider only comparative equilibrium states. But, this is not the way I wish to look at the problem in this paper. We need not assume, strictly speaking, a two-factor world. Our analysis is not one of comparative statics in which only alternative equilibrium states are considered. To begin with, there is an interest cost component in capital goods, and for this reason, the cost of capital inputs may not rise in the same proportion as the cost of labour inputs as the consequence of a wage increase.[1] In addition, we may assume that there exists at any time a stock of capital goods, and that when the price of labour goes up this only increases the cost of the additions to capital, but not necessarily the cost of the existing stock of capital. Consider the following possibility: suppose that the ratio of capital to labour in the production of consumption goods industries is one to one; but suppose that the ratio of capital to labour in the production of capital goods is three to one. Now, in this case a rise in wages will obviously affect the cost in consumer goods for the given technique to a larger extent than it will increase the cost of capital goods. Therefore, there will be an inducement to substitute capital for labour if such substitutions are possible. Similarly, bowing somewhat in the direction of realism, we should assume the existence of other stocks such as land, which are used in different proportions in producing capital and consumer goods, so that a change in the price of labour can result in an increase in the relative price of labour to capital. These remarks are in conformity with the general spirit of this paper — which is not to present results that prove the case, but rather to point to some possibilities that I believe are worth considering.

[1] Cf. Joan Robinson, *The Accumulation of Capital*, London 1958, chapters 10-12.

The Economics of Take-off into Sustained Growth

IV. TECHNICAL PROGRESS AND THE PRODUCTION FUNCTION

Why should the production function have the shape indicated above? We have already suggested one piece of evidence based on underemployment. I want to consider now the following question: Where on the production function is the likely locus of invention? We may look upon a production function as the end result of all of the inventions that have been made in the past. With this in mind, let us consider how inventions determine shifts in the production function, and the relation between the new production function after the invention and the old one prior to the invention.

What will the shift in the production function as a consequence of an invention look like? Some textbooks illustrate such an event by a shift of *all* points of the isoquant to the left. For example, in Fig. 2 below this is illustrated by the shift from Q to Q'. But in fact, I suspect, this is not what is likely to happen. There is no reason why we should anticipate that the improvement in, say, a given type of machine should shift all the points on Q to a new set of points on Q'. A given type of machine may not be used at low wage rates at all, nor perhaps, will it be used at very high wage rates.

Suppose there is an improvement in such a machine. Clearly such an improvement will lead to the machine being used at the same wage rates as previously and perhaps at some slightly lower wage rates than before. If our production function is discontinuous and the particular technological alternative for which this machine is utilized is represented by a point on it, then that particular point will be shifted to the left as a consequence of the improvement. Similarly, those segments of the curve involving the utilization of the machine will also move to the left. There is no reason for the entire curve necessarily to do so. This is the first aspect of my argument. Namely, that in many cases the consequence of an innovation is for only a small portion of the production function to shift rather than for the entire function to do so.

Next we want to consider at what points on an isoquant inventions are most likely to take place. We should distinguish between two types of inventions: those that are of a spectacular sort and result in great

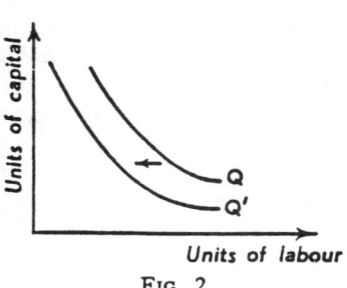

FIG. 2.

Leibenstein — Technical Progress and Development

potential shifts in the production function, and those that are improvements in machines, equipment, implements or other aspects of the production process, which are relatively small and which occur frequently — in some cases almost on a day-to-day basis. Inventions of the spectacular type may be of great importance not only to economies in which the capital-labour ratio is high, but also to those in which the capital-labour ratio is low. Such spectacular innovations are, in a sense, historical accidents. We cannot possibly say much that is of a systematic nature about them. The remarks that follow are limited, for the most part, to the latter variety of inventions — those that involve small improvements which occur almost continuously in an advanced economy, and which can occur to some extent in a backward economy. Such inventions are easier to achieve when the processes involved are simple rather than complex. Indeed, among the most important means of affecting productive efficiency are specialization, standardization, and simplification of processes and commodities. But specialized and standardized processes are more likely to be employed at the higher regions (i.e. higher capital-labour ratios) of the production isoquants. Standardization and specialization usually imply a specialized type of capital good, which is efficient precisely because it is labour saving. Hence, it occurs at those points at which the capital-labour ratio is high. Frequently the most efficient types of machines and devices are those that substitute non-human mechanical energy for human or animal energy. But in such cases also this is likely to occur where the capital-labour ratio is high. Further, inventions and innovations are likely to take place where the process is sufficiently simplified so that it becomes easy to see the next potential improvement — and again, this usually means at the higher points on the curve. These ideas are illustrated in Fig. 3. The three isoquants have a common segment at the low capital-output ratios, at which no inventions take place, and branch out at the higher capital-labour ratios at which inventions do take place.

Thus Q is the initial isoquant, Q' is the isoquant that results as a consequence of an innovation on Q, and Q'' is the isoquant resulting from an innovation on Q'. The main notion is that in the state of relative backwardness few techniques are known. As the country does develop it shifts to higher capital-labour ratios, and the new techniques, as they are discovered, become incorporated into the ever-changing production functions (*mostly*) at the higher capital-labour ratios.

The implications of this thesis are two-fold. First, it contains an argument for a production function in which the greatest

The Economics of Take-off into Sustained Growth

discontinuities occur at the points where the capital-labour ratio are lowest. Second, it enables us to illustrate the possibility of inventions taking place, or of new production processes becoming available, without their being used in the economy.

Let us return to Fig. 3. Suppose that the wage is low so that the budget line is E_1, then we could readily see that it is quite possible for a series of changes to take place in the upper portions of the production isoquant without in any way producing new points of tangency between the isoquant and the budget line. By the same token, if the wage were initially a higher one and the point of tangency with the isoquant were also higher, then each invention would have

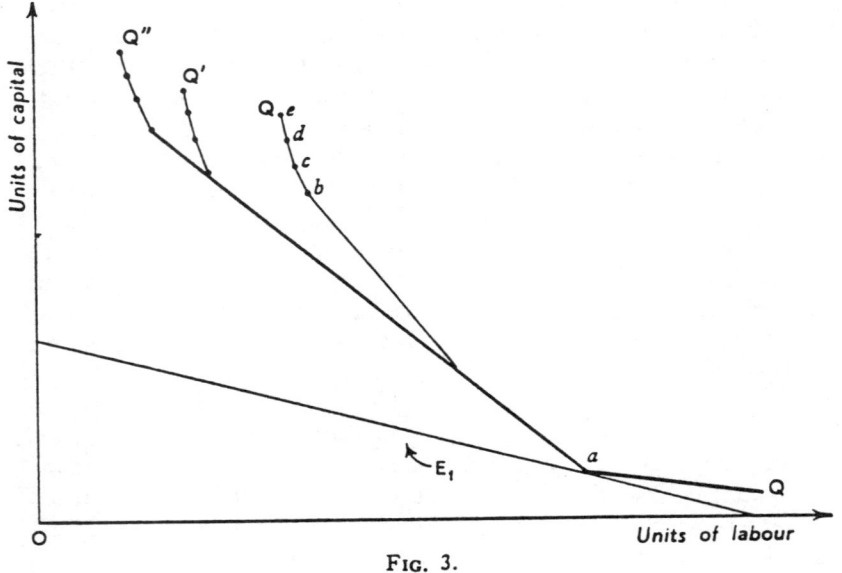

FIG. 3.

produced a new point of tangency, which in turn implies a new technique being adopted. In other words, at the relatively high wage, technical progress would be turned into practical innovations whereas at the low wage, it has no influence whatsoever.

How does all of this affect the rate of investment? The basic argument is that (1) the shape of our production function, and (2) the relationship between inventions and the production function, create a situation in which there is greater inducement to adopt inventions at high capital-labour ratios than at low. Let us look at the low wage rates situation first. Suppose, for a moment, that all commodities have the sort of production functions that we have

Leibenstein — Technical Progress and Development

described. Under such circumstances small changes in wage rates will not lead to the adoption of new techniques. For any given commodity the same technique will be employed. This means that the capital-labour ratio will be the same. This does not necessarily mean that no net investment will take place. But the net investment that does take place will be of the 'capital widening' variety rather than the capital deepening type. It is even possible under these circumstances for *per capita* output to increase, *up to a point*, by increasing the degree to which the labour force is employed. But *per capita* output per man *employed* will remain almost the same. In any event, although *per capita* output can be increased, there are very strict limits to the extent to which this can be done without shifting to more capital-using techniques, and without taking advantage of the technical progress that takes place. Quite clearly, if we are to expect sustained growth to occur then these last two types of investment must also occur. However, at high wage levels, firms will be induced to substitute capital for labour as wages rise, thus increasing output per man. In addition, they will also be induced to take advantage of the technical progress that occurs.

Let us look at the matter from the point of view of a single firm in an economy in which wages are rising. To the individual firm, taking advantage of some types of inventions is a cost-reducing procedure. The firm that does this first has a slight edge on its competitors. We can visualize a Schumpeterian process taking place in which the initial cost-reducing innovator is pursued by a host of followers who adopt the same new technique in order to remain in competition. There are two things to observe here. First, such innovations will increase output per man. Second, they may decrease the useful life of capital goods through the process of obsolescence. In either event, one can readily see that we would have a greater rate of investment in this situation as against the one in which taking advantage of technical progress is not possible. In addition, we might keep in mind the possibility that technical progress, by decreasing costs, increases the marginal productivity of capital, and hence, we would expect it to increase the rate of investment and savings accordingly.

Not only does technical progress increase investment in the industry in which it occurs, but it is likely to increase investment in at least some industries that are complementary to it. The effects of technical progress are often transmitted from the initial industries to related industries — for example, to those industries that use the outputs of the technically advancing industry. In this case

The Economics of Take-off into Sustained Growth

the cost reduction that occurs in the first industry results in a further
cost reduction of a lesser degree in the second industry. If cost
and price are reduced 50 per cent in industry A and industry B
uses 50 per cent of industry A, then costs per unit in B may be
reduced by 25 per cent. This cost-reducing procedure may, in
turn, expand the demand for the commodity and increase output.
Whether, in fact, this will or will not happen in particular cases will
depend on a variety of circumstances. What is important for our
purposes is that in such instances we have at least situations that
can lend themselves to the creation of further investment opportunities.

V. KNOWLEDGE, SCALE EFFECTS, AND COMPLEMENTARITIES

In the usual conception of the production function it is assumed
that the firm is aware of all of the technical alternatives that are
available. In fact, of course, this is unlikely to be the case. However, our argument will not be based simply on the point that the
existing theory assumes perfect knowledge. What is important is
not that entrepreneurs have imperfect knowledge of production
alternatives, but that this knowledge is likely to be *different* for different segments of the production function in use — i.e. for different
capital-labour ratios. I will try to argue that at low capital-labour
ratios relatively fewer technological alternatives are known than at
high capital-labour ratios. By 'known' I mean known in sufficient
detail to enable the firm to shift successfully and with ease from one
production technique to another.

The technique that a firm knows best will, of course, be the
technique that is currently being employed. And the longer the
period that a certain technique is used the greater the degree to
which that technique is known, and probably the greater the dis-
inclination to shift to other techniques, other things equal. This
is especially likely to be true if there are no alternative techniques
in the neighbourhood of the point that the firm is on. In other
words, if there were quite a few technique alternatives in the neighbourhood of the capital-labour ratio at which the firm is working,
then there is a greater chance of becoming acquainted with those
alternatives and a greater inducement to discover the exact nature
of such alternatives, than if there are very few alternatives in the
neighbourhood.

In addition, the extent to which alternative neighbouring points
on a production function are known is likely to depend on the rate

Leibenstein — Technical Progress and Development

of change. The greater the rate of change, the greater the interest in discovering alternative production techniques. Clearly, a high rate of change already implies that firms are shifting from one technique to another, which in turn, leads to greater knowledge about alternative techniques. We have already argued that at the low capital-labour ratio there is likely to be little change in technique and hence, little effective knowledge of alternative techniques that might foster change, while the reverse is likely to be true at the high capital-labour ratios.

The number of 'employable' points on a production function may also be determined by institutional factors. Educational levels are likely to be lower at lower capital-output ratios, and the institutional factors surrounding labour mobility, such as the existence of a caste system, are also likely to reduce the number of technological alternatives that the firm feels are really available to it. I do not intend to go into detail in this matter. The institutional factor is probably much too difficult to analyse in any event. I mention it simply as an element that probably is in support of our general argument.

There are two more elements which are of great importance and which will often inhibit an under-developed country from readily adopting new techniques of production. These are the scale of plant and the problem of complementary inputs. A great many capital goods, especially of the more capital intensive variety, are economically employable only where the scale of plant and market is reasonably large. It is usually the case that the size variety of plants is likely to be larger in an advanced economy than in a backward economy. In the backward economy there may be many industries in which plants are so small that many types of capital goods cannot be employed and new inventions adopted, even if a consideration of the relative wage rate — apart from scale considerations capital cost factors were such as to favour the adoption of new techniques. Of course, firm growth is not precluded as a possibility, but in a world of uncertainty there are limits to which a small firm can grow in any period, and hence, there are limits to which the small firm and plant can adopt techniques that are more suitable for a much larger plant size.[1] Now, let us refer back to our previous successful dynamic sequence that involved the gradual adoption of more and more capital intensive techniques. It would appear, clearly, that the scale element would be one of the factors

[1] On the limits to the growth rate of a small firm, see my *Economic Theory and Organizational Analysis*, Harper & Brothers, New York, 1960, chapters 16, 18, and 19.

The Economics of Take-off into Sustained Growth

that would cause such a dynamic sequence to break down. In referring to the scale element we are obviously talking, at the same time, about indivisibilities and the notion that inventions may be of a type to increase such indivisibilities. For one of the reasons that firms are small in a backward economy is that where the capital-labour ratio is low, techniques are available in which small firms could operate in competition successfully. Such techniques cease to be available, in many cases, where the capital-labour ratio is relatively high. But it is precisely such indivisibilities that make it difficult for the small firm to grow and increase its output if the stimuli to growth are relatively small rather than large.

Complementarities in the production process play a similar rôle to that of scale. In many capital intensive techniques the type of raw materials, spare parts, maintenance equipment, and labour skills may be different and more specialized than those required for production techniques in which capital intensity is low. A backward economy may not produce all these complementary elements for all industries. Some of these complementary elements may be importable from abroad, but others may have to be produced at home if firms are to be induced to adopt more capital intensive techniques. It is obviously easier for more advanced economies to produce the complementary inputs than for a backward economy in which labour skills, entrepreneurial capacities, and engineering skills are limited. I do not want to work this argument too hard, but I merely mention it in order to suggest that the differential capacities of the backward as against the advanced economy to provide complementary inputs may serve as an additional deterrent to the adoption of such inputs. But it is important to note that the lack of such complementary inputs will reflect itself both in the nature of the production function and in the nature of technological progress. With respect to the production function, clearly, any production technique that cannot be adopted because of the lack of complementary inputs will not appear as a point on the production function. By the same token, improvements in techniques and inventions may require not only intellectual capacities, but also the necessary complementary inputs in order to make intellectual conceptions into realities. Hence, once again, the sort of innovations that can exist will, for this reason, not be created in the backward economy where they are lacking.

Before closing it is important to note that the argument presented does not depend on the notion that all production functions are of the kind that have been described, or that the locus of inventions and innovations is always in the neighbourhood that we have

Leibenstein — Technical Progress and Development

suggested. It depends only on the idea that there are likely to be quite a few production functions of this type so that the overall influence is in the direction suggested.

VI. CONCLUSIONS

Sustained economic growth (in the *per capita* income sense) requires that the firms in the economy shift periodically (and almost continuously) towards the choice of production techniques that yield greater and greater outputs per man. Whether or not firms are motivated (1) to move along the production function towards higher capital-labour ratios, and (2) to take advantage of the inventions that take place from time to time, will depend on, among other things, (a) the wage rate, (b) the nature of the production function, and (c) the locus of inventions. But there are circumstances in which, even if wage rates tend to rise, a shift towards new techniques will not take place. I presented the outline of a model that shows why the inducements to adopt techniques that increase output per man would exist more readily at high incomes per head than at low. The model suggests that one of the potential obstacles to growth faced by a low income country may lie in the nature of some of the production functions, in the locus of inventions and technical progress, and in the degree of knowledge that entrepreneurs may have about such inventions.

On the shape of the production function it was argued that there are considerable indivisibilities and that these indivisibilities are likely to be more significant at low capital-labour ratios than at high; that for a given segment around a point on the production function there will be more distinct techniques available at the higher capital-labour ratios than at the lower ones. It was also argued that this is in part due to the historical locus of 'normal' inventions and production improvements which, in turn, depend on the points on the production function at which there is likely to be a greater degree of specialization and standardization. In other words, it was suggested that there is likely to be a greater incidence of invention at those points where standardization and specialization become economically more feasible. Finally, it was suggested that the firm does not know all of the technical alternatives on its production function. It could only shift easily to those alternatives that it knows. And the nature of the situation is such that it is likely to know more alternatives where the capital-labour ratio is high than where it is low. The small scale of plant in a backward

The Economics of Take-off into Sustained Growth

economy, and the lack of some of the complementary inputs necessary for production were mentioned as additional deterrents to the
adoption of new production techniques. It was suggested that both
of these elements are, in turn, related to indivisibilities in the
production function and to the locus of technological progress. The
point of these suggestions (if they are correct) is that they are consistent with higher sustained rates of investment at the higher
capital-labour ratios.

[17]

Technical Progress, the Production Function and Dualism

1. Introduction

While a great deal has been written in recent years on the problem of economic dualism (*), rather little has been done to connect it with the nature of technical progress. The purpose of this paper is to suggest a view of the production function and its relation to technical progress which may lead to insights into our understanding of the phenomenon of economic dualism.

By economic dualism I have in mind the phenomenon that one segment of a country develops very much more rapidly than another. With respect to Italy, the differential development of the North and South is well known. Clearly it is a phenomenon that is common to a great many underdeveloped countries. The mere

---

(*) There are now a number of famous articles on this subject of which the following are significant: R. S. ECKHAUS, " Factor Proportions in Underdeveloped Areas ", *American Economic Review*, September 1955, pp. 539-565; VERA C. LUTZ, " The Growth Process in a ' Dual ' Economic System ", *Banca Nazionale del Lavoro Quarterly Review*, No. 46, September 1958, pp. 279-324; ALBERT O. HIRSCHMAN, " Investment Policies and Dualism in Underdeveloped Countries ", *American Economic Review*, September 1957, pp. 550-570; W. ARTHUR LEWIS, " Economic Development with Unlimited Supplies of Labor ", *Manchester School*, May 1954, reprinted in Agarwala and Singh ed. *The Economics of Underdevelopment*, Oxford, 1958, pp. 400-449; J. H. BOEKE, *Economies and Economic Policy of Dual Societies*, New York, 1953; J. H. SADIE, " Social Anthropology of Economic Underdevelopment ", *Economic Journal*, June 1960, pp. 294-303; HLA MYINT, " An Interpretation of Economic Backwardness ", *Oxford Economic Papers*, June 1954 and " The Classical Theory of International Trade and the Underdeveloped Countries ", *Economic Journal*, June 1958, pp. 317-337; W. H. NICHOLLS, " Accommodating Change in Underdeveloped Countries ", *American Economic Review*, Proceedings, May 1960, p. 165; LUIGI SPAVENTA, " Dualism in Economic Growth (Development in a country having both an advanced and an underdeveloped sector in its economy) ", charts, *Banca Nazionale del Lavoro Quarterly Review*, December 1959, pp. 386-434.

I am very much indebted to Professor Howard S. Ellis for letting me read an unpublished review paper of his on the question of dualism, and especially for his helpful comments on this paper.

3

fact of differential rates of development in different sections of a country would not itself be surprising. After all, there is no reason why at any one time all segments of a country should develop at the same rate. What is puzzling is that this differential should persist for very long periods of time. This is especially so if we look at the problem from the viewpoint of neo-classical economic theory, since one of the messages of neo-classical theory is that differentials would tend to disappear. For example, the difference in wage rates between one segment of a country and another should induce entrepreneurs to the areas with lower wage rates, and/or induce workers away from areas of lower wage rates. The end result of such movements would be an equalization of real wages.

I do not wish to suggest that the attempts of others to explain dualism in terms of lack of mobility, socio-cultural elements, or in terms of monopolistic influences are on the wrong track. Most likely, it seems to me, these may very well have been, and continue to be in many cases, contributing factors. Rather, the spirit of this paper is to suggest an additional aspect of the situation that helps to explain why dualism may persist for some time. Now, a consideration of economic dualism must include a discussion of investment. What determines the differential rates of investment in different areas? It is common to divide the analysis of investment into two parts: The propensity to save, and the inducement to invest. A low propensity to save is, in a low income country, a sufficient reason to explain a lack of high investment. But this is not an especially compelling reason in circumstances in which the country-wide rate of investment is often quite high, but the rate of investment in the less developed segment of the country turns out to be quite low. Under such circumstances it may be useful to focus our attention on the inducement to invest. We recognize, of course, that by concentrating on the inducement to invest we are treating only part of the picture. But, of course, it is a very important part. In other words, I am trying to suggest that part of the reason for dualism is not a lack of savings or a lack of capacity of entrepreneurs to obtain investment funds, but rather, a low inducement to invest because of the nature of the underdeveloped sector. The main purpose of this paper is to analyse some possible relations between the production function and innovations in the underdeveloped sectors, and to show how these relations — if they exist — would lead to a low inducement to invest. In addition, I want to show

4

that while it may be likely for such conditions to exist in the underdeveloped sector of the economy, these same conditions need not exist in the more developed sector. Thus, if it turns out that the over-all savings rate is fairly high, the inducement to invest in the advanced sector may also be fairly high, although the inducement to invest in the backward sector may, nevertheless, be low. In such a case we have reason to expect a differential rate of development. Also, I will want to suggest why this differential rate of development might persist. Clearly, if this possibility could be established, then we will have a possible explanation for non-equalization of sectors, at least for some period of time.

It is of interest to note that on a superficial basis we might expect the existence of technical progress to lead, if anything, to equalization of growth rates rather than to the maintenance of the differential. The backward segment of a country uses more primitive and older methods of production than the more advanced segment. Obviously, the backward sector has more technological " know-how " to borrow than the advanced sector. Such differential opportunities might suggest, on a superficial basis, that the inducement to invest would be greater in the backward area, and hence, that technological progress would work in the direction of equalization. I will want to show why the opposite tendency may persist.

Before setting out the details of the analysis, it is perhaps important to indicate the limited nature of this paper. I shall suggest a *possible* reason for dualism. I do not suggest that it is a necessary one. However, I do believe that what follows is a reasonable, rather than an entirely remote possibility, and that as a consequence, it is a possibility that should be well considered in examining the underdeveloped segment of a given country, and in attempting to work out development policies for such areas.

2. The Production Function

The standard view of the production function is to think of it as a continuous function. In the usual textbook representation of such a function, in terms of two factors, it is usually assumed that the isoquants are continuous and non-kinky (1). This means that

---

(1) Cf. ALFRED W. STONIER & DOUGLAS C. HAGUE, *A Textbook of Economic Theory*, London, 1953, Chapter X.

5

any combination of the inputs are possible, and that for each ratio of inputs a production technique exists. In fact, of course, there are many industries in which there are significant discontinuities in factor inputs, and therefore, not every combination of these inputs leads to a new technique. Of course, the possibility of discontinuities is well known. It is usually assumed that the continuity assumption is only made for mathematical convenience. The sort of production function that I wish to present here does not differ so much in the fact that it is discontinuous (2), but in the fact that it is more discontinuous where the capital-labor ratio is low than where it is high. I want to show that, if the production function is of such a nature, this has consequences for the differential inducement to invest between the backward, as against the advanced sector.

Before going into the details of the argument, we might ask the question — why should we care about the nature of the production function in connection with development? If we interpret development as increases in income per man employed, then obviously, we have to examine how such increases are achieved. One usual way of achieving such increases is through the augmentation of the amount of capital that each worker has to work with, *i.e.* via increases in the capital-labor ratio. But increases in the capital-labor ratios imply a movement from some production techniques to other production techniques. It is the shifts along the production function towards higher capital-labor ratios which, in great part, increase output per man. If the production function is assumed to be continuous, then such shifts can be made with relative ease.

But, can shifts along the production function always take place if the latter is highly discontinuous? Consider, for a moment, the extreme case in which there is only one technique. Obviously, under such circumstances, no matter what the inducements are, there is no possibility of shifting to an alternative technique. On a less extreme level we may assume two techniques — one in which the capital used is very cheap and rather primitive, and the other in which capital used is expensive and complicated. Under such circumstances, it is clear that a large discontinuity exists that may inhibit move-

---

(2) The mere existence of discontinuities in the production function as part of the explanation of dualism is not new. See, for example, the interesting and well known articles by Eckhaus and Hirschman previously cited. It is the differential discontinuities that I stress, which is a somewhat different matter.

6

ments along the production function. Usually, looking at the matter from the micro-economic viewpoint, we would suppose that a rise in wages relative to capital cost would lead a firm to substitute capital for labor. But, obviously. this need not take place if there are very few productive alternatives available. If the increase in relative wages to capital cost is small, but the alternative technique involves, let us say, a tripling of capital stock, then it may clearly not pay for the typical firm to shift to the alternative technique. Thus, we have a case in which there is an inducement to substitute capital for labor, but the production function does not permit that that be done. This is one of the essential ideas of this essay. Namely, we want to examine circumstances under which there might be inducements to increase capital per man, and hence, inducements to increase output per man, but in which the nature of the production function (and the locus of technological progress) does not permit firms in the backward sector of the economy to respond effectively to such inducements.

Now, for analytical purposes, we want to contrast two possible dynamic sequences. Under one, successful capital accumulation takes place, and capital per man increases, period after period, while under the other, successful shifts towards more intensive techniques are blocked at various points. Consider the former possibility first. Suppose that in a given industry the normal course of events is for output and the wage rate to rise by 5% per year. Clearly, such increases can only continue, in the long run, if output *per man* also increases. Suppose, for the moment, that the labor force is constant. Hence, if the firm can substitute capital for labor (*i.e.* instead of increasing both labor and capital by 5% each period to get the output increase) then it is possible to obtain the requisite output increases. Under such circumstances, we might visualize a smooth adjustment process taking place in which the capital stock per man increases every year, output increases every year, and wages increase every year. No problems arise as long as, period by period, the firm can shift from techniques which are less productive per man to techniques which are more productive per man. However, the possibility of such a sequence taking place obviously breaks down as soon as the firm finds that there is not any technique close by that would permit it to increase output at the requisite rate. If output cannot be increased, the entire wage increase must come out of profits, and in a very short time, the

profitability of such firms would disappear. Obviously, such wage
increases would be resisted, and the inducement to substitute capital
for labor would also disappear. In any event, we can certainly see
that where there are discontinuities, such sequences of improvement
cannot take place, or if they do take place, they fairly soon reach a
point at which they break down. We assume that in the advanced

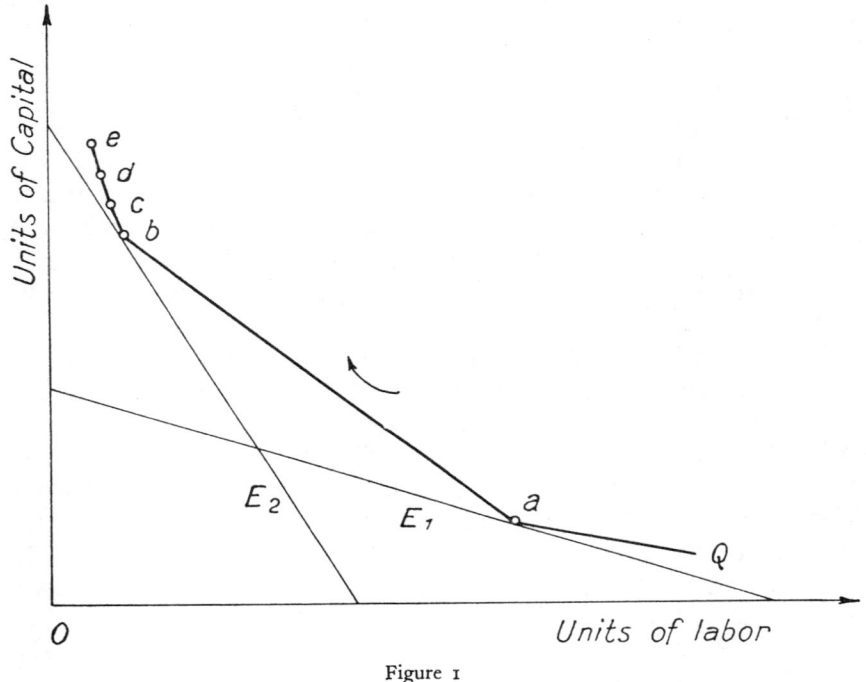

Figure 1

sector the successful (and gradual) growth sequence can take place.
Entrepreneurs expect, period by period, a certain expansion of the
market, and they expand output in accordance with their expectations. Firms can expand output either with the same technique
or with a new technique. Now, if individual firms attempt to expand output, they increase the demand for labor, and we would
expect wages to rise. It is this effect that should lead to the substitution of capital for labor (3). The increased output per man

---

(3) We assume that in both sectors some types of labor will not be in infinitely elastic
supply in the short run. This may still be true, even if unemployment exists for many
groups in the backward sector.

would then permit an increase in real wages. Thus, the expectations of output growth may be self-fulfilling if it is possible to shift easily to more labor intensive techniques. Clearly, this process would not be self-fulfilling if such shifts are not possible — that is, if there are no neighboring (more capital intensive) techniques that could readily be adopted.

The curve Q in the figure 1 is an illustration of one of the isoquants of the production function in question. The points (a), (b), (c), (d) and (e) represent alternative distinct techniques. That is to say, we assume that the capital comes in distinct and indivisible units, and that with each different outfit of capital, we associate a given quantity of labor necessary to produce the output Q. The line E_1 is the usual expenditure line, on the basis of given prices for the capital inputs and labor inputs. The slope of the line reflects the ratio of the input prices. E_2 is another such expenditure line which reflects the fact that the relative wage rate is, here, considerably higher than at E_1. Now, the isoquant Q is drawn in such a way that there are relatively few distinct production techniques available when the capital-labor ratio is low and relatively many are available when it is high. The lower part of the isoquant would be relevant for the backward segment of the economy, since in this segment the capital-labor ratio is low, while the upper part of the curve may be relevant for the advanced segment. Now, a small shift in the relative prices of labor to capital will not induce the firm to change its productive technique. This is clear if we compare the line E_1 as against the line E_2. In both cases the tangency of the expenditure line and the isoquant exists. But note that it takes a rather large increase in the relative wage rate in order to induce the firm to shift from technique (a) to technique (b).

Now, let us look for a moment at the line E_2. Here we find that a relatively small shift in the wage rate would induce such a firm using technique (b) to shift out of (b) and into (c). In other words, if the indivisibilities were as illustrated in the diagram, then a small wage change in the backward sector would not induce firms to substitute capital for labor, but a relatively small wage change in the advanced sector would do so. Hence, under such circumstances, many firms in the backward sector are *not* induced to increase the amount of capital per man, while this would be the case in the advanced sector.

9

Before closing this section, let me review the main point. Increases in output per man, in the long run, in a sector of an economy necessitate increases in productivity per worker. But this in turn, requires an increase in the capital stock per worker. This increase in the capital stock will come about if there is an inducement to substitute capital for labor. But, even if this inducement may exist — and there would be such inducements for the typical firm if the wage rate relative to capital cost went up — the productivity per man could still not be increased if there are not any more capital-intensive productive techniques that could be attempted and warranted by the input price changes. The existence of significant indivisibilities in the outfits of capital goods that could be used, reflects a situation in which it may often not be possible to shift from one production technique to another. In sum, small stimulants to growth do not induce permanent shifts in technique in the backward sectors, although they may do so in the advanced sector.

Expanding our argument to the economy as a whole, we can see in the existence of indivisibilities, the possibility of differential rates of growth between the two sectors of the economy. If, at the outset, there is a differential in the degree of development in the two sectors of the economy, then the sort of production function that we have depicted should result in an increase of this differential. Where will the investment funds go? By and large, they cannot go to the backward sector because in the backward sector it is impossible, under our assumption, to increase the capital-labor ratio except by making extremely large increases in capital. Clearly, there will not be an inducement for firms to make such large increases. Such increases would occur only if firms anticipate that the wage rate will rise significantly, and if they anticipate that markets will grow significantly (4). But, obviously, there is little reason for such anticipations unless productivity per man rises. In the advanced sector, however, an anticipated increase in wages will lead to an inducement to invest, which in turn, will increase output per man. At the same time, since this results in an increase in wage rate, it also results in an increase in markets for the increased output. Thus, in the advanced sector we can visualize a sequence

---

(4) This view is also consistent with my " critical minimum effort principle " that I have developed elsewhere. See my *Economic Backwardness and Economic Growth*, New York, 1957, Chapter VIII.

of events in which there is a persistent and gradual increase in the capital-labor ratio. We have already suggested why this cannot take place in many industries in the backward sector. In other words, indivisibilities in the backward sector form a bottleneck for a sustained gradual growth sequence in at least some industries, even if such a sequence could be initiated.

3. Technical Progress and Dualism

Probably the major means through which productivity and income per man have increased, in the long run, has been technical progress — through the creation of new techniques by firms. But, whether or not new techniques are adopted depends on the existing capital-labor ratio, the price of inputs — which determines the cost of alternative techniques — as well as other elements within the firm's purview. We want to show in this section, parallel to the ideas expressed in the last section, the possibility of technical progress which occurs in such a way that it is not adopted in the backward sector of the economy (5).

A common diagrammatical approach is to assume that technical progress leads to a shift of all points on the production function. However, it is quite possible — indeed, it is likely — that specific technique improvements shift only some points on an isoquant, but not all points. This possibility is illustrated in figure 2 below.

The curve Q' results from inventions made after the curve Q in figure 2. If the invention is fairly capital intensive, but the current technique is at a low degree of capital intensity, then it is quite likely that the invention will result in a shift in that portion of the isoquant associated with fairly high capital-labor ratios, but it will not shift that portion of the isoquant associated with low capital-labor ratios. Let us return again to figure 2 and observe the curve Q'', which represents an invention after Q' becomes the production function. Now, if the expenditure slope of the line E_1

---

(5) The reader should note that although we shall proceed to employ discontinuous isoquants many of the arguments that follow, with respect to technical progress and dualism, would be just as valid if we assumed continuous production functions. For example, in figure 2 a set of continuously non-kinky isoquants of the branched type would yield some of the same results. In other words, the burden of the arguments do not all of them rely entirely on discontinuities.

reflects the existing ratio of labor cost to capital cost, then we see that the shifts in the isoquant noted in the figure have no effect on choice of technique. In other words, we have illustrated the possibility that the locus of technical progress may be such that it would affect the choice of technique in those cases in which the cost of labor to capital is high, but not when it is low. The same inventions, when they take place in the advanced sector of the eco-

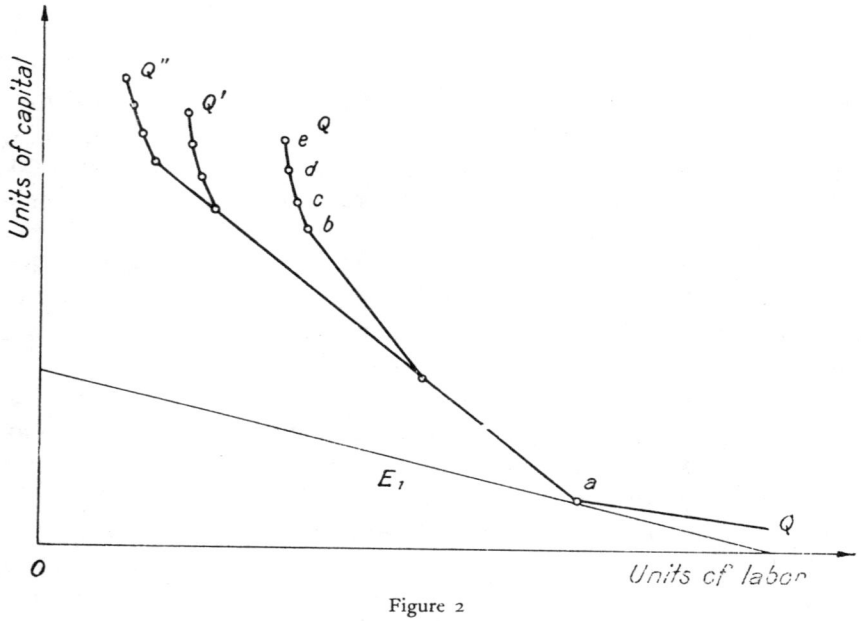

Figure 2

nomy, would be adopted, but they would not be adopted in the backward sector of the economy.

Now, is technical progress likely to be of the kind that we have just illustrated? Here we have to make a major distinction between at least two types of technical progress. The first type we might consider is that of a major over-all invention such as the steam engine or the internal combustion engine or the electric motor. Secondly, there is the gradual type of technical progress which takes place year after year, and in which there are no drastic changes in machines or implements employed, but, through redesign and general improvement, the effectiveness of given types of machines and implements are increased. It is probable that more of the technical progress that occurs in an economy is of the gradual kind, where through small changes, year after year, the eventual technique that emerges is very much superior to the initial technique. Now, the spectacular innovations may be of the type that may affect all, or at least a great many, points on the production isoquant (6). But, in general, the gradual type of invention and improvement is more likely to affect that portion of the isoquant associated with lower capital-labor ratios. There are at least two reasons why this may be the case. First, gradual technical progress is likely to take place where there is already a sufficient division of labor so that entrepreneurs, inventors, and others, could see the possibility of improving those machines and implements which are sufficiently specialized as to be within their purview. The idea here is that the more specialized the machinery or the implements, the easier it is for someone to understand it sufficiently so that it is possible and likely for improvements to occur to people. In any event, it is likely that inventions will take place in the less traditional and more educated sector of the economy, and such inventions are more likely to be close to those techniques already utilized in the advanced sector.

4. Technical Progress, Knowledge, Scale of Plant, and Complementary Inputs

The previous remarks about gradual inventions and improvements are not intended to suggest that inventions of a spectacular type will have an equal impact on both the advanced and the backward sector. The point made, with respect to spectacular inventions, is that some of them may affect the entire production function — or a great many points on it — so that such inventions may be adopted both in the backward and the advanced sector. It does seem to me, however, that in general, the advanced sector is more likely to be in the position to adopt inventions even of a spectacular kind. This is likely to be true, among other things, if we take into account such considerations as sufficient size of

---

(6) For example, we often find in some backward sectors, some small scale firms using small electric motors. Obviously, the invention of the electric motor can influence more than just the advanced sector of an economy.

plant and the existence of complementary inputs necessary to adopt some types of new capital goods. In other words, some inventions result in capital goods that are sufficiently large to be adopted more readily in larger rather than smaller plants, and the advanced sector is the more likely to have the larger rather than the smaller plants. A similar argument holds with respect to complementary inputs.

We have already touched on the matter of knowledge. The higher the degree of education that the labor force has, the greater its chances of hitting on inventions, and in addition, the greater its capacity to see the possibility of the useful adoption of inventions in production processes. All of these aspects are likely to be more prevalent in the advanced rather than in the backward sector. It is not only the degree of education that is significant, but also the variety of knowledge available to individuals. Since the advanced sector of the economy is likely to employ a larger variety of productive techniques, hence, the variety of productive knowledge in the sector will accordingly be larger. Therefore, it is more likely that this greater degree of knowledge will yield more inventions and improvements suitable to the advanced sector.

We have already stressed the importance of indivisibilities in potential productive techniques. But, further indivisibilities may be created by the new type of capital goods that come on the market. In other words, there may be a certain minimum size in which new outfits of capital can be produced economically. Certain improved machines or implements may be larger than the existing machines or implements that do a similar type of job less efficiently. The consequence of this possibility is that a large firm of sufficient scale finds that it would pay for it to adopt the new technique, whereas a small firm finds that it could not do so. The variables involved here are the existing size of the firms, the possibilities for expansion, and the size of the market. All of these elements are clearly likely to be greater in the advanced sector than in the backward sector, and hence, to the extent that scale is a consideration in the adoption of an invention, such inventions will more readily be adopted in the advanced, rather than in the backward sector.

For a capital good to be used efficiently, it is often necessary that other capital goods, or other types of labor be employed at the same time. Obviously, to operate a complicated type of capital good such as a linotype machine requires the existence of skilled operators. Similarly, many types of capital goods, for their successful adoption and utilization, require the existence of skilled maintenance people and repair crews who have to be available in time of need. Every type of complicated machinery usually requires the simultaneous existence of a reasonably large spare parts industry. All of these inputs are more likely to exist in the advanced sector. Hence, on this basis, the type of innovations that will take place will, more often than not, be of the kind that could most readily be adopted in the advanced, rather than in the backward sector.

Finally, we might consider that the capital goods that could be adopted do not run the gamut of all *possible* types and sizes of capital goods. Firms are limited in many of their choices to those types of capital goods that are actually produced. To the extent that they utilize industrial machinery and equipment, the backward sector of the economy is likely to be a net importer of such machinery and equipment. But, what types of machines and equipment are in fact being produced? Apart from those traditionally produced for the backward sector, it is likely that the new type of capital goods produced will not be most suitable for that sector where markets are undeveloped and uncertain, but rather, they will be the type of capital goods suitable for the production conditions and the variety of labor available in the advanced sector. Hence, the backward sector faces the additional handicap in that it has to import capital goods, when it wants to do so, of a type not especially designed for its own factor availabilities.

In sum, the locus of inventions is likely to be such that they are more readily adoptable in the sector with the higher capital-labor ratios. In addition, the locus and nature of many inventions helps, in part, to explain the differential degree of indivisibilities in production techniques that are likely to exist in different parts of the production function.

5. Closing the Gap

Thus far our analysis has aimed at explaining the increasing gap between the advanced and backward sector in the dual economy. This has been the main aim of this paper. " The closing of the gap " is a tantalizing problem but it involves many new considerations, and it must be left for another occasion. Nevertheless, I would like, at this juncture, to offer a few brief remarks in that connection.

I suspect, that in part, the increasing gap and the growth of the advanced sector contain the seeds that eventually lead to the closing of the gap. This happens when more and more markets within the economy become close to being national markets. That is to say, as the economy advances, more and more industries in which there are considerable economies of scale, become important. Also, the average size of firm increases simultaneously. However, the mere existence of economies of scale is not sufficient to create a national market. Economies of scale must become sufficiently large so that their significance is greater than the transportation costs that have to be overcome in supplying national, or almost national, markets. Now, as the advanced sector grows, and as more transportation facilities are built all around (and transportation facilities are themselves subject to economies of scale), a point will be reached at which the economies of scale are more significant than differential transportation costs, and as a consequence, locational advantages other than closeness to markets (or to inputs) gain primacy in determining plant location. When this occurs, the wage differentials between the advanced and the backward sectors come into play, and as a consequence, there is a greater inducement for such industries to locate in the backward sector. At the same time, the wage differential induces more and more workers from the backward sector to move to the advanced sector. All in all, we can readily see that a point will be reached in such a process at which the tendency towards equalization sets in.

6. Summary and Conclusions

Others have used indivisibilities as a means to explain under-employment and the utilization of primitive techniques in backward areas (7). But I suspect that my approach differs somewhat from that of others. In the first place, I am primarily interested in showing that indivisibilities may affect the inducement to invest. Second, a great deal of my emphasis is on technological progress and the fact that the nature of technological progress may *differentially*

(7) See especially the works by Eckhaus and Hirschman, cited previously.

16

affect the inducement to invest in different sectors. In addition, my analysis is not, strictly speaking, of the comparative static type. Rather, what I have in mind are alternative dynamic process analyses of a kind where in the advanced sector the process, which in this case, not limited by the inducement to invest, succeeds in yielding a certain rate of growth in the long run. In the backward sector, the same process must proceed either at a slower rate, or practically not at all, because of the stifling effect that I have attributed to indivisibilities, to the locus of technical progress, and as a consequence, to the lower inducement to invest. I have tried to suggest that the nature of the production function and of technological progress may serve, in the extreme case, as a bottleneck to the inducement to invest, and in the less extreme case, as a factor that stifles, in some degree, the inducement to invest in the backward sector as compared with the advanced sector. In addition, we have considered other elements which are closely linked to the inducement to invest, and which operate in a differential manner between two sectors. These were, differences in productive knowledge, differences in scale and in the capacity to take advantage of new techniques because of scale limitations, and differences in the availability of complementary inputs.

Finally, let us review briefly some of the initial assumptions and elements in the analysis. First, we assumed that the relative position of the two sectors, at the historical point at which we break into the analysis, is one in which a gap already exists. We suggested reasons for the gap to increase. We emphasized the fact that many more productive alternatives are likely to be available in the advanced sector (where the capital-labor ratio is high) than is the case in the backward sector. In addition, we assumed, what it is also likely to be true historically, that the size-variety of firms is greater in the advanced than in the backward sector. In other words, the backward sector is more likely to be handicapped in its expansion by the size limitations of existing plants.

Before closing, a word should be said about entrepreneurship. It is often argued that entrepreneurship is lacking in the backward sector. Whether or not entrepreneurs are in some sense less readily available in the backward sector I cannot say at present. However, it is of interest to note that our analysis would suggest one conclusion with respect to entrepreneurship. The variety of entrepreneurial opportunities, as well as the number of such opportunities, is clearly likely to be greater in that sector in which the inducement to invest is greater — namely, in the advanced sector. As a consequence, since there is usually a possibility of entrepreneurial mobility, we would expect that entrepreneurs from the backward sector would migrate to the advanced sector in search of such opportunities. Thus, even if intrinsic entrepreneurial talent were, at the outset, evenly distributed between the two sectors, this talent would cease to be so distributed in view of the inducements established by the dual economy.

Berkeley   HARVEY LEIBENSTEIN

[18]

THE PROPORTIONALITY CONTROVERSY AND THE THEORY OF PRODUCTION

By Harvey Leibenstein

In the theory of the firm much is made of the observation that certain factors are lumpy. In fact, many writers have gone so far as to attribute both increasing and decreasing returns solely to this phenomenon. Professor Chamberlin challenged this view in a well known article, but defenders of what may be called the "proportionalist position" were quick to reply.[1] (By the "proportionalist position" we refer to the notion that, given divisibility, the multiplication or division of all factors by a constant will yield proportional returns; in other words the idea that, given divisibility, production functions are necessarily homogeneous.)[2] A recent article by Messrs. Whitin and Peston reinforces the Chamberlinian view by describing "several situations where the rational entrepreneur will vary certain factors less than proportionately with output."[3] But in these discussions an important methodological point has been missed. In this note we shall explore this point and show how it can help to clarify some aspects of the problem.

One of the reasons why controversies on theoretical issues are often difficult to settle is that the theory, in its development towards greater and greater generality, becomes so terse that it does not permit certain significant distinctions to be made. As a result implicit assumptions go unrecognized and appear to lead inevitably to what are in fact wrong conclusions. We suggest that this is the case with the conventional theory of production of the firm. When the necessary distinctions are made, some of the central issues in the controversy are clarified, and we shall see that, once these distinctions are accepted, the "proportionalist position" becomes untenable.

1. E. H. Chamberlin, "Proportionality, Divisibility and Economies of Scale," this *Journal*, Feb. 1948, pp. 229–62; "Comments" by A. N. McLeod and F. H. Hahn, "Reply" by E. H. Chamberlin, *ibid.*, Feb. 1949, pp. 128–43. The first article is incorporated in *The Theory of Monopolistic Competition*, 6th ed., as Appendix B.
2. What the outcome of the debate has been is not at all clear. If the writer can judge on the basis of conversations he has had with some economists on the problem, he must conclude that the "proportionalist position" is still held quite tenaciously in some quarters.
3. T. M. Whitin and M. H. Peston, "Random Variations, Risk, and Returns to Scale," this *Journal*, Nov. 1954, pp. 603–12.

619

620

1. *The Issue.* According to the proportionalist argument if the factors of production are infinitely divisible then this inevitably leads to long-run constant costs. Since there is some optimum combination of the factors that will yield an output at lowest average unit cost, then, given infinite divisibility, it follows that we could obtain greater or lesser outputs at the same average cost simply by dividing or multiplying the optimum combination by an appropriate constant. At first blush this appears to be an eminently reasonable point of view. Yet it is quite incorrect.

2. *The Meaning of Factor Divisibility.* Before embarking on our analysis proper we have to indicate what is meant by a fractional unit of a factor. Assuming that all units are homogeneous, the question that arises is how to define half units where it is not meaningful to divide a unit physically. In this case we may, for the sake of argument, accept what appears to be the "proportionalist position" and define half units in terms of efficiency. Namely, one hundred half-men are equivalent to fifty whole men, and this equivalence is in terms of what they can do. Thus, the entrepreneur who hires one hundred half-men, is just as well off as he who hires fifty whole men or two hundred quarter-men, etc. In other words, our definition implies that *under similar circumstances* fractional units, no matter how finely divided, operate just as efficiently as whole units. Surely this meets the proportionalist ideal of perfect divisibility, and yet we shall see that proportional returns to scale do not follow.

Before presenting the elements of our model two aspects of the problem must be made explicit. First, it must be understood that the controversy is about the divisibility of *factors* and its consequences, and not about *other* aspects of the productive process. In other words, when writers on the subject speak of the divisibility of factors we assume that we are to take them literally and that they *are* speaking about factors of production. Second, we assume that the theory we are considering is not merely a formal matter but that it has to do with the productive process as it exists in the real world, although the theory may abstract from many aspects of that process.

3. *The Production Model.* The theory of production is in terms of two polar categories, inputs and outputs. While it is true that writers on production theory are aware that there is more to the process than merely combining inputs and obtaining outputs, and they sometimes allude to intervening elements, it nevertheless remains the case that the formal theory is usually presented in terms of inputs and outputs. For many problems the input-output approach is

sufficient. But with respect to the controversy under discussion a model in which the intervening categories are made explicit is the more adequate.

Recalling that the issue at stake is the contention that complete divisibility is a sufficient condition for constant long-run average costs, it follows that to disprove this proposition we need conceive of merely a single possible case in which this is not so. Thus, if we can visualize a model of the production process in which the proposition at issue need not hold, then we have proven our case.

And now to our model. The definitions of the basic categories of our model follow:

(1) A *commodity* is the entity that is the object of the productive process, and that has a specific set of attributes or specifications.

(2) An *activity* is our primitive concept. It refers to those necessary acts carried out by a factor, or functions of a factor, necessary in the productive process. We define a set of related activities as an *operation*.

(3) A *process* is any specific set of operations used to produce the commodity in question. There may be a number of possible alternative processes.

(4) A *factor* is an entity, units of which can be purchased on the market, that has the capacity to carry out one or more activities.

(5) By a *firm* we refer to the entity that purchases factors, creates commodities, and sells commodities.

Our vision of the productive process is this: The firm purchases all the necessary factors. The firm's purpose in doing so is to create some quantity of a commodity which can be defined in terms of a set of attributes. The attributes are created by a set of operations. We refer to any specific set of operations as a process. The operations are performed by or made up of activities. Our notion of an activity is a rather broad one so that it contains any contribution to the creation of the commodity. For example, we conceive of some specific raw material, say a piece of wood, as capable of performing the activity of becoming the necessary physical matter out of which the commodity, say a bench, is made.

Since we assume perfect divisibility, the firm can purchase its factors in any conceivable combination. For some given output the commodity is produced at minimum costs for that output and with a specific ratio of the factors. The question is whether the firm can also produce any other output at the same cost per unit if the factors are purchased in exactly the same proportion as the alternative out-

622

puts. The answer depends on whether the quantity of any activity
that has to be carried on is a function of the output of the commodity.
Now clearly in any conceivable productive process *not all activities or
operations need be functions of output*. Indeed, it is unlikely that
there is any modern productive process in which *all* the activities or
operations depend entirely on the quantity produced. Once we
accept this possibility then we can quite readily see that perfect
divisibility of *factors* (provided we accept the distinctions between
factors, activities, and operations) is not a sufficient condition for
long-run constant costs.

The number of times any activity has to be performed may vary
directly with the amount of any given factor that is hired, the variety
of the factors, the number of operations, or the number of other
activities. The relationship need not be a proportional one. For
example, the activities of starting and stopping may be functions of
the number and variety of operations that are performed. Nor need
we assume that any particular activity need always be carried on
for any particular output. Some activities may have to be carried
on regardless of output while other activities and operations may be
required when some other variable in the production process reaches
a certain minimum size, while still others may grow or decline in a
nonproportional fashion to other variables. The extent to which the
condition just alluded to holds depends on the nature of the productive process.

The critical reader may assert that all we have done is simply
to shift our grounds from lumpy factors to "lumpy activities" and
operations. But this is not the point. For what we come out with
is that there is something inherent in the productive process and not
in the divisibility of factors that is the cause of nonhomogeneous
production functions.

Furthermore, we have not really shifted ground by changing
the definition of a factor, for the issue is one of *meaningfulness* and
not of definition. There is meaning to a "lumpy factor" but there
is *no* meaning to a "lumpy activity" or to a "divisible activity."
Consider, for example, the production process of publishing a book.
One of the activities is proofreading. Once it is done it need be done
no more, regardless of the number printed, the thickness of the pages,
or any other quality of the book. It is meaningless to say that proofreading is a lumpy or indivisible activity. It is simply an activity
determined by the technical requirements of producing a book. The
fact that it has to be done only once irrespective of the number of

copies produced is entirely unrelated to the bulkiness or divisibility of the factors of production employed. It is just as meaningless to half proofread something as it is to half kick a ball. You either kick it or you do not. An activity is either performed or it is not. The fact of its performance has nothing to do with the size of the ball, the size of the kicker, or their divisibility or lack of it. Something is not proofread if only half the pages are read. In a similar vein to "half-switch" on a light is a meaningless idea. Without belaboring this notion further it should be clear that some combinations of words simply have no meaning and it is a methodological error to act as though they had. By making inadequate distinctions, or by leaving certain elements implicit, some writers seem not to have realized that they were indirectly advocating combinations of ideas that really make no sense.

An objection that may be raised is that our definition of a factor involves an unnecessary distinction; that the firm really purchases the activities performed, and therefore, the activities and the factor are one and the same thing.

In reply we argue that it is surely legitimate to distinguish what is in fact distinguishable. The factors of production that are hired in the market are in fact not the same thing as the uses to which they are put. The factors may be divisible and yet the activities that they perform are discreet. It may take multiple (or fractional) units of a factor to carry out an activity. Under such circumstances we do not violate the assumption of the divisibility of a factor.

But even if we think of factors solely in terms of the bundle of activities performed it does not change the basic argument. The crucial distinction to be recognized is that the nature of the factors supplied must be separated conceptually from the nature of the activities *needed* in the production process. The nature of the factors supplied is determined by conditions outside the production method under consideration. For example, the attributes and specifications of the commodity need not, and do not, determine the characteristics of the factors. But, the attributes and specifications of the commodity do determine, in part at least, the activities and operations necessary for the production of that commodity. That is, the activities and operations required in the production process are determined, to some extent, by technical considerations. Furthermore, the technical considerations may be such that they require operations and activities to be performed that are nonproportional to output.

In order to sharpen the argument it may be useful to classify

624

activities into three categories. (1) Direct proportional activities: those activities which are involved in operations on the commodity in question, and where the quantity of the particular activity is proportional to output. (2) Direct nonproportional activities: these are activities that are directly connected with producing the commodity but where the amount of the activity is not proportional to output. (3) Indirect activities: here we have in mind activities such as personnel administration, record keeping, and others that do not involve contact with the commodity but are necessary to the operation of the firm.

Now the implicit assumption of the "proportionalist position" must be that if factors were completely divisible then *all* activities would be direct proportional activities. This implies that all direct nonproportional activities and all indirect activities carried on by firms at the present time are entirely due to the indivisibilities of factors. But this last implication of the "proportionalist position" is most difficult to believe if we consider some of the specific nonproportional activities that have to be carried on by firms. For example, such activities as production planning, the issuance of orders to personnel, keeping records, the channelling and collecting of information internal to the firm, the channelling and collecting of information external to the firm, the administration of personnel, the administration of credit and finance, as well as a host of similar control activities need not be, and probably are not, directly proportional to output. Many of these activities have to be carried on regardless of output and one cannot see how the fact that factors were divisible would either eliminate their need or transform them to proportional activities. Consider factors that have some degree of durability. Surely the appropriate depreciation formula would not always be of the form $D = NQ$, where D is the amount of depreciation and Q the quantity produced. The "proportionalist" view would imply not only that all depreciation costs are user costs, but also that user costs are always proportional to output if factors are divisible. But the fact of the matter is that the physical nature of durable goods is not of this kind. Some depreciation takes place for reasons other than use. The case is especially clear with respect to obsolescence. The risks of obsolescence, and the fact of obsolescence, surely do not depend on the divisibility of factors. Another interesting possibility is a chemical process where a catalytic agent is involved. Again, the amount of the catalytic agent need not be proportional to output. This is a matter of the laws of chemistry and not of economics or of

625

the divisibility of factors. Other interesting examples in this vein, especially for cases where risk and random variations are involved, are mentioned in the article by Whitin and Peston.[4]

In sum our argument boils down to the fact that many production processes necessitate indirect activities and operations, as well as direct nonproportional activities. The issue at stake is not a matter of definition. Essentially, it is both an empirical matter and a question about the meaningfulness of ideas. The empirical aspect depends on what the firm has to do in order to produce a commodity and maintain the firm as a continuing entity, and this does not depend entirely on the divisibility of factors. It does depend on the objective nature of commodities and production activities, and on the technical requirements of production processes, which in turn depend in part on the laws of physics and chemistry and on the arts of engineering and administration.

The lack of meaningfulness of some of the assertions about the consequences of factor divisibility have not been recognized heretofore because they were based on a theory in which there are inadequate distinctions. As a result it was not recognized that certain implicit elements in the argument implied combinations of ideas that were in essence nonsensical. By breaking down the theory into more elements we are enabled to make these necessary distinctions and thus bring to the fore the meaningless nature of some of the arguments. Specifically, we have seen that while it may often be sensible to speak of the divisibility of the factors it is quite meaningless to think even implicitly in terms of divisible activities. And since activities need not be proportional to output if factors are divisible, then factor divisibility need not lead to constant returns to scale.

HARVEY LEIBENSTEIN.

UNIVERSITY OF CALIFORNIA,
BERKELEY

4. Whitin and Peston, *op. cit.*

Part VI
Welfare

[19]

NOTES ON WELFARE ECONOMICS AND THE THEORY OF DEMOCRACY [1]

WELFARE economics is an apparatus of thought for dealing with the choice of economic policies. Strangely enough, at a time when there is a great deal of intervention by democratic governments in the economic life of the community there is almost no use of this particular apparatus. (This is in sharp contrast to the employment of macro-economic theory in the analysis of public policies.) Why should this be the case? It is of interest to consider at least one important aspect that may have a bearing on the matter: namely, the relation between a common interpretation of democracy—non-minority rule—and contemporary welfare economics criteria. This is the problem that we shall pursue here. In doing so we will also touch on the use of voting in this connection, since voting is a customary procedure in determining degree of consent and in the operation of non-minority rule. [2]

Of course a great deal has been written on voting and welfare economics in connection with Professor Arrow's justly famous " impossibility theorem." The emphasis there is on the fact that a social-welfare function, constructed by aggregating individual preference orderings, and that simultaneously met certain standards suggested by Arrow, did not turn out to be transitive in all possible cases. My concern here is with the somewhat larger and less technical question: namely, whether the non-minority rule interpretation of democracy is consistent with economic choice criteria implicit in the normative aspects of micro-economic theory to the extent that these are made explicit by modern welfare economics. Surely economists in a democracy must face the question whether or not the social choice rules derivable from democratic ideals are consistent with the prescriptions derivable from welfare economics. Despite the possibility that in some cases non-transitive social choices may appear, I expect that we can agree on some compromise rules, albeit somewhat arbitrary ones, for deciding such cases. In other words, I suggest that for present purposes it may be of interest to put the possible non-transitivity aspect of the problem in the

---

[1] The author is indebted to Professors Julius Margolis, Robin Marris, Benjamin Ward and Robert Dorfman for helpful comments after reading various versions of this essay.

[2] On the political implications of contemporary welfare economics, Kenneth Arrow's *Social Choice and Individual Values* (1), and the number of articles that it has inspired, is, of course, basic. A recent paper by James Buchanan, " Positive Economics, Welfare Economics, and Political Economy " (2), which looks at the problem from a different viewpoint than that taken here, is of special interest. In the same connection, see also Gordon Tullock's " Problems of Majority Voting " (6). On the interpretation of the meaning of democracy, see Robert A. Dahl, *A Preface to Democratic Theory* (7), especially Chapter II on " Populist Democracy." For further references on the meaning of democracy, see Dahl (7, pp. 36–7).

background and concentrate on the issue of the consistency of non-minority rule and welfare economics.

The issue is especially important if we look upon welfare economics as a formal interpretation of at least some of the prescriptive suggestions contained in micro-economic theory. Certainly some of the words and phrases employed in micro-economics; for example, " efficiency," " the optimal allocation of resources " and " an increase of income " are value-laden terms. Looking at the matter from this viewpoint, it appears that welfare economics has made a significant contribution, since it has helped us to clarify what we could mean by such terms, as well as to suggest their limitations. But this process of clarification could be carried further by comparing the social choice criteria developed by welfare economics with those taken from the fields of either ethics or politics. Such clarification is especially important if we are ever to apply economics to the actual determination of social policies. This paper is intended as a step in that direction.

In the usual approach, concern over the " share of the pie " (income distribution problems) is separated from the concern with the " size of the pie." This separation may bias the results. Whether or not this is so, it is something that is worth investigation. Consequently, I begin with the assumption that people care *simultaneously* about the relative position of their income as well as the absolute level. Although many of the notions that follow have been stated before, as far as I am aware they have not been considered to any great extent in connection with the latter assumption.

The word " Notes " in the title suggests the very modest aim of this paper—to consider some elements of a very large problem area, on many aspects of which the literature is large and growing.

I. PARETO COMPARISONS AND CONSENT AREAS

The underlying notion of contemporary welfare economics is " The Pareto Comparison." If between two states of the economy, S and T, some people are better off in S than in T and no one is worse off, then S represents a " higher welfare level " than T, and S is preferred to T. " Better off " and " worse off " are usually interpreted in terms of bundles of commodities, income or some other economic index. If some people are better off and some are worse off in S than T, then S and T are non-comparable states. Schemes such as the compensation principle are techniques for transforming some non-comparable situations into comparable ones.

In this connection it may be worth noting that there is a possible ambiguity created by the language often employed. For example, it is sometimes stated that point S is Pareto superior to T if at least one person " feels " better off in S and no one feels worse off. What is not clear in such a statement is whether in determining " feeling better off " we take into account how the person feels about the *distribution* of income. However, the literature almost always implies that in making such comparisons we visualise individuals who consider only the magnitude of their own income and not their relative share in the income pie.

Now we can distinguish clearly three types of comparisons: (1) *Pure* Pareto comparisons in which each individual takes into account his own income but no one else's; (2) " the share of the pie " comparisons in which each individual takes into account the income distribution from a relative point of view but not the absolute magnitude of his income; and (3) the " compromise Pareto comparison " [1] in which individuals take into account both the absolute magnitude of their income *and* their relative income position. To each type of comparison we may visualise indifference curves which embody the same ideas. Indeed, we will now develop the notion of the compromise Pareto indifference curves that take into account the distributive aspects of the problem.

Most people are not likely to care only about their share of the pie, nor by the same token are they likely to be entirely indifferent to the distributive aspect. Such common emotions and considerations as envy, compassion, relative status and so on do determine in part the utility that we derive from the outcome of economic events. To get a more accurate reflection of how people feel, we should include both the size of the income [2] as well as the distributive element in determining an individual's indifference curves. In other words, within limits we might expect an individual to be willing to substitute a greater absolute income for a smaller share of the pie, and vice versa. Fig. 1 illustrates this possibility for individual A. We start with the state x in Fig. 1. a_1 represents the *pure* Pareto indifference curve and a_2 the " share of the pie " indifference curve for the individual. Since, by definition, A does not care about B's income in the case of the pure Pareto indifference curve, a_1x is a locus of points of A's income and B's income between which A is indifferent. Similarly, if A cares only about the " share of the pie," then the ray xa_2 represents the locus of points in which A's proportionate share of the pie is the same. xx_1 is the indifference curve representing the compromise between a greater income and a greater share of the pie. He is indifferent between all points on that line.

We now turn to compare the implications of " compromise " indifference curves as against pure Pareto indifference curves. Consider Fig. 2 below. Once again x is our initial point. a_1x is the pure Pareto indifference curve

---

[1] I use this because a better term does not readily come to mind. It suggests roughly that individuals compromise their desire for absolute income in order to gain a superior *relative* income status. On the fact that many people do care about their relative income status, see Barbara Wootton, *The Social Foundations of Wage Policy* (8, pp. 28–34).

[2] In what follows we will use real income as our economic index. We frankly by-pass some of the subtle problems that enter in the definition of real income. For our purposes y_2 will be deemed to be a higher income than y_1 if every bundle of goods that could be purchased for y_1 could also be purchased for y_2, but if every bundle of goods that could be purchased for y_2 could *not* be purchased for y_1.

302   THE ECONOMIC JOURNAL   [JUNE

for person A, and similarly b_1x is the pure Pareto indifference curve for person B. All points on or above the curve a_1xb_1, other than the point x itself, are Pareto superior points as compared to x. But all such points are not superior points from the point of view of our compromise indifference curves. Only points bounded on the left or below by the figure a_2xb_2 are

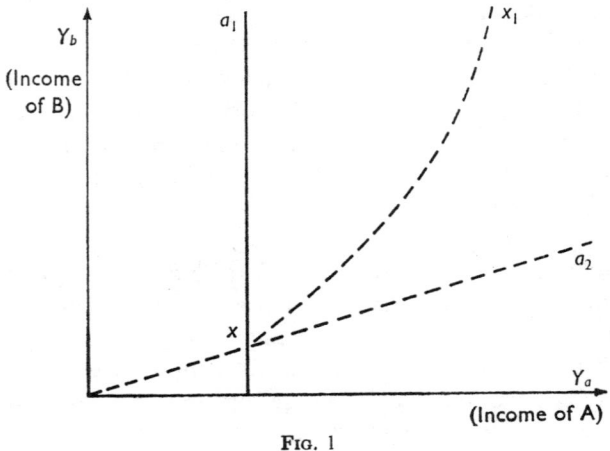

FIG. 1

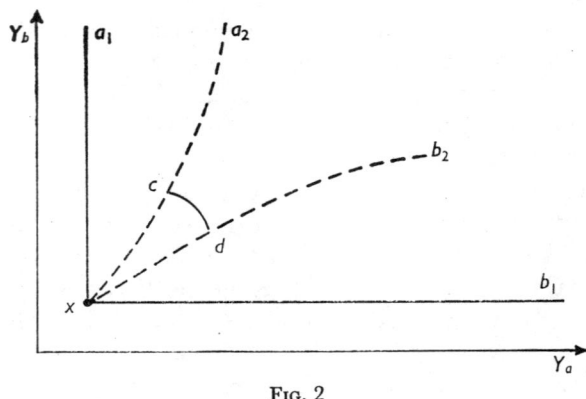

FIG. 2

really superior points to x when feelings about income distribution are simultaneously taken into account. Now, the set of points that are bounded by the compromise indifference curves (a_2xb_2) may be said to form a consent area. That is, both individuals agree that any of these points are superior to, or as good as, the initial point x. The compromise consent area is obviously narrower than the pure Pareto consent area bounded by a_1xb_1. Henceforth we will refer only to the compromise consent areas as the " consent area," since in determining consent it appears proper to take into account feelings about equity and relative status, which, after all, do enter into people's actual utility functions. Points in a consent area are obviously points to which both parties would not be averse to move.

In passing we note that if *cd* (Fig. 2) is a portion of a new income possibility curve, then both parties would consent to a shift from *x* to a point on *cd*. Of course, points on *cd* closer to b_2 are better for person A, and those closer to a_2 are better for person B. If both parties could agree on a point on *cd*, then that should be the point they should choose, and they should make arrangements that would enable them to reach that point. But since between any two points on *cd* one point is to the benefit of one party and at the expense of the other, they may have great difficulty, or find it impossible to reach agreement. Yet agreement is superior to remaining at the point *x*. In view of this, it may be sensible for them to pick a third party (*e.g.*, government) to choose a point on *cd* for them, or to establish a procedure for reaching such a point (*e.g.*, a market mechanism), and agree

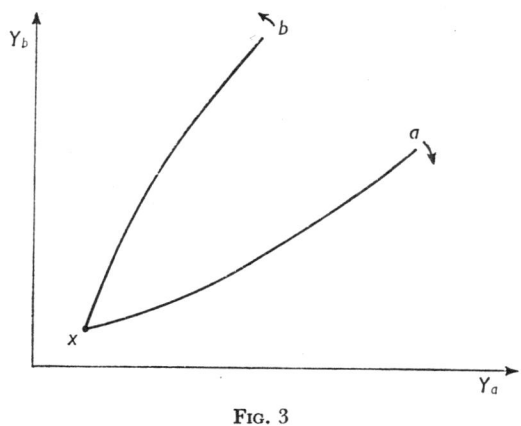

Fig. 3

in advance to abide by the decision. This is a technique that has many precedents, and one that is well known in labour disputes. Here, clearly, is a possible role for governmental activity—to make such arrangements or rules or to set up general procedures so that the parties affected can reach superior points within their consent areas. But will a consent area necessarily exist?

Whether or not there is a mutual consent area will depend in part on how people feel about the existing state in which they find themselves. This is a point that seems to be ignored, for the most part, in the literature. To examine this question, let us continue for a moment with our two-person world. In the situation illustrated in Fig. 3 there is clearly no mutual consent area. Person B would accept points on *xb* or to the left of *xb*, while A would accept only points on *xa* or to the right of *xa*. Clearly there is no point that would raise the incomes of both parties on which they would agree. But why should this ever be the case?

Such possibilities may appear reasonable if we consider how one might behave if one is motivated by feelings of envy, inferiority, revenge and so on.[1] Suppose that A feels that he is twice as productive as B, and that therefore he should receive twice B's income, and, in turn, suppose that B feels that he is just as good as A. If x is a position in which they have equal incomes, then A would certainly be unhappy with x, and his feelings of unhappiness and perhaps revenge might make him unwilling to move to a higher income position where his relative income status did not improve. Another, and perhaps more likely possibility, is that if the change gave him a very large increase in income, he might move; but for a small increase he would not move *unless* his relative position improved (see Fig. 4). Such attitudes are not entirely unknown.

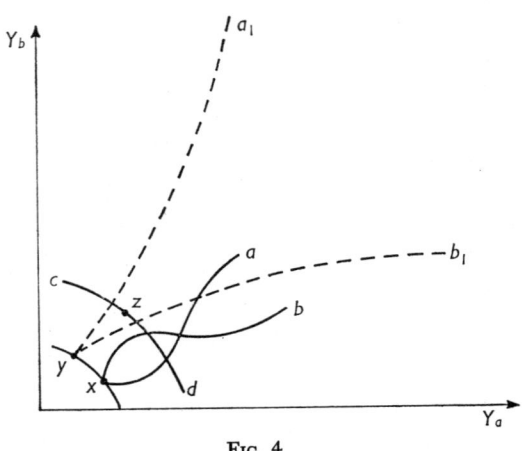

FIG. 4

Fig. 4 (curve *axb*) illustrates the possibility where there is no mutual consent area for small increases in income but where there is one for large increases in income. In addition, it is worth noting that the income possibility curve may not be in the mutual consent area. Feelings about the current state may not only determine the magnitude of the consent area, but the accompanying attitudes of envy and regard for relative status may in turn also determine how people feel about the income distributions associated with potential changes. It is possible that some income redistributions may enlarge the majority consent areas even though they do not increase national income. Such enlargements may be desirable because they ease the path for future improvements. In other words, we visualise changes that are made up of two steps: one step that enlarges the consent area and another that takes us into the enlarged consent area on a higher income possibility curve. Fig. 4 also illustrates this possibility. The shift

[1] Professor Melvin W. Reder mentions this possibility, *en passant*. See K. Boulding, " Welfare Economics," comment by M. W. Reder in *A Survey of Contemporary Economics* (3).

from x to y enlarges the consent area (note new consent area a_1yb_1), while the shift from y to z gets us on a higher income possibility curve.

II. Many-person Consent Areas

In a many-person world our compromise indifference curve will depend in part on the income distribution of all other individuals. Of course, I may feel quite strongly about the relative shares received by some individuals and almost indifferent to those received by others. For example, I may feel strongly about my relative income status *vis-à-vis* other members of my profession, but feel much less strongly about my relative income status and that of people in some other occupation.

A state of the economy, for our purposes, can be represented by a vector or point in which there is one place for everyone's income. Let $x_0 = (y_1, y_2, \ldots y_t, \ldots y_n)$ be such a point, where y_t is the income of the ith person, for all i. Suppose that x_0 is the present state. For a typical individual, let us call him individual A, all possible states can be divided into three sets: the set of points that are from A's viewpoint inferior to x_0, the set of points that are as good as x_0 and the set of points that are superior to x_0. Now, clearly an individual would not agree to shifts from x_0 into his inferior set, but he would consent to shifts from x_0 into his *superior* set, or into his " as good as " set. Thus we have for each individual a consent set [1] whose elements are points representing states of the economy, such that the individual in question would consent to a change from x_0 to a point in his consent set.[2]

Each person has his consent set. The intersection of two consent sets would give us a two-person mutual consent area. In a similar way, we can conceive of three-person mutual consent areas, and an n-person mutual consent area *provided*, of course, *that the intersections involved are non-empty*. To illustrate what we have in mind, let the points in a circle in Fig. 5 (*a*) below represent the set of consent points of an individual. Suppose there are only three people in our population. Then the intersection of the three-consent area (the shaded area in the figure) is a three-person mutual consent area.

To avoid complicating matters unnecessarily, we should limit ourselves to states of the world that are possible: *i.e.*, to the income feasibility function. By the income feasibility function we mean the set of all achievable incomes and achievable distributions that are possible with given resources. Of course, what is achievable depends on permissible (institutional) changes

---

[1] The reader should remember that, except where it is otherwise stated, each individual is assumed to care about his relative income position as well as his absolute income position.

[2] Unless otherwise stated, we assume in the rest of the article that x_0 is not Pareto superior to all points, for all individuals, in the feasible point set. If x_0 were Pareto superior to all points, for all individuals, then everyone would prefer x_0 to every feasible alternative, and as a consequence, everyone's consent area would be empty. The choice problem in the latter case is obviously trivial. In order to have a problem of interest we assume that at the very least there are always some non-empty individual consent areas.

that can be brought about. Unless otherwise stated, the reader should assume in the discussion that follows that we have in mind only the set of *feasible* points within a mutual consent area when we use the term consent area.

We can distinguish at least six possible sets of points:

> (1) universal consent points;
> (2) maximal consent points;
> (3) majority consent points;
> (4) minority consent points;
> (5) universal *preference* points;
> (6) majority *preference* points.

(1) The universal consent points are those states of the system that *everyone* would agree would be superior to or as good as the existing state. For instance, in Fig. 5 (*a*) a point in the shaded area would be a universal consent point in a three-person world. However, there may not always be a feasible universal consent point.

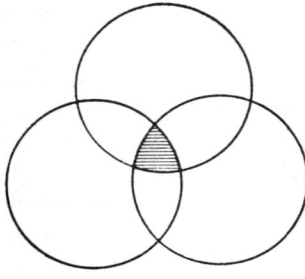
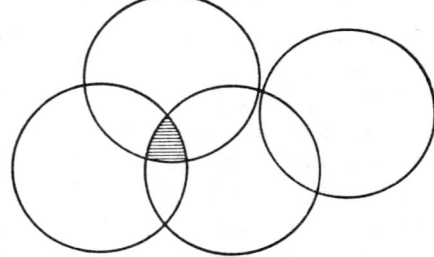

Fig. 5 (*a*).   Fig. 5 (*b*).

(2) There must still be a maximal consent point. By this we mean the point, or set of points, that the greatest number of people would agree is superior to or as good as the existing point. In Fig. 5 (*b*), which is limited to a four-person world, there is no universal consent point. However, points in the shaded area are maximal consent points. They are three-person consent points, while the points outside the shaded area are either two-person or one-person consent points.

(3) Majority consent points are those considered by a majority as superior to or as good as the existing point.

(4) Minority consent points are, of course, points that only a minority of the population would agree to be superior to or as good as the existing state.

(5) Among the universal consent points some would be preferred to others within that class. While everyone agrees that all points in that class are superior to or as good as the existing point, they may not be indifferent between these points. We can partition the universal consent set into two

subsets $\bar{U}$ and $\underline{U}$; the subset $\bar{U}$ contains the universal preference points, if there are any, and $\underline{U}$ contains the other universal consent points. A point $\bar{u}$ is a universal preference point if: (i) there is no other point (except another universal preference point) that some people prefer to $\bar{u}$, and (ii) with regard to any other point (that is not a universal preference point) at least one person prefers $\bar{u}$ to it. To illustrate what we have in mind, consider a case in which there are five universal consent points. Let us denote these points by u_1, u_2, u_3, u_4 and u_5. Now, by definition, everyone prefers u_1 to x_0—the existing point. Similarly, everyone prefers u_2 to x_0, and the same holds for u_4 and u_5. By $u_1 P u_3$, we will mean that u_1 is preferred to u_3. Now suppose that:

$u_1 P u_3$ by all individuals, $\qquad u_2 P u_3$ by all individuals,

$u_1 P u_4$ by all individuals, $\qquad u_2 P u_4$ by all individuals,

$u_1 P u_5$ by all individuals, $\qquad u_2 P u_5$ by all individuals.

But suppose that u_1 is not preferred to u_2 by all individuals, and that u_2 is not preferred to u_1 by all individuals. Then, we call u_1 and u_2 universal preference points. They are preferred by everyone to the other three points in the universal consent set.

(6) We designate as majority *preference* points those within the majority consent set that a majority of the population prefers to or feels that they are as good as any other points in the set. Suppose that m_1, m_2, m_3, m_4, m_5 are the points in the majority consent set. Then, $m_1 R x_0$ (m_1 is preferred to x_0 or thought to be as good as x_0) by a majority of the population, and similarly, $m_2 R x_0$, $m_3 R x_0$, $m_4 R x_0$ and $m_5 R x_0$ by a majority of the population. But between members of the majority consent set the following might hold:

$m_1 R m_2$ by a majority

$m_1 R m_3$ by a majority

$m_1 R m_4$ by a majority

$m_1 R m_5$ by a majority

In this case m_1 is the majority preference point.

Now that we have our six classes of points, let us define Pareto superior points and Pareto optimal points. We will want to compare as we proceed our various classes of points with the ideas of Pareto superiority and Pareto optimality.

Pareto Superior: A point y is Pareto superior to another point x if at least some people prefer y to x and no one prefers x to y.

Pareto Optimal: A point is a Pareto optimal point if there is no other feasible point that is Pareto superior to it.

Now, only universal consent points can be Pareto superior points to x_0, the existing state. For if a point is not a universal consent point, then at least one person does not feel that it is superior to or as good as the existing state, and hence at least one person will prefer the existing state to the point in question.   Now we can show that a universal preference point is a Pareto optimal point if we make the usual assumptions of connectivity and transitivity with respect to individual preferences.[1]   Also, Pareto optimal points must be universal consent points if the initial state x_0 is not Pareto optimal.

III. Democratic Choice and Majority Preference Rule

How should we judge democratic choice?   The answer must depend, of course, on what our interpretation of democracy happens to be.   It is probably reasonable to argue that most people would think of democratic rule as at least *non*-minority rule.   Even though this may not be a sufficient condition for democracy, it may be conceived as a necessary one.   In any event, let us assume for the time being that by democracy we mean non-minority rule.[2]   With this in mind, I want to show in this section that this interpretation of democracy implies that the social choices that occur must be majority preference points where such points exist.

If it is correct that majority preference points are those that should occur if the choice-making machinery is democratic, then we could examine whether any choice-making machinery, including the mechanism for making economic choices, does in fact result in the choice of majority preference points.   In addition, we could compare the actual choice-making machinery with " Pareto criteria."   We could also compare the " Pareto criteria " with our interpretation of the correct democratic criteria.

A slightly different way of looking at the matter is to ask the following: does democracy imply doing things that can win as much support as possible when compared with the existing state, as against those alternatives which win less support but which nevertheless carry a majority?   In other words, does democracy imply majority preference rule?   In the following I want to argue that if we agree that non-minority rule is a necessary condition for democratic choice, then this implies majority preference rule rather than maximal consent.   More important, maximal consent procedures that are not consistent with majority preference rule will be shown to be forms of minority rule.   In the instances to be considered the maximal consent points referred to are also assumed to be majority consent points.

To begin with, a crucial distinction must be made between maximal consent and majority consent points.   Maximal consent points are not always the points preferred by the majority.   Consider this case: the feasible alternative points are A, B and C, and the existing point is C. Suppose that A is a universal consent point so that 100% of the population prefers A to C, while only 60% prefers B to C.   But the same 60% may

---

[1] See Appendix I.   Also note that, since we are employing *compromise* Pareto comparisons, the consent areas that emerge are likely to be much narrower than under *pure* comparisons.   That is, the chances of universal agreement for a move to a new point are likely to be considerably less if we take into account feelings about the distributive element.

[2] In a later section we will relax this assumption somewhat.   See Dahl (7), *op. cit.*, on this point.

prefer B to A, and hence the majority consent point B is preferred by the majority to the universal and maximal consent point A.

Whether or not a certain choice-making mechanism will turn out to be democratic, according to our interpretation, will depend: (*a*) on the alternatives that get on the ballot explicitly and implicitly,[1] and (*b*) on the system of scoring—that is, the rules that determine among the alternatives on the ballot which alternative is the winner. In many voting procedures, such as bills in a legislature or a referendum, a single alternative is offered, and if carried by the majority it displaces the existing state of affairs. Such procedures are obviously equivalent to pitting the alternative to be voted upon against the existing state. Now, let us suppose that the alternative that gets on the ballot is the one that the proponents think has the maximum chance of carrying; that is, it is the one that will receive the greatest vote against its implicit rival, the existing state. This, clearly, is equivalent to having a rule that the maximal consent point should be the one adopted.

Consider the following: suppose that out of five alternatives, A, B, C, D and E, that A is a maximal consent point, B is a majority preference point and C is the current state of the system. Granted rule in accordance with maximal consent, point A will be adopted. But once A is adopted, A then becomes the current state of the system; and B is a majority consent point with regard to A. But B may or may not be a maximal consent point with regard to A. Suppose that both D and E have a higher degree of consent than B with regard to A. Then the possible sequence of choices is as follows: D is adopted over A and it becomes the current point, then E is adopted over D and it becomes the current point. But in the end, B, by the definition of a majority preference point, must be adopted over E. Thus, any

---

[1] How things get on the ballot is obviously important. If a majority-preference point, say, the point M, cannot get on the ballot, then a democratic choice cannot be made. But let us assume for the time being that M does get on the ballot. This will not necessarily guarantee that M will be the winner, even in the case of a majority scoring rule. For example, people may not actually vote their preferences. Although some may prefer M to, say, N, they may vote for N over M because they may believe that N has a better chance of winning, and they prefer N to, say a third alternative, P, which is also on the ballot. Such behaviour is quite likely to be the case where M is a minimal majority consent point and N is a maximal consent point. It is also possible, of course, for the majority to split their votes between M and N in such a way that a third candidate which they did not desire wins on a plurality basis.

The above is not entirely unrelated to the question of the alternatives that get on the ballot. Frequently a group will try to get on the ballot not the alternative that is the majority-preference point, but the alternative that they believe will have the greatest *chance* of winning over, say, the existing alternative. This, too, will usually be something closer to a maximal consent point. The same phenomenon may also occur as a result of log rolling. That is A will vote for B's proposal if he could get his own proposal accepted, and B will behave similarly. They may, therefore, end up with a combination of the two as the final proposal that they both support, but each of them really prefers their own proposal to the combined compromise proposal. Nevertheless, since they believe the combined proposal to have a better chance of winning, they support that one rather than their own proposals, although it may be the case that one of their own proposals would have been a majority-preference point. Thus we see that where people try to support the most likely or surest winner they may, in fact, be supporting an alternative that is not a majority-preference point.

system of maximal consent rule will eventually lead to a majority preference choice being adopted if preferences remain the same. A maximal choice procedure, rather than a majority preference rule, is simply a delaying action in the circumstances indicated. Unless there is good reason for such delay, it is clear that majority preference rule really reflects the democratic choice.[1] That is, it is the only rule that is ultimately consistent with " non-minority choice." This follows from the fact that any technique used to prevent the majority preference point from being the one adopted ultimately implies a technique in which a minority is able to enforce the adoption of the point it wants over and above a point that more people prefer to it, that is, a majority preference point. Hence, the mere notion that democratic choice implies non-minority choice means that democratic choice implies the majority preference choice, if a majority preference point exists.

IV. PARETO CHOICES VERSUS DEMOCRATIC CHOICE

By a Pareto choice we have in mind one made on the basis of our compromise Pareto comparisons. Let us contrast and compare briefly our democratic choice criterion as against the Pareto choice criterion. Since Pareto superior points and Pareto optimal points are universal consent points, such points are inconsistent with democratic choice in all instances in which a majority preference point is not a universal consent point.

The burden of the argument is that there may be points which are majority preference points with respect to, say, p, a point in the set of Pareto optimal points. Of course, such majority preference points are not universal consent points. Hence, such points cannot be Pareto superior to p, but a majority of the people would prefer them to p. Hence, a welfare criterion that advocates the point p would, in the suggested circumstances, favour a point preferred by the minority over some other point that was a majority preference point.

It is, of course, possible and in many cases likely that there would not be any Pareto optimal points or Pareto superior points in the sense in which we have defined them. Namely, if some people are concerned about their relative income shares as well as their absolute level, then there may not be any point that would command universal consent as against the existing state. In this connection, consider the well-recognized contention that Pareto choices implicitly involve a prejudice in favour of the *status quo*.[1] Operating on the basis of Pareto comparisons gives a veto power to anyone who might lose by a change, or to anyone who *thinks* that he might lose by a change. For example, in a shift from x to y one person, say, a very rich one, may lose, but most people gain. Should the rich person be permitted to exercise a veto against the wishes of the majority? Pareto choice gives

---

[1] See Appendix II for proof.

a veto power to anyone opposed to a change.[1] Such a person would merely have to say that he feels worse off by the change. (And this may be true for changes, even if compensations *à la* compensation principle are included in the changes.) *E.g.*, the introduction of a progressive tax would probably never be justified on the basis of Pareto choice.

Now, it may be argued that contemporary welfare economics really does not imply giving a veto power to every individual. Namely, it may be argued that all contemporary welfare economics says is that where universal consent does not exist, then welfare economists simply are unable to declare whether there has been an increase in welfare in the cases in which some people feel better off and others feel worse off. It would seem to me that this really amounts to saying that in most cases welfare economics is irrelevant. If the Pareto choice rule is assumed to be relevant at the outset, then we have to admit that it implies minority rule, and further, it gives a veto power to every individual whenever there is a choice to be made. At the very least it would seem that the Pareto choice criterion gives every individual the right to declare that this criterion is not relevant to the situation in question. In other words, there are only two possible interpretations of the Pareto choice rule. If it is to be interpreted that there is no decision in which there is not universal consent, then everyone can decide whether or not the rule is to apply. If the rule is to apply, then it certainly involves a veto power of everyone in favour of the *status quo*, and hence it implies minority rule. We can seriously question whether a rule is really a good rule if everyone has the opportunity to disqualify the application of the rule if he wants to. In sum, either the Pareto choice rule is presumed to be applicable from the outset, in which case it implies a veto power to everyone who favours the *status quo* (*i.e.*, minority rule); or alternatively, everyone can veto the applicability of the Pareto choice rule.

V. The Majority Tyranny Problem

Is the new welfare economics essentially undemocratic in all contexts? Suppose that the majority preference point is not in the universal consent area, then a minority will oppose a shift to the point in question. According to the Pareto approach, such a shift would not be recommended. Indeed, this would be the case if only one person opposed the shift. This is clearly minority rule. Thus, we must conclude that as a *general principle* Pareto choice does appear to go counter to the theory of democracy.

But we must not be hasty in our judgment. We have to distinguish between Pareto choice as a general principle and Pareto choice as a democratically chosen rule to be applied in certain areas. As a principle, Pareto

---

[1] Boulding (3, p. 94), also K. Arrow (1, p. 45). It does not help to be told that what we need is a social-welfare function in order to solve such problems. This merely masks our ignorance unless we are told how to obtain such functions. As far as I am aware, authors who employ social-welfare functions have not as yet presented us with workable procedures for the derivation of such functions.

choice will often be undemocratic; but Pareto choice may conceivably be desired by the majority as a choice procedure, in which case it will be in conformity with majority rule.

One fear in using the majority preference rule is that of " ganging up " on the minority. It is no help to a minority that is " exploited " to know that this is being done by majority preference rather than some other basis. Clearly, the majority preference criterion could, and perhaps should, be qualified in some way to take care of this legitimate fear. An essential condition is that an individual's consent area must be *independent* of his belief or knowledge as to whether or not it intersects with the *majority* preference point. This would prevent changes that involve collusion at the expense of the minority. Of course, other qualifications could be added to the democratic choice criterion that would protect minority rights. Indeed, we might expect the majority to vote for such protections if the voters see themselves just as easily in the minority as in the majority. But again, as previously suggested, there are other rules that might be chosen that protect minority tastes to some extent. Individuals may not know whether their interests will lie with the majority or with the minority in the future. Hence, as a hedge against the possibility that their interests may lie with the minority, they may choose a scheme that will protect minority interests. In addition, people might be in favour of protecting minority interests on purely compassionate grounds.

One has to distinguish between determining the rules of the game, as against applying the rules to determine the outcome. To make up a fair set of rules the rule maker should not take into account how he personally will fare under them. If those who make up rules visualise that they may at times be at the wrong end of the outcome of a game, then they may wish to set up rules that would not make such an eventuality too onerous.[1] If qualifications to the operation of the majority preference criterion were developed from that viewpoint, then it seems that many of the possible objections to it based on potential sympathy with a minority would disappear.

An extreme form of protecting a potential minority interest is to give everyone a veto power. But this last is the same as the Pareto choice rule. Thus, a group that is especially sensitive to potential minority interests might adopt, on the basis of majority consent, a set of rules or procedures consistent with Pareto choice in certain areas of their activities.

But the above must not be taken to suggest that concern for minority interest implies the necessary adoption of a Pareto choice rule. While Pareto choice, which implies universal consent, does protect minority in-

---

[1] For instance, the majority may favour economic rules of the game consistent with free competitive enterprise, but fear that this would lead to an income distribution under which some individuals and their families might face starvation. As a consequence, they may favour an additional rule which would subsidise those people who under a free competitive enterprise system would receive an income below some predetermined minimum level.

terests in the face of prospective change, it is an extreme position. Between majority rule and the complete protection of minority tastes there are obviously a wide variety of compromises possible. Since the obverse side of universal consent is a veto power given to everyone, a choice rule involving a lesser degree of consent may be preferred in many cases, since it may avoid the cost of catering to exceedingly eccentric tastes or to extreme positions. The exact degree of consent deemed desirable, or optimal, will depend on a variety of considerations, among which are the importance attached to protecting minority interests and the assessment of probable costs of permitting a minority to obstruct changes desired by the majority. Our main point here is not to suggest how the optimal degree of consent rule is to be determined, but rather to emphasise the fact that the choice rules suggested by modern welfare economics are really of an extreme nature.

VI. PLURALITY PREFERENCES AND DEMOCRATIC CHOICE

A special set of problems enters the picture in those cases where a majority preference point does not exist. There will, nevertheless, be a plurality preference point. Two problems are involved here: (1) how do we interpret democratic choice in such cases? and (2) what do we do in those cases in which the " social preferences " appear to be non-transitive? [1]

The major criterion of democracy with which we started was non-minority rule. That is, no alternative should be chosen which is preferred by a minority against another alternative favoured by a larger number of people. Let us examine this aspect in connection with a non-majority plurality preference point. [2] Suppose that 40% prefer A over B and C, while 30% prefer B over the two other alternatives, and another 30% prefer C. If A is chosen, is there another point that can be preferred to it by a larger number? Clearly this is a possibility. We know from the initial assumption that 30% prefer B over A. Another 30% prefer C over B, but the same 30% may nevertheless prefer B over A. Hence, in this case 60% prefer B over A. Therefore, if A is chosen it would go against the wishes of the majority.

Now suppose that B is chosen. This, too, may be a minority choice. 30% prefer C to B. In addition it is quite possible that, say, ¾ of those that prefer A to B also prefer C to B; and C will be desired by 60% of the population over B. Likewise, C versus A may lead to a similar result. If C is chosen it is desired initially by the 30% who prefer it to any other choice. However, 40% prefer A to C, but the 30% who prefer B to A may nevertheless prefer A to C. Once again, C will be a minority choice. This

---

[1] The problem has been examined most interestingly and in considerable detail by Professor Arrow (1, pp. 2–3). The case that follows is very similar to the one discussed by Arrow (1). See also Duncan Black, *The Theory of Committees and Elections* (4, Chapter VII, pp. 46–51).

[2] A point is a plurality preference point if, among a set of points, it is preferred by more people than any other point in the set, but by less than a majority, when all the points are considered simultaneously, and when any one person can " vote " for one, and only one, point.

example illustrates both aspects of our dilemma. We see that no choice can have majority approval; and, in addition, we see that if we had a voting system in which the alternatives were taken two at a time, the social preferences would be non-transitive. In an election between A and B, B would be the winner. But in an election between B and C, C would be the winner. However, in the election between C and A, A would be the winner and so on. In other words, whatever point is chosen, there is always another point outside which is preferred by the majority. There is really no solution to this problem. It represents a situation in which the majority is unhappy with whatever exists at the moment.

The other aspect of this situation is: what the majority wants depends on the initial situation. If the existing state is C, then they prefer A; if it is A, then they prefer B; and so on. Clearly a series of elections would lead to the society shifting in a circle from one choice to another and never settling down to a specific choice. If their preferences remain firm in the process, then one must conclude that they prefer this round of shifting from one choice to another. However, there is the alternative of asking people whether they prefer the stability of a single choice, whatever it is, to the instability of the existing situation.[1]

Plurality choices may not have the characteristic we have just discussed.[2] It is possible and perhaps common for the plurality choice to be transitive. Suppose that in the previous example, where 40% preferred A to B, the ones who preferred C to B nevertheless also preferred A to B. In that case, if A is chosen, then it would get 70% of the votes over B. Similarly, the ones who prefer B to A may, at the same time, prefer A to C. Again A would be a majority winner over C. Although in this case A is only a plurality preference point, it does meet our criterion of a democratic choice, namely that of non-minority rule. We might conclude, then, that where only a plurality preference point exists, if it is one that is transitive with respect to the other alternatives, then it meets the democratic choice criterion, at least in the sense that when such a plurality point is chosen there is no alternative point that the majority prefers to it.

VII. DEMOCRATIC CHOICES VERSUS COMPETITIVE MARKET CHOICES

Thus far we have assumed that the alternatives are fairly discrete; but in many instances it is conceivable for a continuous range of alternatives to exist. Indeed, the alternatives in the market-place often approximate

---

[1] In this case a rule that favoured the *status quo* for a given period, say, four years, would at least have the virtue of giving stability, and people may prefer stability to constant change. Transferring this idea to the political sphere in such a situation, people may prefer an American type constitution that gives the executive a long term in office rather than a parliamentary system in which any government formed would fall whenever it came to a vote of confidence. Clearly the desirability of certain types of constitutional provisions will depend on the likelihood that the political system will develop non-transitive pluralities.

[2] Cf. Duncan Black (4, pp. 46–51).

this character and, as a consequence, provide possible compromise solutions between majority rule and minority interests. The following artificial example will illustrate the points involved.

Suppose that a country producing exceedingly poor cigarettes and cigars considers permitting importation as an alternative for local production. Assume that the maximum amount that can be imported is limited by balance-of-payments considerations and that it is a small amount relative to their demand at reasonable prices. The alternatives open are to import only cigarettes, or only cigars, or a combination of the two, or none. Assume that 80% of the voters are cigarette smokers and 20% are cigar smokers. If the majority preference point is to rule, then they would import only cigarettes, since the majority would clearly be in favour of cigarettes. Cigar smokers would favour, of course, the exclusive importation of cigars. A competitive type market that employed the price system to ration imports would normally provide a mixture of cigarettes and cigars in relation to the demand elasticities of the two groups. If we assume that the income and average tastes for non-tobacco products within the two groups are the same, then a market system would normally provide roughly for 80% of the import quota on cigarettes and 20% on cigars. Since the existing condition of local production provides cigarettes and cigars of very poor quality, the alternative to import *both* cigarettes and cigars will be a universal consent point. Everyone prefers this combination to exclusive local production. However, cigar smokers might prefer the importation of neither to the exclusive importation of cigarettes, and similarly for cigarette smokers.

An interesting aspect of this example is that majority rule conflicts with the universal consent point. A choice made in accordance with Pareto optimum considerations would be a choice consistent with the universal consent point rather than the democratic choice point. Clearly the universal consent point in this instance does have an appeal, because it gives something to everybody, and it appeases minority tastes. As previously suggested, we have to distinguish between decisions on specific issues and decisions on rules under which specific issues are to be decided. Thus, a democracy may very well decide by majority consent that in the economic sphere, or in certain economic areas it will operate in accordance with rules of choice that are consistent with universal consent points. But again, as previously suggested, there are other rules that might be chosen to protect minority tastes to some extent.

In this connection, observe that real markets do not always operate in accordance with universal consent points. For instance, if there are considerable economies of scale the variety offered in the market will often be less than the variety possible or desired by various minority groups. For example, in some towns not all possible sizes of various types of clothing may be available. The shops will cater more to the average than to the extreme, and their reactions to risk may be such they will not stock any extreme sizes. The lack of newspaper variety in many cities is an obvious example. Another example is the theatre. Although a minority may prefer a professional theatre in many communities, the majority desire for motion pictures or television eliminates the possibility of a non-subsidised professional theatre. To the extent that there are cost advantages in mass production, to that extent it is likely that majority tastes may be catered for to the exclusion of minority tastes. Of course, this is hardly surprising, since only perfectly competitive markets are consistent with universal consent points, and non-competitive markets, which are implied by decreasing cost industries, will work more in the direction of majority rule. In other words, in such industries there will be, at the very least, a cost disadvantage because one has minority tastes. Sometimes the cost differential may be sufficiently great so that minority tastes are not catered for at all.

The connection between cost functions and universal consent points can be considered from a slightly different viewpoint. We have suggested that universal consent is a means of protecting minority interests. Now, expansions and contractions in output in constant-cost industries do not affect the costs and prices of commodities to those who have minority tastes. Similarly, in the case of increasing costs an expansion in output increases the cost for those with majority tastes. But the exact opposite is the case for industries of decreasing costs. The expansion of output in a decreasing cost industry that catered to the majority, and the simultaneous contraction of a decreasing cost industry catering to minority tastes will result in a reduction in cost to the former and in increase in cost to the latter. This is usually the case in mass-production industries. An economy made up of such industries will often cater to minority tastes only at very high cost to the minority. For example, in the course of economic development a shift of labour from personal services to factory workers producing mass-produced goods may actually worsen the condition of those with minority tastes who previously indulged heavily in personal services. From this point of view, many members of a middle class, or upper middle class, may become worse off as a consequence of economic development.[1]

VIII. Summary and Conclusions

(1) The choice rules suggested by contemporary welfare economics are really ethical rules of an extreme nature: at the very least, they give everyone a veto to declare whether or not the rule is applicable in a particular instance. If the " Pareto choice " rule is assumed to be applicable at the outset it will be inconsistent in many instances with a reasonable interpretation of democratic choice.

(2) We interpreted the idea of democratic choice as non-minority choice, and saw that this implied the adoption of a majority preference point in

[1] Cf. Tibor and Anne Scitovsky, " What Price Economic Progress? "

those cases where there was one. By contrast, we saw that Pareto superior points and Pareto optimum points implied universal consent points. Indeed, a Pareto optimal point is a universal preference point among the universal consent points. From this it follows that, in general, democratic choices are not usually consistent with choice in accordance with modern welfare economics, since majority preference points are unlikely to be universal consent points.

(3) Considering voting as a means of determining democratic choice, we pointed out the possibility that many voting procedures would not lead to the eventual choice of majority preference points. This is especially likely when alternatives on the ballot are those that are put there because they are believed to have a maximum chance of winning.

(4) If a majority preference point does not exist, then the special problem of a non-transitive plurality may arise. This situation cannot be interpreted as definitely consistent with democratic choice: any choice made on this basis would be one for which the majority preferred some other alternative. If periodic elections are permitted in such circumstances, then such choices are inherently unstable and the society might prefer some other scheme in order to preserve stability. However, when non-majority pluralities are transitive the plurality choice is in conformity with democratic choice.

(5) A universal preference point rule does have an appealing feature: it protects minority tastes in the process of change. We suggested the importance of distinguishing between choices about rules of choice and choices with respect to specific alternatives. It was argued that a group might make a democratic decision in favour of a universal preference choice rule in some areas of the economy if the majority could not tell whether their interests would lie with the minority or the majority, and if they wish to protect their interests should they find themselves in the minority. (They may also do so on compassionate grounds.) But such a choice rule is an extreme one for the protection of minority interests. A society has open to it the infinite number of choice rules, lying between majority preference and universal preference, that are more or less compromises between strict majority rule and the complete protection of minority interests.

(6) Finally, we saw that, while purely competitive markets are equivalent to universal preference choices, some actual markets, especially those in which decreasing cost industries are involved, may be said to operate more in the direction of majority preference-point choices. That is, shifts in output towards decreasing-cost industries may be in the interest of the majority but at the expense of those with minority tastes.

HARVEY LEIBENSTEIN

University of California,
Berkeley.

REFERENCES

1. Kenneth Arrow, *Social Choice and Individual Values* (New York: John Wiley & Sons, 1951).
2. James Buchanan, "Positive Economics, Welfare Economics, and Political Economy," *Journal of Law and Economics*, October 1959.
3. K. Boulding, "Welfare Economics," comment by M. W. Reder, *A Survey of Contemporary Economics*, Vol. II, Bernard F. Haley, Editor.
4. Duncan Black, *The Theory of Committees and Elections* (Cambridge: Cambridge University Press, 1958).
5. Tibor and Anne Scitovsky, "What Price Economic Progress?", *Yale Review*, autumn 1959.
6. Gordon Tullock, "Problems of Majority Voting," *Journal of Political Economy*, December 1959, pp. 571–580.
7. Robert A. Dahl, *A Preface to Democratic Theory* (Chicago: University of Chicago Press, 1956).
8. Barbara Wootton, *The Social Foundations of Wage Policy* (London: George Allen & Unwin, 1955).

APPENDICES

I. We want to show that a universal preference point is a Pareto optimal point. The notation follows that used by Arrow (1).
Notation:

xP_iy means x is preferred to y by person i.

xR_iy means x is preferred to or as good as y by person i.

u is any point in U, the universal consent set.

$\bar{u}$ is any universal preference point contained in U.

x_0 is the existing state of the economy.

v is any point in V, the set of all points not in U, and excluding x_0.

xR_iy and yR_ix implies that x is indifferent to y.

To show that $\bar{u}$ is Pareto optimal we have to show that there is no point that is Pareto superior to $\bar{u}$. In effect, we have to show that neither u, v nor x_0 are Pareto superior to $\bar{u}$. With respect to every individual's preferences between different points we make the usual assumptions of connectivity and transitivity (cf. Arrow 1, pp. 13–14).

We observe at the outset an obvious necessary condition for Pareto superiority: If x is Pareto superior to y, then xR_jy for all i.

(a) Consider u different from $\bar{u}$.
By definition of a universal preference point $\bar{u}$ is in U.
Also by definition of a universal preference point for someone, say person j, $\bar{u}P_ju$.
Therefore it cannot be true that $uR_i\bar{u}$ for all i.
Therefore u is not Pareto superior to $\bar{u}$.

(b) Since v is not in U, v is not a universal consent point.
Therefore for at least one person, say person j, x_0P_jv.
But we also know that $\bar{u}R_jx_0$.
By the transitivity assumption if $\bar{u}R_jx_0$ and x_0P_jv, then $\bar{u}P_jv$.
Therefore $vR_j\bar{u}$ cannot be true.
Therefore v is not Pareto superior to $\bar{u}$.

(*c*) By definition of a universal-consent point, $\bar{u}R_i x_o$ for all i.
Therefore no value i exists for which $x_0 P_i \bar{u}$.
But $x_0 P_i \bar{u}$ for some i is a necessary condition for x_0 to be Pareto superior to $\bar{u}$.
Therefore x_0 cannot be Pareto superior to $\bar{u}$.
If x_0 is itself a Pareto optimal point, the class U is vacuous.
We have therefore shown that neither x_0, u or v can be Pareto superior to $\bar{u}$.

II. The other major proposition employed in this paper is as follows: If a majority preference point exists and it is not in the universal consent set, then the choice of a universal consent point (say, the universal preference point) implies minority rule. (For our purposes it is sufficient to assume that there is at least one majority preference point.) To prove this we want to show that the following more general proposition is true: The choice of any point, other than a majority preference point, when there is such a point, implies minority rule.
Additional notation:

$xP_{(n)}y$ means x is preferred to y by n persons. N is the set of those n persons.
$xR_{(n)}y$ means x is preferred to y or thought to be as good as y by n persons.
$\sim xP_j y$ means not $xP_j y$, i.e., $xP_j y$ is not true.
q is the total number of persons to be considered.
M is the majority consent set.
$\bar{v}$ is any majority preference point in V.
$w \neq \bar{v}$ is any point in M other than a majority preference point.

Now, $V \subset M$, and $\bar{v}$ is in M.
By definition of a majority preference point (p. 12):

$\bar{v}R_{(n)}w$ for some $n > \frac{1}{2}q$.
Let j be the jth person in N.
Then $\bar{v}R_j w$ implies $\sim wP_j \bar{v}$ for all j in N.
Therefore at most $wP_{(q-n)}\bar{v}$.
But since $n > \frac{1}{2}q$, $(q - n)$ is a minority of q and $wP_{(q-n)}\bar{v}$ is a minority preference between w and $\bar{v}$.
Since w is any point in M other than $\bar{v}$ and $\bar{u}$ is in M.
Therefore $\bar{u}P_{(q-n)}\bar{v}$ is a minority choice between $\bar{u}$ and $\bar{v}$.

2

Long-run Welfare Criteria

by Harvey Leibenstein*

Established welfare economics has reached an impasse. There is no generally accepted rule for judging situations in which some people gain and others lose. The attempt to flank this problem by the compensation principle, which turns some of these situations into others where some gain and nobody loses, comprehends few realistic situations. I suggest an approach that enables us to get around "distribution judgment" difficulties of a specific character, as these are currently conceived, by using what I hope will turn out to be an important class of cases. The emphasis is on the development of criteria for long-run welfare decisions rather than on the technical aspects of deducing conclusions from established criteria.

Now, it is quite possible that no welfare criterion will cover all cases. But this is a question that need not be settled at present. It may be useful to consider criteria that suit some cases as an initial step in the research process and only eventually worry about whether there are common principles underlying various criteria.

In what follows I have been motivated by two considerations. First, it is desirable to develop a welfare principle (or set of principles) that would receive a high degree of consent. Whether or not the principles considered below would earn such consent is an empirical question, but it is a factor that I have kept in mind. A high degree of "basic consensus" is necessary for economic welfare policies to be applicable. But the subject matter on which we need consensus has not been determined. Kenneth Arrow, in his Social Choice and Individual Values (see reference 1), makes the point that " . . . it must be demanded that there be some sort of consensus on the ends of society, or no social welfare function can be formed." In this connection he points to the writings of philosophers such as Kant, Rousseau, and Green, who emphasize the significance of an underlying consensus or common interest needed somewhere as a guide for social action. In addition, George Stigler has argued against contemporary welfare economics on the grounds that it does not take into account consensus on ends. The diffi-

---

*University of California.

culty arises from the lack of specificity of ends. In other words, what is meant by "social ends"? Arrow paraphrases Kant: "The moral imperative corresponds to our concept of the social ordering, in a sense, but it is also an individual ordering for every individual; it is the will which every individual would have if he were fully rational." But what is the relevant subject matter of this will that rational people would agree upon? This essay may be looked upon as an attempt to elaborate a suggestion as to where we might, in fact, look for the necessary high degree of consensus. *

The second consideration that I have kept in mind is the desirability of making welfare economics an empirical rather than a purely deductive science. I believe that the ideas outlined below are steps in that direction.

PAYOFF PROBLEMS VERSUS CHOICE OF GAME PROBLEMS

One of the main difficulties in welfare economics lies in the fact that the theory has focused on one type of problem. To be specific, welfare economics theory has concentrated on what might be called "payoff" problems rather than "choice of game" problems. By shifting the problem focus new areas of research in welfare economics may be opened.

Payoff Problems

The essence of "payoff" problems is that a change of some sort is contemplated, and as a result of this change some people gain and others lose. It is possible that redistributions can be made so that some gain and no one loses. These are still essentially payoff problems because we are asked to choose between the payoffs to individuals before the change as against one or more possible payoffs after the change.

Payoffs and distributions are frequently linked in a critical way. If the aggregative payoff is larger after the change than before, and the distribution is "no worse," then the change is deemed desirable. But there is lack of agreement as to what is meant by a "no worse" distribution. Frequently pay-offs and distributions cannot be separated. Ultimately we have to choose between different payoffs as they are specifically distributed to specific indiv-duals. When we use the word "payoffs" in what follows we shall have in mind specific distributions to specific individuals.

Choice of Game Problems

There is, however, a different set of problems we might consider: "choice of game" problems. A sample problem from such a set exists among people who enter a gambling establishment. Assume that in a hypothetical gambling establishment all the games are fair in the sense that the odds are in accordance with the mathematical probabilities of winning. Some people will prefer some games to others. Each person has to choose a game. Mathematically expected return is exactly the same for all games. Applying this idea to economic situations, we argue that it may be easier for people to choose (on the

---

*The ideas that follow are in some respects similar to the "Economic Theory of Constitutions" developed by Buchanan and Tullock (see reference 2). However, the emphasis and some of the conclusions are in many respects quite different.

basis of mutual consent) between "economic games" than to choose (on the basis of mutual consent) between payoffs.

In the simplest types of games such as zero-sum games or income-redistribution games the difficulty involved in choosing among payoffs is immediately obvious. What one gains the other loses. We have no way of determining whether the one that gains is in any way "worthier" than the one that loses. If one gains utility and the other loses utility, we have no way of deciding whether this is desirable or undesirable. There is no reason why we should want to maximize the utility of the two individuals together by taking utility from one and giving it to the other. To the loser, such a principle, and others like it, is likely to appear as purely arbitrary. Furthermore, there is no reason for people to agree on such a principle, if they focus their attention on utility redistribution or income redistribution.

We have to distinguish games for which the outcome is known as against those for which it is unknown. The difficulties we have just mentioned disappear in connection with choices of games for which the outcome is not predetermined. Suppose A and B are both chess players and each derives a great pleasure from winning and slight displeasure from losing at chess. Also suppose it is known to both players that A is a very much superior player to B. Will A and B agree to play? They obviously will not. B immediately anticipates the outcome of the game and hence will not agree to play. However, the same two players, knowing nothing about each other's strength as players, might quite readily agree to play for some period of time. But this agreement would only be temporary. Pretty soon B would discover that he is the inferior player and he would cease to agree to continue to play. Now suppose that A and B are evenly matched. In some cases A wins and in some other cases B wins. If they both get some pleasure out of chess in addition to the pleasure of winning, then they are quite likely to agree to play with each other.

Now, consider a given change in an economy's "rules" under which the outcome is known. Say, an increase in tariffs which would make producers competing against domestic imports, better off while making consumers and exporters worse off. If the outcome is known, then we immediately focus our attention on the change in the payoffs, and there is no way of deciding between those that gain and those that lose. (We assume realistically that in all the cases we shall mention the compensation principle is not applied.) People might possibly agree to the change if they have no way of determining who would gain as against who would lose. For example, suppose consumers and exporters are misled at the outset about the consequence of such a change. As soon as the facts became clear the losers would object to the change and would urge a reversal to the previous set of rules. Once again we are faced with a basic conflict, which, in essence, involves shifting utilities from some people to others. Only in rare cases would we expect that both those that lose and those that gain would agree to the shift.

What are the kinds of games that we could agree on? Clearly, we could agree on games for which the utility of the payoff or the utility of the expected value of the payoffs is zero or positive to all players, and for which the utility of playing the game is greater than zero for all players. Once stated, this would appear to be obviously true. The main point of this paper is to show how we could apply an extension of this principle to a large variety of problems. Quite clearly this principle works with a great many gambling situations. In games involving fair gambles, the expected value of the payoffs to any individual is close to zero, and for those who enjoy the activity, the utility of the games is greater than zero. Thus, the obvious popularity of the large variety of gambling games organized in homes and clubs. This does not mean that everybody will agree to play such games. For some people the dis-utility of the possible losses is greater than the utility of the possible gains, a situation most likely to be true where large amounts of money are involved. Thus, people will generally agree to play for small stakes but not for large.

OBSTACLES TO CONSENT IN ECONOMIC GAMES

The next problem is to interpret this principle from the point of view of what might be called economic games. Here, there are three elements involved, two of which are, in an important way, not comparable to the gambling situation considered above. First, in economic games, the sum of all the payoffs is greater than zero. Second, people are able to make some assessments of the actual payoffs in advance. Third, from some points of view the games are not fair, since some people have advantages at the outset (before the play, so to speak) over others. The last two elements stand in the way of achieving mutual consent for economic or socioeconomic games.

Most people need to earn an income for their livelihood and thus, engaging in an economic game is better than not playing at all. But this will not lead to mutual consent for any particular game. Also, economic games obviously have a redistributive aspect. There is not only one payoff possible but a variety of payoffs. This means that there are a number of ways of adding taxes and sub-sidies so as to change the payoffs and still keep everybody in the game. Finally, some people start with more innate ability and other resources than others. This gives them an advantage over other players. Thus, players are aware at the outset of some of the elements that will determine the payoff. If changes are made in these economic games, they help some people and worsen the condition of others. Clearly, we are unlikely to get unanimous consent for such changes. Our problem is to separate those elements of the game for which there is mutual consent as against those for which there is not.

In mutual consent games everybody approves of the rules. In non-mutual consent games at least some do not approve of the rules but they may be power-less to change them. In both cases we assume that non-approval of the rules does not exist out of ignorance. In other words, we abstract from those forms of economic protest which are based on misconceptions about the nature of economic games. Presumably we want, if possible, unanimous consent or a high degree of consent for the set of socioeconomic games to be played.

There are many obstacles to consensus. For example, there may be a lack of consensus because people respond to emotional rather than rational considerations, or consensus may be absent because there is misinformation, or because different individuals know different aspects of the factual situation. But problems of this type are not unique to welfare economics. For the purpose of this paper we should limit ourselves to those aspects especially related to the context in which proposals for economic change occur. What is central to the welfare economics context, as the problem is usually conceived, is the consider-ation of "mid-game" situations rather than "pre-game" situations. This distinc-tion is crucial for the argument in this paper. In the middle of a game, players are less likely to agree on changes in the rules, because they see a closer connection between such changes and the outcome of the game than would be the case if such changes were considered prior to the game. In other words, the basic consensus that is relevant in the long run is the consensus that would occur were we not caught in the middle of the game when we had to make a decision about a change in the rules.* In economic affairs in the short run we are always caught in the middle of the game, as it were.

"PRE-GAME" MAXIMAL CONSENT

Criteria for the Game

Can we invent, conceptually, an economic game which would be a mutual or maximal consent game? The first problem is to eliminate the "mid-game" knowledge of the specific payoffs. Let us, therefore, conceive of a Robinson Crusoe type situation in which a large number of shipwrecked children (without parents) are placed on an island on which the only existing residents are aged adults. An economist in the adult group has to advise on the nature of the economic institutions that will be adopted for the next generation: the children in question. We assume that no information exists about the nature and individual tastes of these children, but as a group the distribution of tastes is similar to that found among other children. There are no filial connections between the children and the adults on the island. Our problem is to invent an economic game for these children that would be the best game possible.

Consider briefly the information that we are assumed to know about these children. We do not know their individual utility functions. Similarly, we do not know their individual capacities. We do know the resources that they start with. We assume knowledge of the production functions of the economy. This last includes the production of acquired qualities in human beings. Namely, we are assumed to know the kinds and amounts of training that would lead to the acquisition of various kinds of skills and improved general capacities. We assume a knowledge of the distribution of the innate capacities of the group. We also assume knowledge of the distribution of utility functions but not the utility functions of specific individuals.

Given these facts we have to create an economic game (or set of games), which is really another way of saying an economic system, that will achieve maximum consensus from the children were they able to understand what it was they were getting into. While we cannot be certain what characteristics would achieve consensus without empirical research, we can speculate on some of the characteristics that would probably do so. First, it should be a fair game. Second, there should be no coercion. Third, if possible, it should be a game that would permit each and every one of them to achieve a livelihood at some

---

*A somewhat related idea has been developed by John C. Harsanyi (see reference 3). Harsanyi is concerned with the nature of moral choice. In this formulation a moral choice requires that each person put himself in the place of every one of N persons, with the probability of being in a specific place of $1/N$. Under such circumstances each person would have a similar composite utility function, which would reflect the utility functions of the N individuals, under which every individual's utility function would carry the weight of $1/N$. Under such circumstances an individual's behavior would not depend on what I have called his "mid-game" position, since he attaches equal weight to everyone else's mid-game position. However, my formulation is different from Harsanyi's, in that I see people having separate rather than composite personalities. Even though in the pre-game situation each individual cannot determine what situation he will find himself in during the game, he is not visualized as adopting the tastes of other people, hence each person's evaluation of his being in any specific situation is different, even if the probability of getting into it is the same for all people. This formulation does not really argue with Harsanyi, since we are concerned with different types of problems. Mine is not a problem of moral choice, in the strict sense.

agreed upon minimum level equal to or above subsistence even for those individuals who, without intent to do so, played the game very poorly. And fourth,
it should be the best possible game in some sense that we shall discuss later.
Let us assume for a moment that we invented such a game and see how it would
differ with respect to the problem of consent found in contemporary welfare
economics. The first thing we note is that the bedeviling feature of welfare
economics does not exist in this situation. That is to say, we do not have to
decide between the benefits of shifting the payoff from one specific person to
another. The payoffs are assumed to be known in a general sense but not in a
specific sense. This is similar to the situation in various types of gambling
games. We do not decide that blackjack is a good or a bad game because player
A will win and B will lose. Rather, we decide this on the basis of whether A
and B enjoy the game before we know the outcome of the game. Similarly, the
economist in our illustration does not know whether an individual child will end
up as a winner or loser.

We have distinguished in passing between <u>specific</u> distributive problems
and <u>general</u> distributive problems. To take income from a specific person A
and give it to a specific person B is a <u>specific</u> distributive problem. The choice
between an equal income distribution and a certain unequal one (but one which is
not defined in terms of the exact income going to specific individuals) is a
general distributive problem. The criteria necessary to decide specific distributive problems are quite different from those necessary for general distributive
problems. The potential payoffs are important in determining the desirability of
the game but it is not the specific payoffs that are involved. Individuals prefer
some types of gambles to others, and in the same sense, individuals prefer some
types of possible economic payoffs to others. For example, complete laissez
faire may lead to some people receiving 100 times the income of others. There
may be a type of adjusted laissez faire possible under which the maximum income
deviation might be that some people receive only, let us say, 10 times the income
of others. Individuals may possibly prefer the latter type of game to the former.
But this choice is made without any knowledge as to who will, in fact, end up
with the higher, as against the lower, income.

Let us now return to the characteristics of our possible maximal consent
game. We have already mentioned fairness. Briefly put, given full knowledge
no player should feel that he starts with some <u>removable</u> disadvantage as
against any other player. In addition, no player should feel that he is in some
sense forced to play a particular game. This requires that there be a sufficient
choice of economic games so that the player can find that particular type of
game he really prefers, if that is possible.

Evaluating the Game

Now, under what conditions can we say that we have a best possible game?
For any individual player the best possible game would have at least three
characteristics. First, the general payoff distribution would be the one that he
likes best, given the possibilities. Second, the expected value of the payoffs is
the maximum for the particular payoff distribution that he likes best within the
possibility set. Third, the roles that he will take, or the nature of the plays
that he will make will also be best, given his capacities and the possibilities
available. Where these qualities are not obtainable simultaneously, then trade-
offs between such qualities of games have to be considered. Let us consider the
optimal payoff distribution. A prudent player may not wish to play for stakes so
small that he gains little by participating in the game, nor for stakes so high

Harvey Leibenstein

that he faces the possibility of suffering a great deal should he turn out to be a
"loser." In economic terms, a player of this type would not prefer a situation
in which all incomes were equal, nor would he prefer one in which there were
vast income extremes. For instance, he might not prefer an economic game
under which he faced the possibility of starving, although under it he also had
some chance of becoming a millionaire. For different individuals we might
expect that the ideal payoffs would differ. Now, for any payoff distribution we
would expect an individual to prefer a higher expected value of the payoff rather
than a lower one. The payoff distribution has, within it, motivational features,
and as a consequence, the value of the payoff distribution is related to the nature
of the distribution. Completely equal pay for all jobs might not motivate people
to either work hard or to be willing to accept unpleasant types of employment,
and as a consequence, output would be less than with some other distributions.
In addition, an efficient allocation of resources depends on using differential
monetary incentives. Thus, up to some point, we would expect a connection
between the payoff distribution and the expected value of the payoff.

Another element in determining the best possible economic game is the
nature of the role structure and career structure open to individuals. This
means that the value of the game depends also on the nature of the game and
not only on the expected value of the payoff. In economic terms this element
recognizes the importance that people are likely to attach to the sort of work
they do and to the status that may be associated with the work done or with the
title and position connected with a job. The value of a job depends in part on
what other jobs it leads to. Therefore, we have to think of sequences of jobs
or roles; that is, we must think in terms of potential alternative careers. There
is no way of determining in the abstract what would be an optimal set of career
alternatives.* The important point, however, is that this is an empirically
researchable question. If we ask researchable questions, there is some hope
of getting answers. First, we have to determine the set of possible career
pattern-payoff combinations. This is a type of possibility set assumed in all
types of welfare economics. Second, we have to determine the career pattern
preferences of a representative sample of people. Here, we do not want their
preferences at the present moment, given the special context in which they find
themselves, but rather the sort of preferences of career pattern-payoff opportunities that they would like to see exist for their grandchildren or great-grand-
children. That is, we want the pre-game preferences. We also have to determine the tradeoffs between better career patterns and worse payoffs and vice
versa.

A question that arises is one of variety. Some recent sociological studies
suggest the possibility that large numbers of people in different countries may
have rather similar career pattern preferences. Prestige patterns and status
patterns related to various types of careers receive similar rankings in many
countries (see references 5 and 6). For many people (perhaps a majority) it
may be possible to erect career-pattern alternatives in different organizations
that would be optimal for them. Very clearly, these preferences would influence the nature of the organizational structure of the firms and the efficiency
of firms. The variety of career-pattern alternatives desired by people need not
be the same as the distribution of occupations that would maximize output. A
tradeoff between the distribution of career patterns desired and the cost of providing for such a set of alternatives, in terms of output foregone, would have to
be determined.

---

*For a discussion of careers from the careerist viewpoint as against the organization's or
firm's viewpoint, see my Economic Theory and Organizational Analysis (reference 4).

Additional considerations easily come to mind, but there is little point at this juncture in expanding the list. The previous paragraphs are intended to be illustrative rather than exhaustive.

Game-Suggested Research Possibilities

We are not concerned here with answering in detail how it would be possible to determine the nature of the optimal economic casino, so to speak. We are only concerned with pointing out that this is a researchable question. However, a few comments in this direction are offered. The sense in which it is research-able is that it is possible that when people look back at their lives at various junctures in their careers they may be able to specify how they would have liked things to be, in terms of economic opportunities, rules, payoff distribu-tions, and constraints, if they had it to do all over again. In other words, they may be able to give information of a psychological and factual character that would enable trained investigators to assess what their pre-game preferences are like. For any given role it should be possible to discover how people like that role as well as to discover what changes they would like to see made in it. We could also discover what people are willing to give up in order to be, in what they believe, is a superior role. Similarly, we should be able to discover at various points in a person's career the extent to which he would like to see changes made in those aspects of his career that he has already experienced, as well as his reactions to what he believed was the payoff distribution open to him. This could be done for a representative group of individuals. Once again, some assessments of costs and tradeoffs should be possible. Through such information it may be possible to develop a ranking of career characteristics and career types. The next question that has to be answered is what career opportunities people would have liked before starting their career. In other words, "What were their preferences at various junctures with respect to access and changeover to alternative careers?" We do not know what degree of unanimity exists within a representative group of individuals about their pre-game preferences for possible economic games. Even if, in principle, there is no guarantee that everyone could agree on a set of economic games it is conceivable that there exists a set of possible games that would command a very high degree of consent. Of course, nothing could be said at this point about the degree of precision with which such questions could be answered or the value of the inferences that could be made from such data. Nevertheless, these are potentially researchable areas.

But even if unanimity does not exist for an economic game set that everyone considers to be optimal, unanimity or a high degree of consent may exist for a change from one game set to a preferred one. By allowing for tradeoffs between individuals with different views, one could increase the degree of consent for moving to a new game set. What degree of pre-game consent should rule the adoption of a new game set cannot be determined in advance. If pre-game consent criteria were adopted, then perhaps experience could tell us what degree of consent leads to sensible legislation. However, there is no reason for insisting on strict unanimity on a priori grounds.

CAREER-PAYOFF DISTRIBUTION INSURANCE

To return to our gambling metaphor, we can say that there are two aspects to our problem. First, can we invent an "optimal casino" of economic games?

Second, can we determine whether any specific change is in the direction of a better casino rather than away from it? The answer to the first question would be easy if economic games were as independent of each other as gambling games, in fact, are. The difficulty arises because such independence may not exist. Strictly speaking, to provide separate economic games would mean to provide separate economies for potential players. Players would be free to migrate from each economy to every other one. Such separateness might bear an exceedingly high cost. In addition, to suit everybody's tastes, the variety of economies that would have to be set up might be rather large. Even in an actual gambling casino, where independence between games is easily achieved, the variety of games is quite small. Clearly, beyond some point, variety is costly.

Social inventiveness may lead to some degree of accommodation to the variety of tastes about payoffs, careers, and activities, even in cases where setting up completely separate economic games is impossible. For example, insurance schemes might enable some people to choose career-payoff distributions that have a greater variance than those that most people bear. In principle, it should be possible to insure, to some degree, against the lack of a sufficient degree of inequality in the earned income distribution. The "moral hazard" principle in insurance would prevent the possibility of insuring against too much inequality in any given income distribution.

Consider a hypothetical example: Suppose that there are ten career grades and that salaries are proportional to the career grade involved, so that those in grade 10 receive ten times the salary of those in grade 1. Assume, also, that those in grade 5 receive the mean income. In the extreme case no one would be willing to set up a firm that would sell "equal income" insurance, because, given the distaste for effort, people could still obtain the income of grade 5 though they only worked hard enough to get into grade 1. However, insurance in the opposite direction is, in principle, a possibility. We have to assume that effort alone is not enough to achieve any grade. Luck also matters. Suppose that only one out of a hundred can be chosen for the top supervisory position, which merits grade 10. Even if all had the same capacity to rise to that position, only one would be chosen. Hence, luck or probability would, of necessity, enter the situation.

Now, the career-payoff function that we have just described may be too egalitarian for some tastes and too inegalitarian for others. If there are enough people for whom it is too egalitarian, then this becomes an insurable matter. Such people should be able to purchase, for a premium, at the outset of their careers (or at other junctures) a policy that would give them a lesser salary at lower grades than the given career-payoff function and a higher salary at the higher grades. To the extent that some people could be provided with such policies, which would give them a career-payoff function that they would prefer to the one available, then this would appear, on the surface, to be desirable. This is the equivalent of extending the variety of economic games open to people. The uni-directional nature of such insurance would suggest the possibility that society provide career-payoff functions biased in an egalitarian direction and then provide facilities for those that prefer a more inegalitarian career-payoff function to purchase an "unequalizing" insurance policy out of their income to the degree desired and possibly available. Such people would be betting in favor of achieving a relatively high grade in their career. In other words, there may exist a set of socially controlled career-payoff functions and insurance arrangements that would enable some or all to choose a career-payoff function that they prefer (and force no one to choose a career-payoff function that he does not prefer) to the career-payoff function dictated by the market.

At least two major obstacles to such a scheme come to mind. One is the risk and outcome measurement problem, and the other is what we might call the "handicapping" problem. If such insurance is to be offered then the various steps in a career would have to be carefully graded, or, alternatively, the percentile in which a person's earned income falls would have to be computed, and the associated probability of achieving a given grade or position in the income distribution would have to be determined. The other problem is that people clearly have unequal capacities at the start of their careers, or at various steps along the way, and hence a specific person's probability of achieving a specific career grade would be very different from that of some other person. In other words, some system of handicapping might have to be used in determining either the insurance premium or the payoff. However, such measurement problems exist in other fields but they do not limit the possibility of applying the insurance principle in those fields. For example, in life insurance a person's health at a given stage biases the probability of survival. These measurement problems complicate and perhaps inhibit but they do not necessarily prevent the application of the insurance principle in such areas. Only empirical research can determine whether the measurement problems can be handled to a sufficient degree of precision so as to make such a scheme practical, if desired.

Effort is another element in career achievement. Ideally, people should be able to play the type of effort-career-payoff game that they desire. For example, some might prefer to put in more effort if the career-payoff function is less, rather than more, equal. Ideally, wider variety of games is provided, to the extent that the application of the insurance principle allows individuals to relate the amount of effort they want to put forth with the career-payoff function that they prefer. Under a market system people are forced, in a sense, to accept the career-payoff function that market forces dictate. We need not, at this juncture, concern ourselves with why the market does not provide career-payoff insurance. To the extent that society could provide it, or encourage private firms to provide it, such insurance would appear to be a desirable mechanism to consider, if it enabled some people to choose those career-payoff functions they prefer to that provided by the market place.

WELFARE DECISIONS — THE BALANCE BETWEEN MID-GAME AND PRE-GAME CONSIDERATIONS

Welfare economics is concerned with the questions that have to be answered in order to make a welfare decision. The notions that we have presented in the previous pages suggest two major considerations that enter into the determination of a welfare decision. We visualize some proposed change and examine how the change scores with respect to these two considerations or aspects: (1) The mid-game aspect — to what extent does the change affect the incomes, careers, and activities of people alive today? (2) The pre-game aspect — to what extent does it change the economic games open to people in the future? The first consideration is similar to the sort of considerations raised in contemporary welfare economics. To the extent that the change involves current income redistributions or wealth redistributions, the question cannot be answered apart from preferences about <u>specific</u> redistributions. As far as one can judge there does not exist any unanimity of opinion on this question. But the long-run element involved does not depend on such considerations. The extent to which the change improves the set of available economic games does not depend on individuals' feelings about how the situation affects them personally. In the long run, the second aspect is likely to be the more important. In other words, if the change has a long lasting impact, then the question of the specific distribution of income or wealth is decreased or disappears as a problem as the current generation leaves the scene. In the long run the utility or preference functions of the current generation need not be taken into account. All that we care about for the long run is the kind of economy created by the changes for generations as yet unborn or for those who have not yet entered the economy.

It is easy to think of a number of examples which fall into this category. For instance, the introduction of a system of universal education may affect some portions of the present generation adversely, but since such a system usually persists, we are concerned eventually with the way that it affects the set of economic games. A system of social security is of a similar nature. Currently, it may take more in taxes from some people than it provides in benefits. In the long run, however, it changes the payoff for the representative individual to something other than it would be without the system of social security. In the long run, the latter or pre-game consideration dominates.

In this context, consider the compensation principle. Suppose that, in some instance, the short-run effect is one for which the short-run monetary gains outweigh the short-run losses and that, in fact, the gains are taxed to some extent and that out of such taxes the losers are completely compensated. If the change were also desirable from the long-run viewpoint, then this would clearly be a type of change that could be recommended on both grounds. However, if compensation is not made, the short-run aspect becomes undecidable unless other criteria, not employed in current welfare economics, are introduced. However, if the reason for a lack of compensation is of a short-run nature, and if the long-run benefits are considerable, then we do have an argument favoring compensation, one based on eliminating any doubt in favor of the change.

In the case in which the short-run losses are greater than the gains, we face a more serious problem. There is no unique way of weighing and choosing between the long-run benefits as against the short-run losses. This paper does not attempt to solve every aspect of the problem. Rather, it adds considerations that may be helpful in reaching a decision in some cases. First, there may be situations in which the long-run considerations clearly dominate. For instance, the short-run losses might be small. Second, there is a connection between the benefits or losses to the current population and the long-run considerations. An individual might be in favor of a change by which he, himself, loses if, by favoring a change, he could be convinced that his offspring will move into a world in which they will be potentially better off.

With respect to the short-run problems, it is conceivable that people could agree, in some class of cases, on welfare criteria that do not flow entirely from their individual self-interest. In other words, frequently individuals have a sense of fairness, which may not dominate when large considerations of self-interest are involved but which exists, nevertheless, and which may be important when the self-interest considerations are relatively small. There are, of course, examples where people vote or make other decisions that are consciously against their self-interest. Charitable organizations are built and maintained on this basis. Also, it is not only force that enables governments to collect taxes. Since pre-game preferences do not reflect current advantage and hence imply a sense of what is fair, they add an additional consideration even to the short-run welfare decision problems.

POSSIBLE APPLICATIONS

We have already emphasized that our concern is with pre-game consensus rather than mid-game consensus. The nature of pre-game consensus is ultimately an empirical question. However, it may be fruitful to speculate on some of the possible applications of this concept in order to indicate its range of application.

We have suggested that pre-game consensus is likely to depend on two major considerations: (a) fairness, and (b) the taste for games that in some sense balances the risk of unfortunate outcomes to a player against his chances of achieving desired outcomes. Fairness criteria dictate that economic games be so arranged that, at the outset, players start as equally as possible.* This, in itself, suggests some applications. For instance, economic projects that minimize the inequalities people may possess prior to their entry into the labor force would be deemed desirable. Special schools for children underprivileged or handicapped as a consequence of birth or errors in nurture might fit this category. Other arrangements that would to some degree counterbalance birth defects (such as blindness) or handicaps that are a consequence of social prejudices (caste, color, or religion) would also fit such categories. Other applications may have to do with changes in the general income distribution. This may be handled by a system of taxes and subsidies, and by the "lack of risk" insurance schemes suggested above. However, there may be some cases where the outcome of the game cannot be counter-balanced simply by income changes. These may occur as a consequence of certain statuses that may arise in playing the game. This would argue for arrangements that would encourage certain roles and careers and discourage others. For example, altering the entry requirements into certain roles or careers may be one such arrangement.

Also, not all possible sequences of play that can occur in the economic game may be deemed desirable. Thus, the rules may be set so as to counteract undesirable dynamic sequences. For example, an urban or regional transportation system that may develop naturally may be one that is not desired if people could have foreseen this development at the outset. This is likely to occur as a consequence of indivisibilities. An argument may conceivably be made that the elimination or curtailment of rail transportation in metropolitan areas as a consequence of competition with other means of transportation should not have been permitted if people had a pre-game choice as to the modes of transportation that would be allowed to survive. These remarks refer to possible examples in order to suggest the area of applicability of pre-game criteria. The examples themselves are not meant to indicate approval of any specific economic policy.

SUMMARY

In this paper, long-run welfare decisions were emphasized. It was argued that such decisions should depend on pre-game values or preferences with regard to the payoffs, careers, and activities implied in alternative desired sets of "economic games." Further, long-run welfare decisions depend on pre-game preferences for general income distributions rather than for specific distributions. An additional point emphasized is that the nature of the problem is, in part, empirical. It is possible that empirical research can tell us the degree

---

*I guess that this is what most people would want. My guess is based on introspection and casual empiricism. It is of course possible that the facts, should they be obtained, would turn out to be otherwise.

of pre-game consent we could expect for various classes of welfare decisions, as well as shed light on the factors that determine the degree of pre-game consent. This in turn may enable us to devise consent rules for the adoption of various measures. There would seem to be little reason to determine such consent rules on a purely a priori basis.

There is probably an egalitarian bias in using pre-game valuations and preferences. Since the emphasis is on potential members of society it is likely that most or all people would want to consider every potential member as the equal of all other potential members. In the absence of other considerations, the equalizing bias would imply that more educational resources be allocated to those with disadvantages of birth or inheritance or early nurture or social prejudice as against those more advantageously placed. To give people an equal start might imply that more money be spent on the slow-witted than the talented. Of course, other considerations might dictate a departure from this conclusion.

The contribution that this paper seeks to make is to indicate the sort of questions that should be asked, and to raise questions which are of an empirical and researchable nature in the hope that we can enlarge the basis on which we make welfare decisions. It argues for the establishment of welfare economics on an empirical basis insofar as this is possible. Finally, this paper argues for a shift in the focus of welfare economics to what should be its main preoccupation — the determination of the economic aspects of the good society.

REFERENCES

1. Kenneth Arrow, Social Choice and Individual Values (New York: John Wiley & Sons, Inc., 1951), pp. 82, 83.
2. James Buchanan and Gordon Tullock, The Calculus of Consent (Ann Arbor: University of Michigan Press, 1962), pp. 77-81.
3. John C. Harsanyi, "Cardinal Utility in Welfare Economics and in the Theory of Risk Taking," Journal of Political Economy, LXI (1953), pp. 434-35.
4. Harvey Leibenstein, Economic Theory and Organizational Analysis (New York: Harper & Brothers, 1960), pp. 276ff.
5. Alex Inkeles and Peter Rossi, "National Comparisons of Occupational Prestige," American Journal of Sociology, LXI (1956), pp. 329-39.
6. Seymour M. Lipset and Reinhard Bendix, Social Mobility in Industrial Society (Berkeley: University of California Press, 1962), p. 14n.

Name Index

Subject Index

absenteeism, 206
advertising 122, 265
agriculture 122, 169, 180, 182, 201-203,
    232, 234, 289
average equal expenditure units (AEU) 2-3

balance of payments 176
balance of trade 127
bandwagon effect 24
banking 6
behavioural relations 60, 64, 73
birth control *see* family planning
business cycles 136

Chicago School 35, 38-47 *passim*
classical economics 139-140
competition 13, 16, 202, 204, 215, 247, 249,
    251-2, 254, 340, 345
complementarity 164, 278, 298, 311-13
congestion 124, 126-8
consumer durables 3, 7, 46
conventions and customs 66-71
costs 48, 66, 220, 253, 263, 266-7, 270-71,
    344
    average 210
    decreasing 127, 179, 345
    social 127, 164, 194-5
    total 126

decision environments 137-8, 143-4, 152,
    155-60, 165-7
demography 35-7, 72, 84, 112-15, 194
diminishing marginal utility 59
dualism 309-316

economic growth 47, 118, 122, 173-200,
    223-4, 256, 277-81, 285-300 *passim*
economic history 137
economies of scale 119, 122, 314-15
education 7, 22, 29, 36, 42, 44, 50, 61, 66,
    74, 84-5, 92-6, 98, 100, 115, 124, 150,
    169, 195, 255, 360
    training 198-9, 267
effort 162, 196, 211, 234-5, 240, 250-51
elasticities
    'claim' 15
    income 9
    price 17-20
employment *see* unemployment
entrepreneurship 82, 97, 105, 240, 242, 247-
    58 *passim*, 259-72, 280, 298, 306,
    315-16, 318
environment
    legal 267
    natural 119, 126-8, 170, 195
equilibrium (and disequilibrium) 17, 52,
    224, 255
    Malthusian 80, 98, 111-12, 119, 121-2,
    127, 193, 199
expectations 136, 291, 350, 354
experience 251
exports 176

family planning 115, 195, 197
family size 5, 24, 42, 85-92 *passim*,
    115, 119, 125, 127-8, 196
female participation 36
franchising 259-72
free rider problem 235

game theory 349-60 *passim*
general capital 124

habit 66
Harrod-Domar growth model 277
Hicksian theory 34, 39
hierarchical structure 65-6, 115, 231-42
housing 10
human capital 6, 60, 95, 98
Hutterites 4, 37